D0960431

SHANNON HALE

# REAL FRIENDS

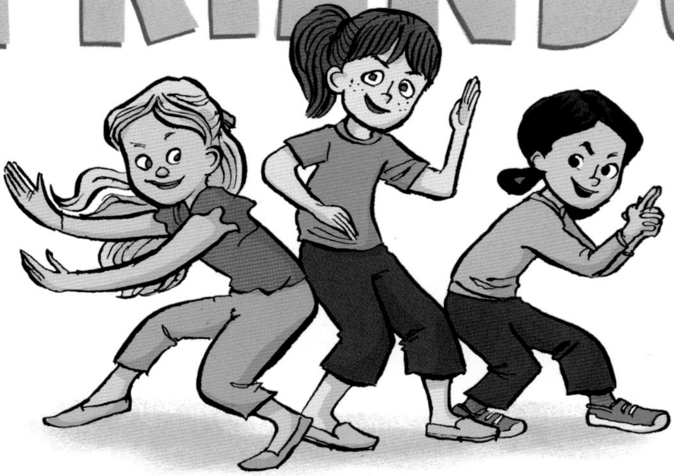

Artwork by
**LeUYEN PHAM**

Color by **JANE POOLE**

:01
First Second
New York

TEXT COPYRIGHT © 2017 BY SHANNON HALE
ILLUSTRATIONS COPYRIGHT © 2017 BY LEUYEN PHAM
PUBLISHED BY FIRST SECOND
FIRST SECOND IS AN IMPRINT OF ROARING BROOK PRESS,
A DIVISION OF HOLTZBRINCK PUBLISHING HOLDINGS LIMITED PARTNERSHIP
175 FIFTH AVENUE, NEW YORK, NEW YORK 10010
ALL RIGHTS RESERVED

LIBRARY OF CONGRESS CONTROL NUMBER: 2016945552

PAPERBACK ISBN: 978-1-62672-785-4
HARDCOVER ISBN: 978-1-62672-416-7

OUR BOOKS MAY BE PURCHASED IN BULK FOR PROMOTIONAL, EDUCATIONAL, OR BUSINESS USE.
PLEASE CONTACT YOUR LOCAL BOOKSELLER OR THE MACMILLAN CORPORATE AND PREMIUM SALES DEPARTMENT
AT (800) 221-7945 EXT. 5442 OR BY E-MAIL AT MACMILLANSPECIALMARKETS@MACMILLAN.COM.

FIRST EDITION 2017
BOOK DESIGN BY LEUYEN PHAM AND ANDREW ARNOLD
COLOR BY JANE POOLE

PRINTED IN CHINA BY TOPPAN LEEFUNG PRINTING LTD.,
DONGGUAN CITY, GUANGDONG PROVINCE

INKED WITH BLACK INDIA INK AND HUNT 103 NIB ON
BRISTOL PAPER AND COLORED DIGITALLY IN ADOBE PHOTOSHOP

PAPERBACK: 10  9  8  7  6  5  4  3  2
HARDCOVER: 10  9  8  7  6  5  4  3  2

FOR YOU
WHEN YOU'RE FEELING LONELY AND WORRIED
SO YOU'LL REMEMBER THAT YOU'RE NOT ALONE
—S. H.


FOR SHANNON
—L. P.

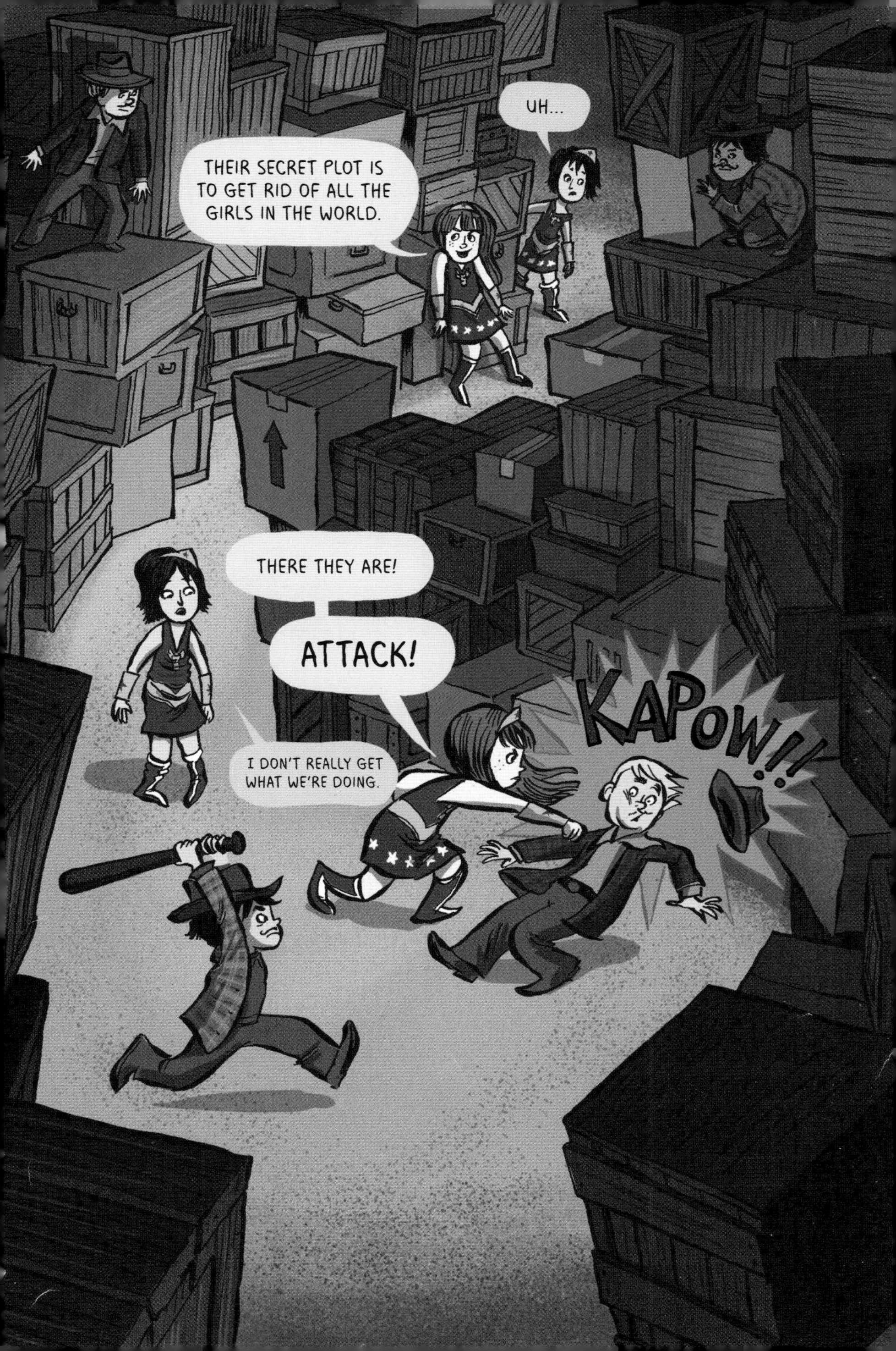
UH...
THEIR SECRET PLOT IS TO GET RID OF ALL THE GIRLS IN THE WORLD.
THERE THEY ARE!
ATTACK!
I DON'T REALLY GET WHAT WE'RE DOING.
KAPOW!!!

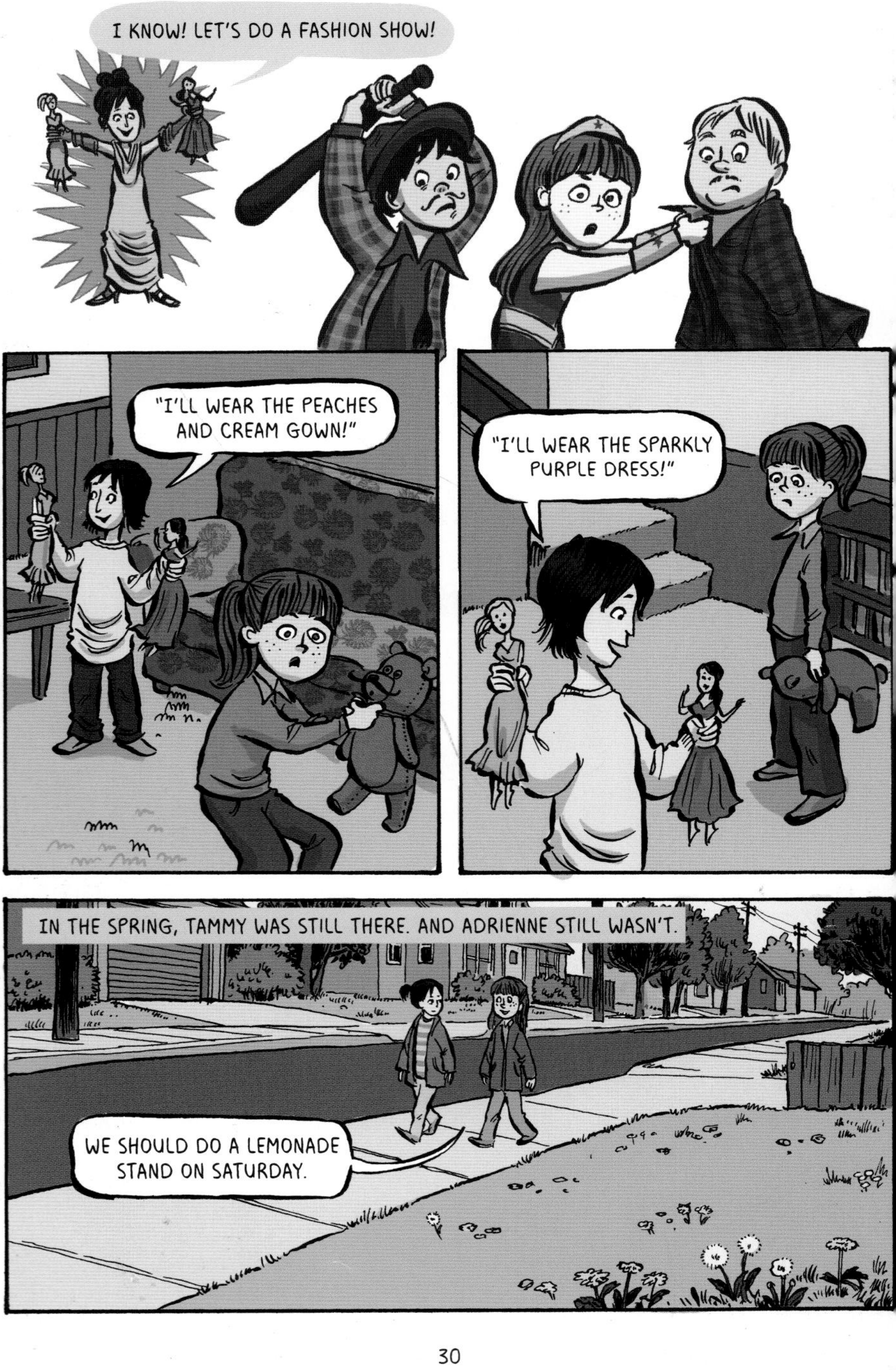
I KNOW! LET'S DO A FASHION SHOW!
"I'LL WEAR THE PEACHES AND CREAM GOWN!"
"I'LL WEAR THE SPARKLY PURPLE DRESS!"
IN THE SPRING, TAMMY WAS STILL THERE. AND ADRIENNE STILL WASN'T.
WE SHOULD DO A LEMONADE STAND ON SATURDAY.

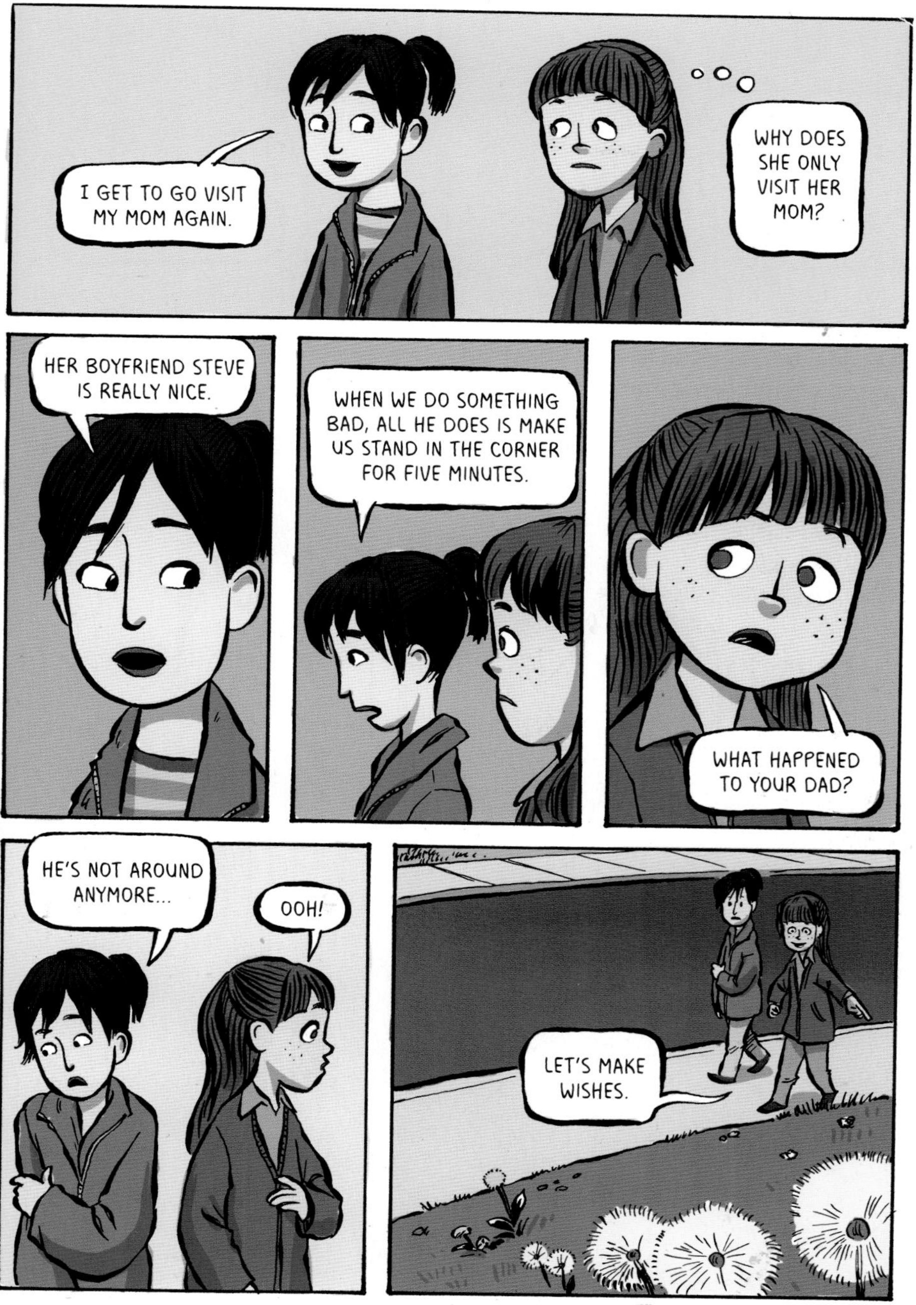
I GET TO GO VISIT MY MOM AGAIN.
WHY DOES SHE ONLY VISIT HER MOM?
HER BOYFRIEND STEVE IS REALLY NICE.
WHEN WE DO SOMETHING BAD, ALL HE DOES IS MAKE US STAND IN THE CORNER FOR FIVE MINUTES.
WHAT HAPPENED TO YOUR DAD?
HE'S NOT AROUND ANYMORE...
OOH!
LET'S MAKE WISHES.

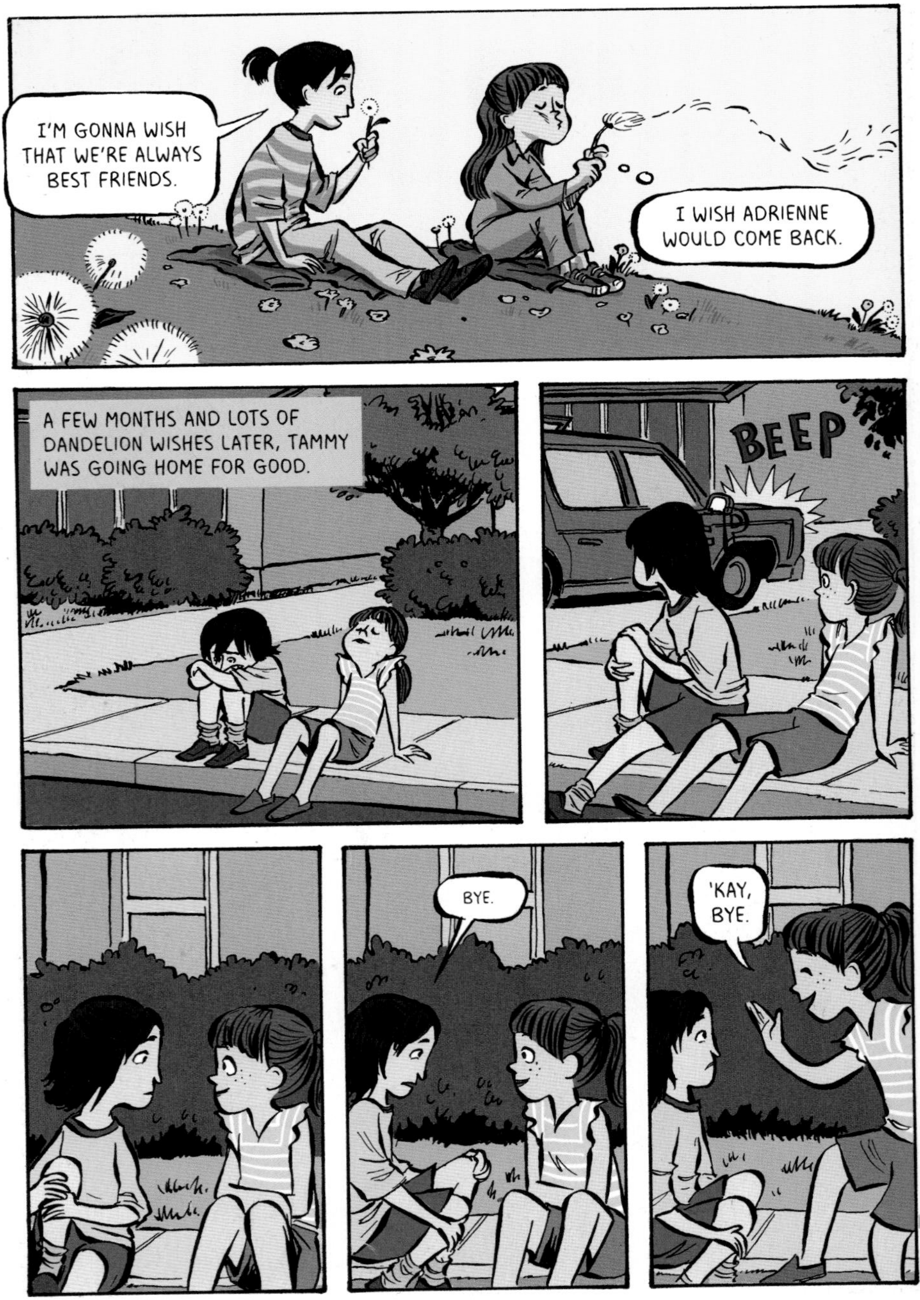
I'M GONNA WISH THAT WE'RE ALWAYS BEST FRIENDS.
I WISH ADRIENNE WOULD COME BACK.
A FEW MONTHS AND LOTS OF DANDELION WISHES LATER, TAMMY WAS GOING HOME FOR GOOD.
BEEP
BYE.
'KAY, BYE.

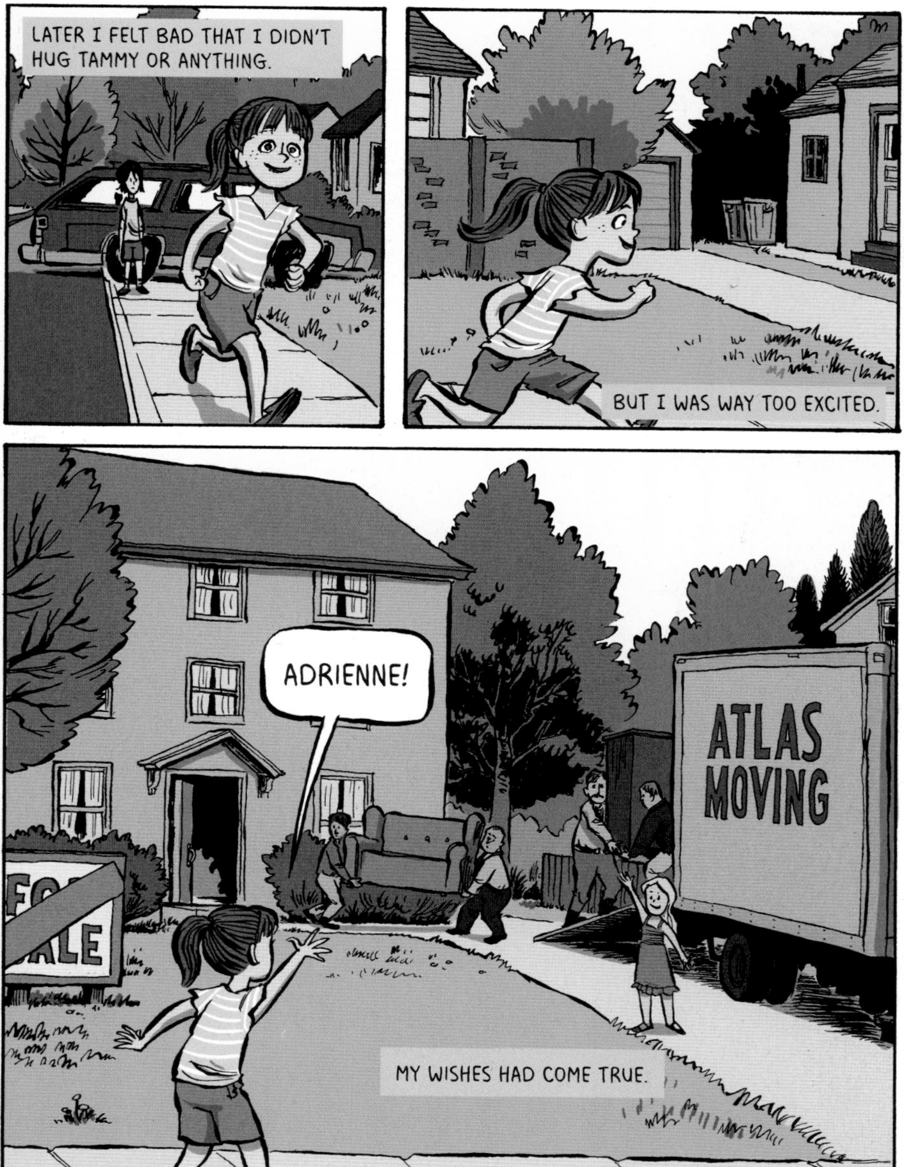

LATER I FELT BAD THAT I DIDN'T HUG TAMMY OR ANYTHING.
BUT I WAS WAY TOO EXCITED.
ADRIENNE!
ATLAS MOVING
MY WISHES HAD COME TRUE.

JEN

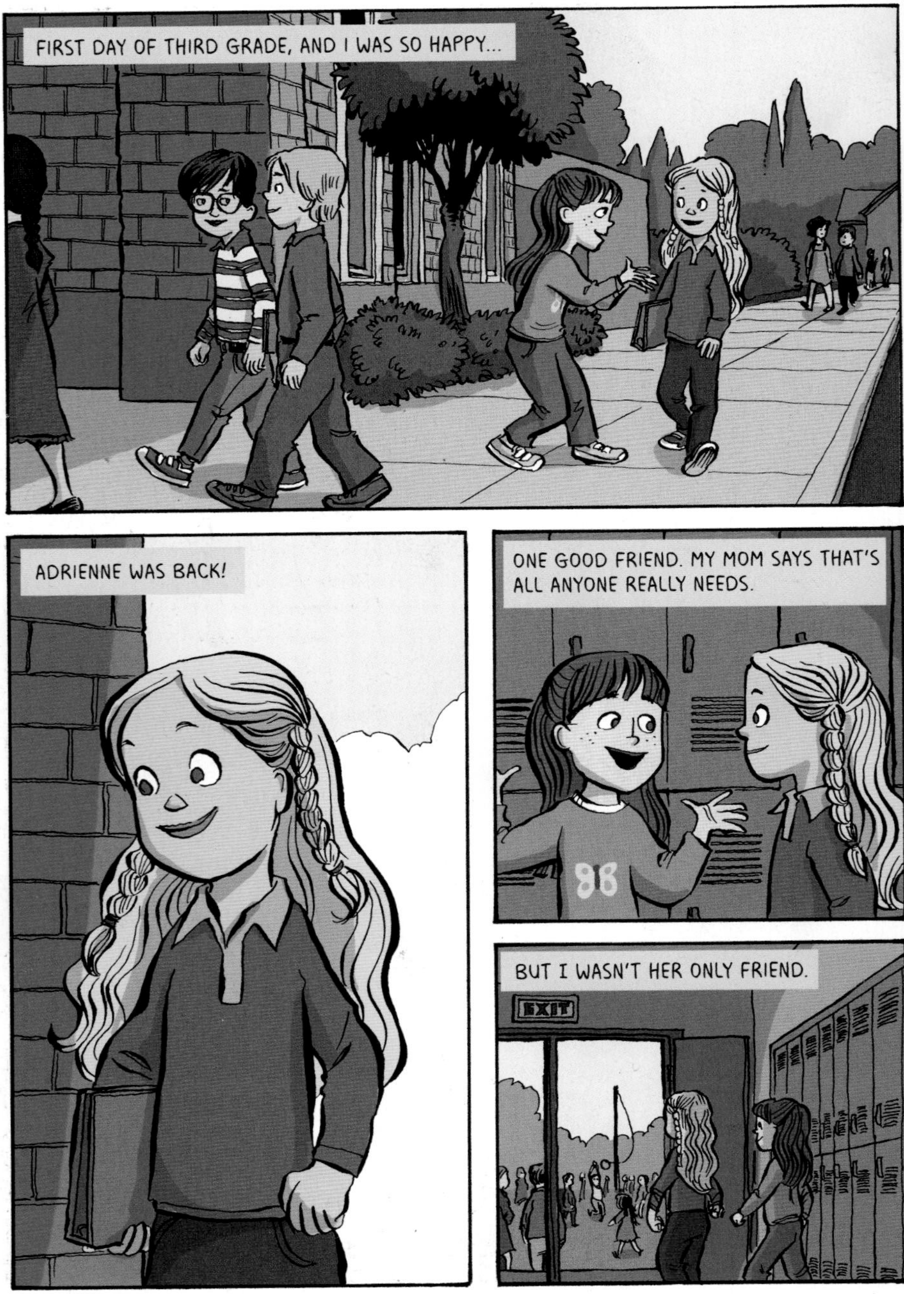
FIRST DAY OF THIRD GRADE, AND I WAS SO HAPPY...
ADRIENNE WAS BACK!
ONE GOOD FRIEND. MY MOM SAYS THAT'S ALL ANYONE REALLY NEEDS.
88
BUT I WASN'T HER ONLY FRIEND.
EXIT

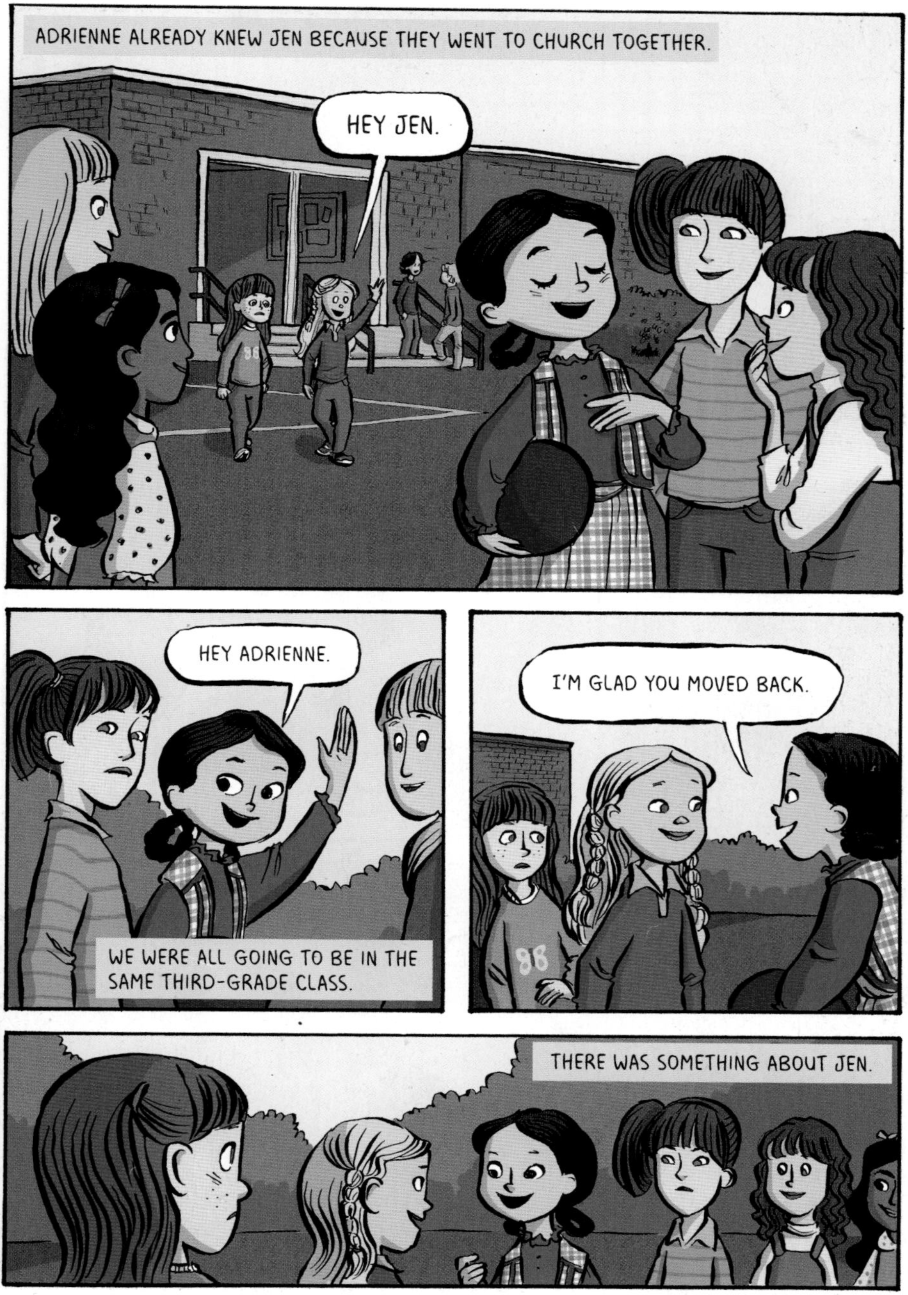
ADRIENNE ALREADY KNEW JEN BECAUSE THEY WENT TO CHURCH TOGETHER.
HEY JEN.
HEY ADRIENNE.
WE WERE ALL GOING TO BE IN THE SAME THIRD-GRADE CLASS.
I'M GLAD YOU MOVED BACK.
THERE WAS SOMETHING ABOUT JEN.

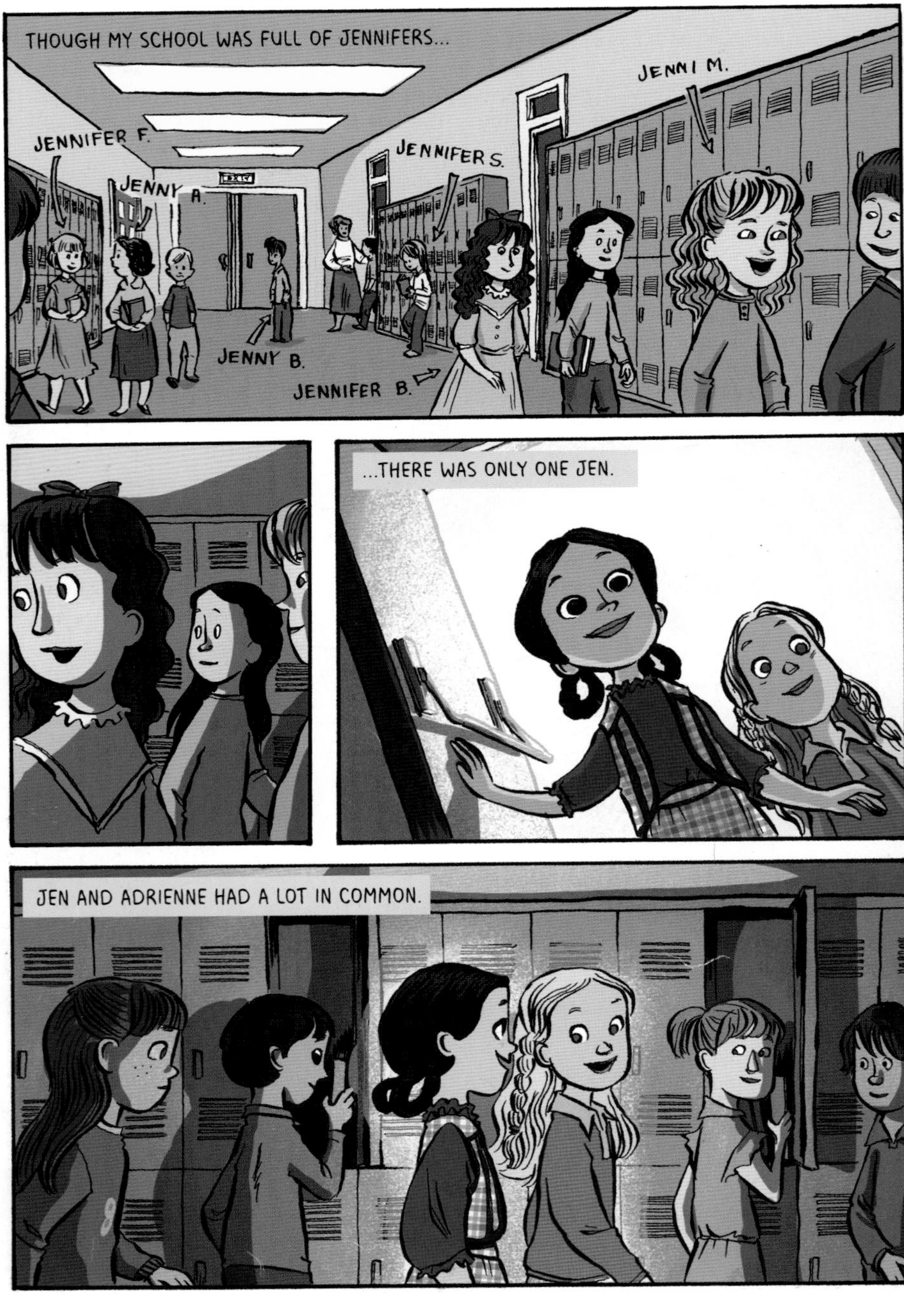
THOUGH MY SCHOOL WAS FULL OF JENNIFERS...
JENNIFER F.
JENNY A.
JENNY B.
JENNIFER B.
JENNIFER S.
JENNI M.
...THERE WAS ONLY ONE JEN.
JEN AND ADRIENNE HAD A LOT IN COMMON.

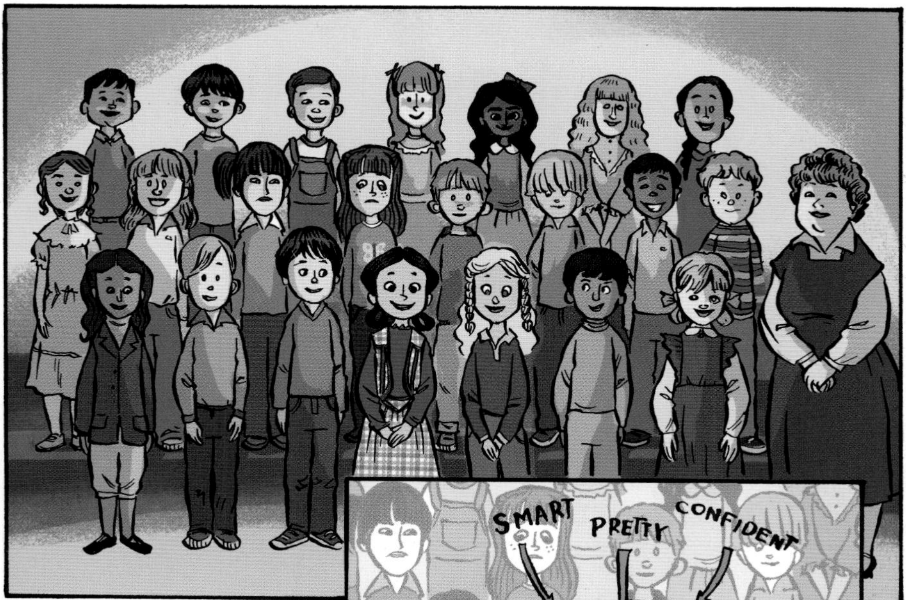

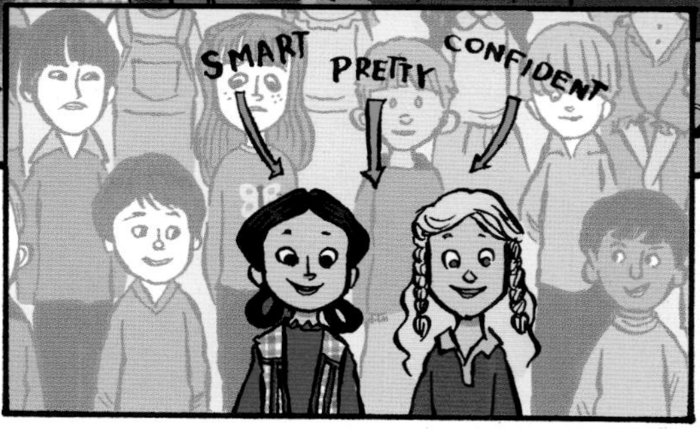
SMART
PRETTY
CONFIDENT

I COULD SEE WHY ADRIENNE MIGHT WANT JEN AS A BEST FRIEND INSTEAD OF ME.

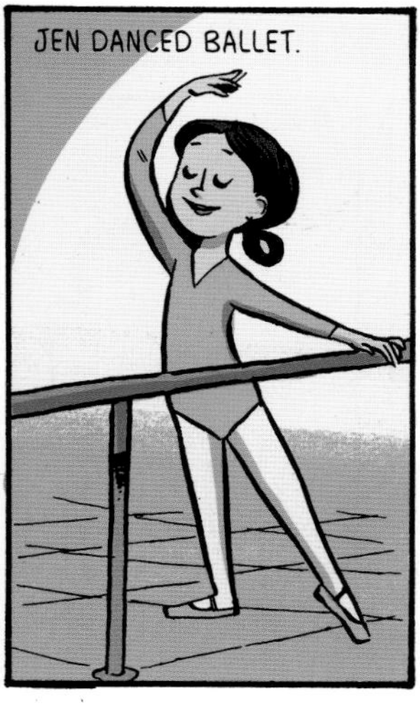
JEN DANCED BALLET.

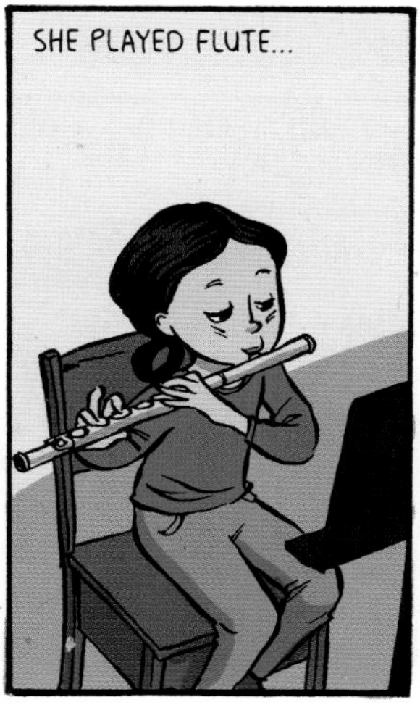
SHE PLAYED FLUTE...

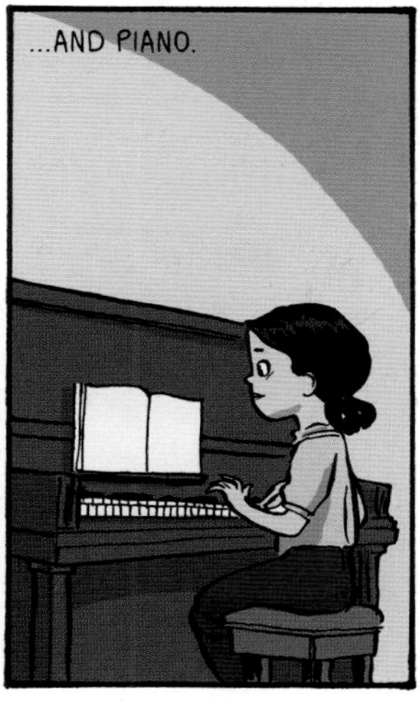
...AND PIANO.

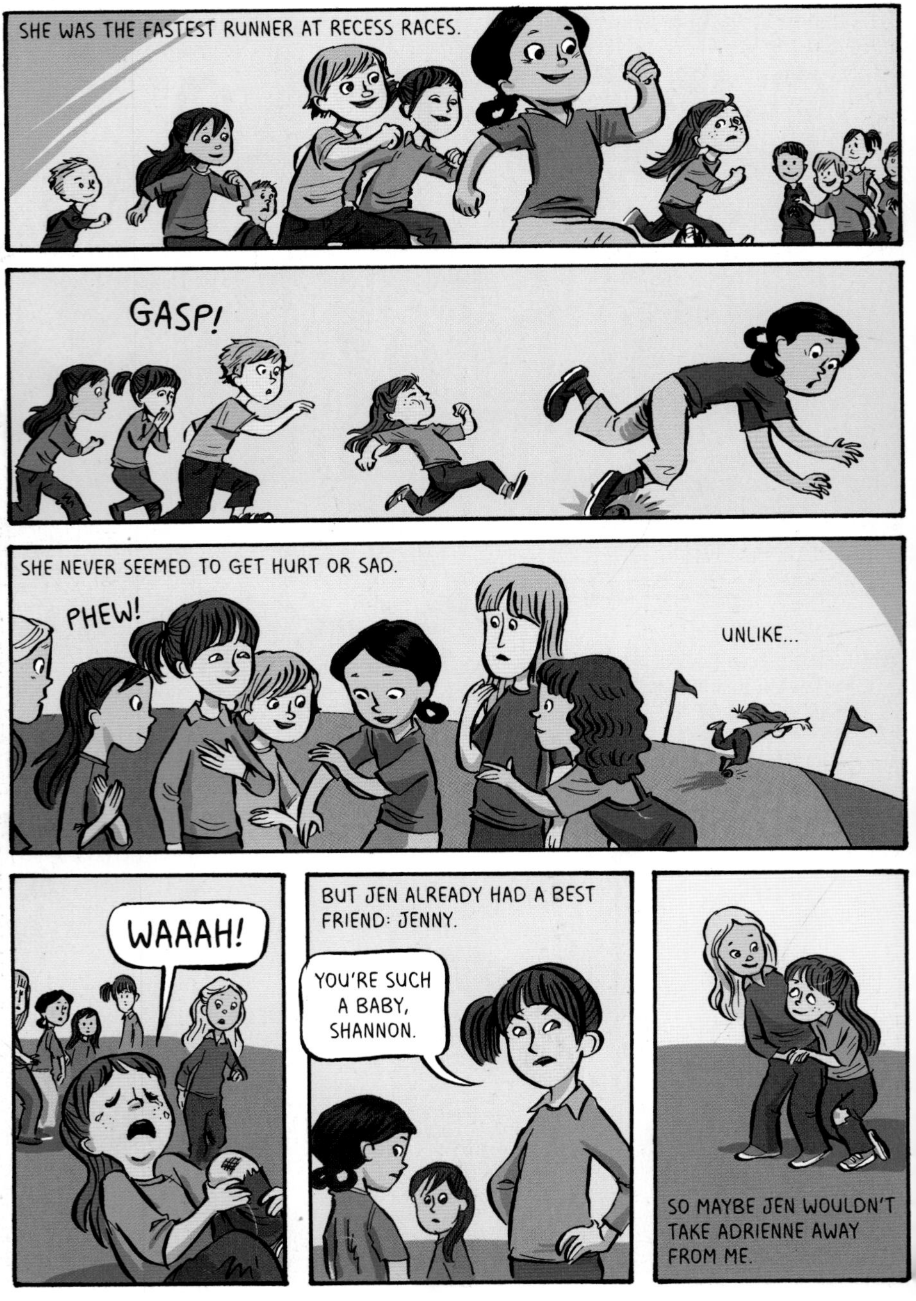
SHE WAS THE FASTEST RUNNER AT RECESS RACES.
GASP!
SHE NEVER SEEMED TO GET HURT OR SAD.
PHEW!
UNLIKE...
WAAAH!
BUT JEN ALREADY HAD A BEST FRIEND: JENNY.
YOU'RE SUCH A BABY, SHANNON.
SO MAYBE JEN WOULDN'T TAKE ADRIENNE AWAY FROM ME.

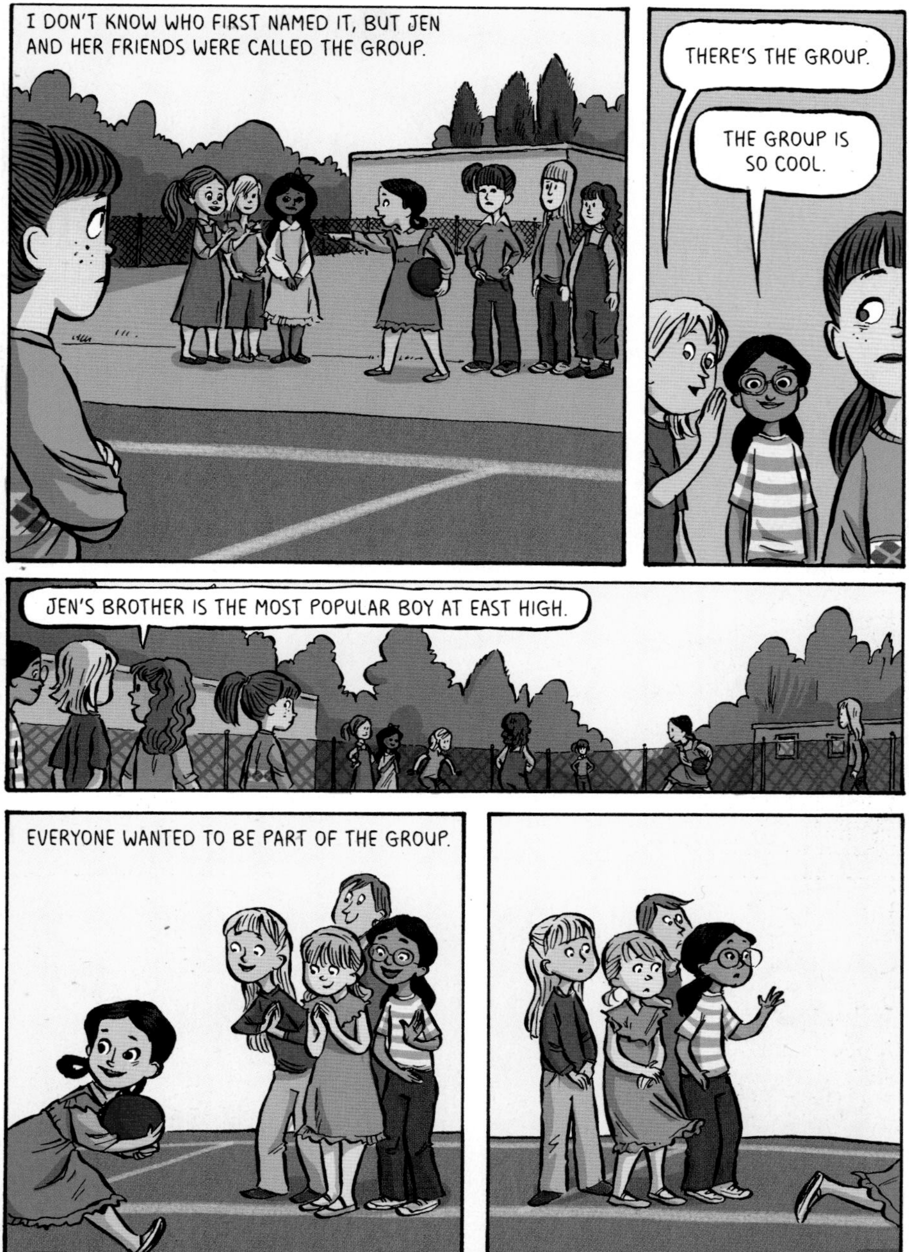
I DON'T KNOW WHO FIRST NAMED IT, BUT JEN AND HER FRIENDS WERE CALLED THE GROUP.
THERE'S THE GROUP.
THE GROUP IS SO COOL.
JEN'S BROTHER IS THE MOST POPULAR BOY AT EAST HIGH.
EVERYONE WANTED TO BE PART OF THE GROUP.

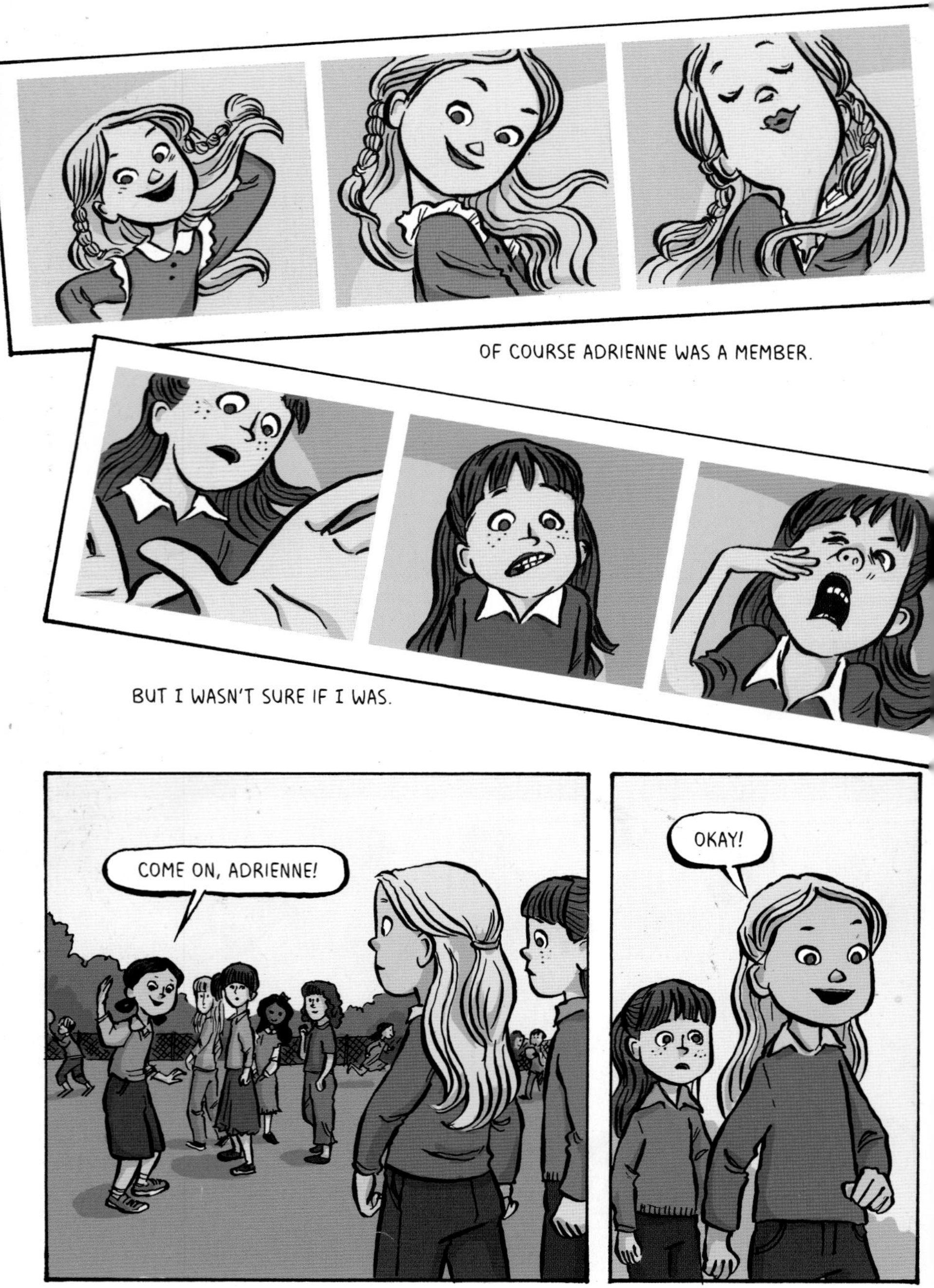
OF COURSE ADRIENNE WAS A MEMBER.
BUT I WASN'T SURE IF I WAS.
COME ON, ADRIENNE!
OKAY!

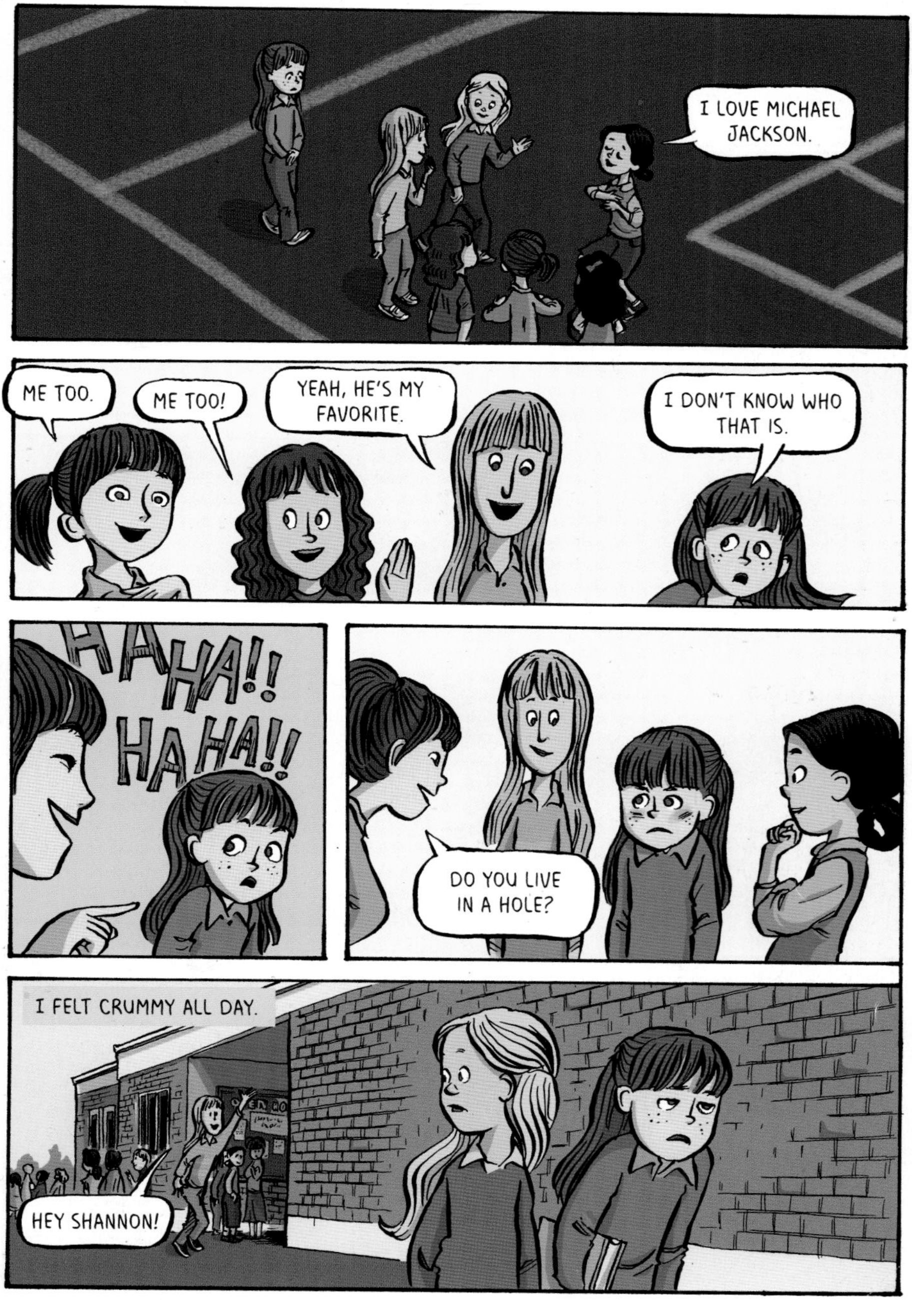
I LOVE MICHAEL JACKSON.
ME TOO.
ME TOO!
YEAH, HE'S MY FAVORITE.
I DON'T KNOW WHO THAT IS.
HAHA!! HAHA!!
DO YOU LIVE IN A HOLE?
I FELT CRUMMY ALL DAY.
HEY SHANNON!

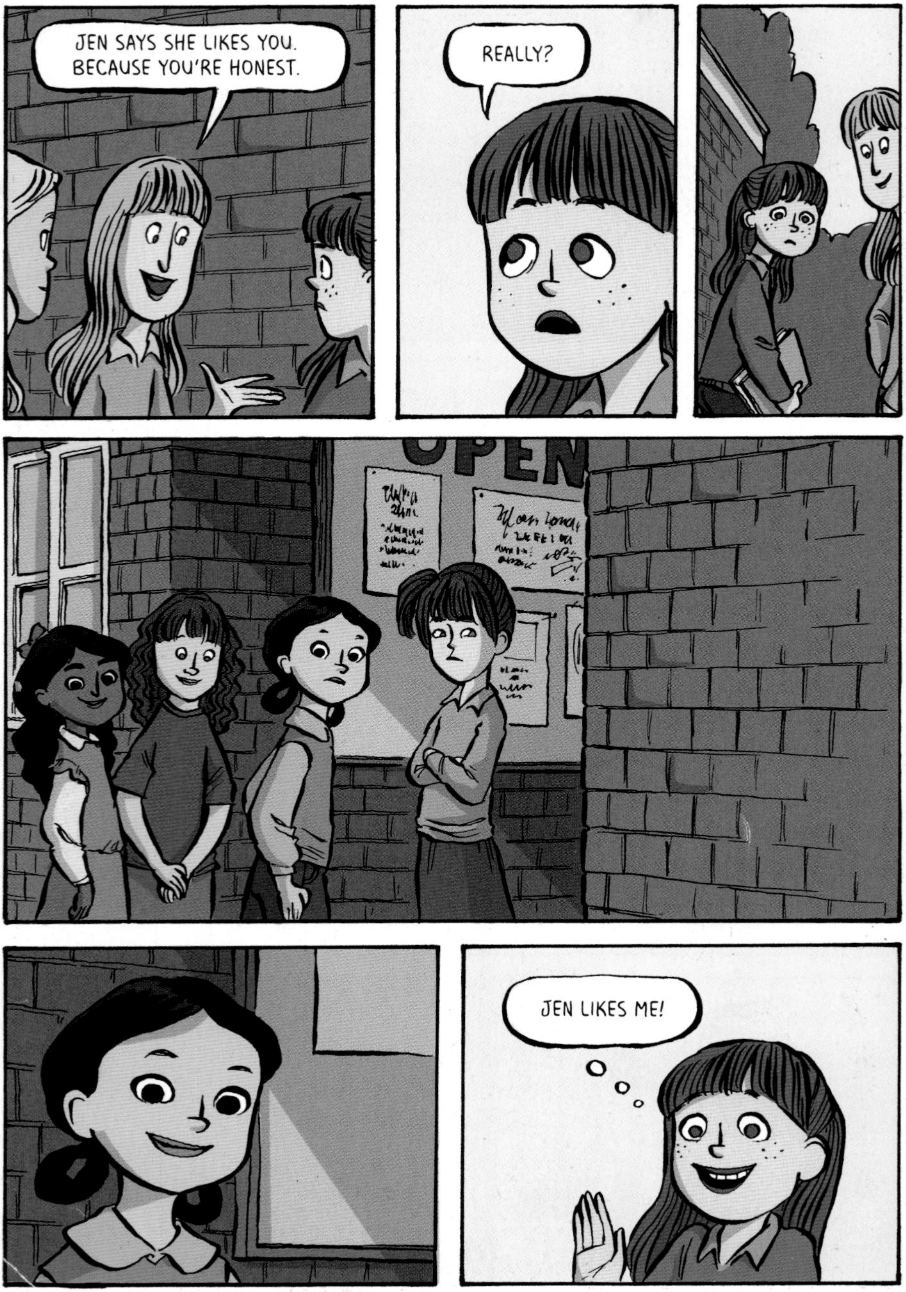
JEN SAYS SHE LIKES YOU. BECAUSE YOU'RE HONEST.
REALLY?
OPEN
JEN LIKES ME!

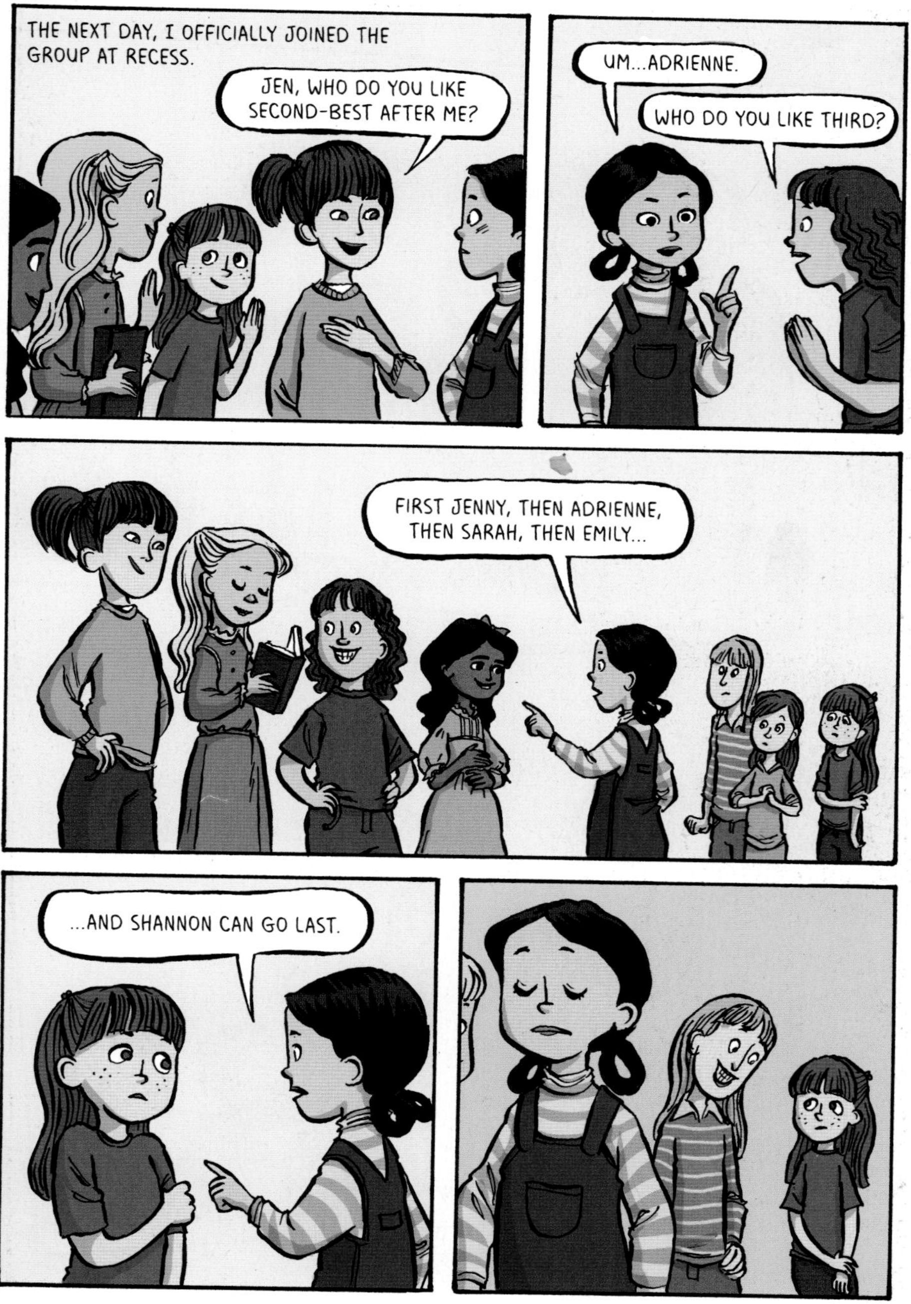

THE NEXT DAY, I OFFICIALLY JOINED THE GROUP AT RECESS.
JEN, WHO DO YOU LIKE SECOND-BEST AFTER ME?
UM...ADRIENNE.
WHO DO YOU LIKE THIRD?
FIRST JENNY, THEN ADRIENNE, THEN SARAH, THEN EMILY...
...AND SHANNON CAN GO LAST.

MY FAMILY DIDN'T EXACTLY LINE UP LIKE JEN HAD HER FRIENDS DO AT SCHOOL...

DAD
MOM
WENDY
LAURA
SHANNON
CYNTHIA
JOSEPH

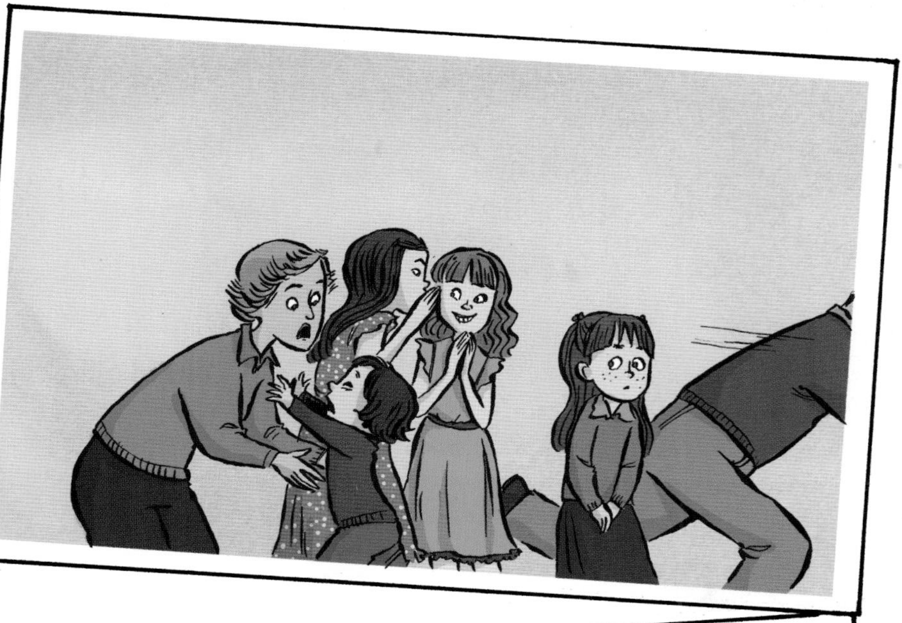

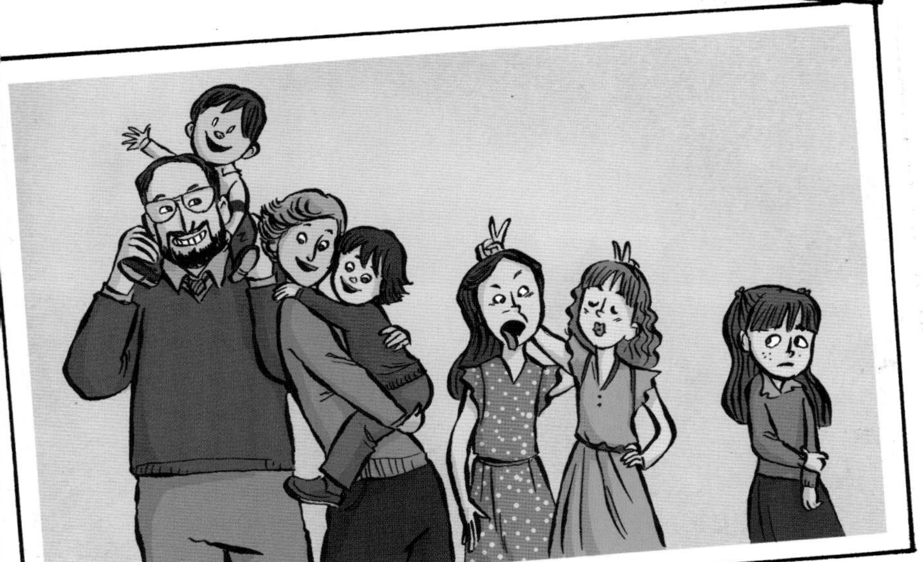

...BUT I WAS USED TO FEELING IN LAST PLACE.

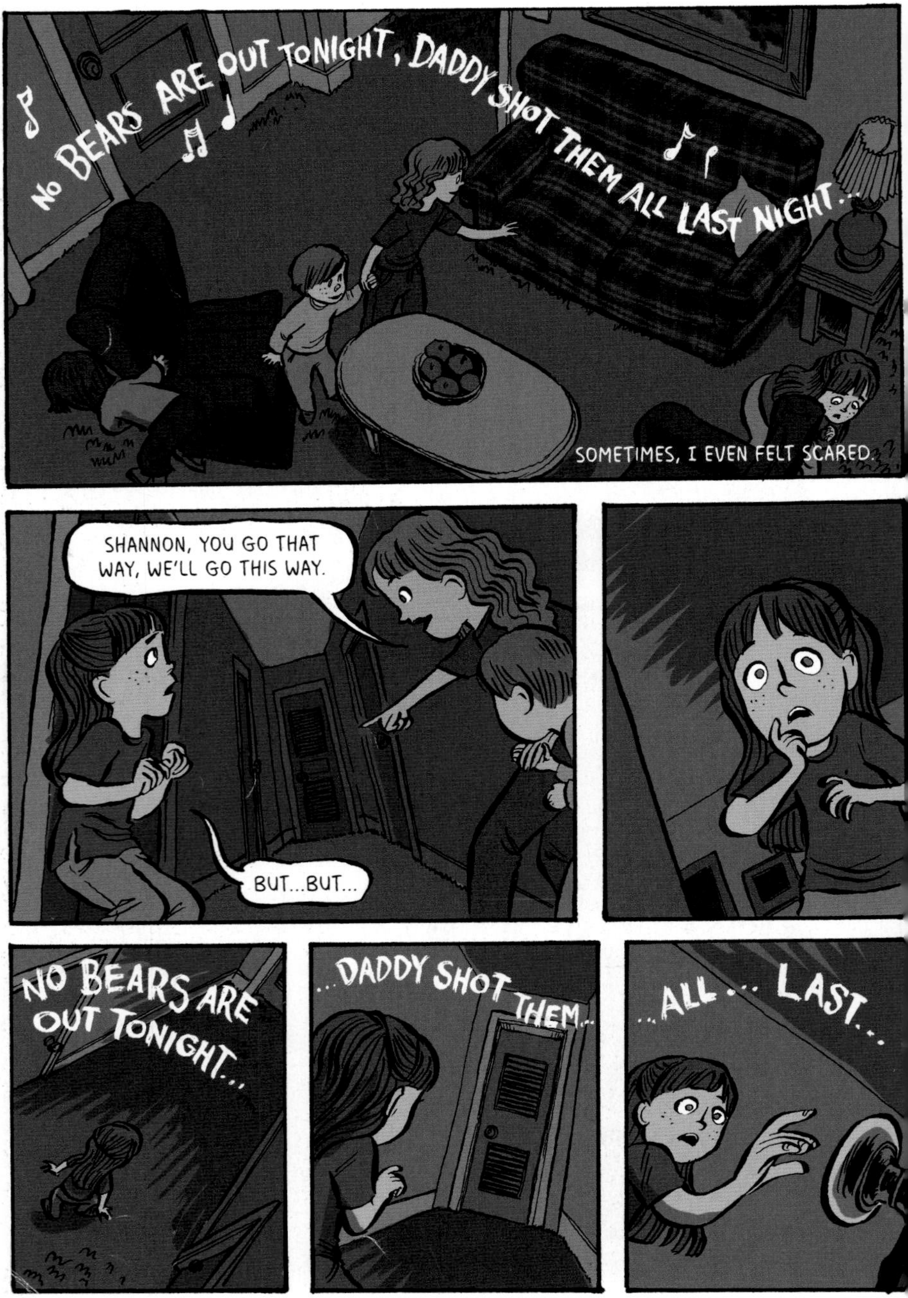
NO BEARS ARE OUT TONIGHT, DADDY SHOT THEM ALL LAST NIGHT...
SOMETIMES, I EVEN FELT SCARED.
SHANNON, YOU GO THAT WAY, WE'LL GO THIS WAY.
BUT...BUT...
NO BEARS ARE OUT TONIGHT...
...DADDY SHOT THEM...
...ALL... LAST...

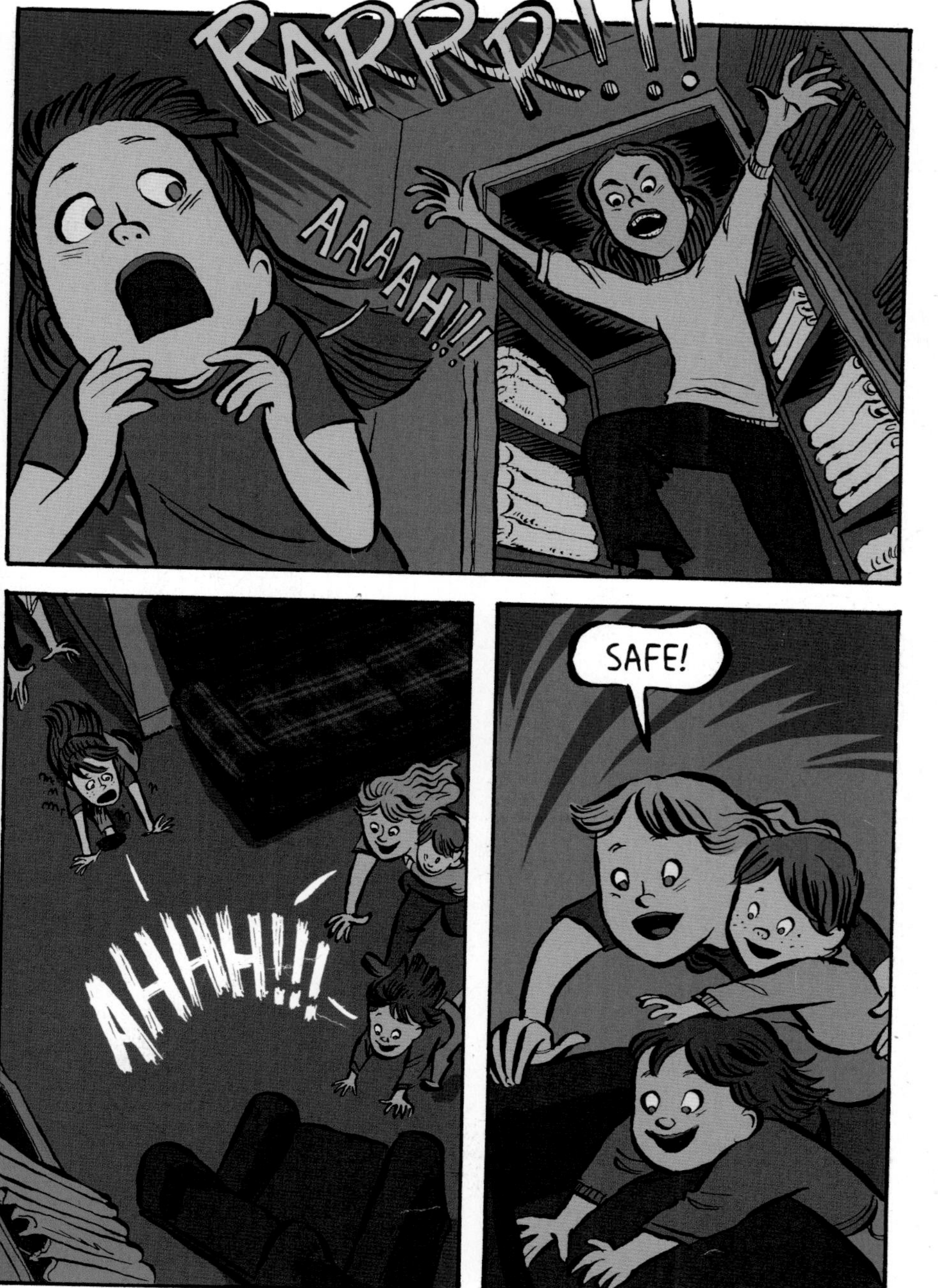
RARRR!!!
AAAAAH!!!!
AHHH!!!
SAFE!

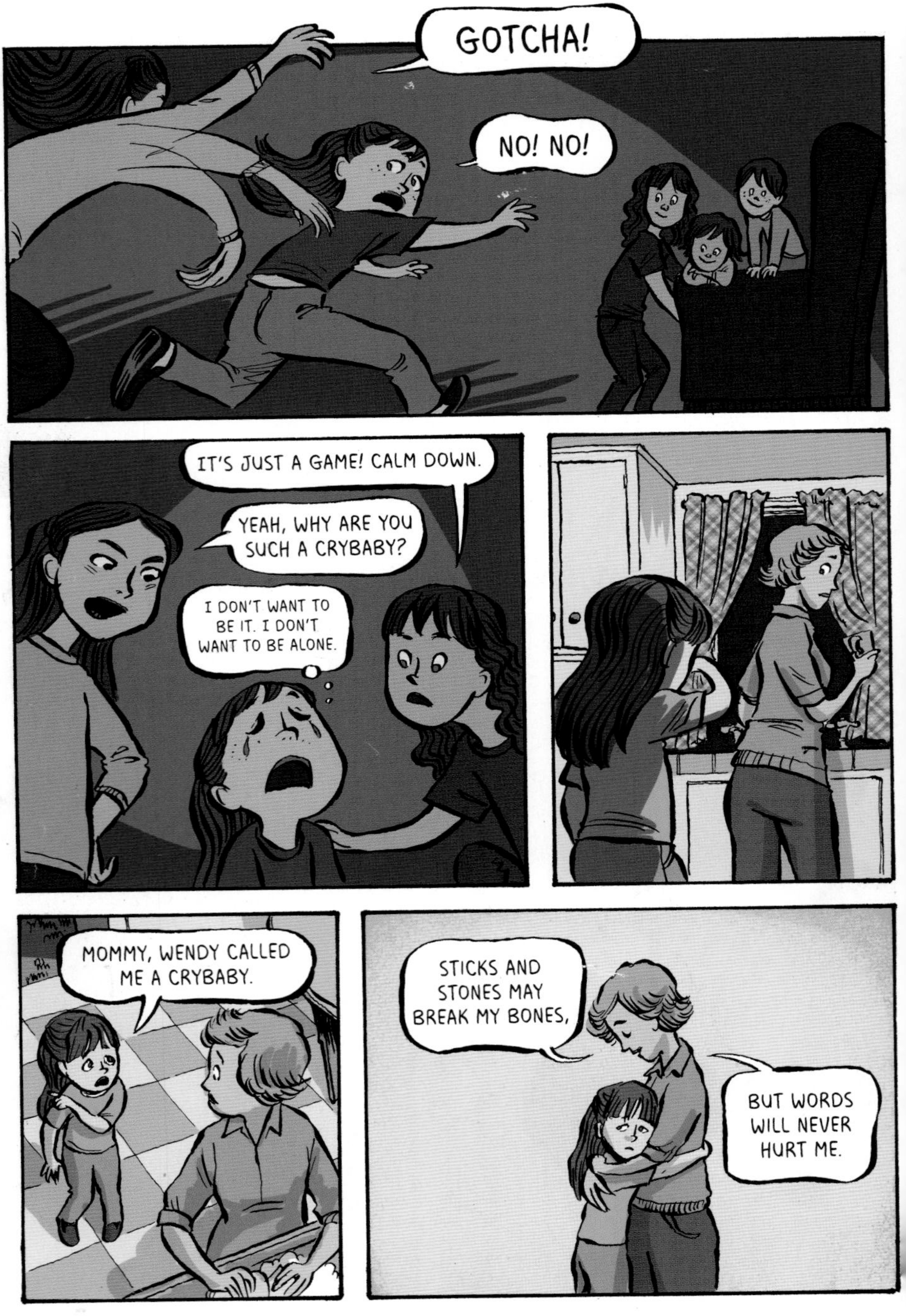
GOTCHA!
NO! NO!
IT'S JUST A GAME! CALM DOWN.
YEAH, WHY ARE YOU SUCH A CRYBABY?
I DON'T WANT TO BE IT. I DON'T WANT TO BE ALONE.
MOMMY, WENDY CALLED ME A CRYBABY.
STICKS AND STONES MAY BREAK MY BONES,
BUT WORDS WILL NEVER HURT ME.

AT LEAST WHEN I WAS PLAYING A GAME, I KNEW THE RULES.

JEN, CAN I SIT NEXT TO YOU AT LUNCH?

SCHOOL LUNCH

come find... hot nutritious!!

THERE WERE RULES FOR MEMBERS OF THE GROUP,

BUT I WASN'T GOOD AT FIGURING THEM OUT.

I ALREADY DIBBSED.

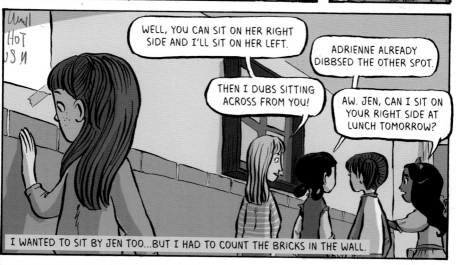

WELL, YOU CAN SIT ON HER RIGHT SIDE AND I'LL SIT ON HER LEFT.

THEN I DUBS SITTING ACROSS FROM YOU!

ADRIENNE ALREADY DIBBSED THE OTHER SPOT.

AW. JEN, CAN I SIT ON YOUR RIGHT SIDE AT LUNCH TOMORROW?

I WANTED TO SIT BY JEN TOO...BUT I HAD TO COUNT THE BRICKS IN THE WALL.

THERE WERE THIRTY-SIX IN A ROW BETWEEN THE THIRD GRADE HALL AND THE LUNCHROOM.

...FIFTEEN, SIXTEEN, SEVENTEEN...

IF I DIDN'T RECOUNT THEM EVERY TIME I WALKED BY, I JUST FELT YUCKY.

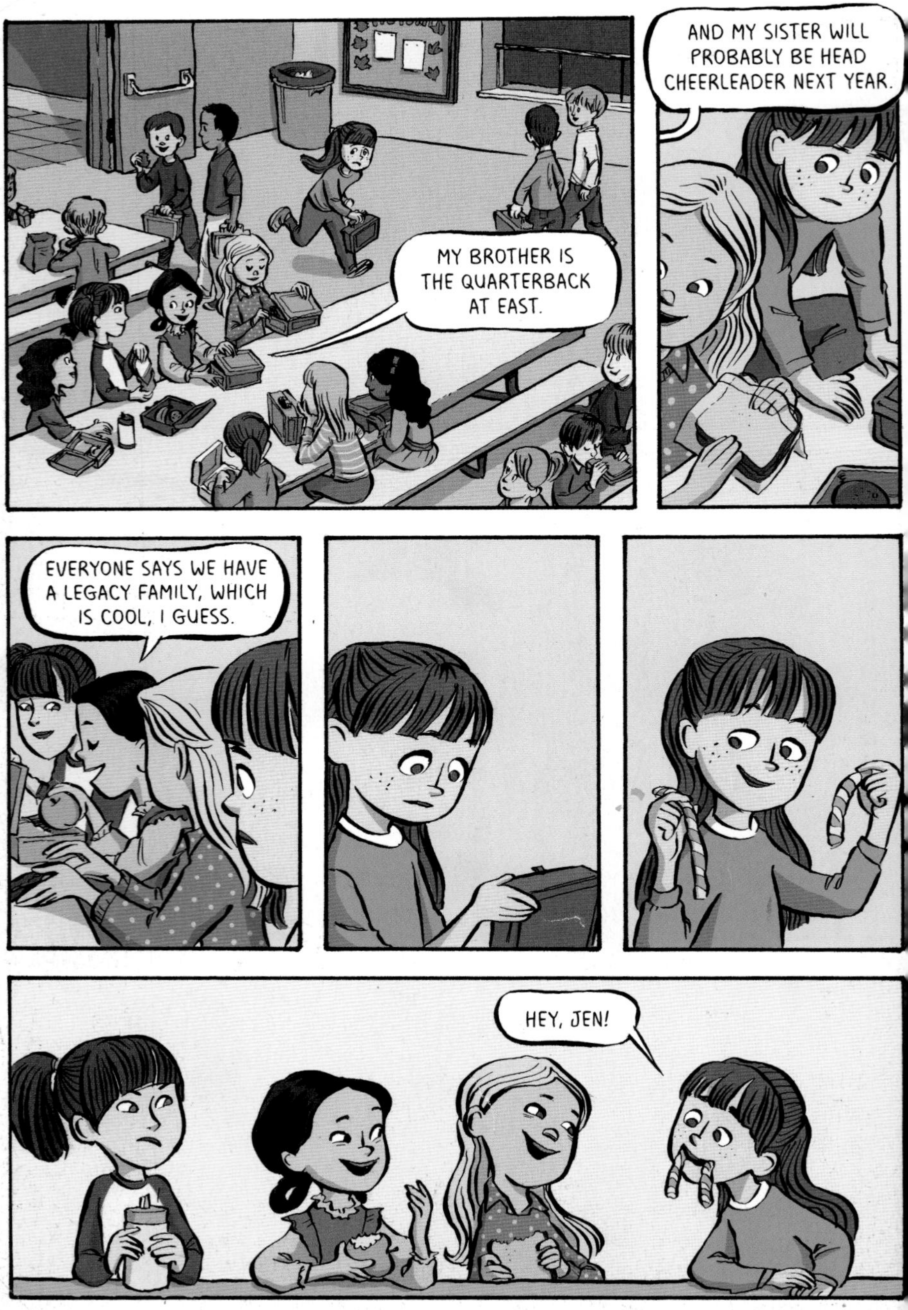
MY BROTHER IS THE QUARTERBACK AT EAST.
AND MY SISTER WILL PROBABLY BE HEAD CHEERLEADER NEXT YEAR.
EVERYONE SAYS WE HAVE A LEGACY FAMILY, WHICH IS COOL, I GUESS.
HEY, JEN!

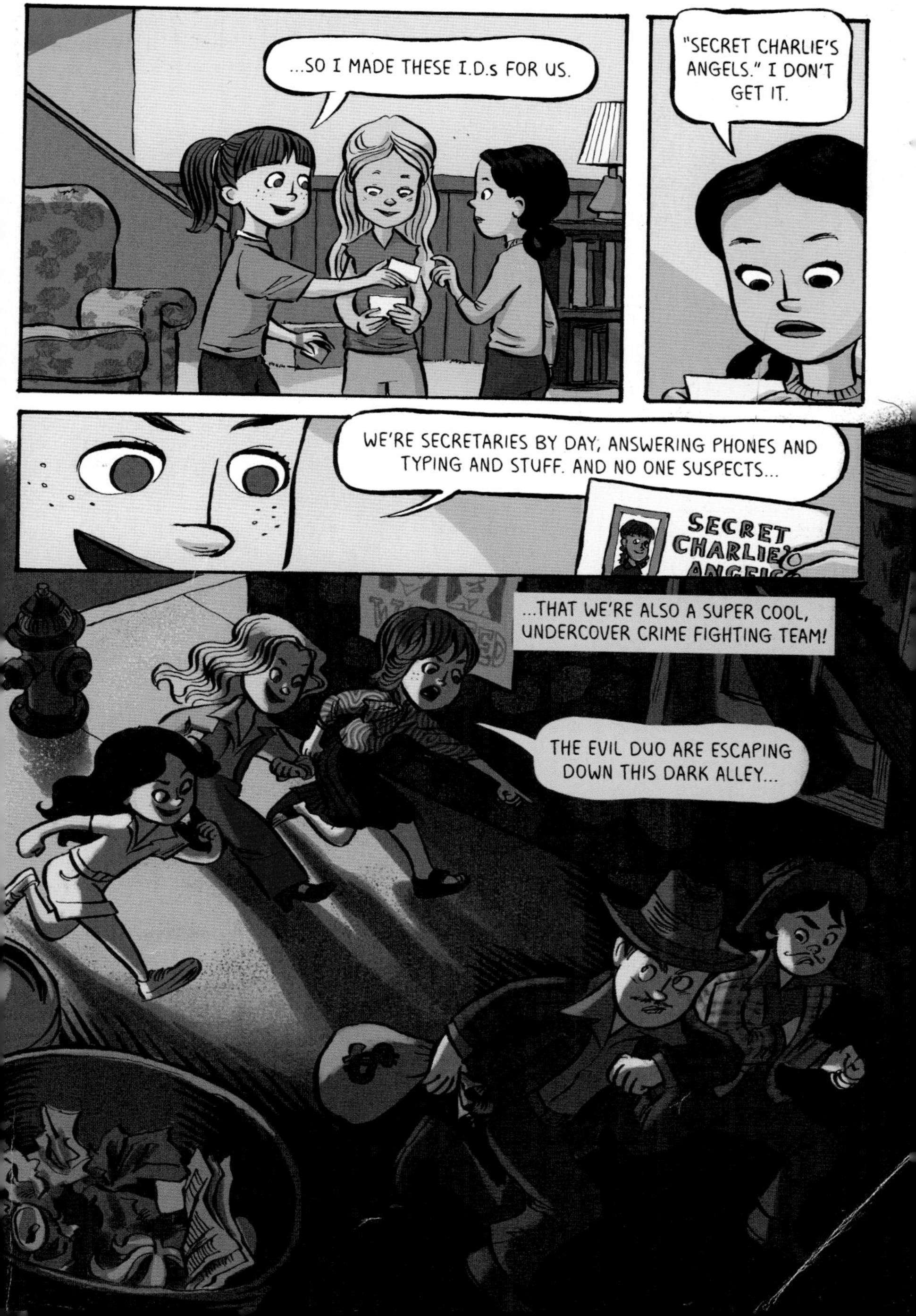

...SO I MADE THESE I.D.s FOR US.
"SECRET CHARLIE'S ANGELS." I DON'T GET IT.
WE'RE SECRETARIES BY DAY, ANSWERING PHONES AND TYPING AND STUFF. AND NO ONE SUSPECTS...
SECRET CHARLIE'S
...THAT WE'RE ALSO A SUPER COOL, UNDERCOVER CRIME FIGHTING TEAM!
THE EVIL DUO ARE ESCAPING DOWN THIS DARK ALLEY...

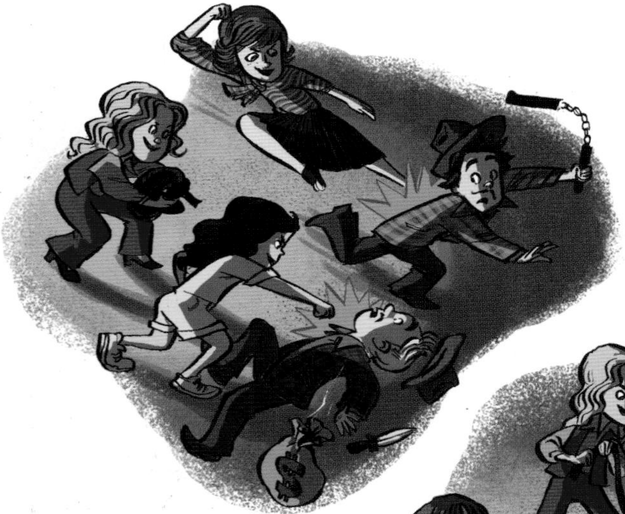

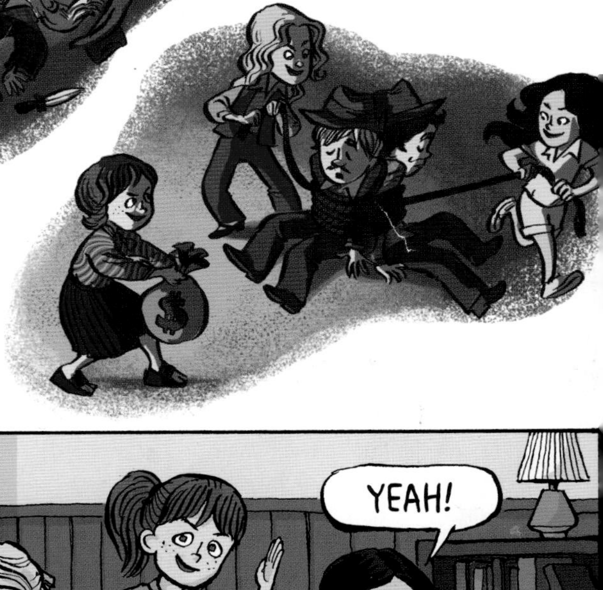

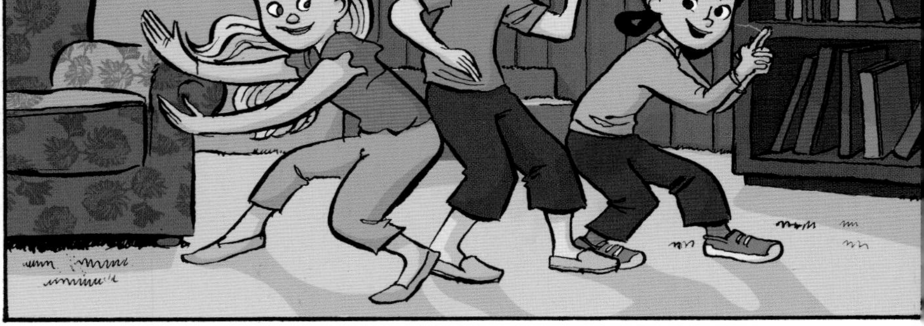
YEAH!

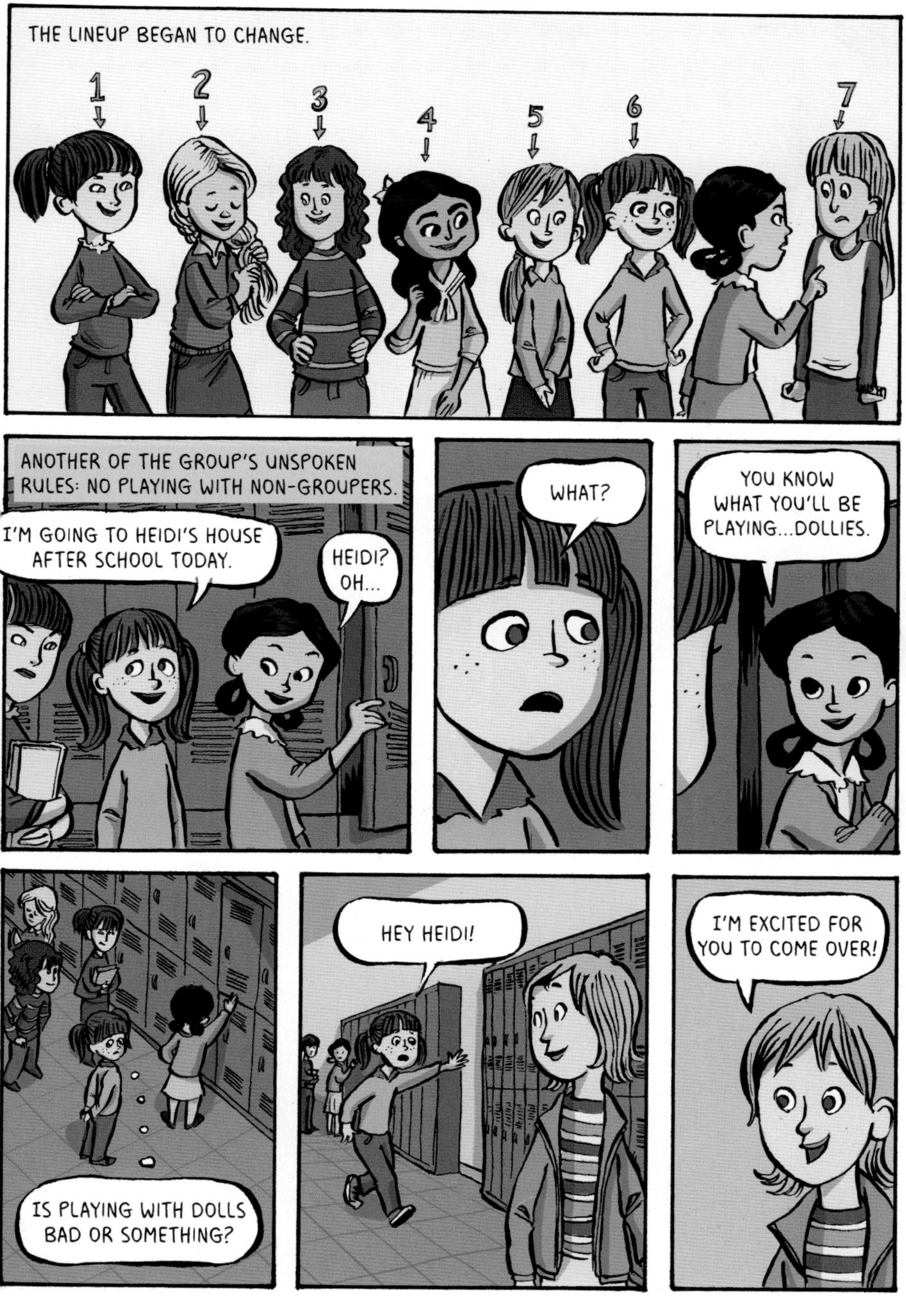
THE LINEUP BEGAN TO CHANGE.
1
2
3
4
5
6
7
ANOTHER OF THE GROUP'S UNSPOKEN RULES: NO PLAYING WITH NON-GROUPERS.
I'M GOING TO HEIDI'S HOUSE AFTER SCHOOL TODAY.
HEIDI? OH...
WHAT?
YOU KNOW WHAT YOU'LL BE PLAYING...DOLLIES.
IS PLAYING WITH DOLLS BAD OR SOMETHING?
HEY HEIDI!
I'M EXCITED FOR YOU TO COME OVER!

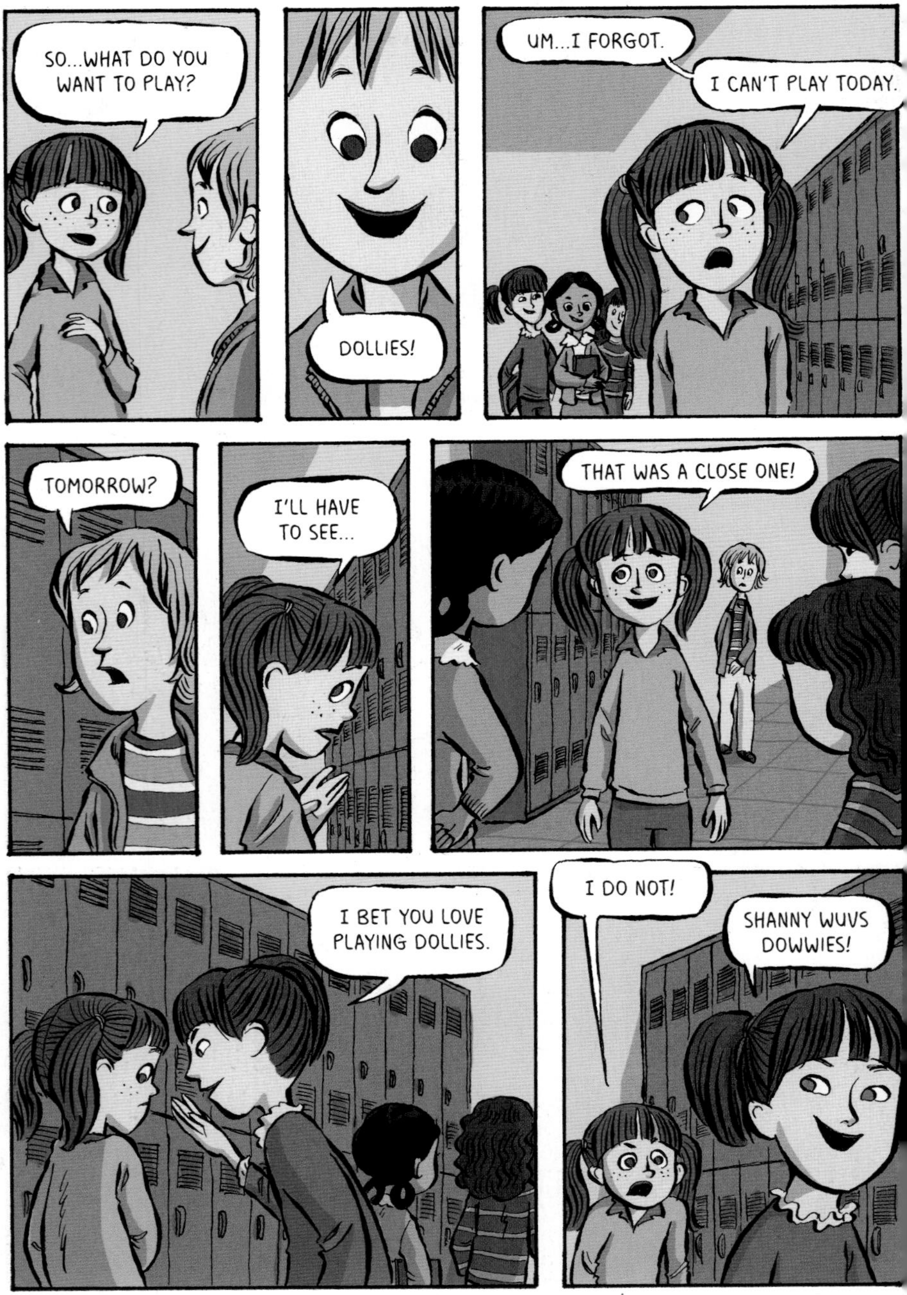
SO...WHAT DO YOU WANT TO PLAY?
DOLLIES!
UM...I FORGOT.
I CAN'T PLAY TODAY.
TOMORROW?
I'LL HAVE TO SEE...
THAT WAS A CLOSE ONE!
I BET YOU LOVE PLAYING DOLLIES.
I DO NOT!
SHANNY WUVS DOWWIES!

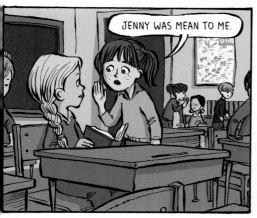

JENNY WAS MEAN TO ME.

DON'T BE SO SENSITIVE.

MRS. WILCOX, I HAVE A TUMMY ACHE.

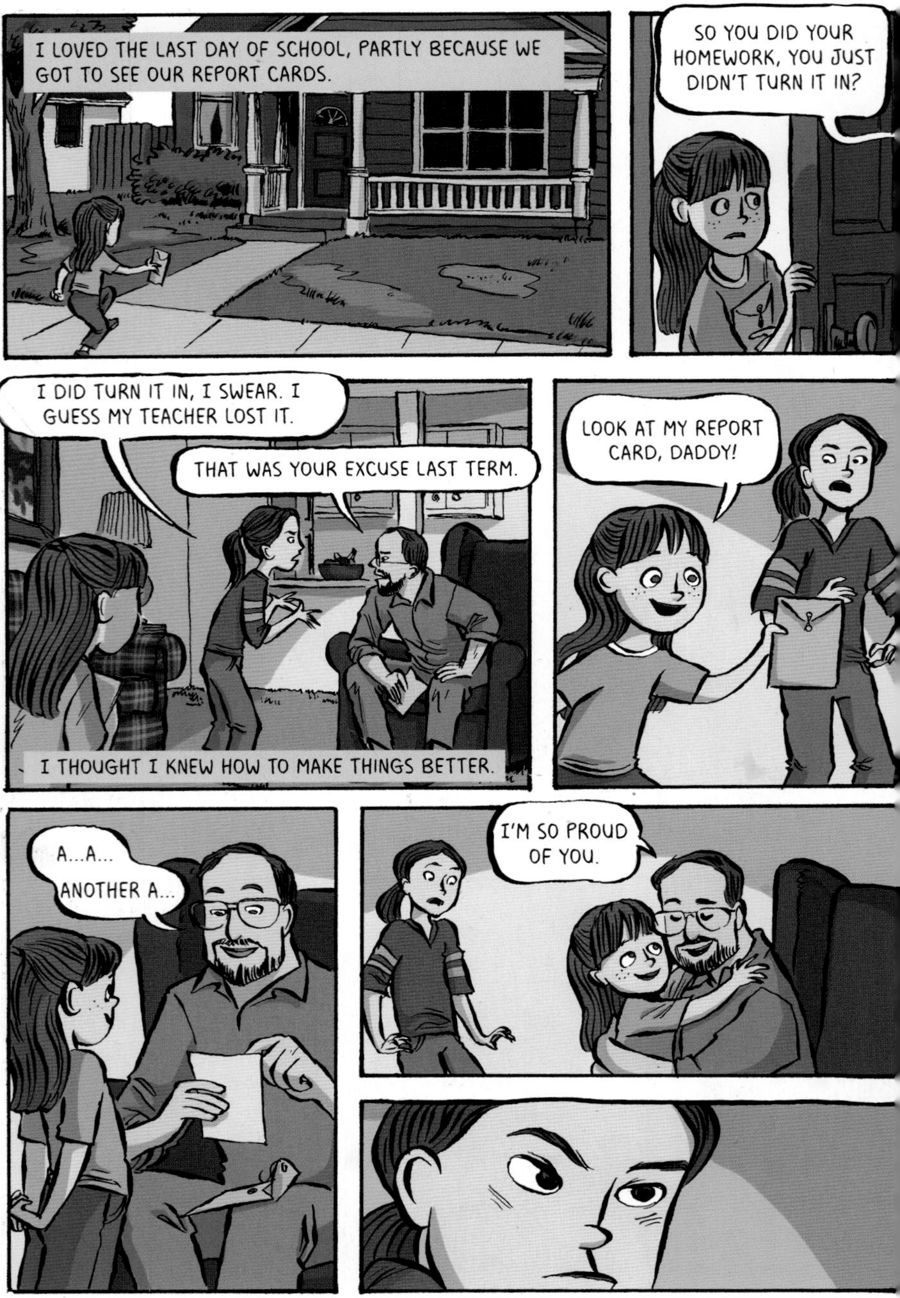
I LOVED THE LAST DAY OF SCHOOL, PARTLY BECAUSE WE GOT TO SEE OUR REPORT CARDS.
SO YOU DID YOUR HOMEWORK, YOU JUST DIDN'T TURN IT IN?
I DID TURN IT IN, I SWEAR. I GUESS MY TEACHER LOST IT.
THAT WAS YOUR EXCUSE LAST TERM.
I THOUGHT I KNEW HOW TO MAKE THINGS BETTER.
LOOK AT MY REPORT CARD, DADDY!
A...A...
ANOTHER A...
I'M SO PROUD OF YOU.

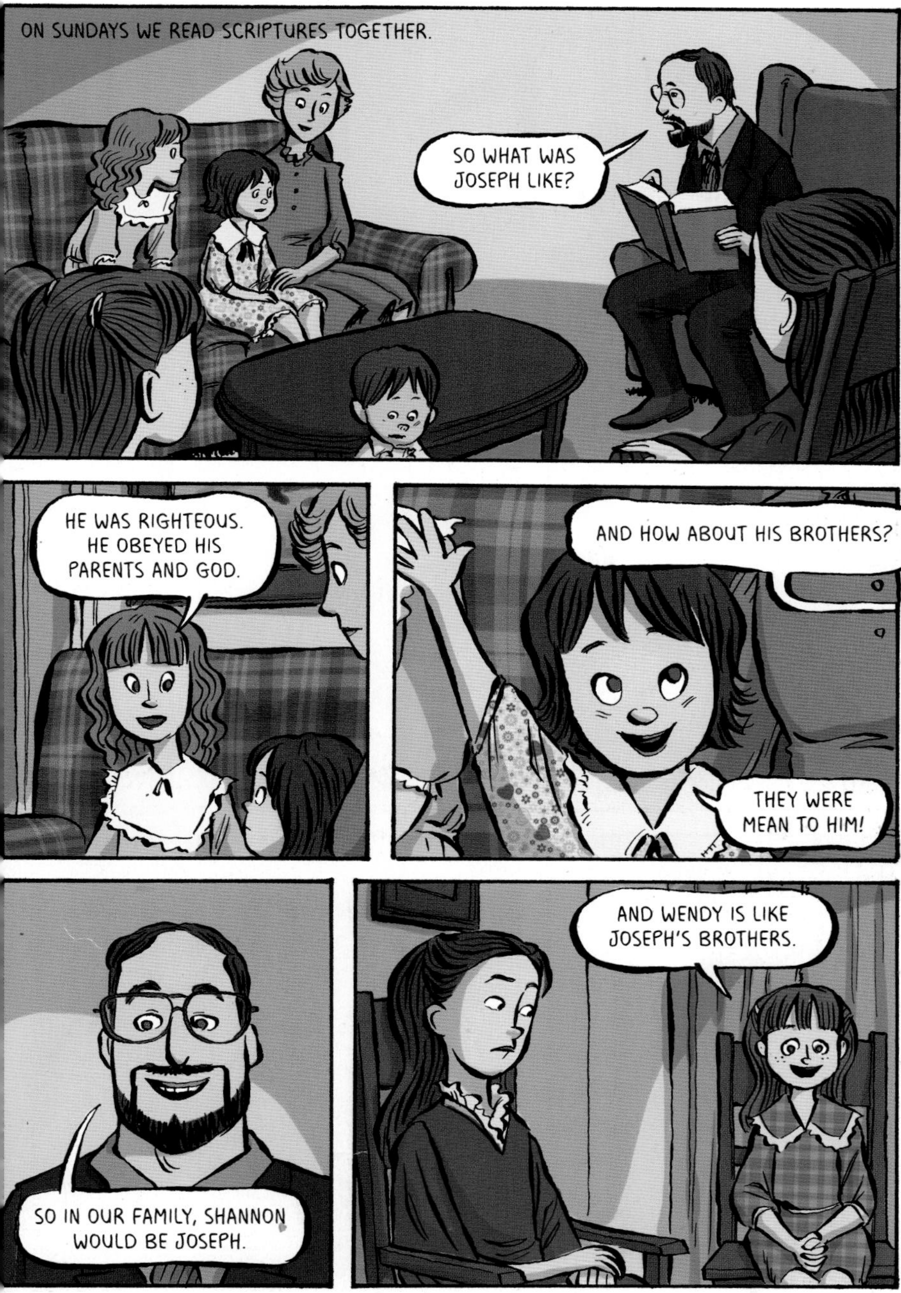
ON SUNDAYS WE READ SCRIPTURES TOGETHER.
SO WHAT WAS JOSEPH LIKE?
HE WAS RIGHTEOUS. HE OBEYED HIS PARENTS AND GOD.
AND HOW ABOUT HIS BROTHERS?
THEY WERE MEAN TO HIM!
SO IN OUR FAMILY, SHANNON WOULD BE JOSEPH.
AND WENDY IS LIKE JOSEPH'S BROTHERS.

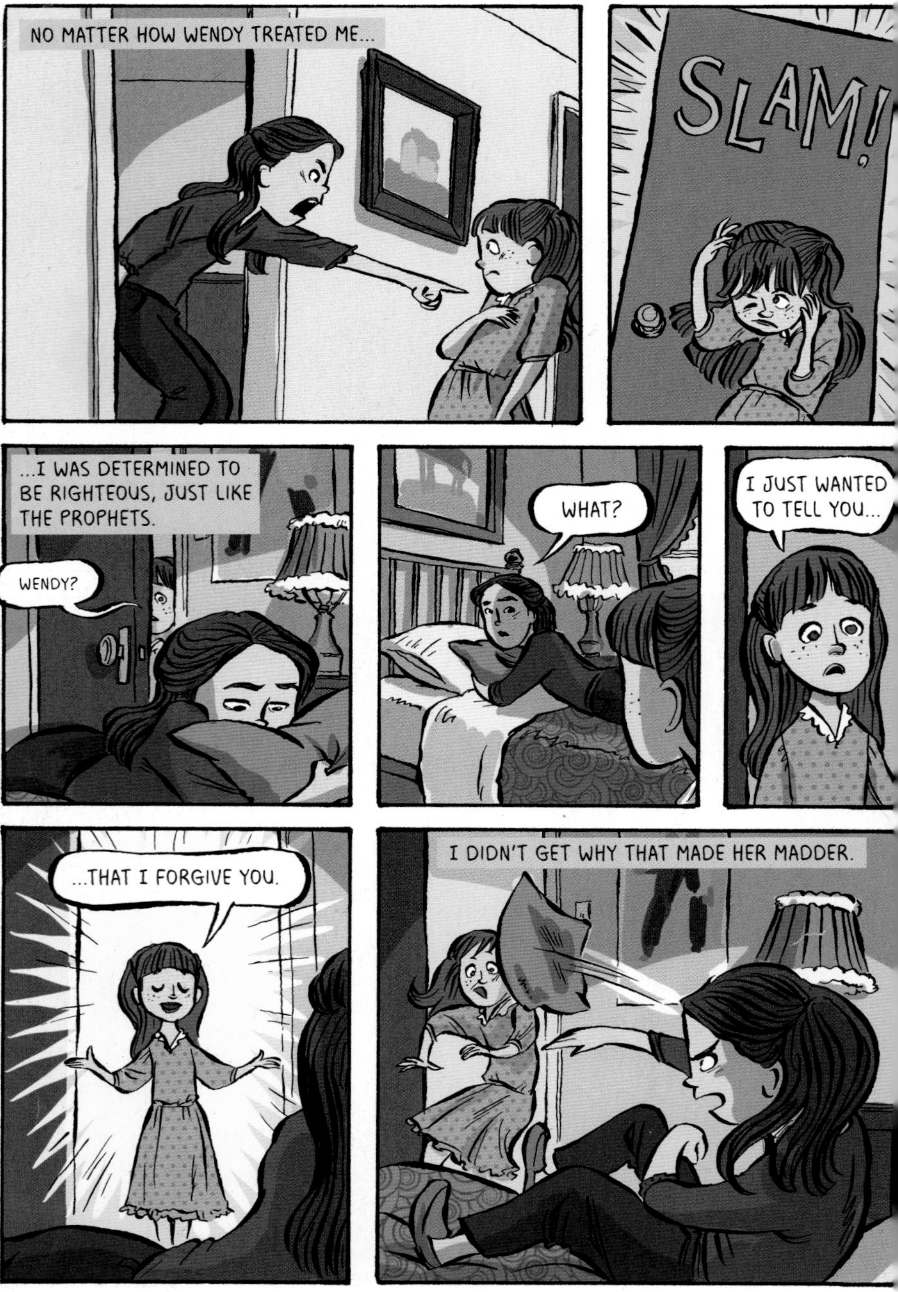
NO MATTER HOW WENDY TREATED ME...
SLAM!
...I WAS DETERMINED TO BE RIGHTEOUS, JUST LIKE THE PROPHETS.
WENDY?
WHAT?
I JUST WANTED TO TELL YOU...
...THAT I FORGIVE YOU.
I DIDN'T GET WHY THAT MADE HER MADDER.

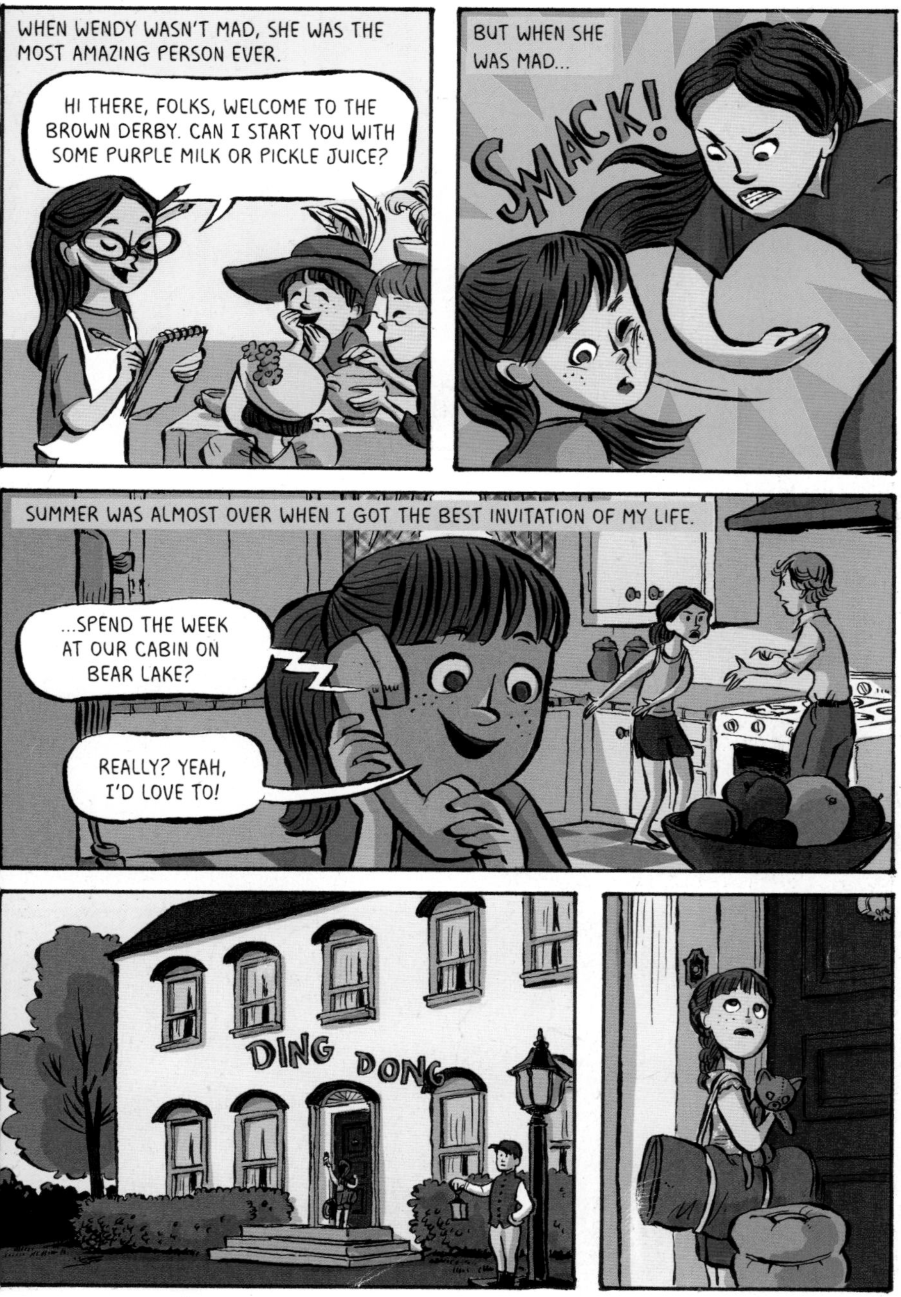
WHEN WENDY WASN'T MAD, SHE WAS THE MOST AMAZING PERSON EVER.
HI THERE, FOLKS, WELCOME TO THE BROWN DERBY. CAN I START YOU WITH SOME PURPLE MILK OR PICKLE JUICE?
BUT WHEN SHE WAS MAD...
SMACK!
SUMMER WAS ALMOST OVER WHEN I GOT THE BEST INVITATION OF MY LIFE.
...SPEND THE WEEK AT OUR CABIN ON BEAR LAKE?
REALLY? YEAH, I'D LOVE TO!
DING DONG

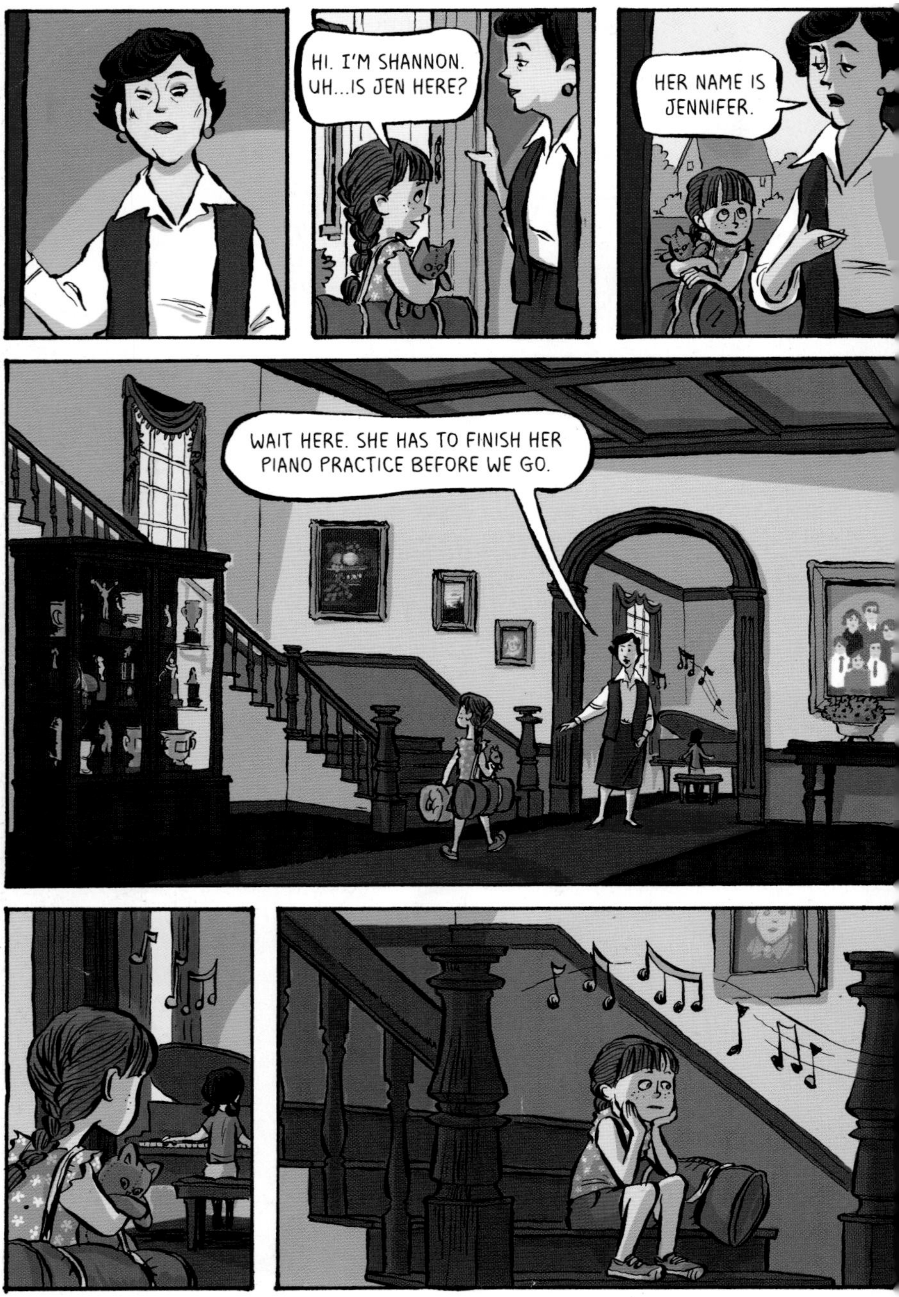
HI. I'M SHANNON. UH...IS JEN HERE?
HER NAME IS JENNIFER.
WAIT HERE. SHE HAS TO FINISH HER PIANO PRACTICE BEFORE WE GO.

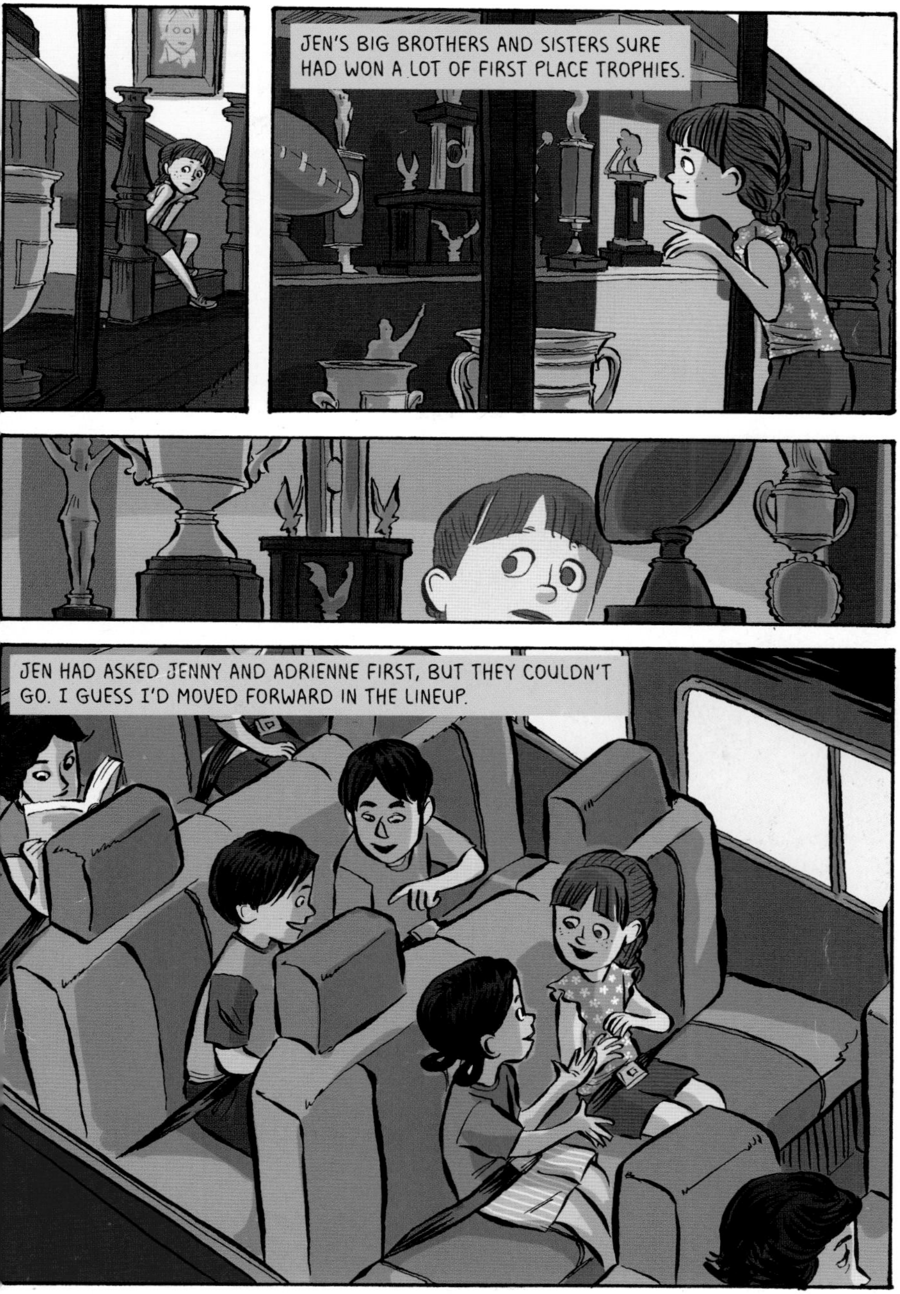
JEN'S BIG BROTHERS AND SISTERS SURE HAD WON A LOT OF FIRST PLACE TROPHIES.
JEN HAD ASKED JENNY AND ADRIENNE FIRST, BUT THEY COULDN'T GO. I GUESS I'D MOVED FORWARD IN THE LINEUP.

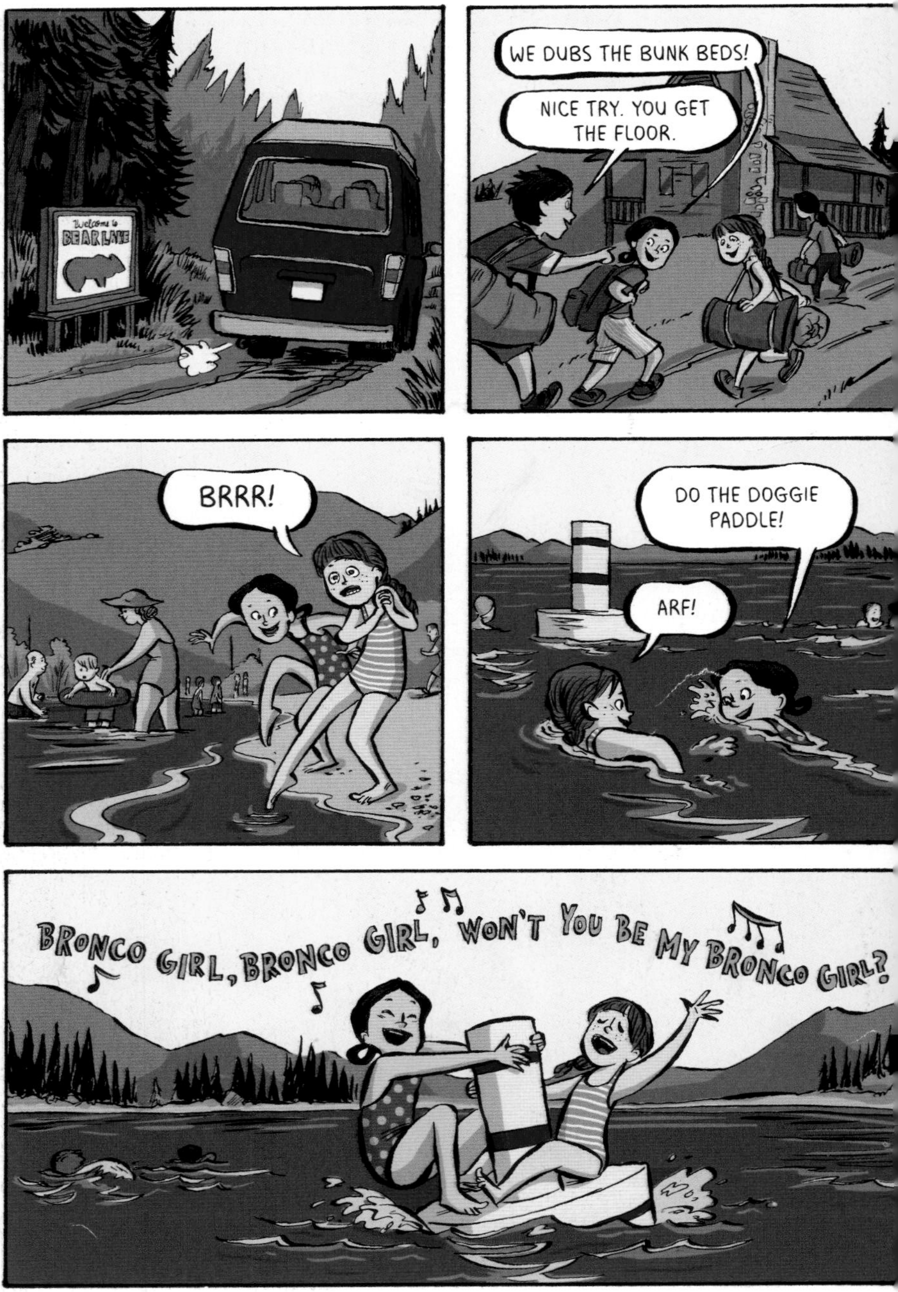

WELCOME TO BEAR LAKE
WE DUBS THE BUNK BEDS!
NICE TRY. YOU GET THE FLOOR.
BRRR!
DO THE DOGGIE PADDLE!
ARF!
BRONCO GIRL, BRONCO GIRL, WON'T YOU BE MY BRONCO GIRL?

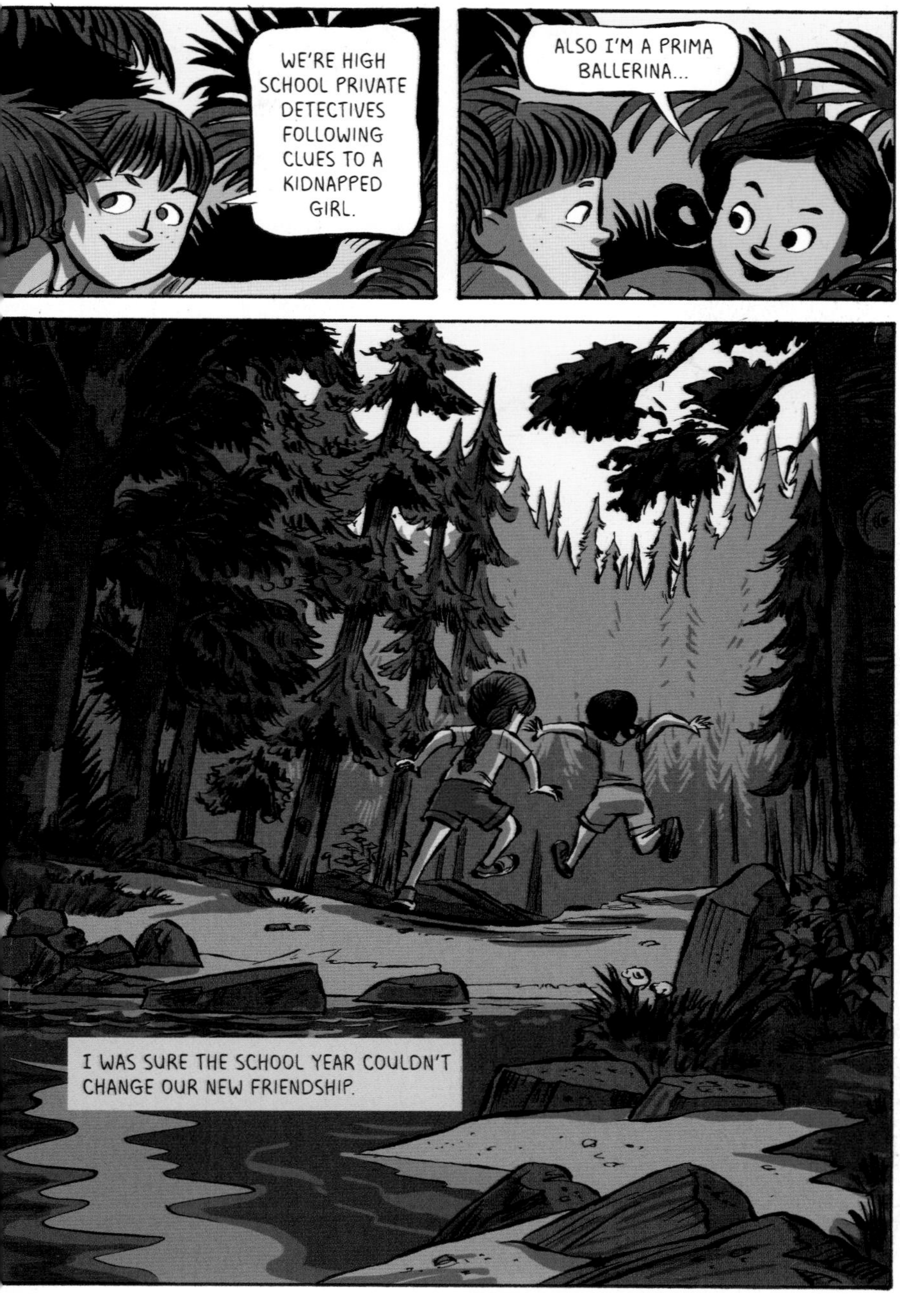
WE'RE HIGH SCHOOL PRIVATE DETECTIVES FOLLOWING CLUES TO A KIDNAPPED GIRL.
ALSO I'M A PRIMA BALLERINA...
I WAS SURE THE SCHOOL YEAR COULDN'T CHANGE OUR NEW FRIENDSHIP.

# JENNY

JUST BEFORE FOURTH GRADE STARTED...

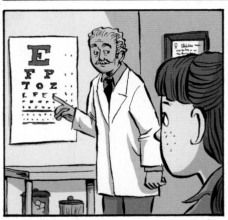

E...P...NO WAIT, F.

OR IS IT H?

I COULD SEE EVERYTHING MORE CLEARLY.

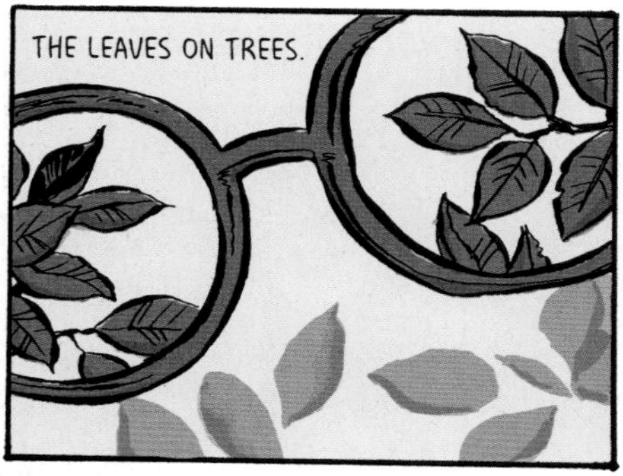
THE LEAVES ON TREES.

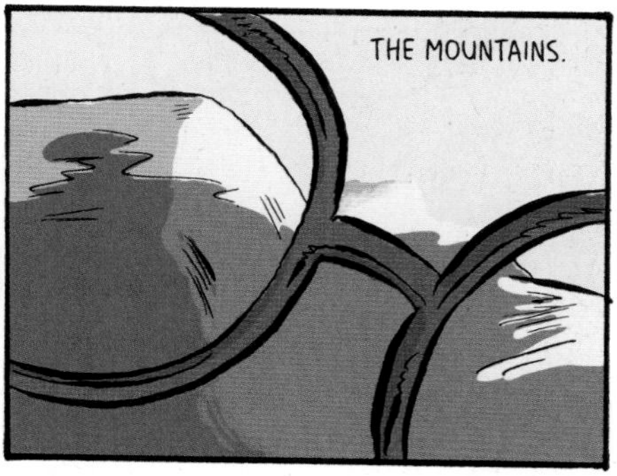
THE MOUNTAINS.

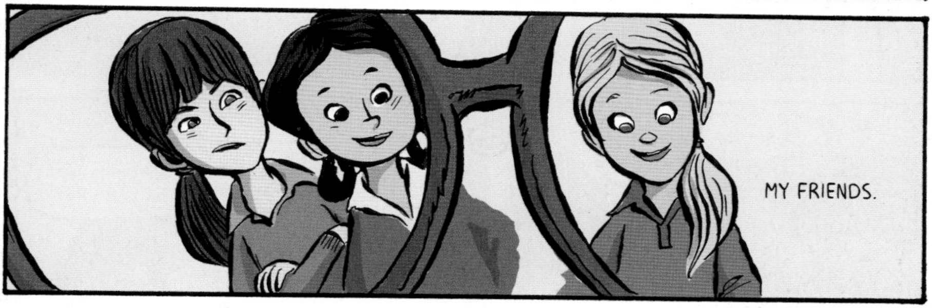
MY FRIENDS.

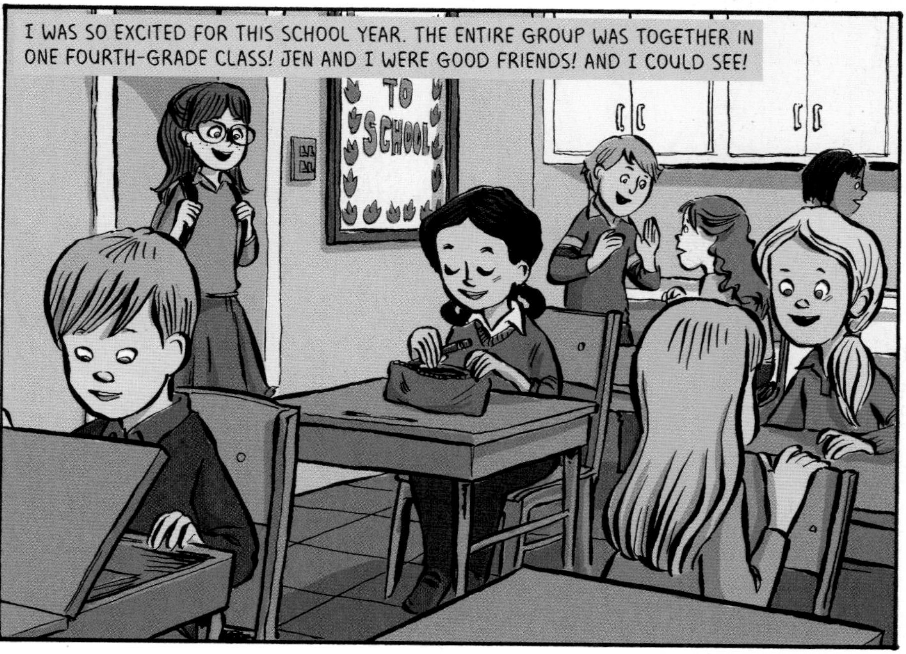
I WAS SO EXCITED FOR THIS SCHOOL YEAR. THE ENTIRE GROUP WAS TOGETHER IN ONE FOURTH-GRADE CLASS! JEN AND I WERE GOOD FRIENDS! AND I COULD SEE!
TO
SCHOOL

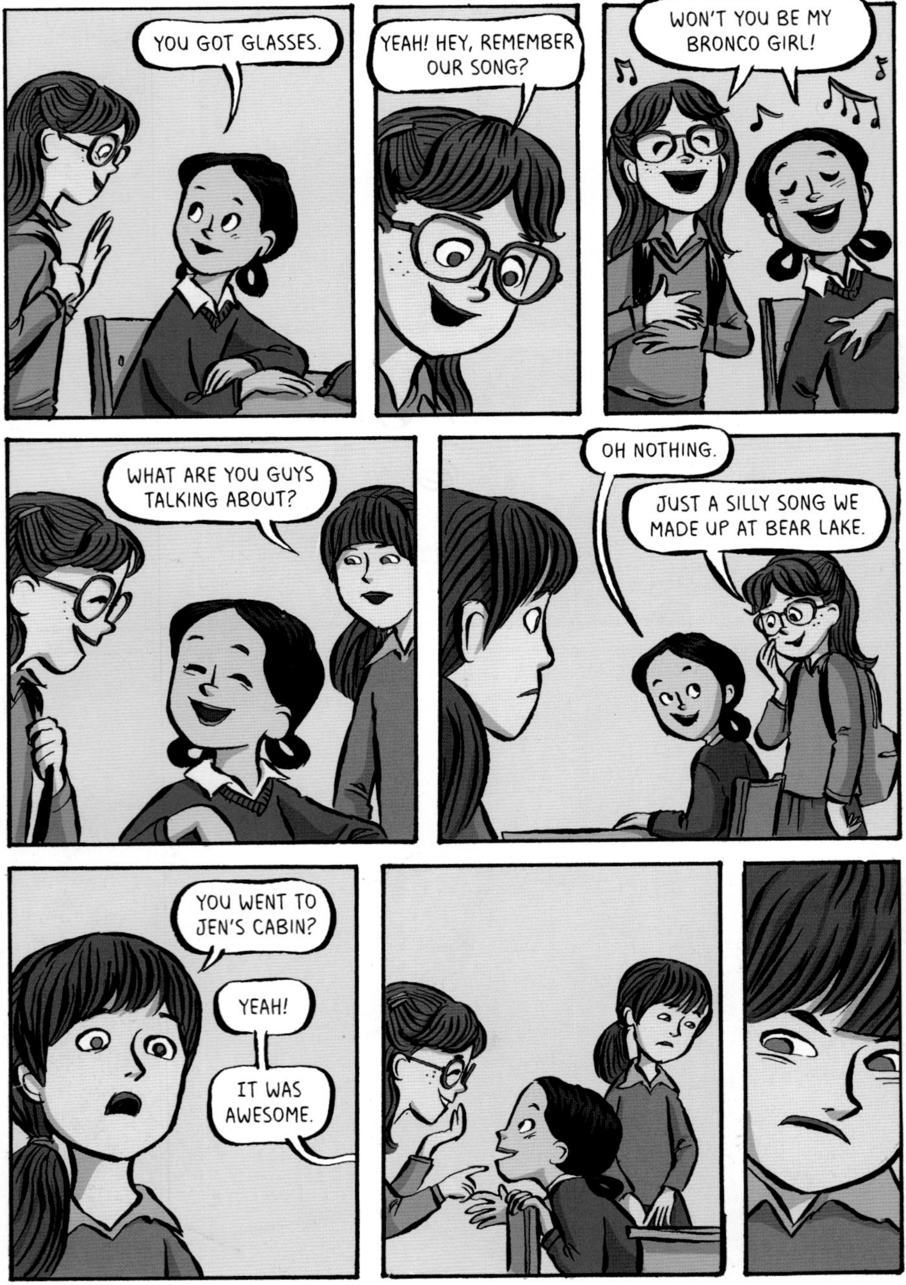
YOU GOT GLASSES.
YEAH! HEY, REMEMBER OUR SONG?
WON'T YOU BE MY BRONCO GIRL!
WHAT ARE YOU GUYS TALKING ABOUT?
OH NOTHING.
JUST A SILLY SONG WE MADE UP AT BEAR LAKE.
YOU WENT TO JEN'S CABIN?
YEAH!
IT WAS AWESOME.

JENNY AND I HAD A LOT IN COMMON.

WE WERE BOTH SORTA POPULAR BECAUSE OF OUR MORE-POPULAR BEST FRIENDS. THOUGH HER WAY MORE THAN ME.

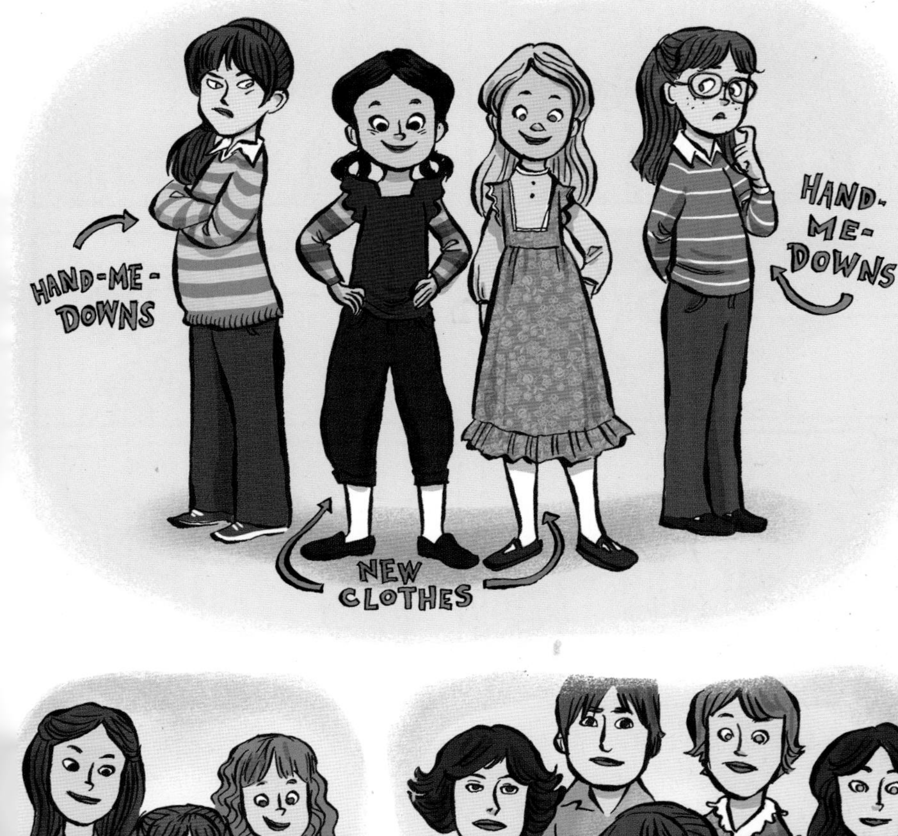

HAND-ME-DOWNS
NEW CLOTHES
HAND-ME-DOWNS


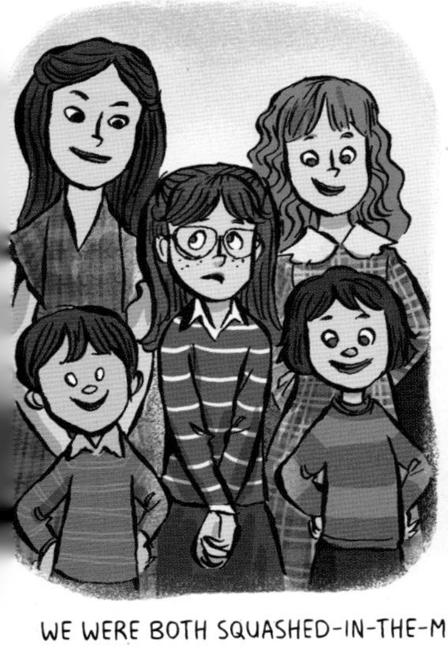

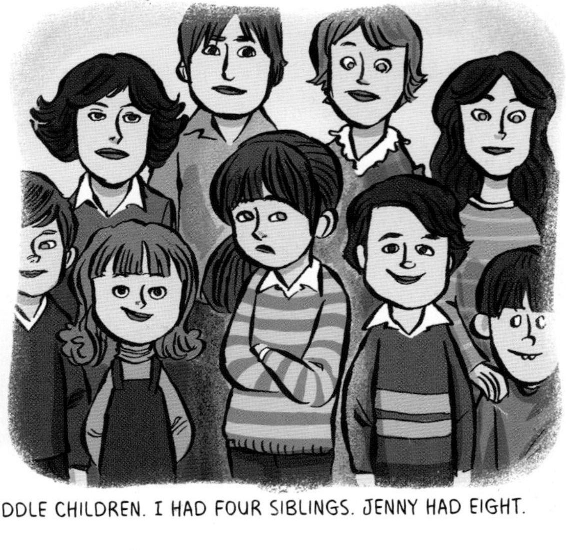

WE WERE BOTH SQUASHED-IN-THE-MIDDLE CHILDREN. I HAD FOUR SIBLINGS. JENNY HAD EIGHT.

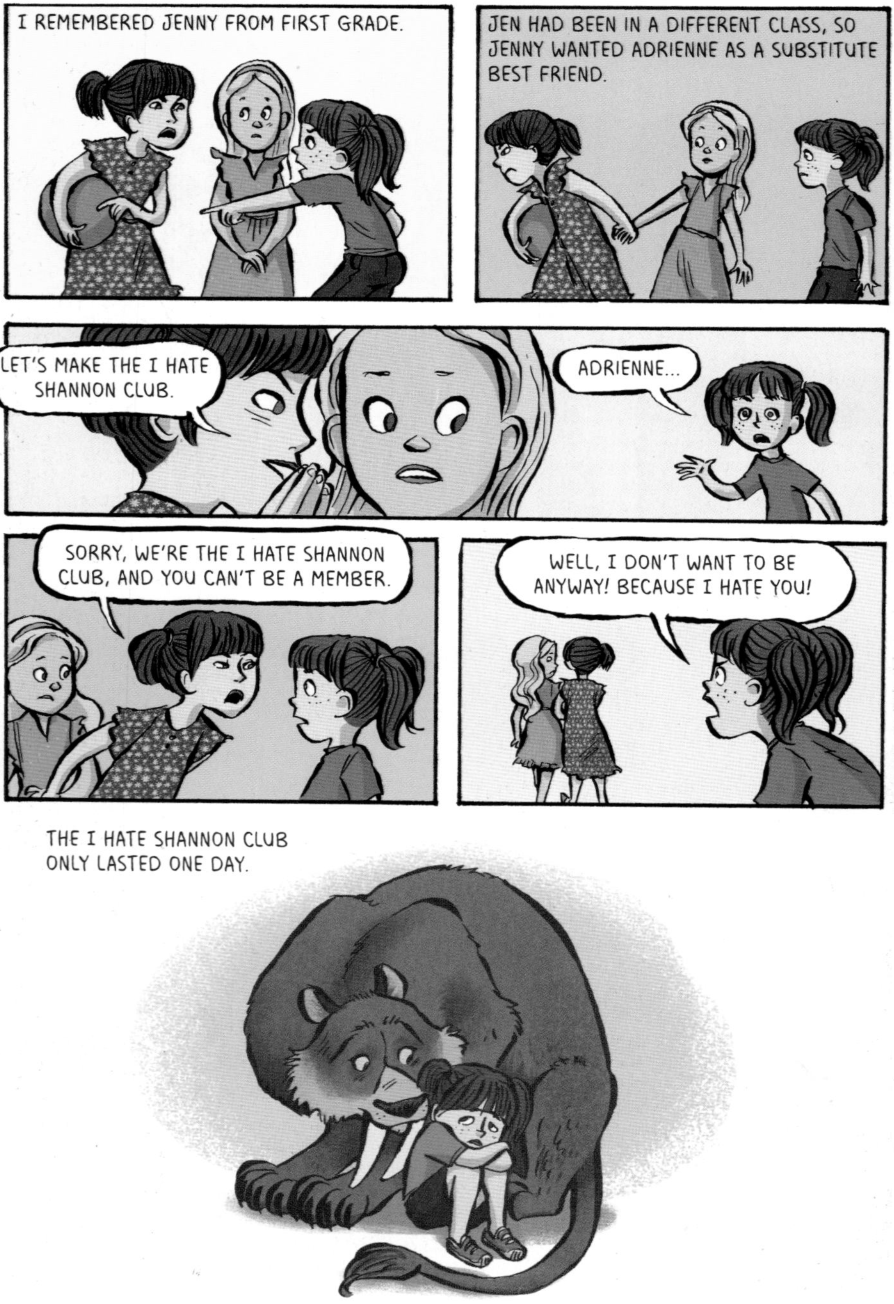
I REMEMBERED JENNY FROM FIRST GRADE.
JEN HAD BEEN IN A DIFFERENT CLASS, SO JENNY WANTED ADRIENNE AS A SUBSTITUTE BEST FRIEND.
LET'S MAKE THE I HATE SHANNON CLUB.
ADRIENNE...
SORRY, WE'RE THE I HATE SHANNON CLUB, AND YOU CAN'T BE A MEMBER.
WELL, I DON'T WANT TO BE ANYWAY! BECAUSE I HATE YOU!
THE I HATE SHANNON CLUB ONLY LASTED ONE DAY.

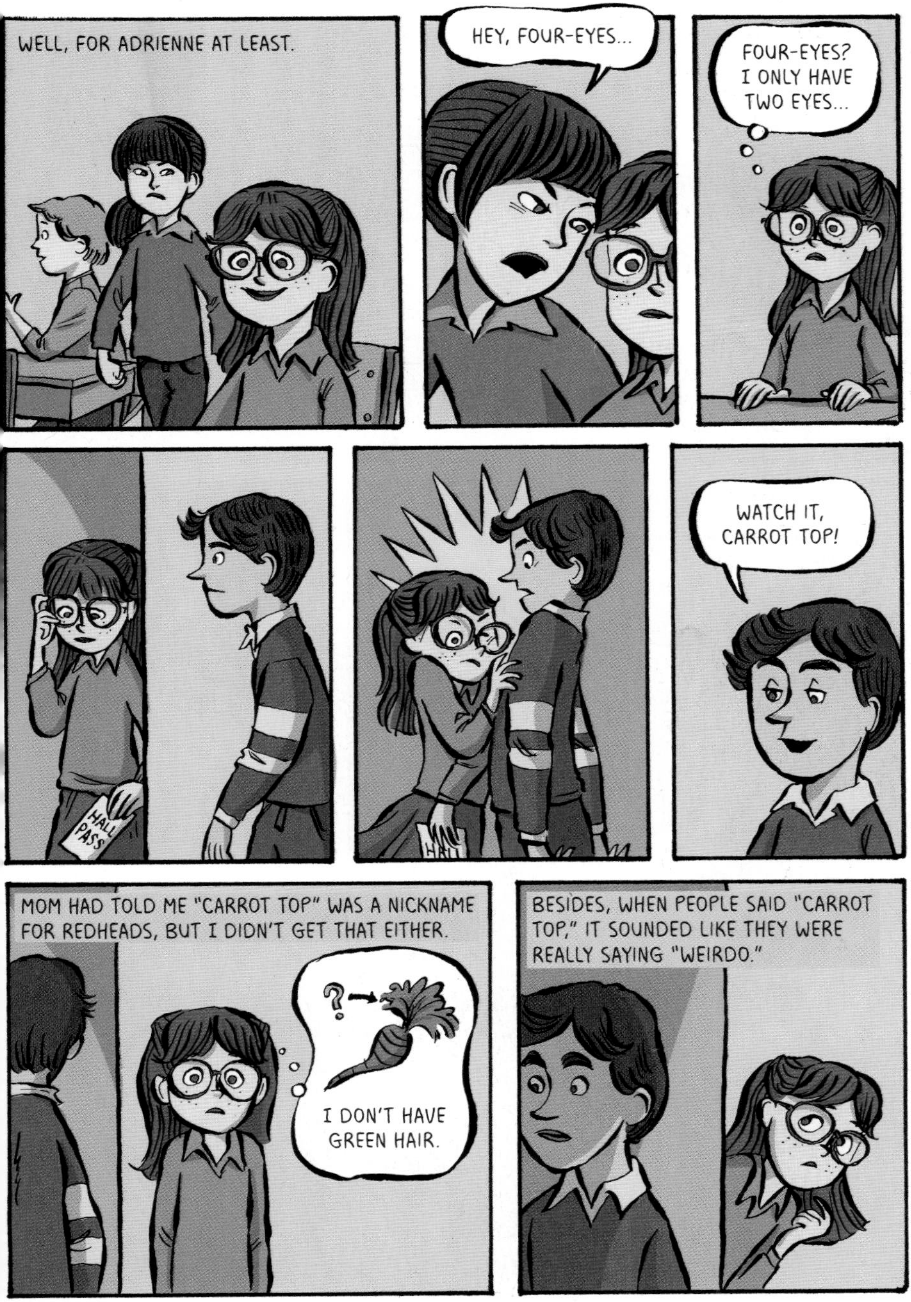
WELL, FOR ADRIENNE AT LEAST.
HEY, FOUR-EYES...
FOUR-EYES? I ONLY HAVE TWO EYES...
HALL PASS
WATCH IT, CARROT TOP!
MOM HAD TOLD ME "CARROT TOP" WAS A NICKNAME FOR REDHEADS, BUT I DIDN'T GET THAT EITHER.
I DON'T HAVE GREEN HAIR.
BESIDES, WHEN PEOPLE SAID "CARROT TOP," IT SOUNDED LIKE THEY WERE REALLY SAYING "WEIRDO."

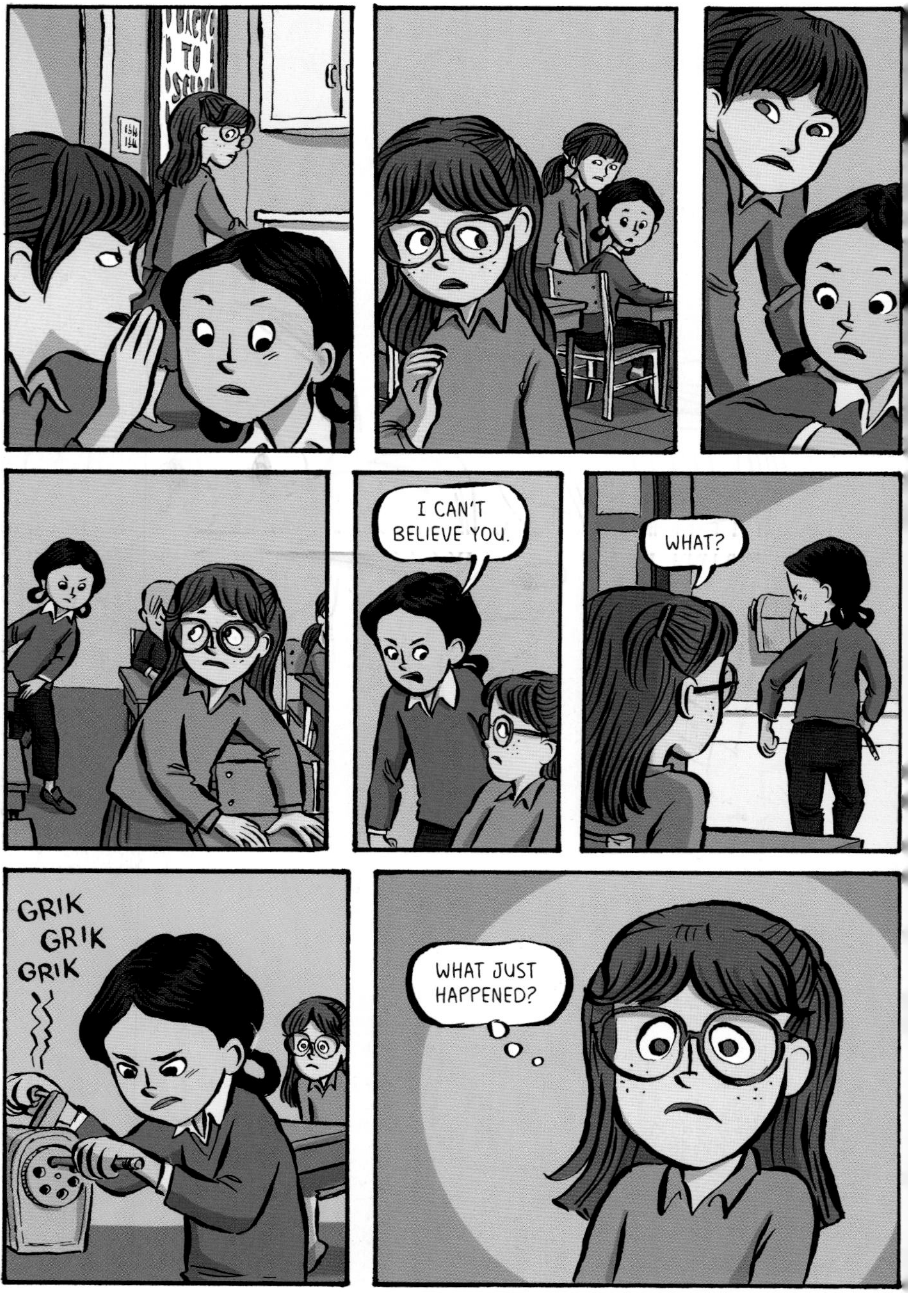
I CAN'T BELIEVE YOU.
WHAT?
GRIK GRIK GRIK
WHAT JUST HAPPENED?

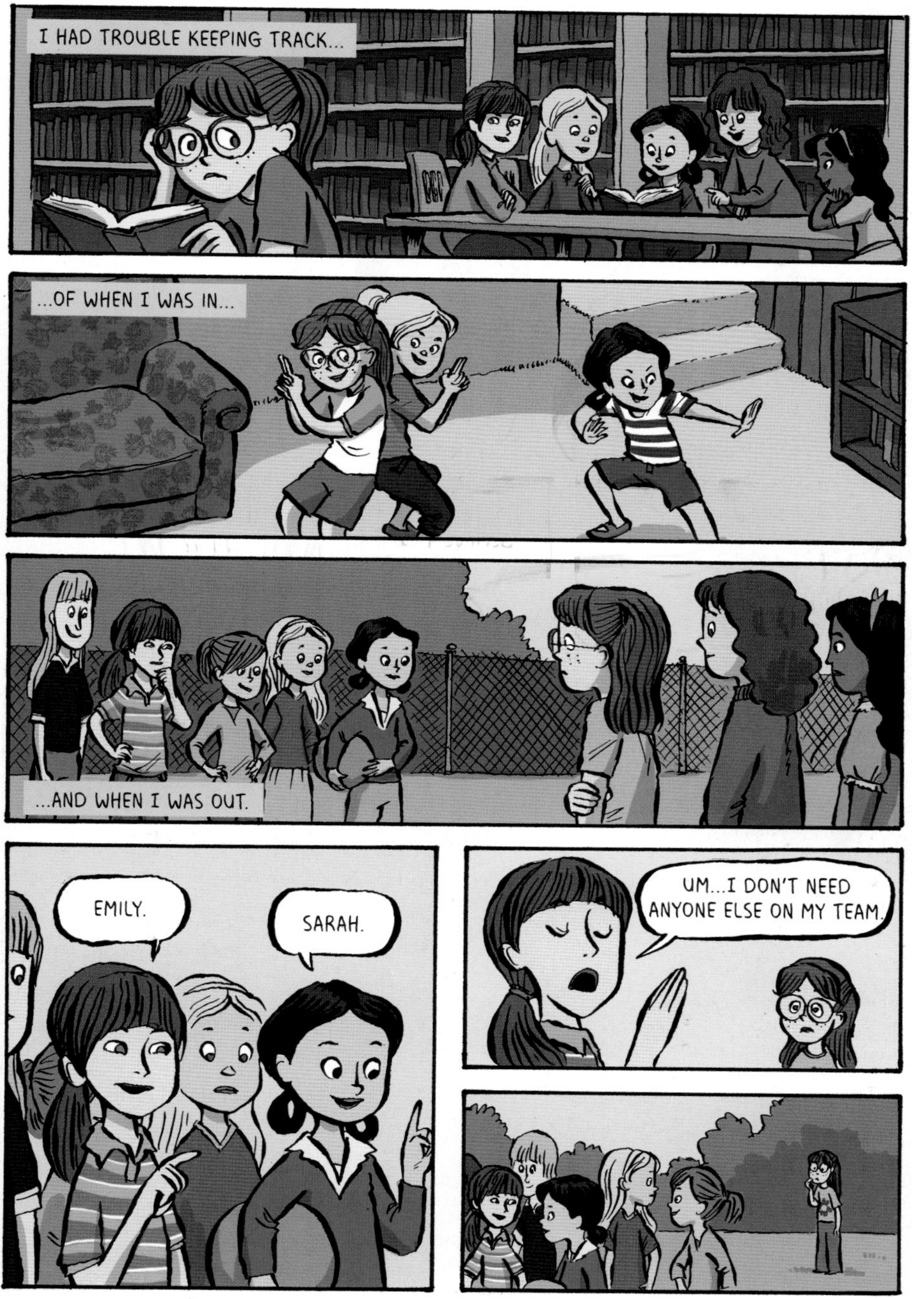
I HAD TROUBLE KEEPING TRACK...
...OF WHEN I WAS IN...
...AND WHEN I WAS OUT.
EMILY.
SARAH.
UM...I DON'T NEED ANYONE ELSE ON MY TEAM.

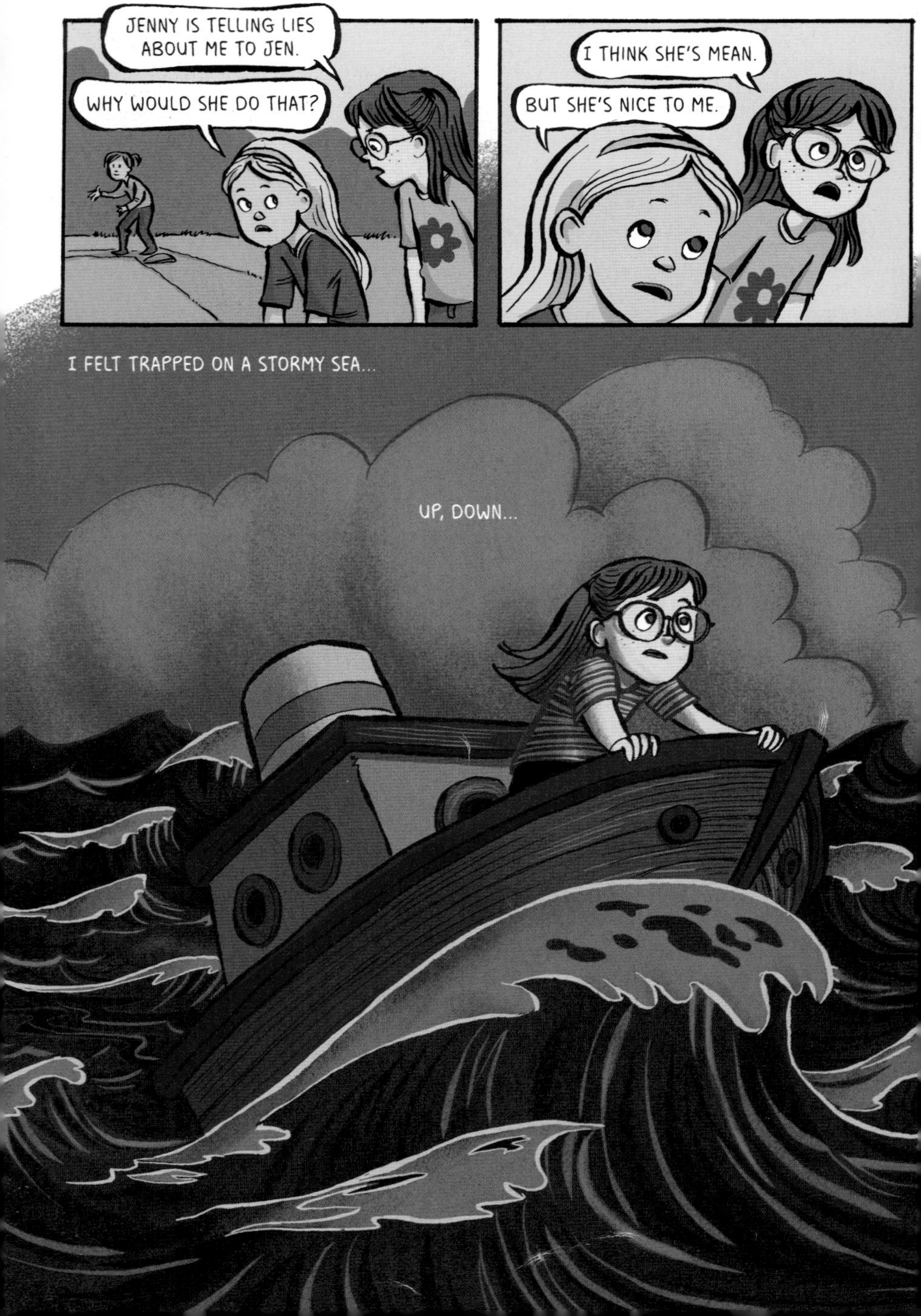

JENNY IS TELLING LIES ABOUT ME TO JEN.
WHY WOULD SHE DO THAT?
I THINK SHE'S MEAN.
BUT SHE'S NICE TO ME.
I FELT TRAPPED ON A STORMY SEA...
UP, DOWN...

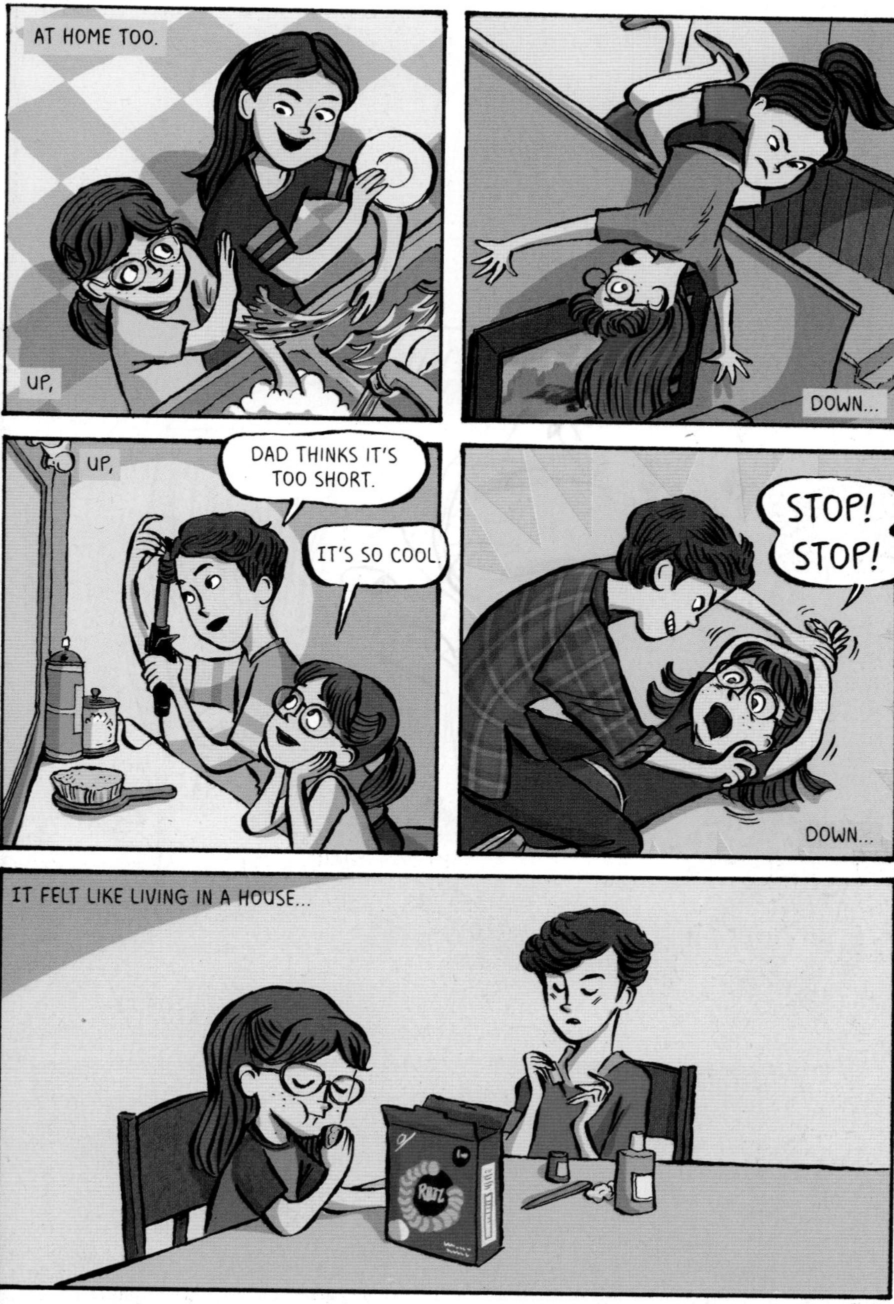
AT HOME TOO.
UP,
DOWN...
UP,
DAD THINKS IT'S TOO SHORT.
IT'S SO COOL.
STOP! STOP!
DOWN...
IT FELT LIKE LIVING IN A HOUSE...

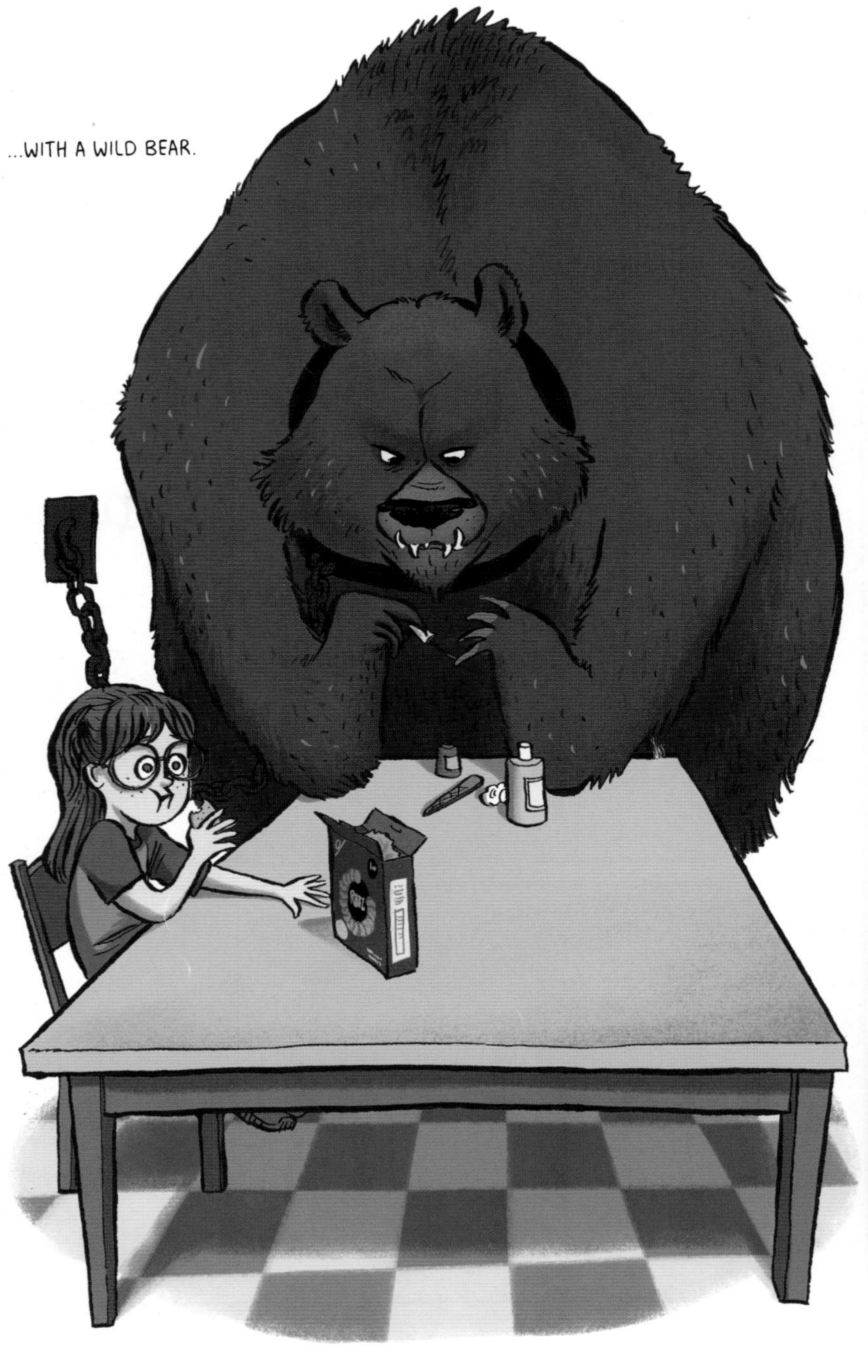
...WITH A WILD BEAR.

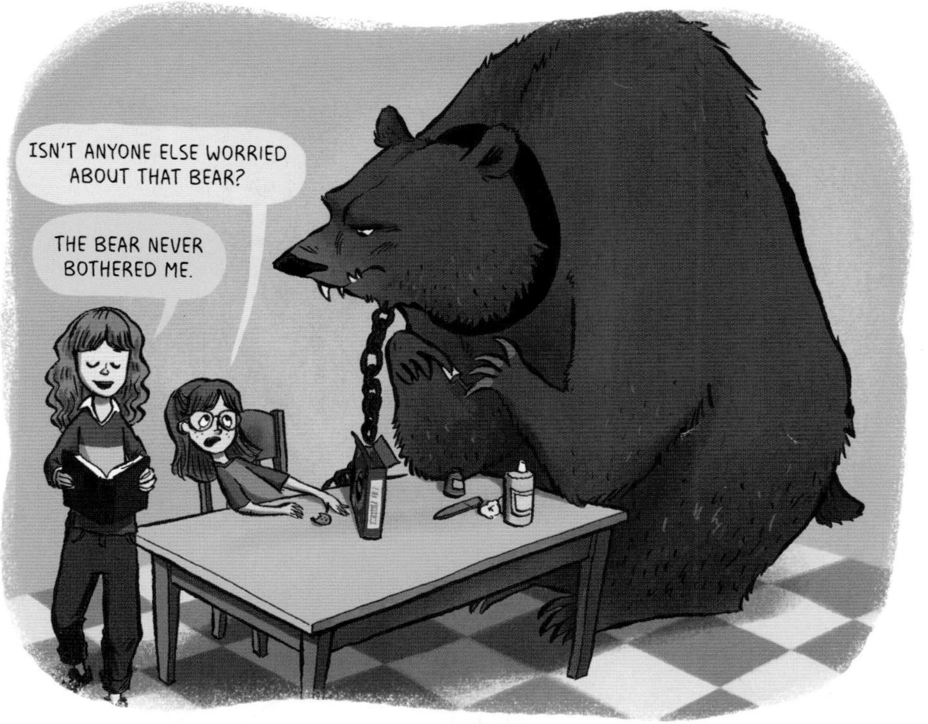
ISN'T ANYONE ELSE WORRIED ABOUT THAT BEAR?
THE BEAR NEVER BOTHERED ME.

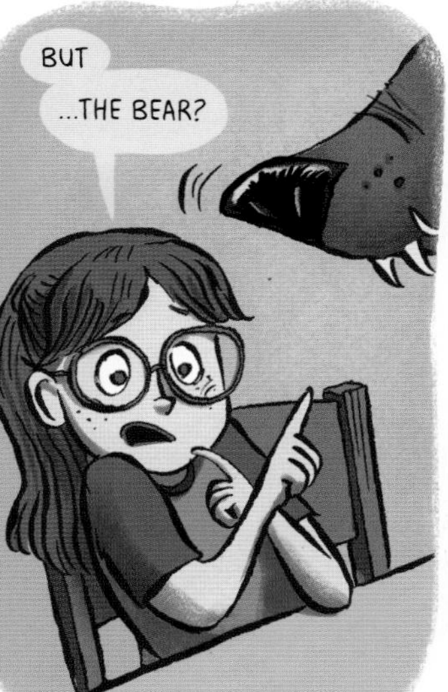
BUT
...THE BEAR?

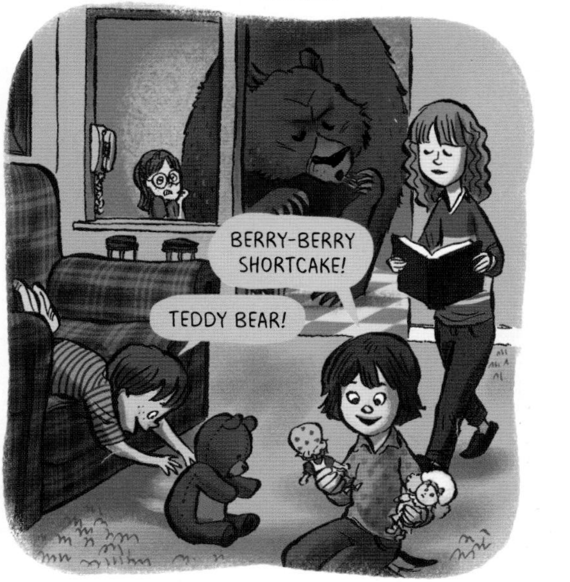
BERRY-BERRY SHORTCAKE!
TEDDY BEAR!

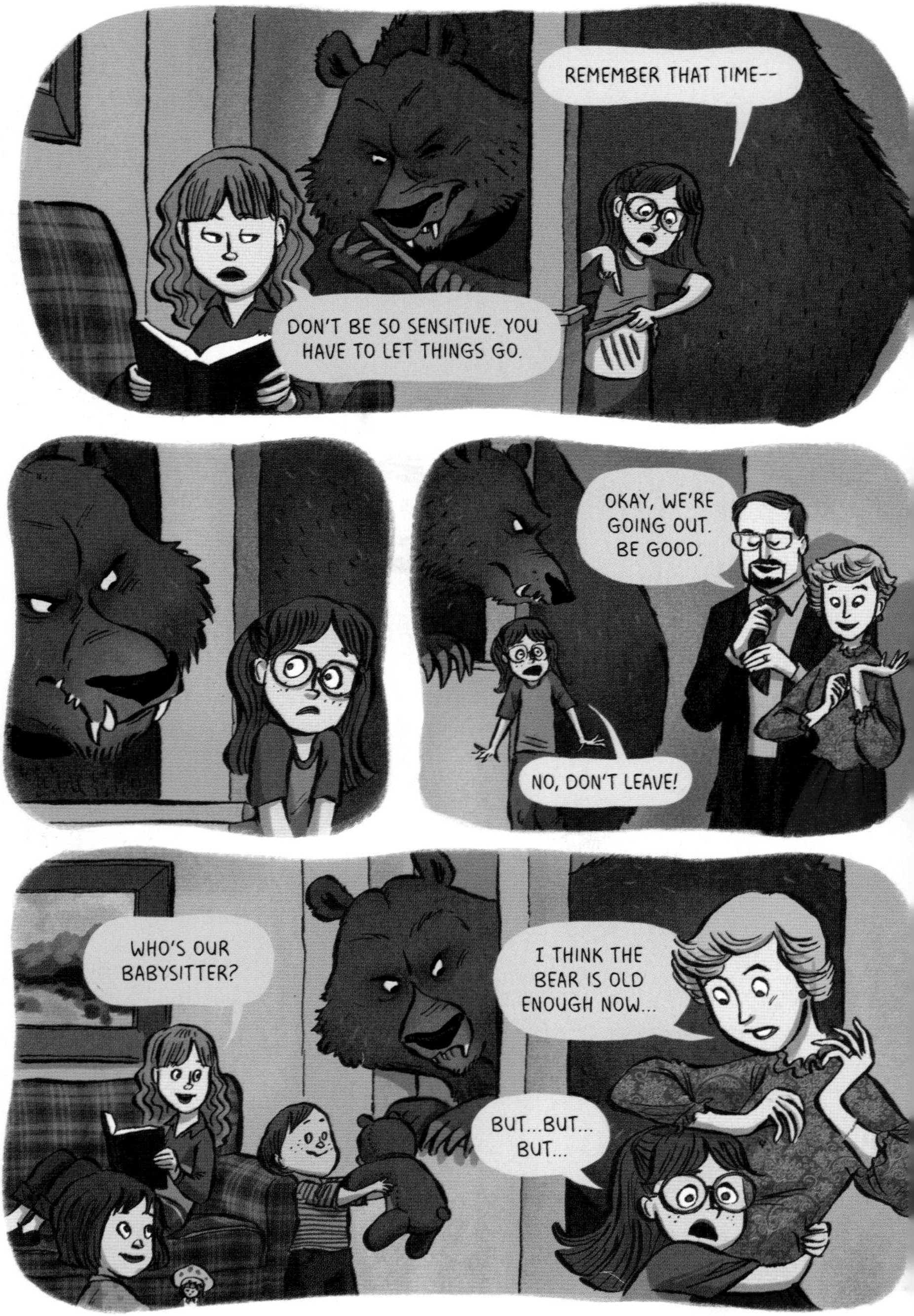
REMEMBER THAT TIME--
DON'T BE SO SENSITIVE. YOU HAVE TO LET THINGS GO.
OKAY, WE'RE GOING OUT. BE GOOD.
NO, DON'T LEAVE!
WHO'S OUR BABYSITTER?
I THINK THE BEAR IS OLD ENOUGH NOW...
BUT...BUT... BUT...

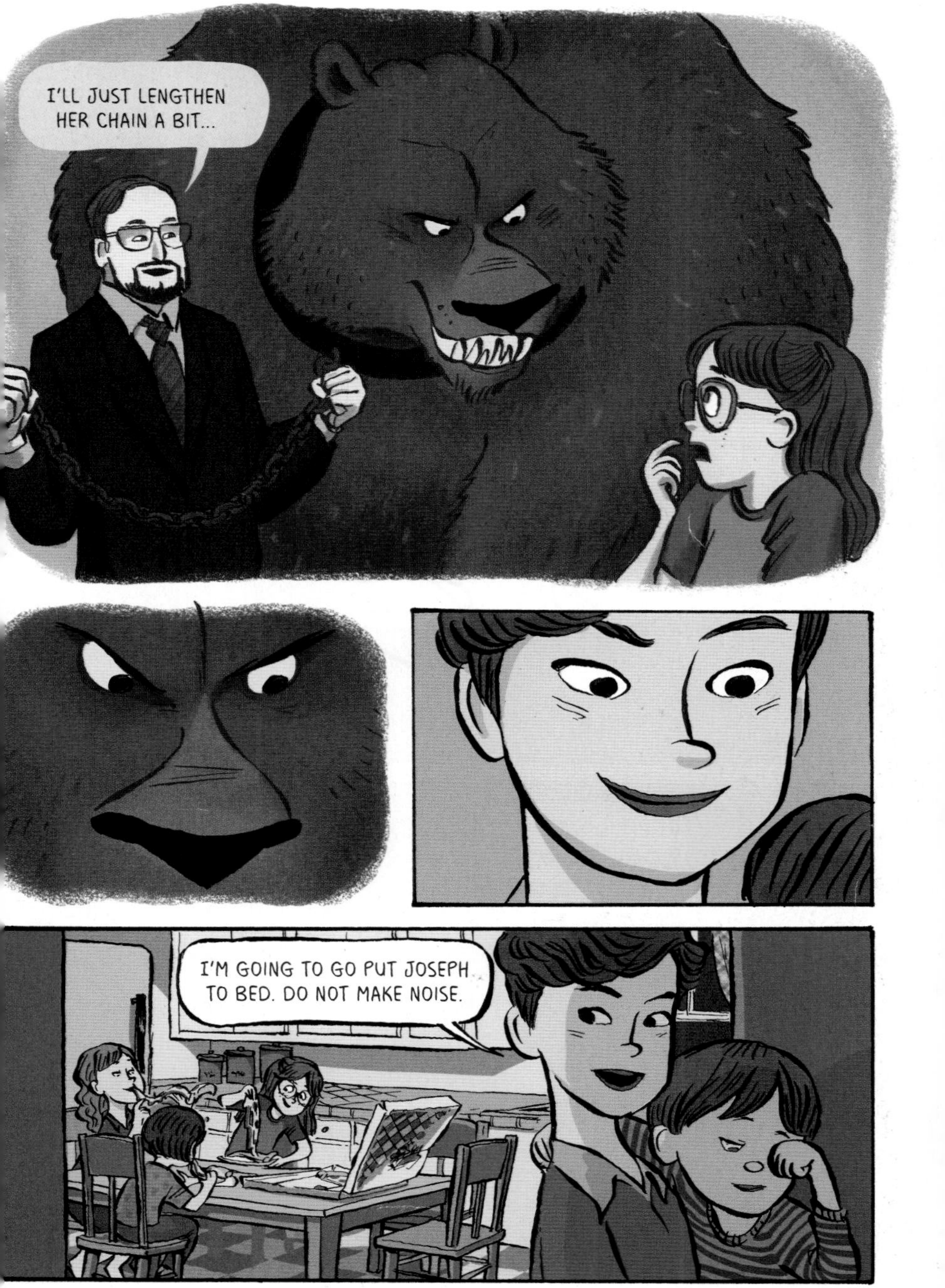
I'LL JUST LENGTHEN HER CHAIN A BIT...
I'M GOING TO GO PUT JOSEPH TO BED. DO NOT MAKE NOISE.

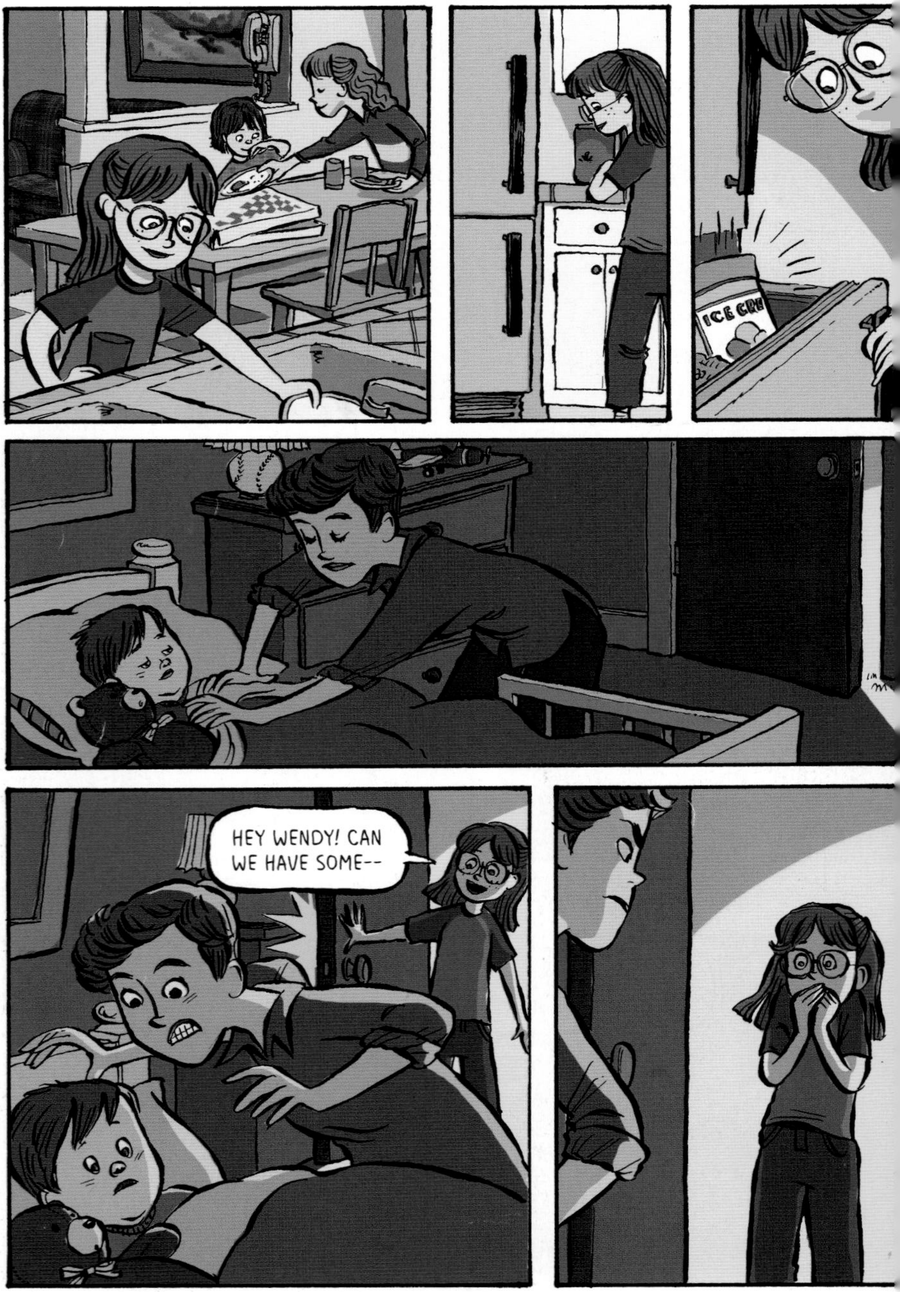
ICE CRE
HEY WENDY! CAN WE HAVE SOME--

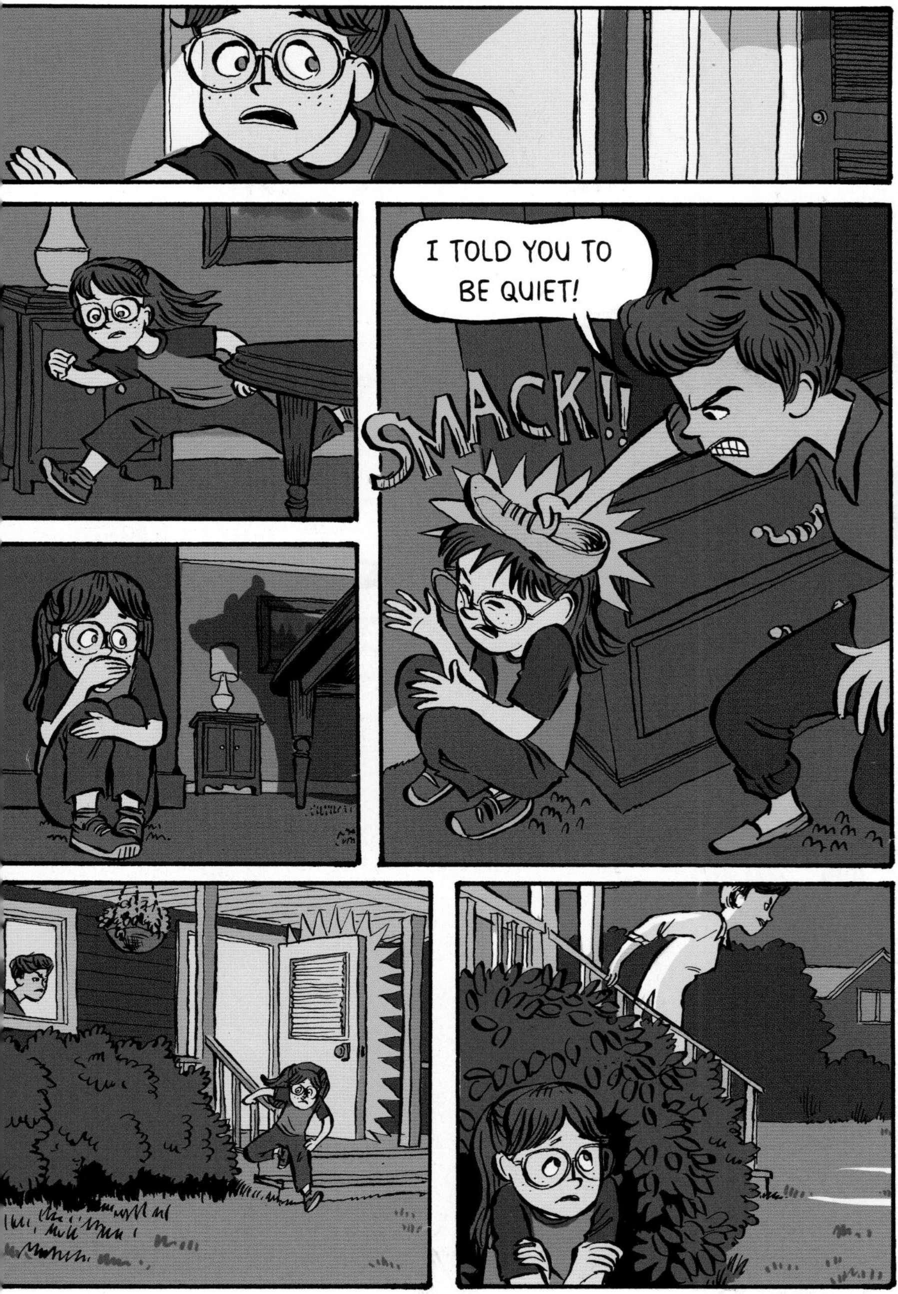
I TOLD YOU TO BE QUIET!
SMACK!!

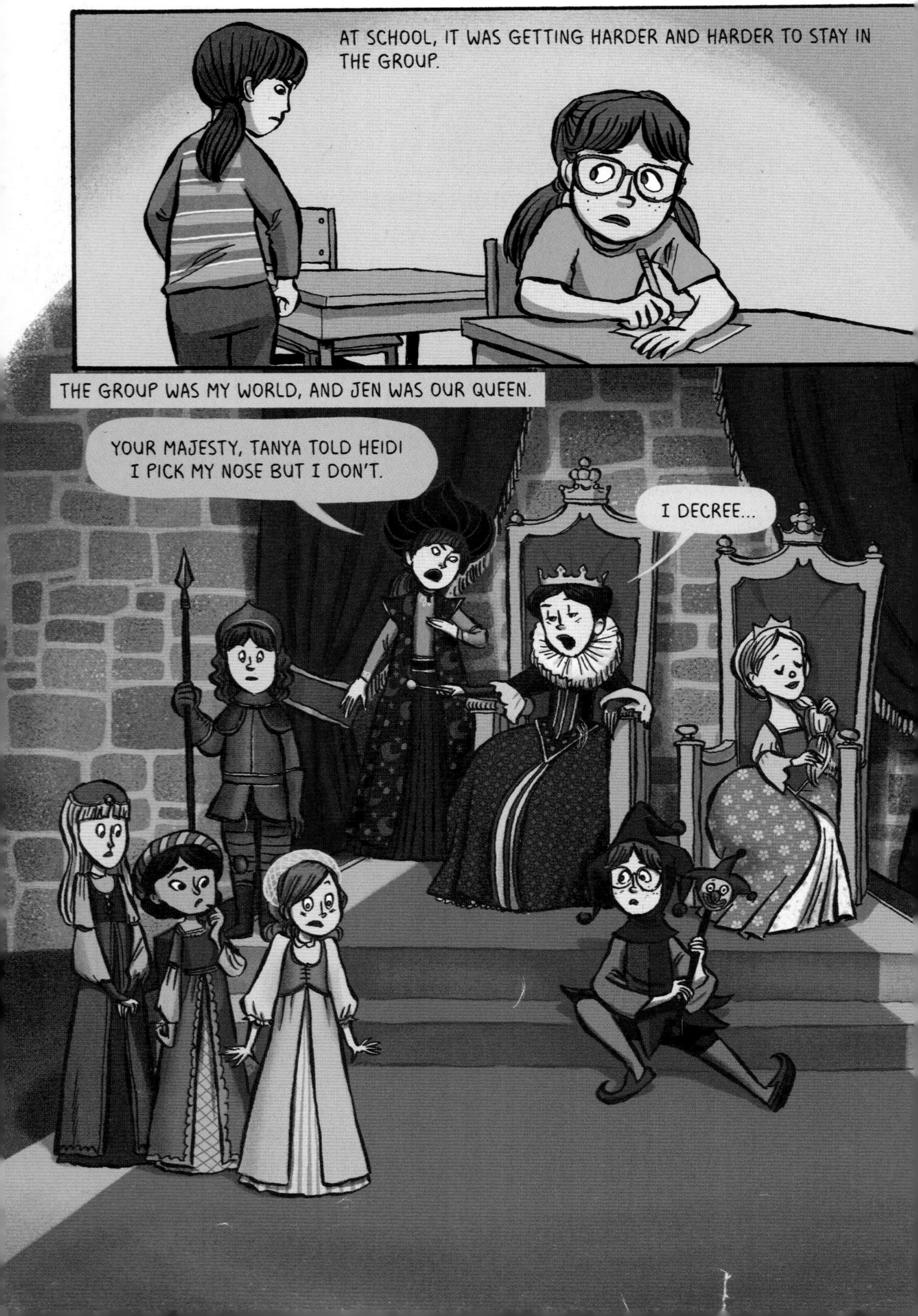
AT SCHOOL, IT WAS GETTING HARDER AND HARDER TO STAY IN THE GROUP.
THE GROUP WAS MY WORLD, AND JEN WAS OUR QUEEN.
YOUR MAJESTY, TANYA TOLD HEIDI I PICK MY NOSE BUT I DON'T.
I DECREE...

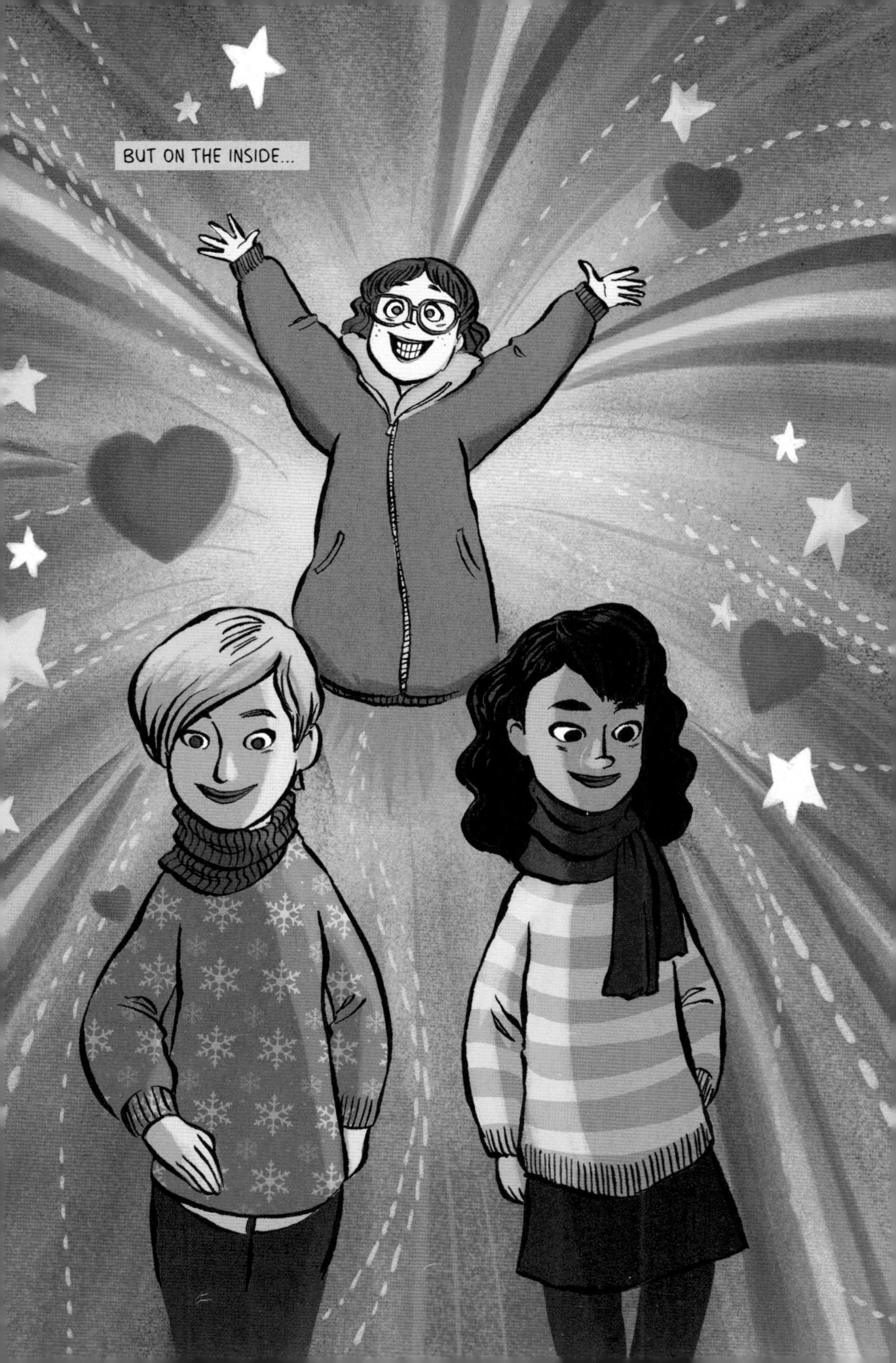
BUT ON THE INSIDE...

ZARA AND VERONICA JUST WALKED AROUND AND TALKED.

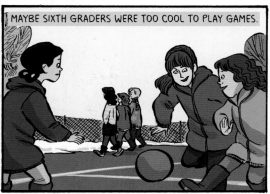

MAYBE SIXTH GRADERS WERE TOO COOL TO PLAY GAMES.

APPARENTLY, SIXTH GRADERS WERE ALSO TOO COOL TO WEAR PARKAS AND MOON BOOTS.

WHO NEEDS A PARKA? NOT ME!

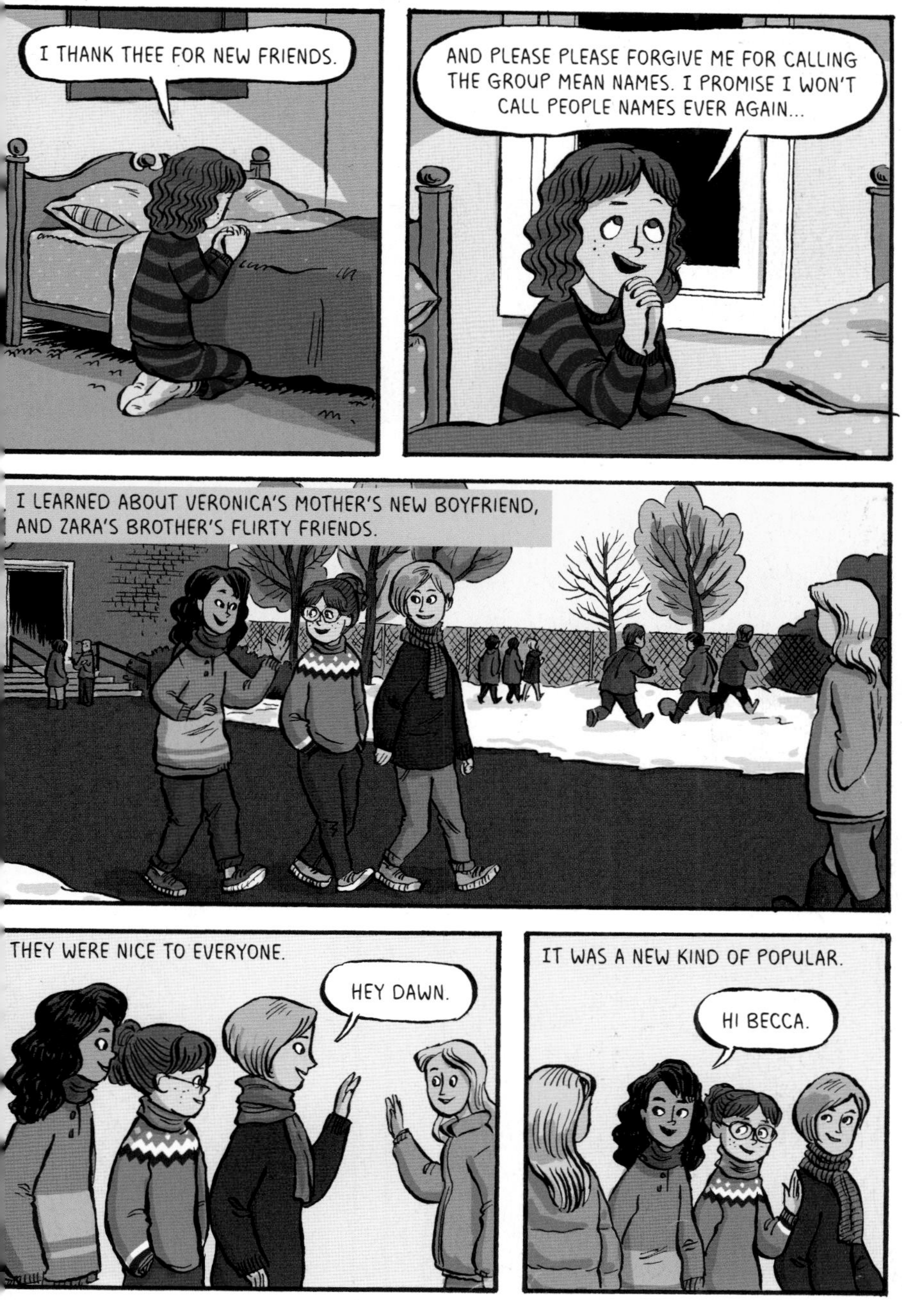
I THANK THEE FOR NEW FRIENDS.
AND PLEASE PLEASE FORGIVE ME FOR CALLING THE GROUP MEAN NAMES. I PROMISE I WON'T CALL PEOPLE NAMES EVER AGAIN...
I LEARNED ABOUT VERONICA'S MOTHER'S NEW BOYFRIEND, AND ZARA'S BROTHER'S FLIRTY FRIENDS.
THEY WERE NICE TO EVERYONE.
HEY DAWN.
IT WAS A NEW KIND OF POPULAR.
HI BECCA.

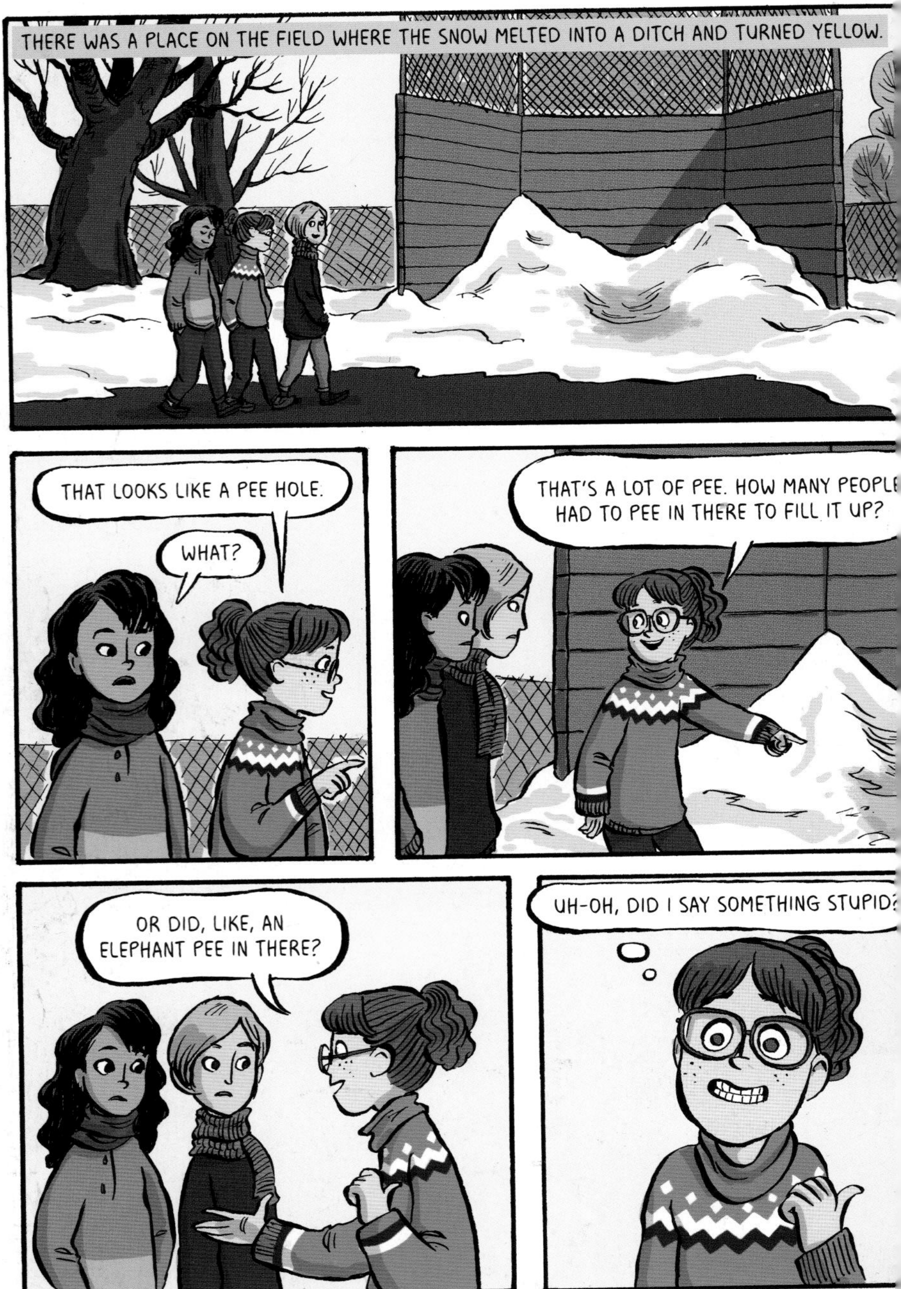
THERE WAS A PLACE ON THE FIELD WHERE THE SNOW MELTED INTO A DITCH AND TURNED YELLOW.
THAT LOOKS LIKE A PEE HOLE.
WHAT?
THAT'S A LOT OF PEE. HOW MANY PEOPLE HAD TO PEE IN THERE TO FILL IT UP?
OR DID, LIKE, AN ELEPHANT PEE IN THERE?
UH-OH, DID I SAY SOMETHING STUPID?

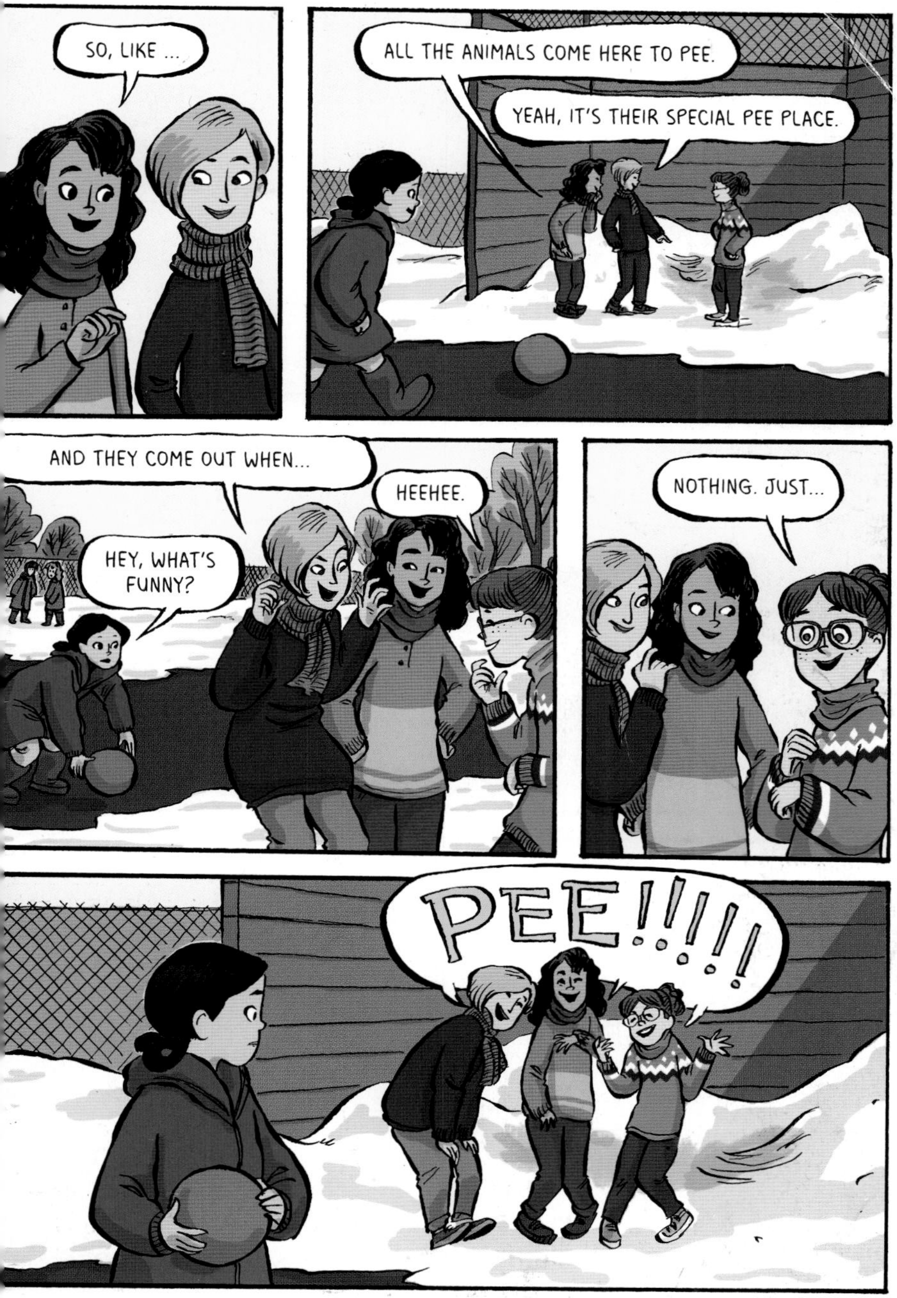

SO, LIKE ...
ALL THE ANIMALS COME HERE TO PEE.
YEAH, IT'S THEIR SPECIAL PEE PLACE.
AND THEY COME OUT WHEN...
HEEHEE.
HEY, WHAT'S FUNNY?
NOTHING. JUST...
PEE!!!!!

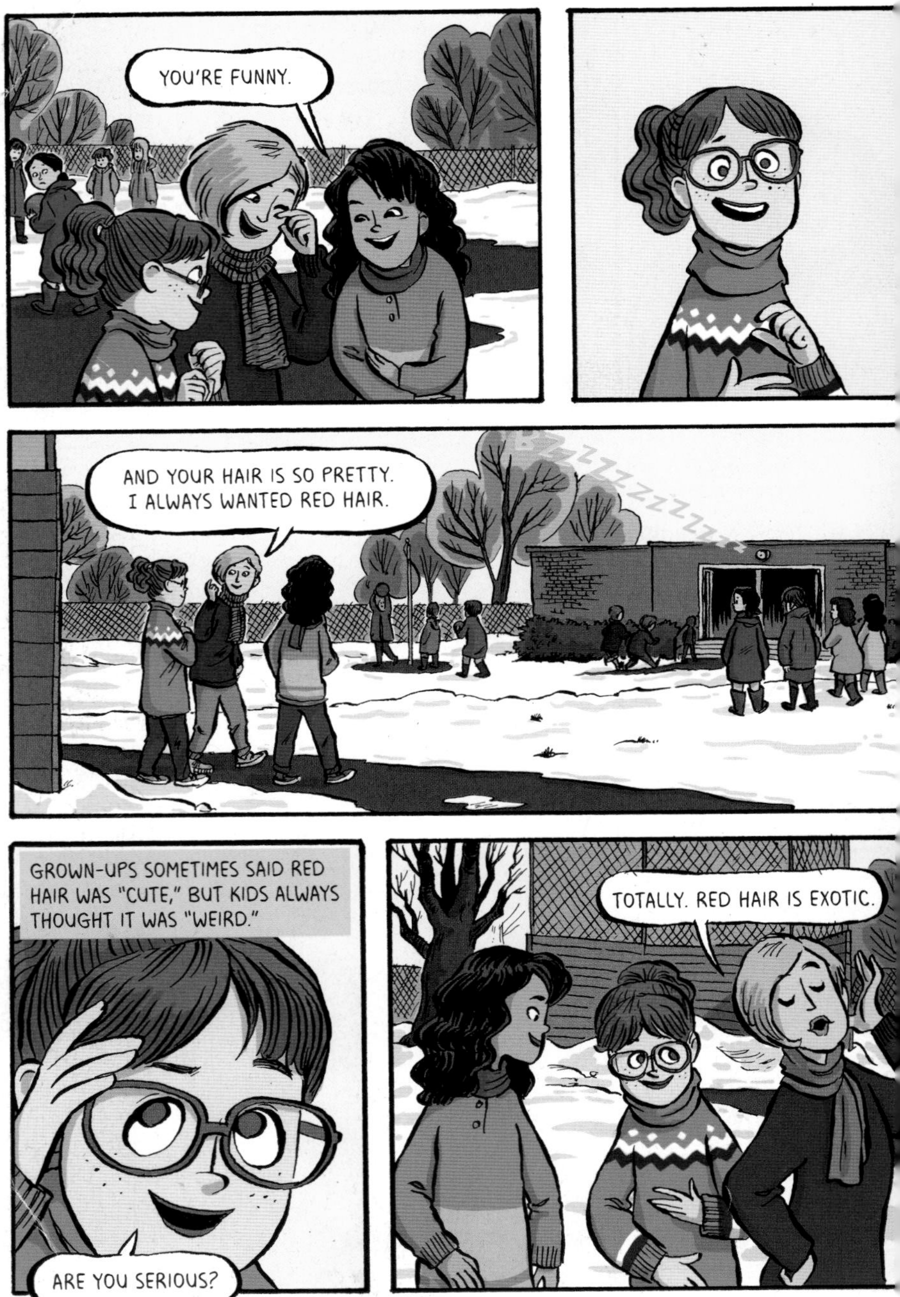
YOU'RE FUNNY.
AND YOUR HAIR IS SO PRETTY. I ALWAYS WANTED RED HAIR.
GROWN-UPS SOMETIMES SAID RED HAIR WAS "CUTE," BUT KIDS ALWAYS THOUGHT IT WAS "WEIRD."
ARE YOU SERIOUS?
TOTALLY. RED HAIR IS EXOTIC.

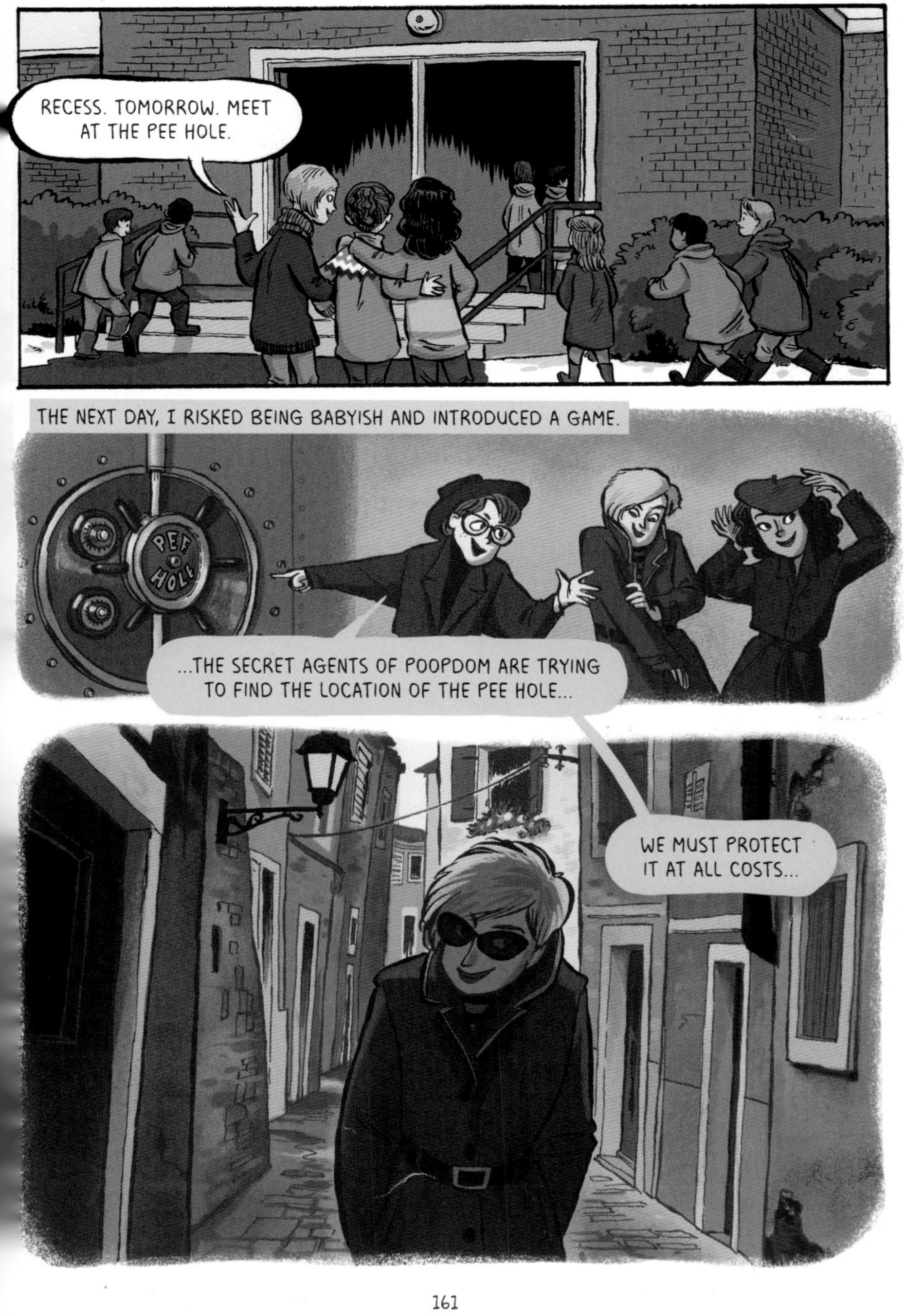
RECESS. TOMORROW. MEET AT THE PEE HOLE.
THE NEXT DAY, I RISKED BEING BABYISH AND INTRODUCED A GAME.
PEE HOLE
...THE SECRET AGENTS OF POOPDOM ARE TRYING TO FIND THE LOCATION OF THE PEE HOLE...
WE MUST PROTECT IT AT ALL COSTS...

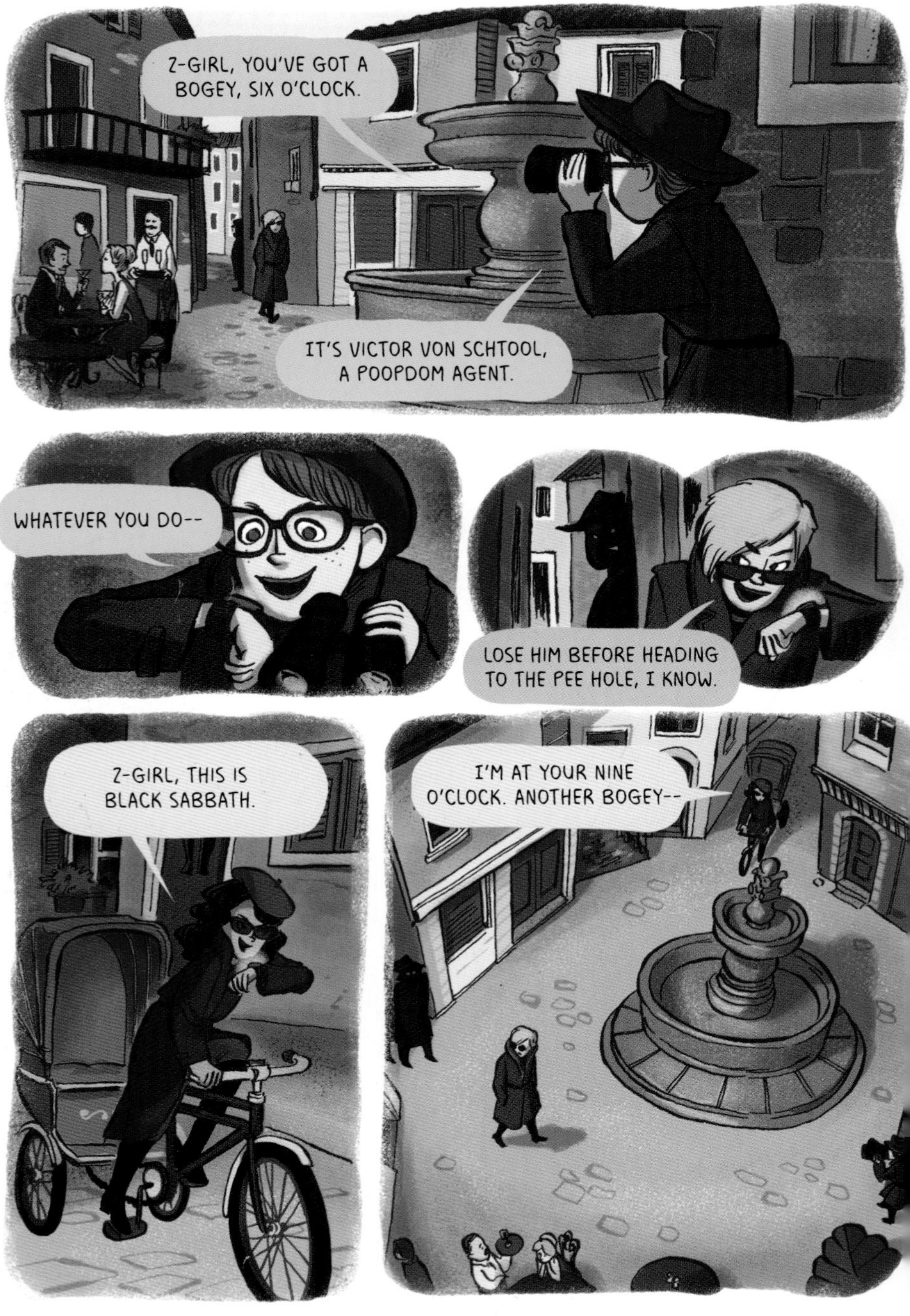
Z-GIRL, YOU'VE GOT A BOGEY, SIX O'CLOCK.
IT'S VICTOR VON SCHTOOL, A POOPDOM AGENT.
WHATEVER YOU DO--
LOSE HIM BEFORE HEADING TO THE PEE HOLE, I KNOW.
Z-GIRL, THIS IS BLACK SABBATH.
I'M AT YOUR NINE O'CLOCK. ANOTHER BOGEY--

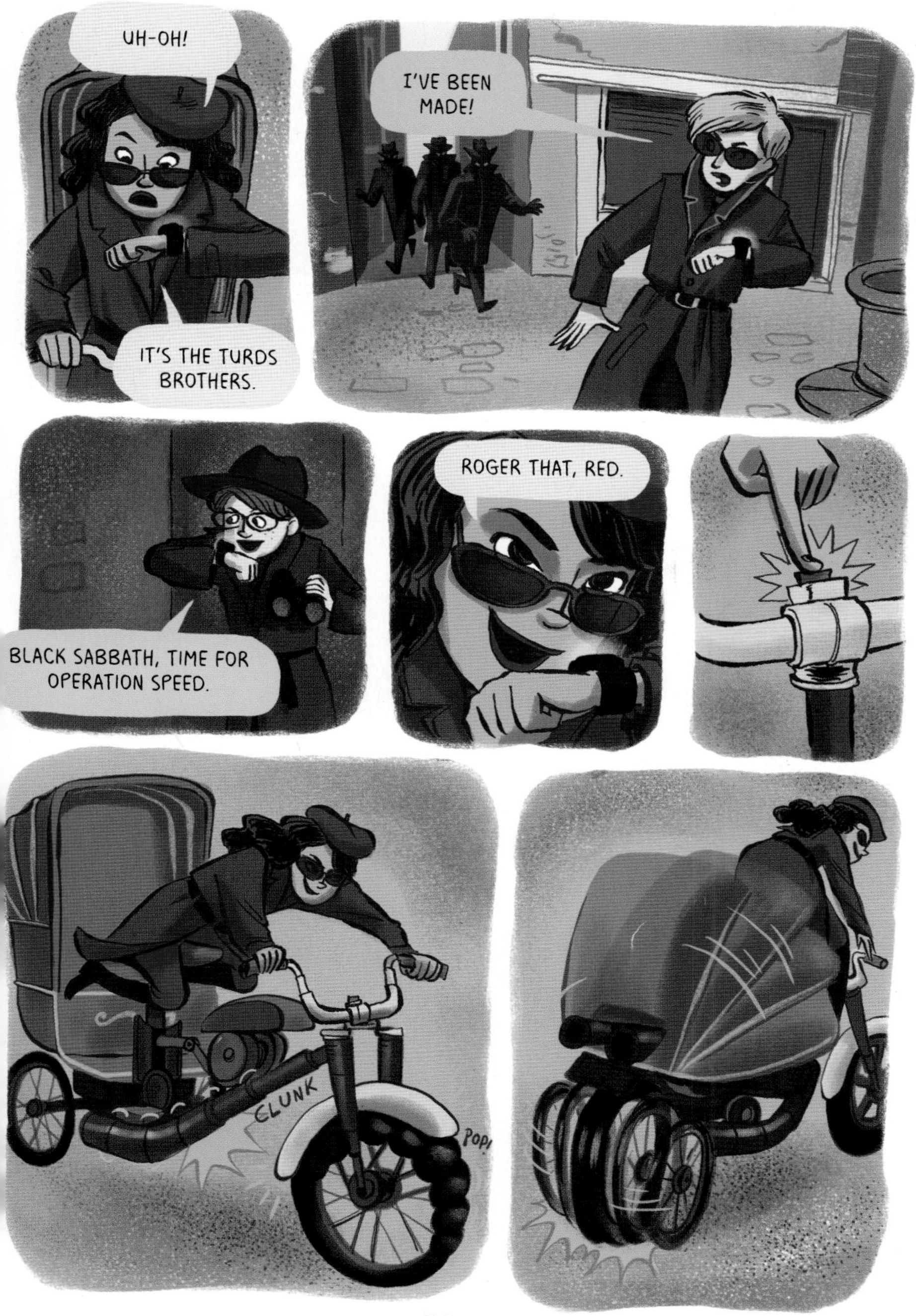
UH-OH!
IT'S THE TURDS BROTHERS.
I'VE BEEN MADE!
BLACK SABBATH, TIME FOR OPERATION SPEED.
ROGER THAT, RED.
CLUNK
POP!

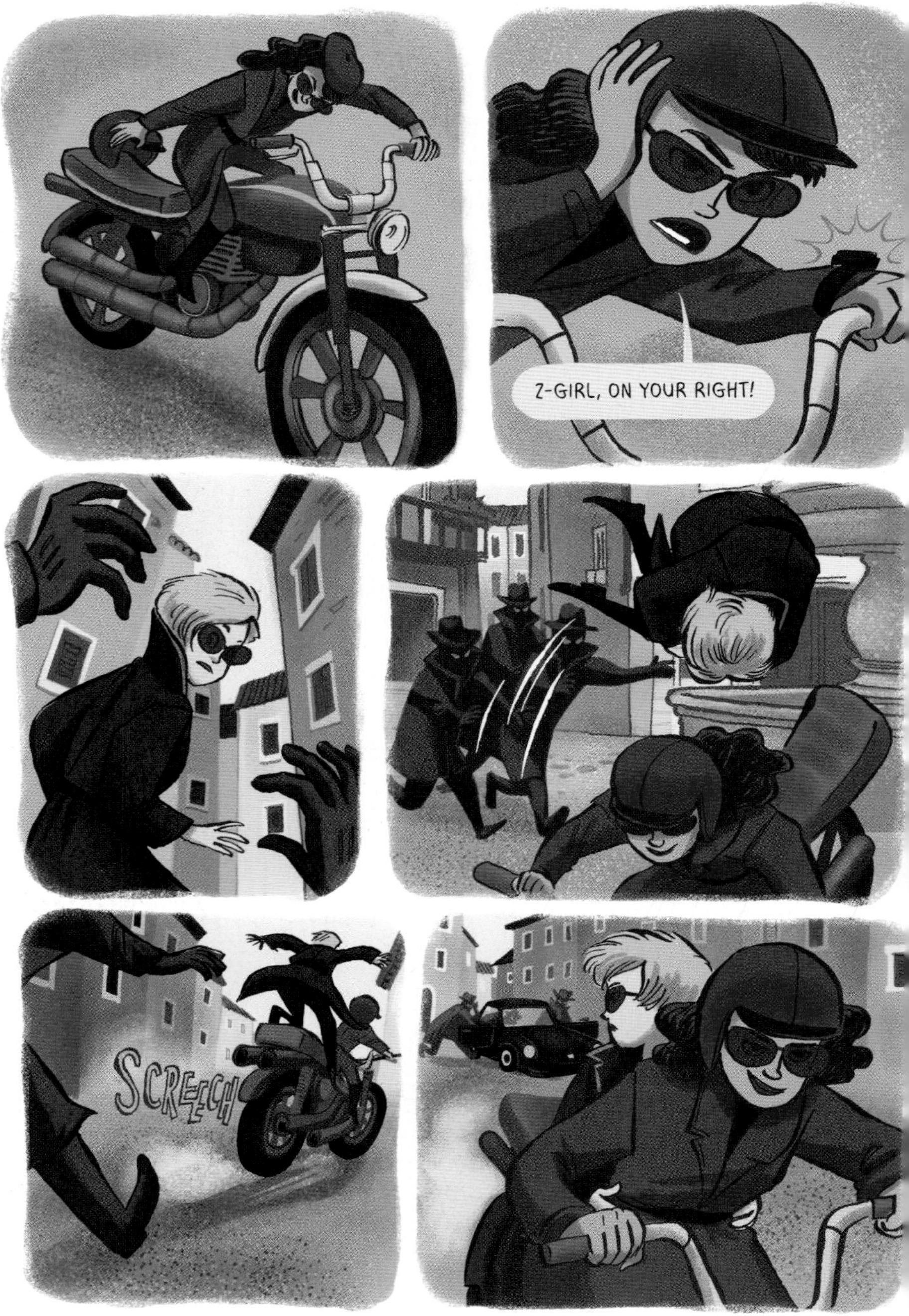
Z-GIRL, ON YOUR RIGHT!
SCREEECH

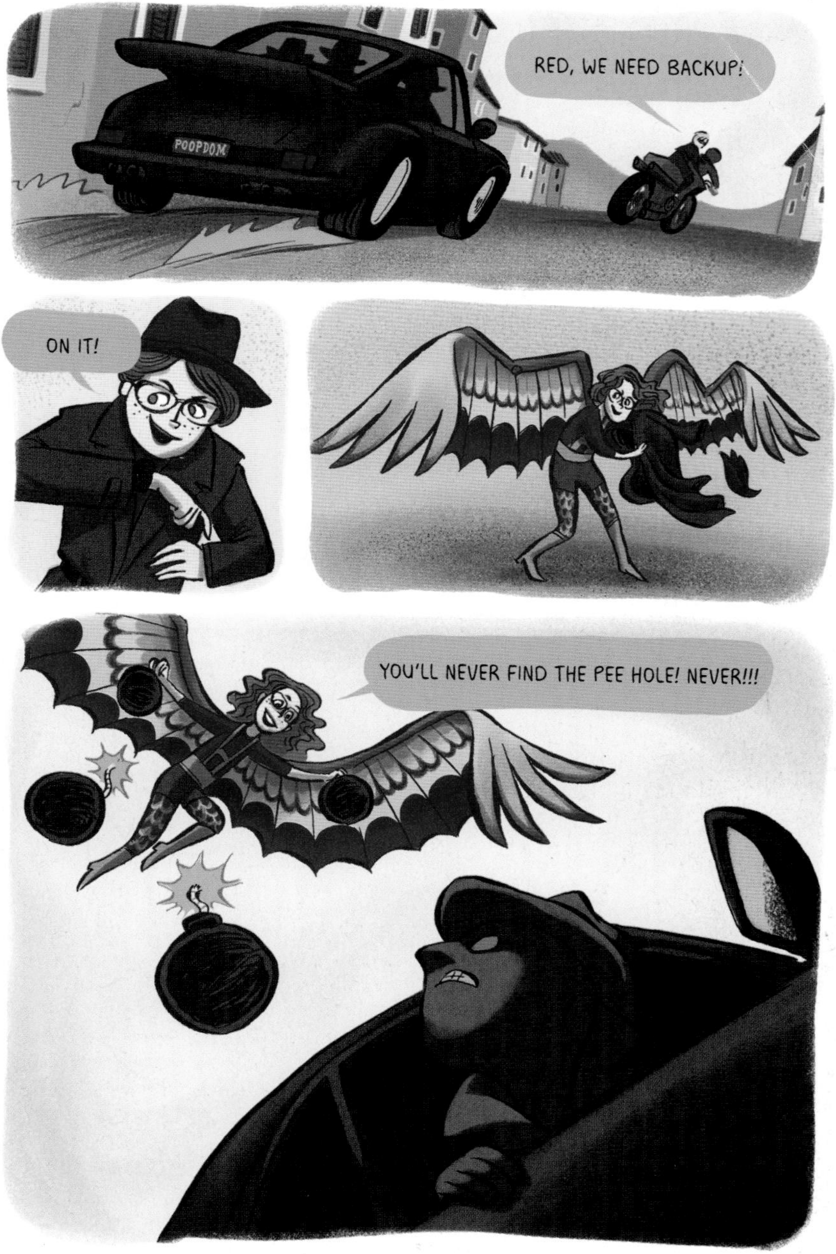
RED, WE NEED BACKUP!
POOPDOM
ON IT!
YOU'LL NEVER FIND THE PEE HOLE! NEVER!!!

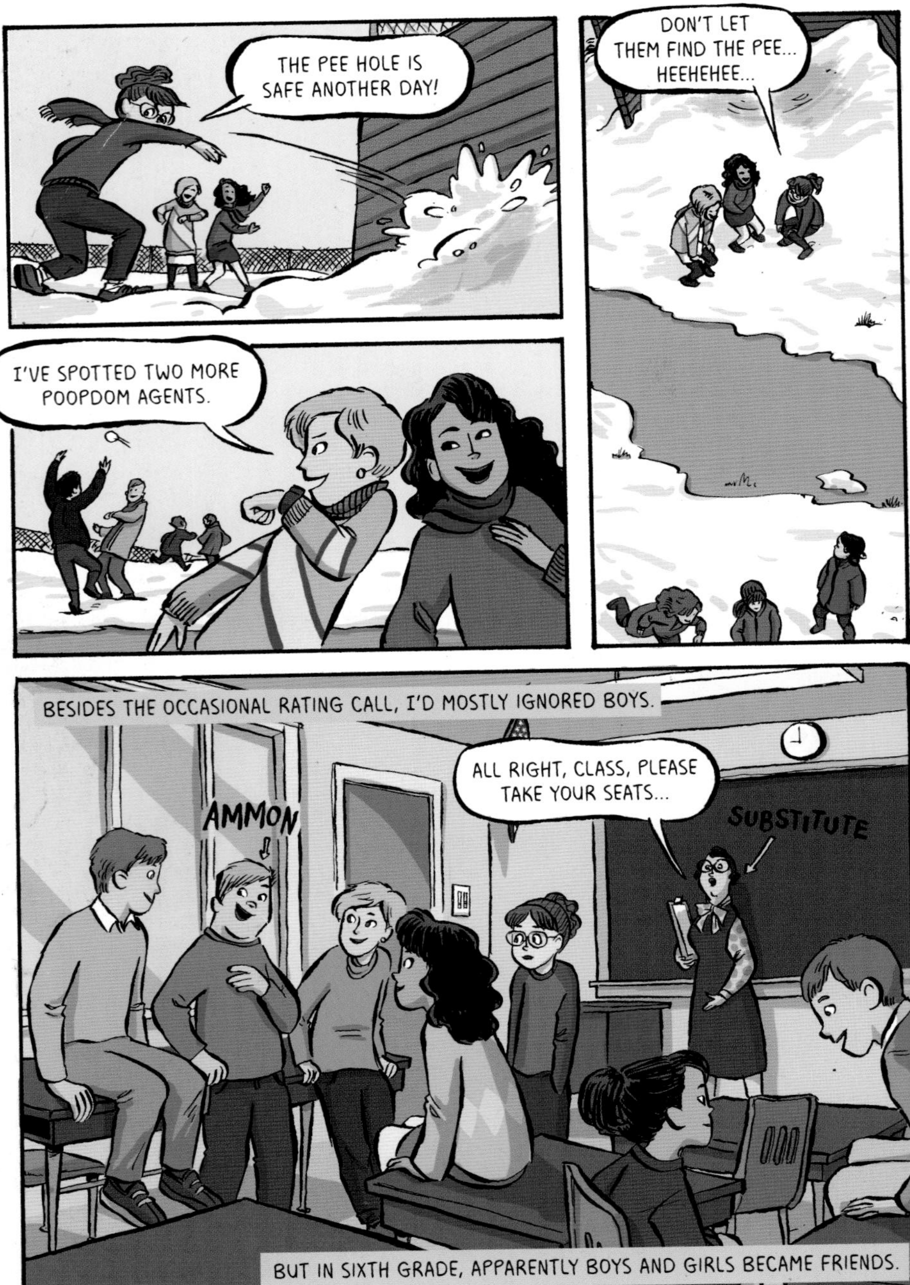
THE PEE HOLE IS SAFE ANOTHER DAY!
DON'T LET THEM FIND THE PEE... HEEHEHEE...
I'VE SPOTTED TWO MORE POOPDOM AGENTS.
BESIDES THE OCCASIONAL RATING CALL, I'D MOSTLY IGNORED BOYS.
AMMON
ALL RIGHT, CLASS, PLEASE TAKE YOUR SEATS...
SUBSTITUTE
BUT IN SIXTH GRADE, APPARENTLY BOYS AND GIRLS BECAME FRIENDS.

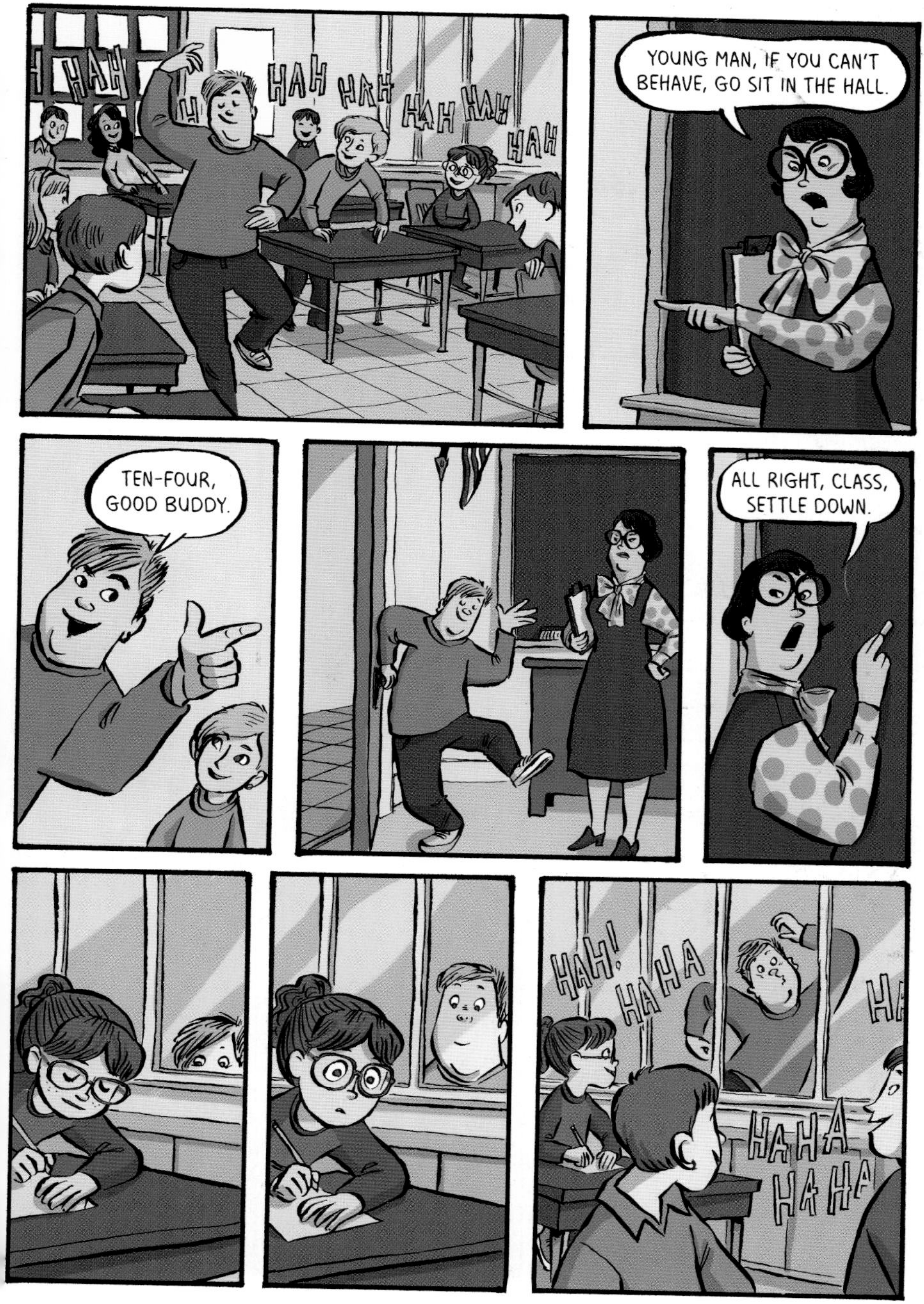
HAH HAH HAH HAH HAH HAH HAH HAH
YOUNG MAN, IF YOU CAN'T BEHAVE, GO SIT IN THE HALL.
TEN-FOUR, GOOD BUDDY.
ALL RIGHT, CLASS, SETTLE DOWN.
HAH! HAHA
HAHA HAHA

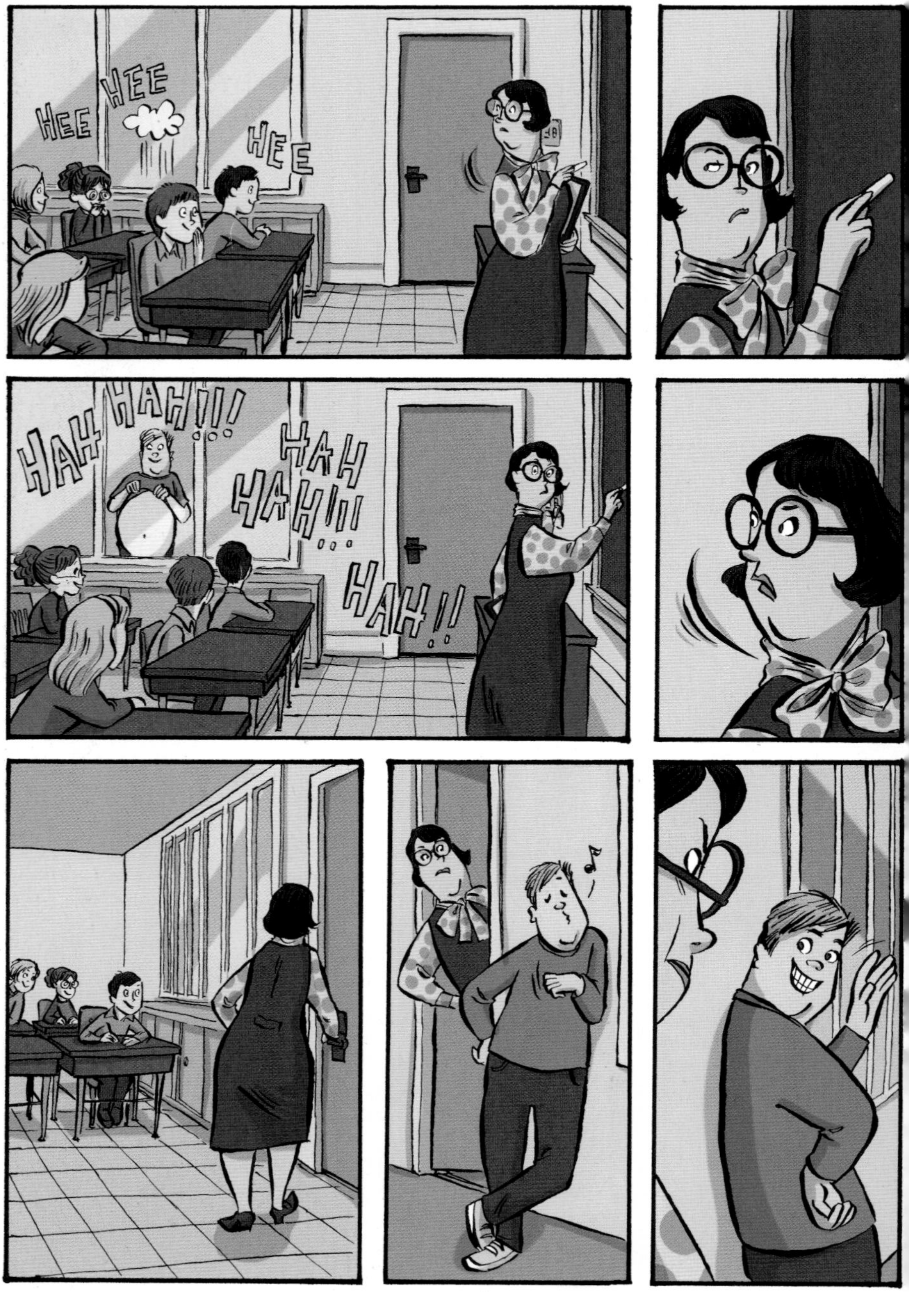
HEE
HEE
HEE
HAH HAH!!!
HAH
HAH!!!
HAH!!

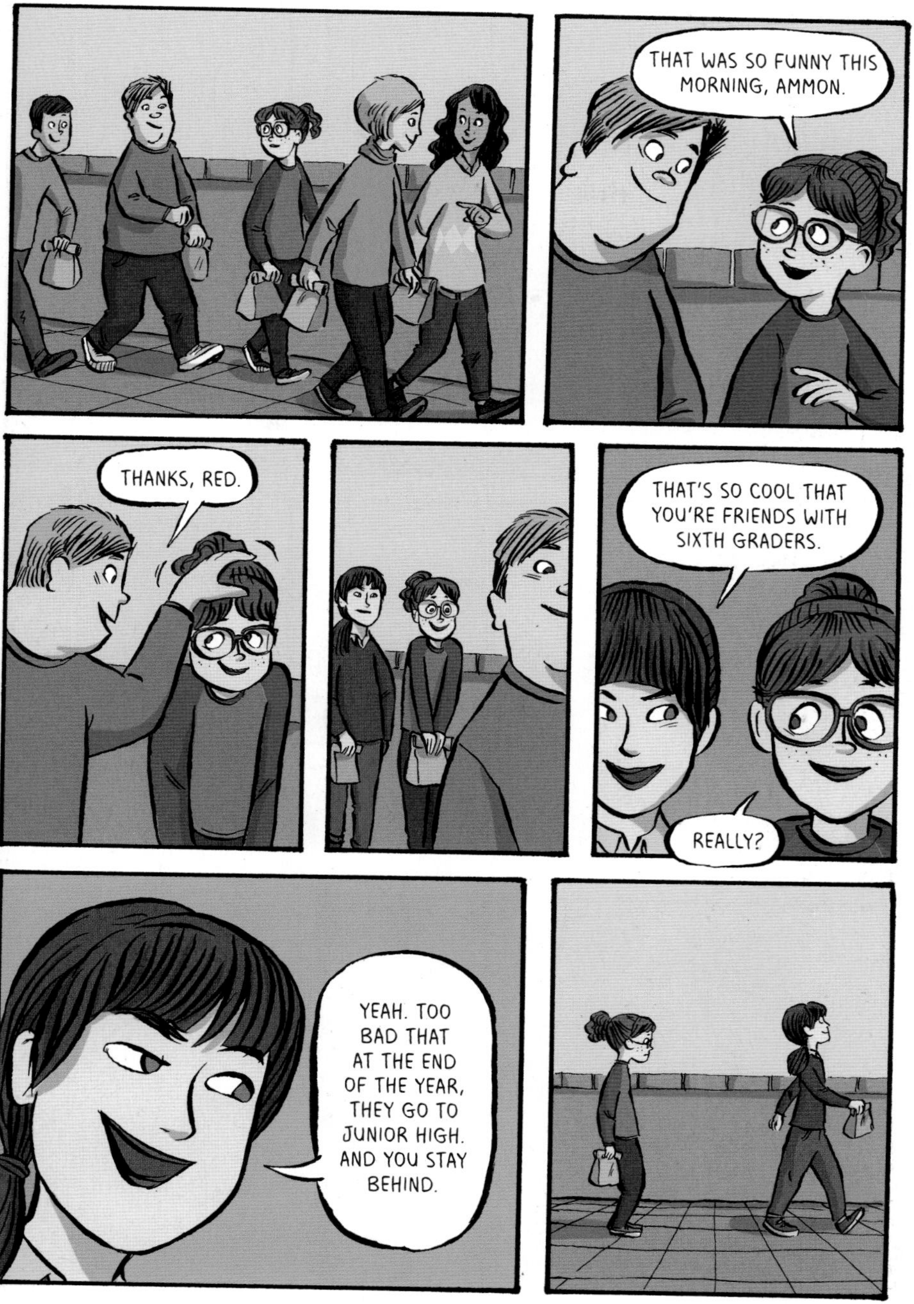
THAT WAS SO FUNNY THIS MORNING, AMMON.
THANKS, RED.
THAT'S SO COOL THAT YOU'RE FRIENDS WITH SIXTH GRADERS.
REALLY?
YEAH. TOO BAD THAT AT THE END OF THE YEAR, THEY GO TO JUNIOR HIGH. AND YOU STAY BEHIND.

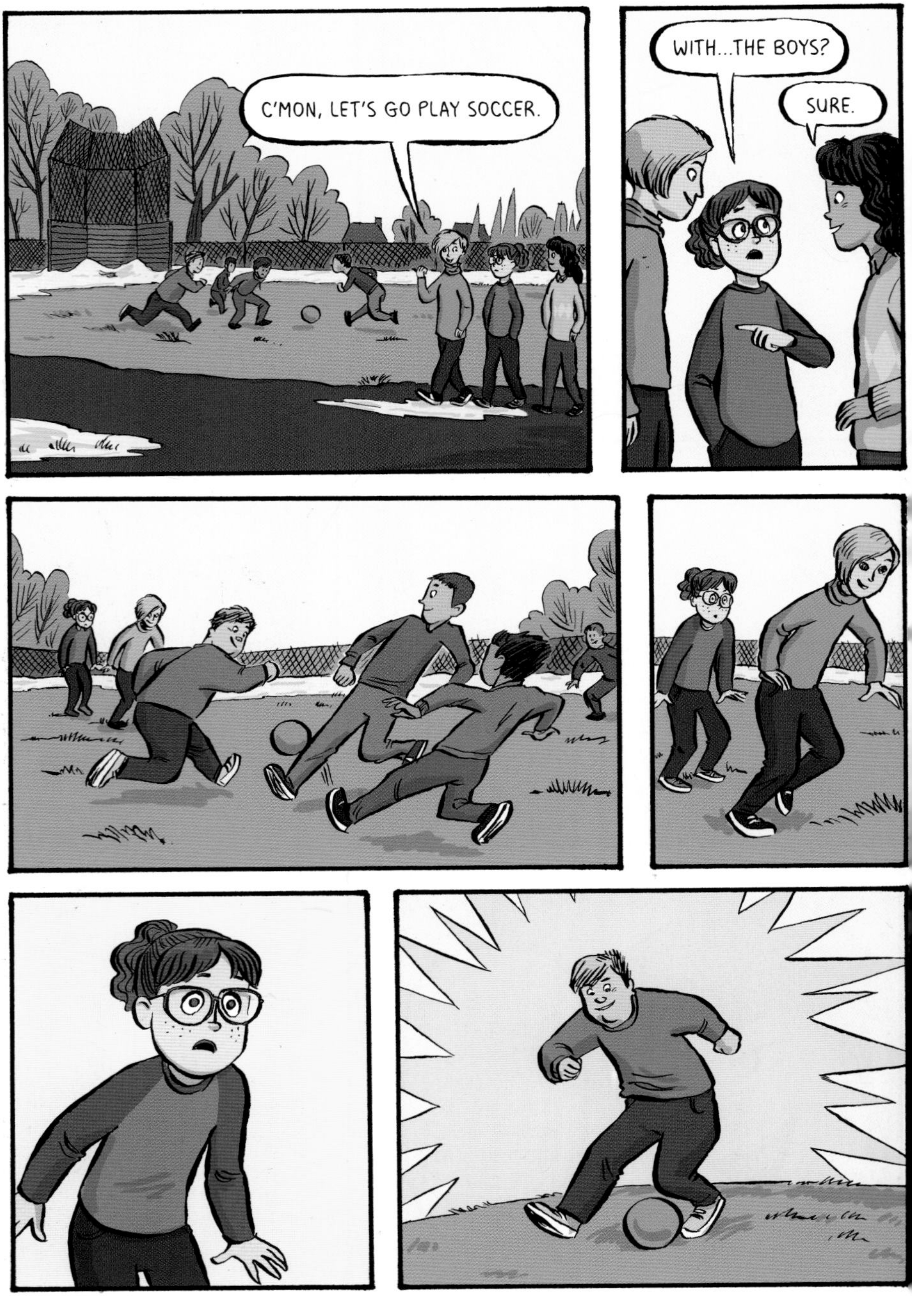
C'MON, LET'S GO PLAY SOCCER.
WITH...THE BOYS?
SURE.

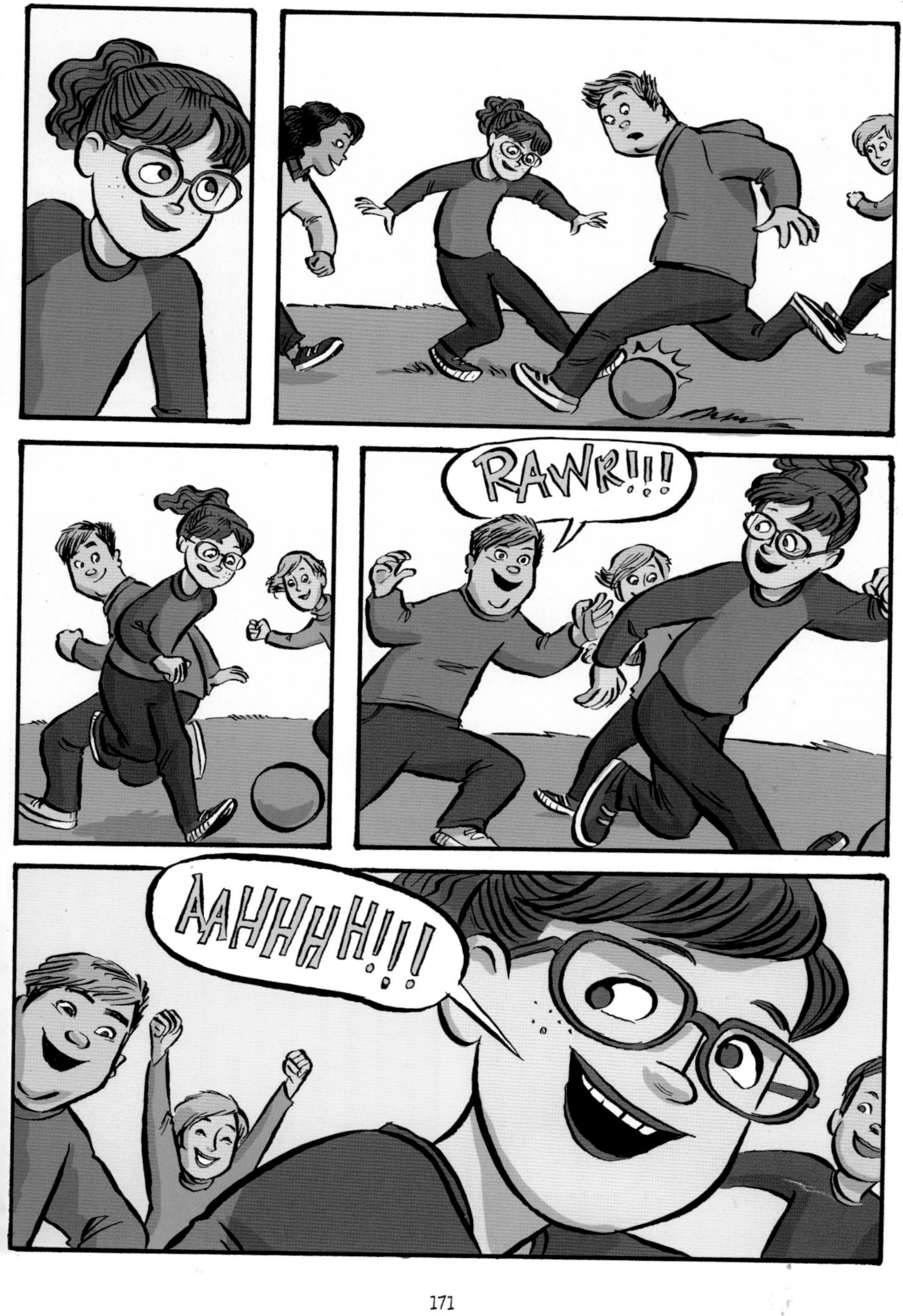
RAWR!!!
AAHHHH!!!

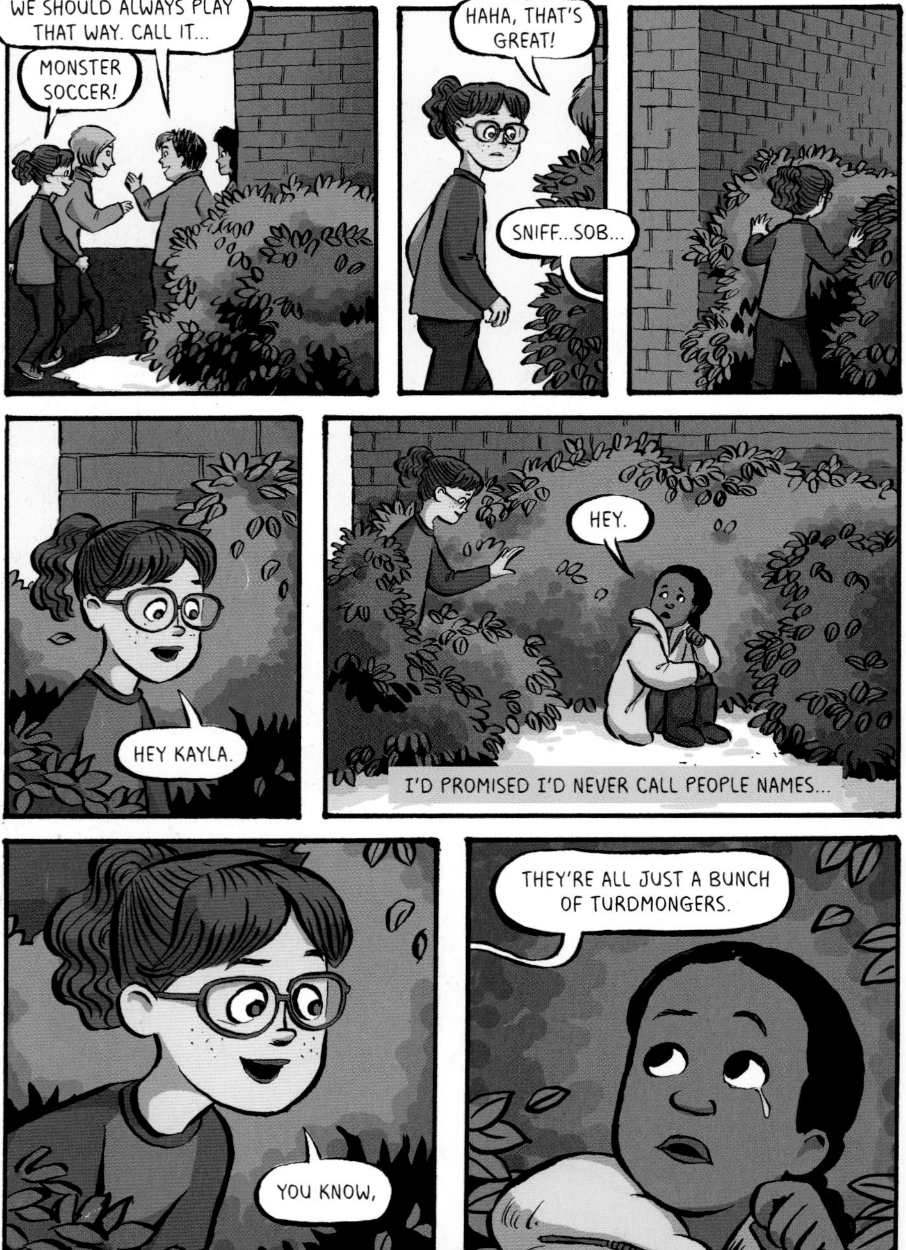
WE SHOULD ALWAYS PLAY THAT WAY. CALL IT...
MONSTER SOCCER!
HAHA, THAT'S GREAT!
SNIFF...SOB...
HEY KAYLA.
HEY.
I'D PROMISED I'D NEVER CALL PEOPLE NAMES...
YOU KNOW,
THEY'RE ALL JUST A BUNCH OF TURDMONGERS.

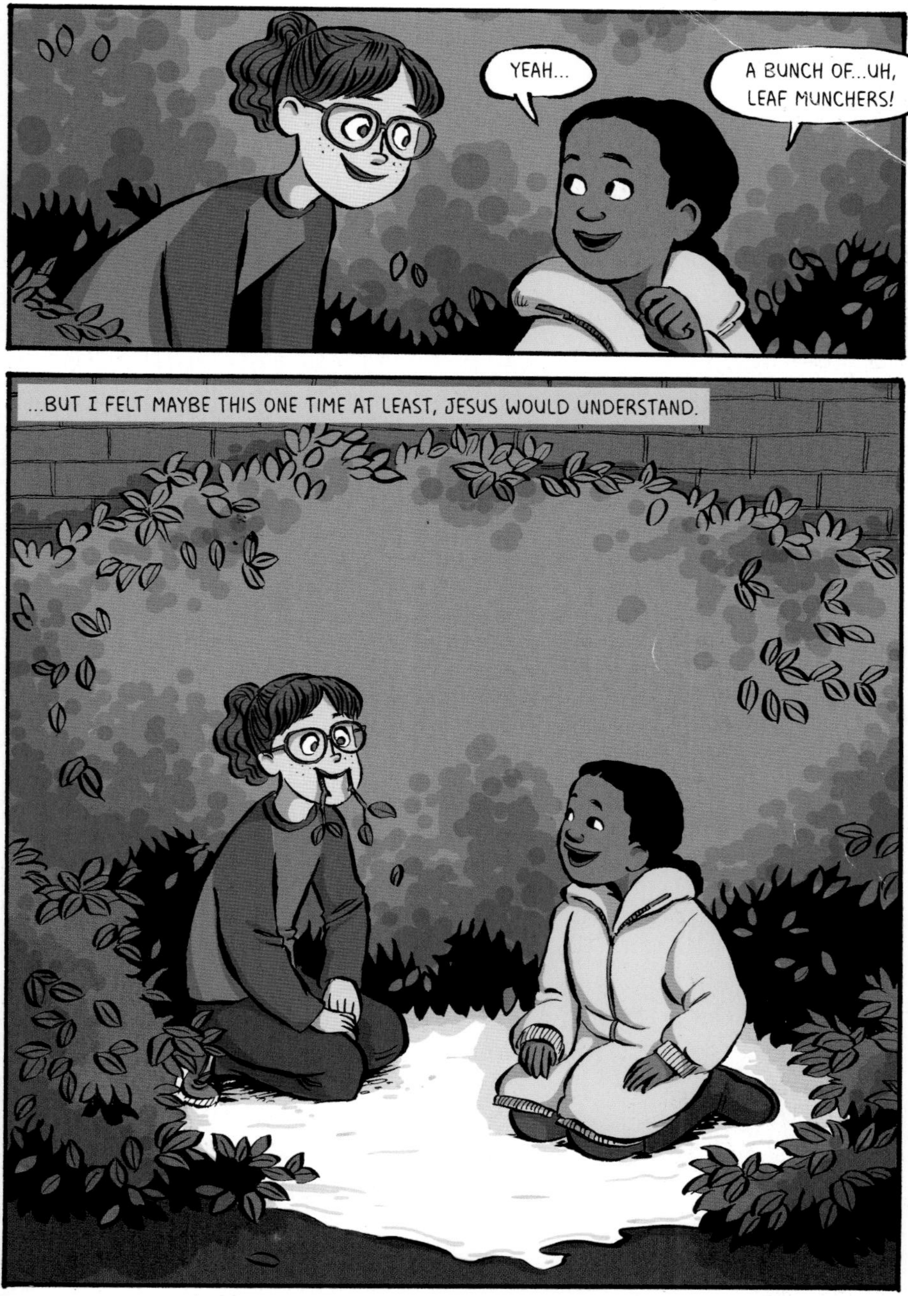
YEAH...
A BUNCH OF...UH, LEAF MUNCHERS!
...BUT I FELT MAYBE THIS ONE TIME AT LEAST, JESUS WOULD UNDERSTAND.

# WENDY

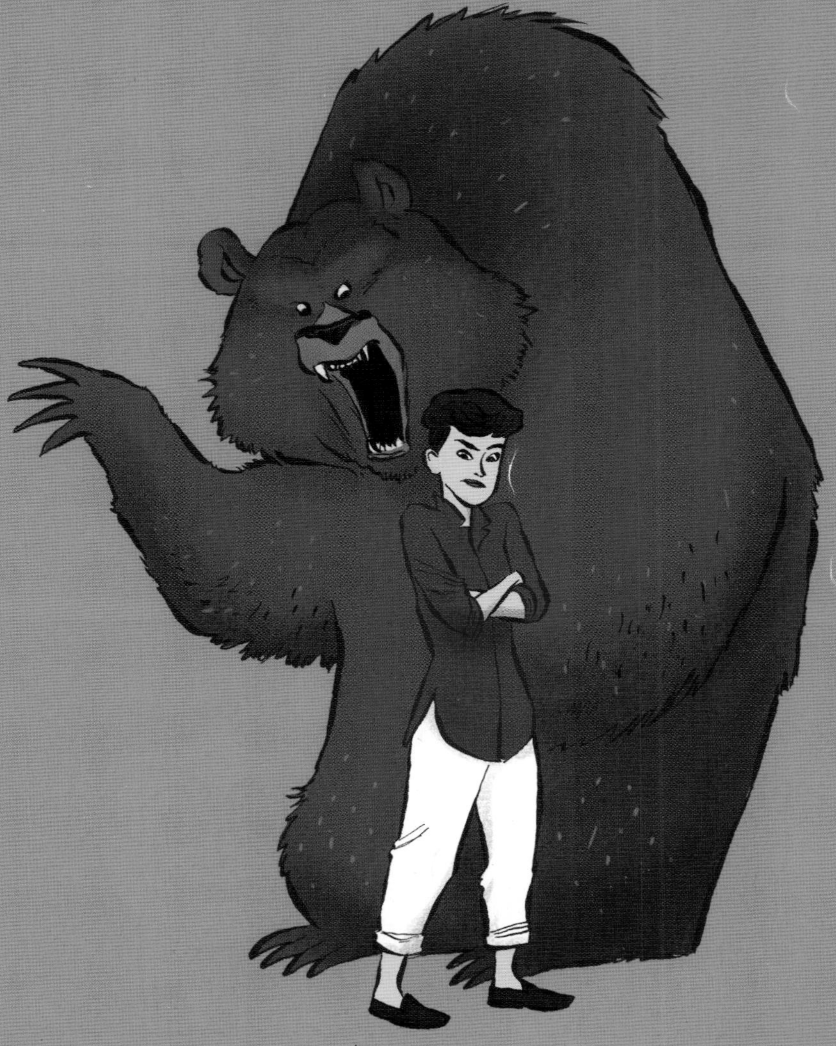

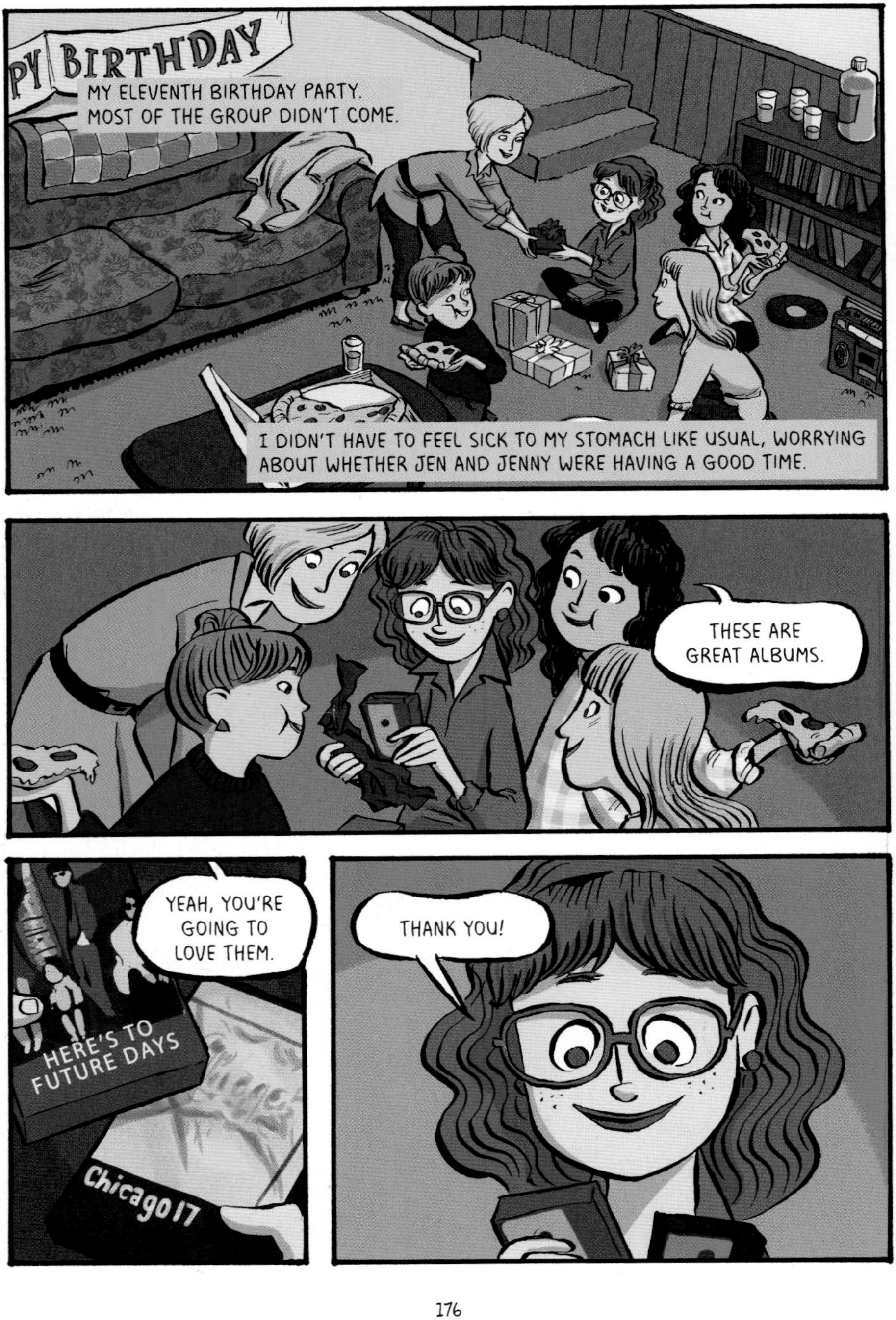
PY BIRTHDAY
MY ELEVENTH BIRTHDAY PARTY. MOST OF THE GROUP DIDN'T COME.
I DIDN'T HAVE TO FEEL SICK TO MY STOMACH LIKE USUAL, WORRYING ABOUT WHETHER JEN AND JENNY WERE HAVING A GOOD TIME.
THESE ARE GREAT ALBUMS.
YEAH, YOU'RE GOING TO LOVE THEM.
HERE'S TO FUTURE DAYS
Chicago 17
THANK YOU!

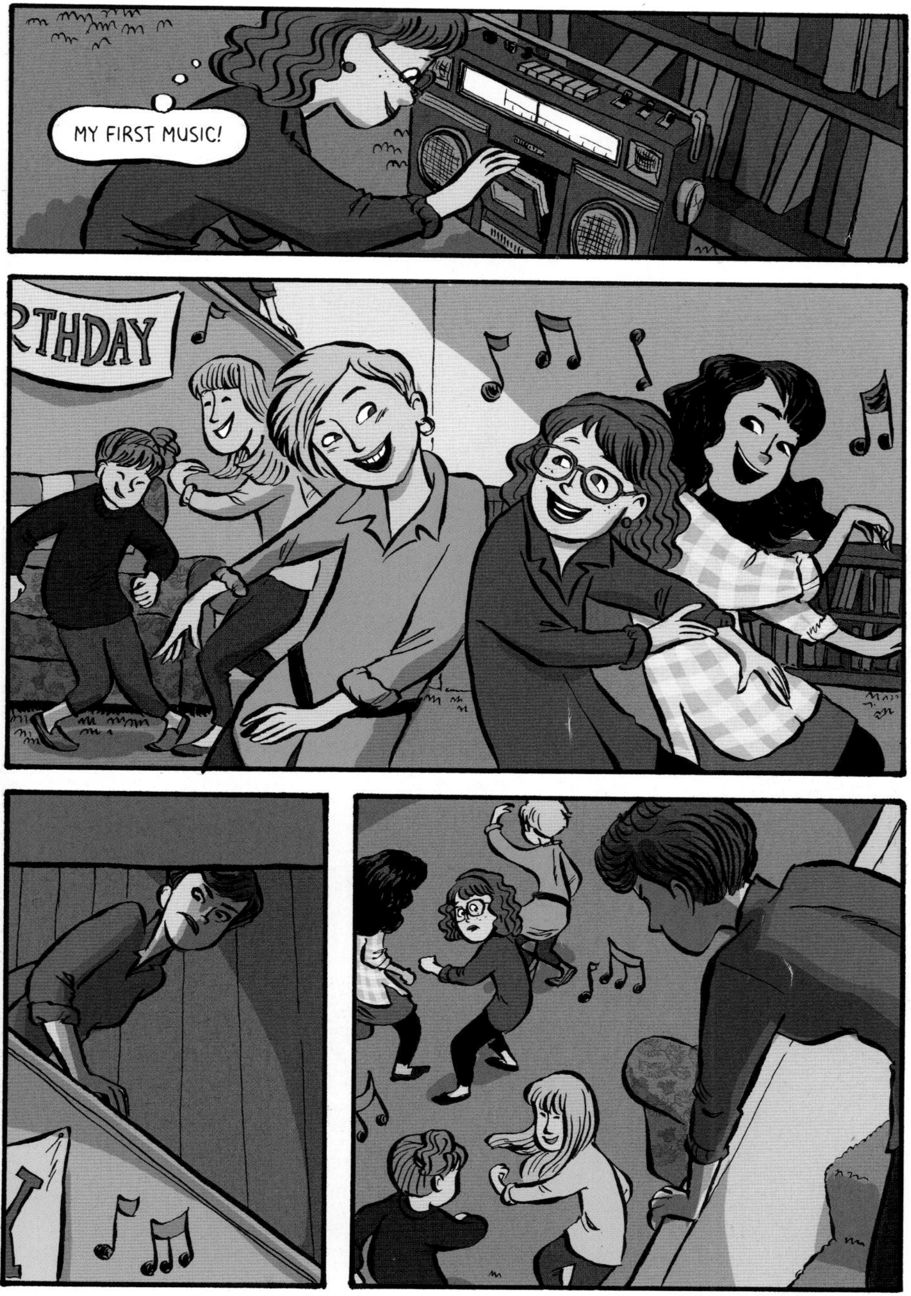
MY FIRST MUSIC!
RTHDAY

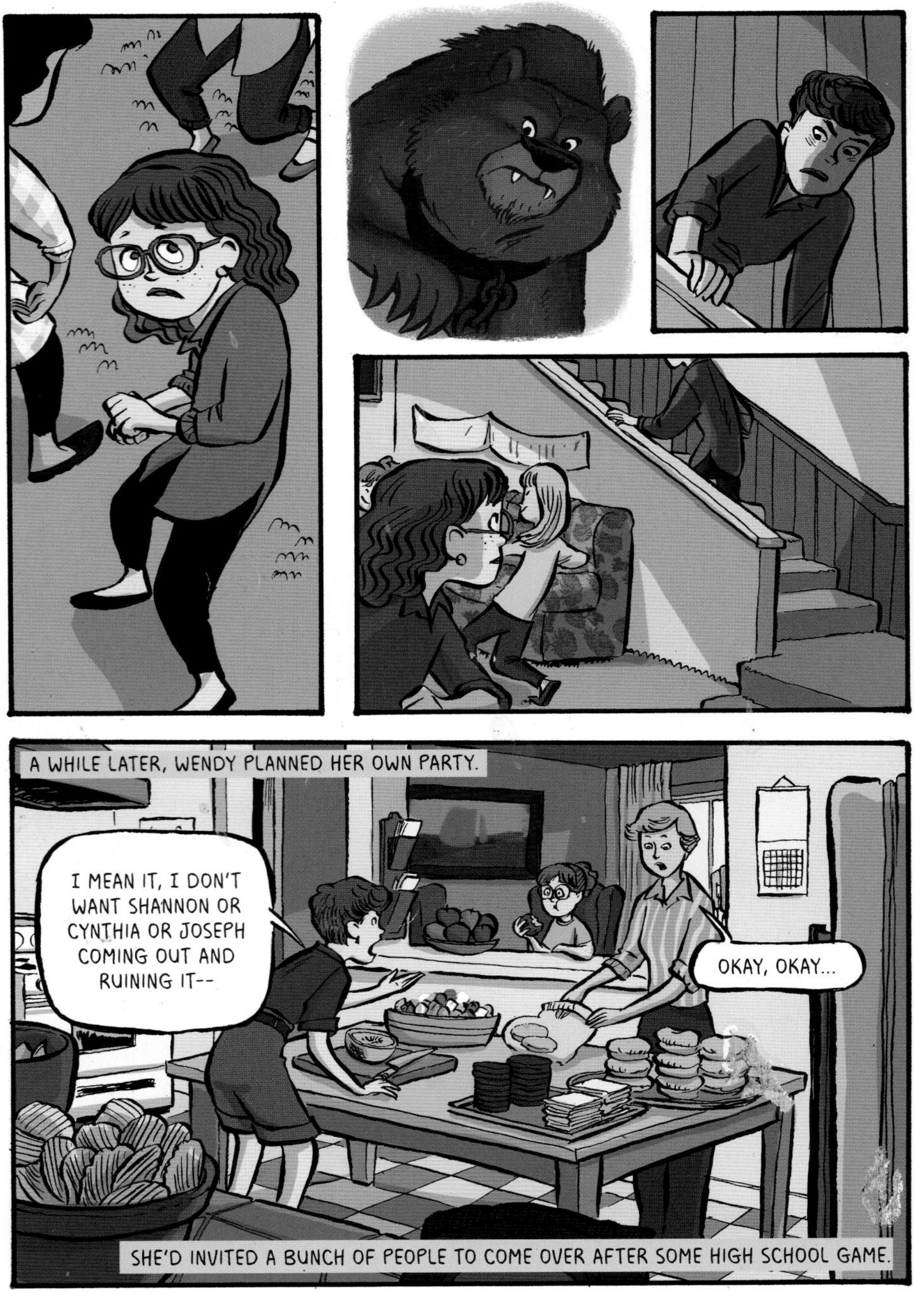
A WHILE LATER, WENDY PLANNED HER OWN PARTY.
I MEAN IT, I DON'T WANT SHANNON OR CYNTHIA OR JOSEPH COMING OUT AND RUINING IT--
OKAY, OKAY...
SHE'D INVITED A BUNCH OF PEOPLE TO COME OVER AFTER SOME HIGH SCHOOL GAME.

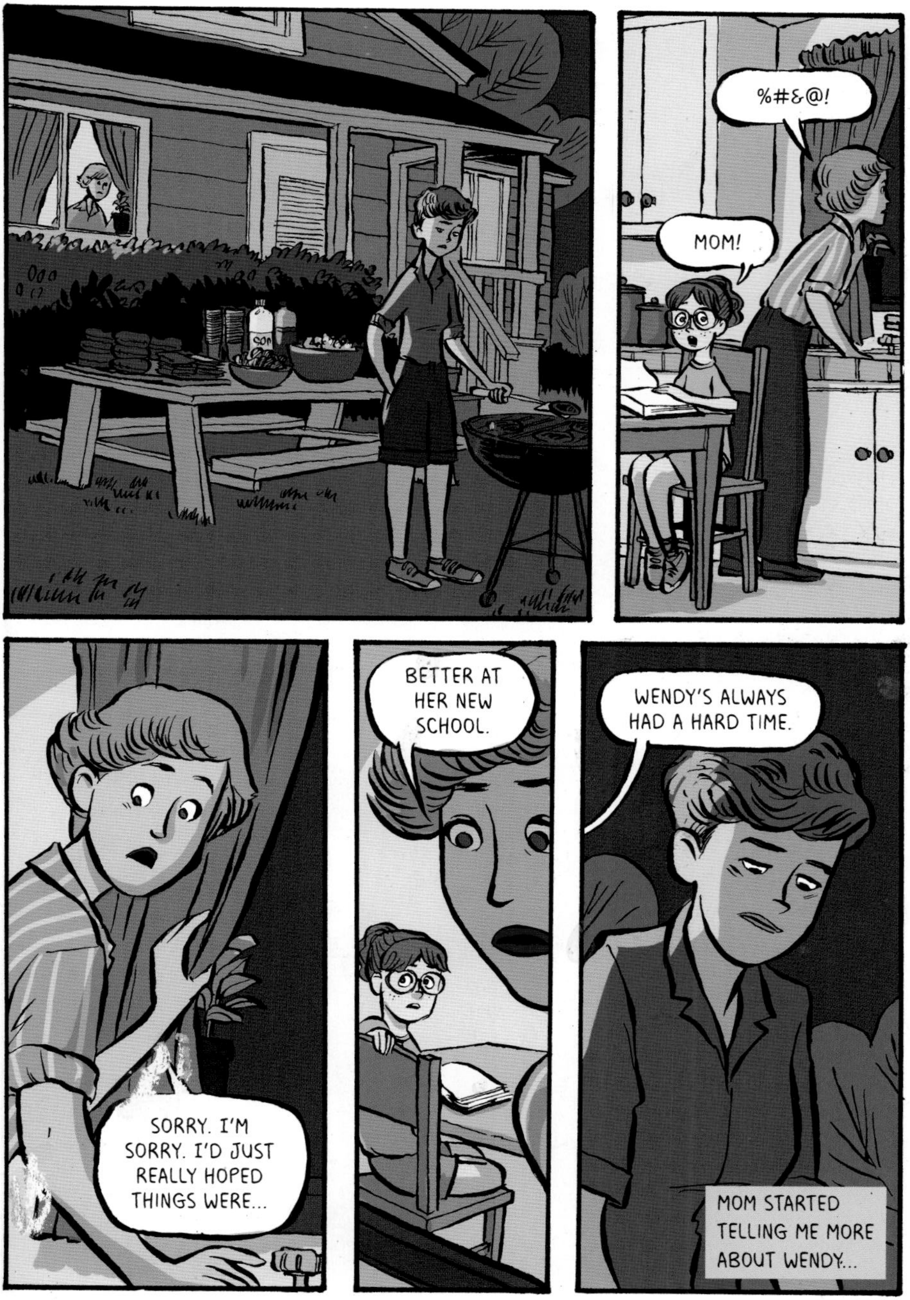
%#&@!
MOM!
SORRY. I'M SORRY. I'D JUST REALLY HOPED THINGS WERE...
BETTER AT HER NEW SCHOOL.
WENDY'S ALWAYS HAD A HARD TIME.
MOM STARTED TELLING ME MORE ABOUT WENDY...

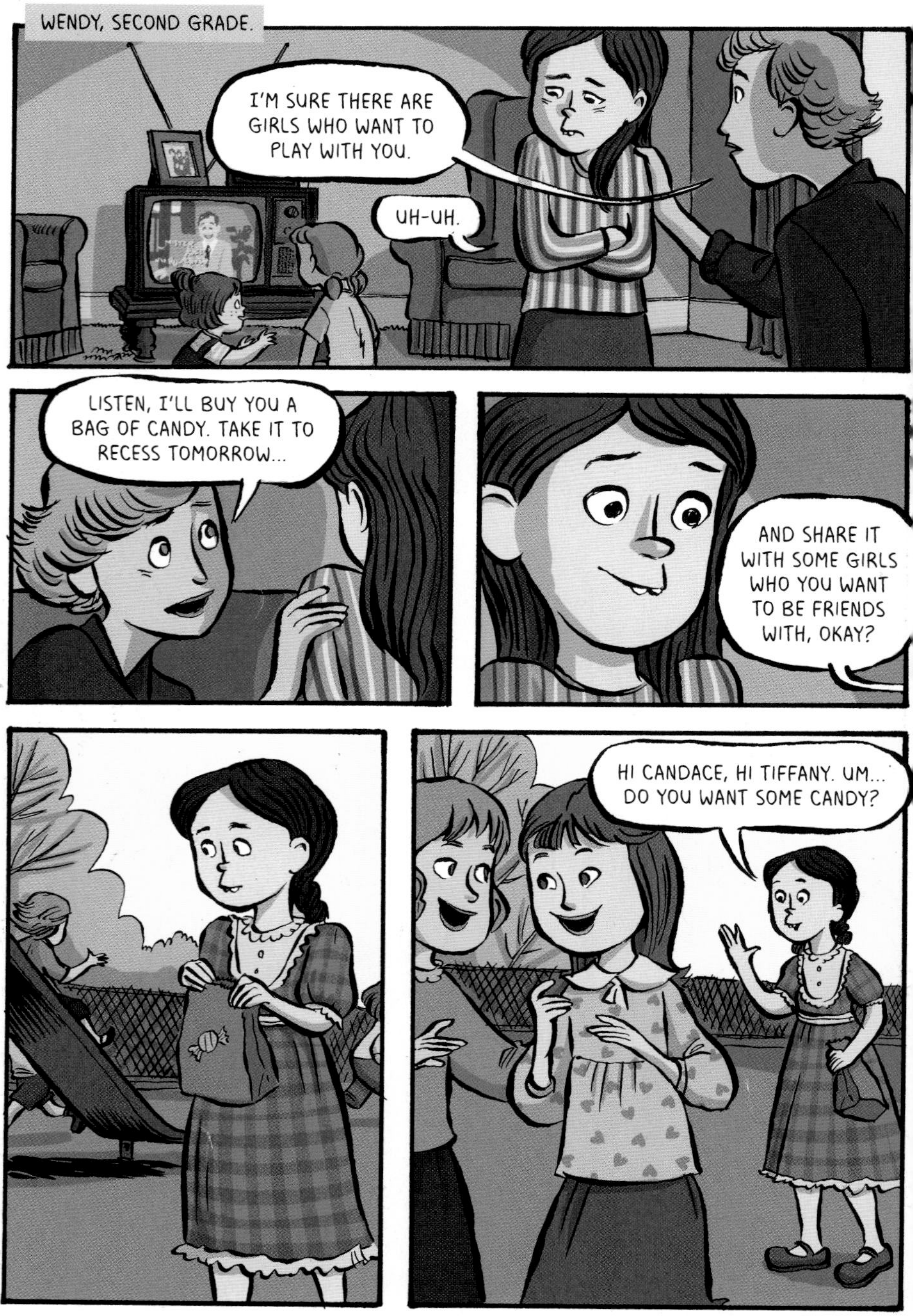
WENDY, SECOND GRADE.
I'M SURE THERE ARE GIRLS WHO WANT TO PLAY WITH YOU.
UH-UH.
LISTEN, I'LL BUY YOU A BAG OF CANDY. TAKE IT TO RECESS TOMORROW...
AND SHARE IT WITH SOME GIRLS WHO YOU WANT TO BE FRIENDS WITH, OKAY?
HI CANDACE, HI TIFFANY. UM... DO YOU WANT SOME CANDY?

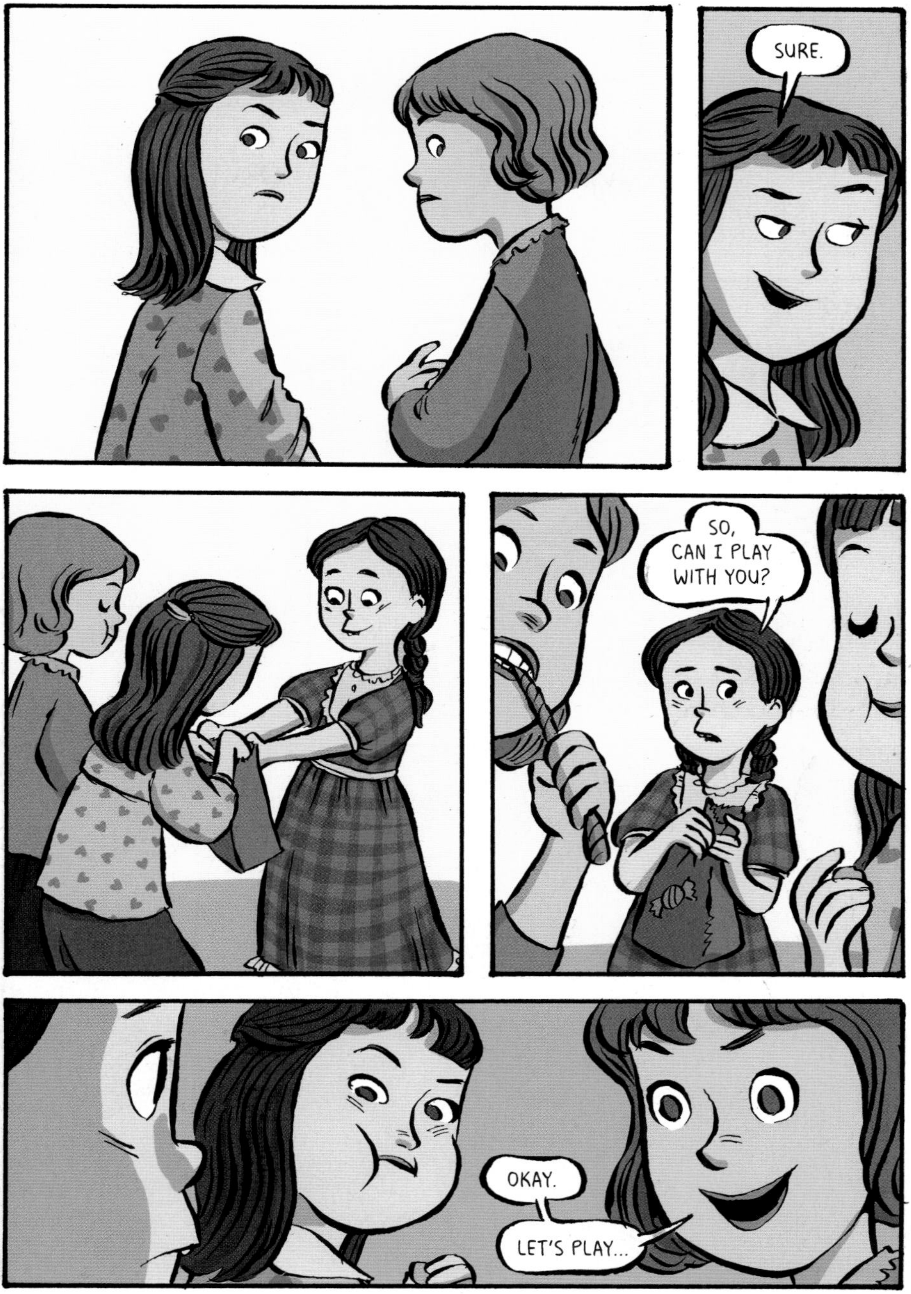
SURE.
SO, CAN I PLAY WITH YOU?
OKAY.
LET'S PLAY...

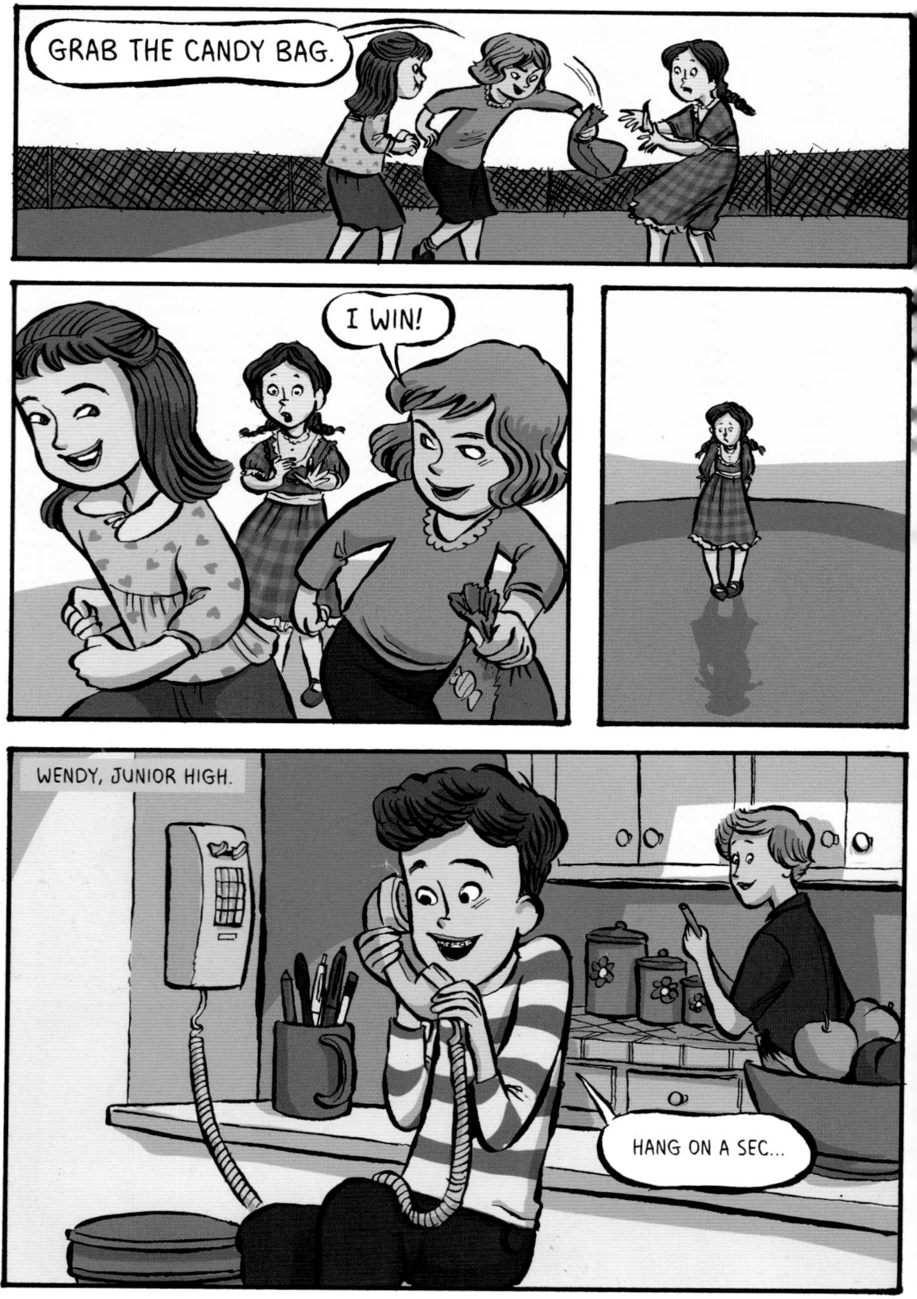
GRAB THE CANDY BAG.
I WIN!
WENDY, JUNIOR HIGH.
HANG ON A SEC...

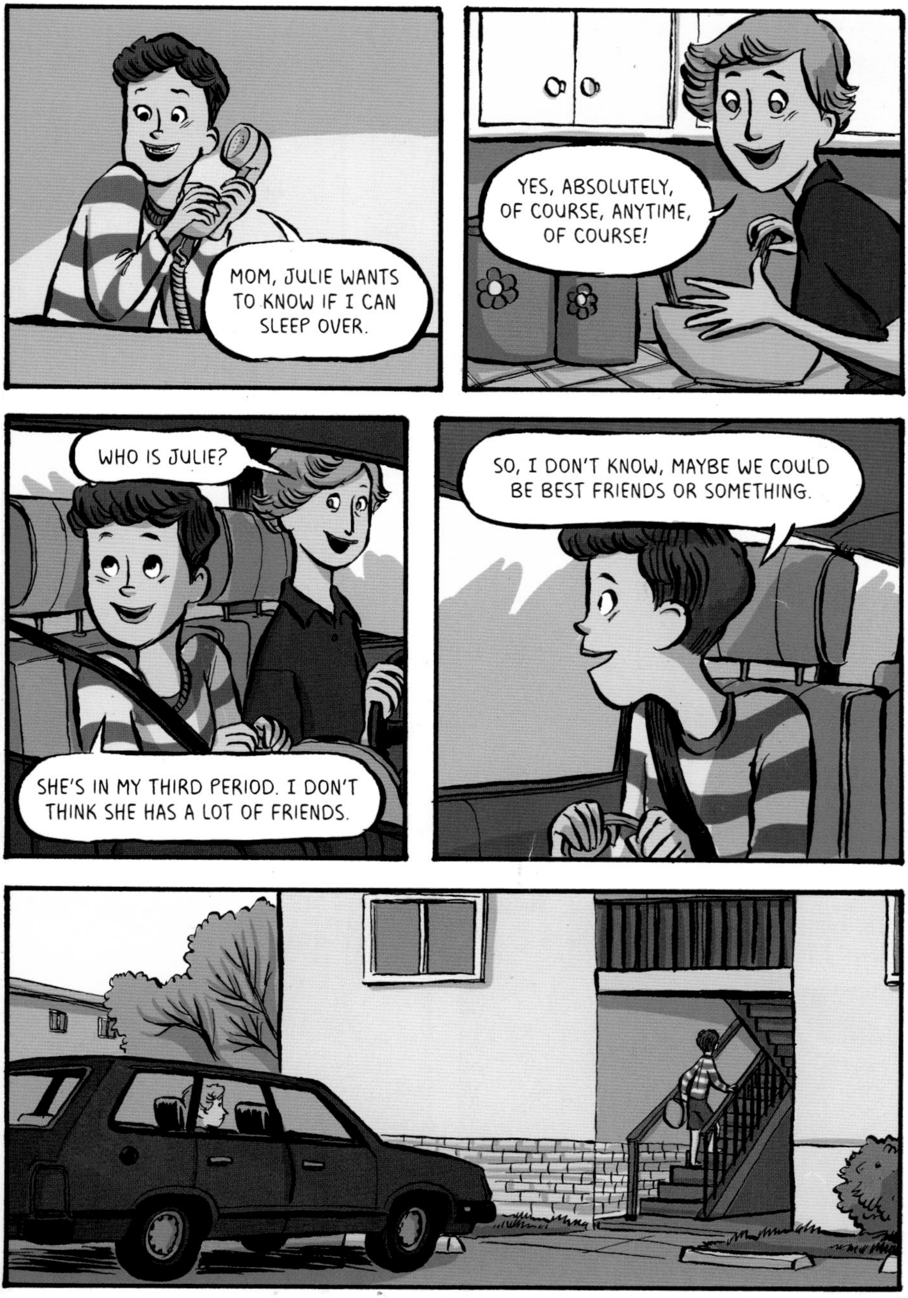
MOM, JULIE WANTS TO KNOW IF I CAN SLEEP OVER.
YES, ABSOLUTELY, OF COURSE, ANYTIME, OF COURSE!
WHO IS JULIE?
SHE'S IN MY THIRD PERIOD. I DON'T THINK SHE HAS A LOT OF FRIENDS.
SO, I DON'T KNOW, MAYBE WE COULD BE BEST FRIENDS OR SOMETHING.

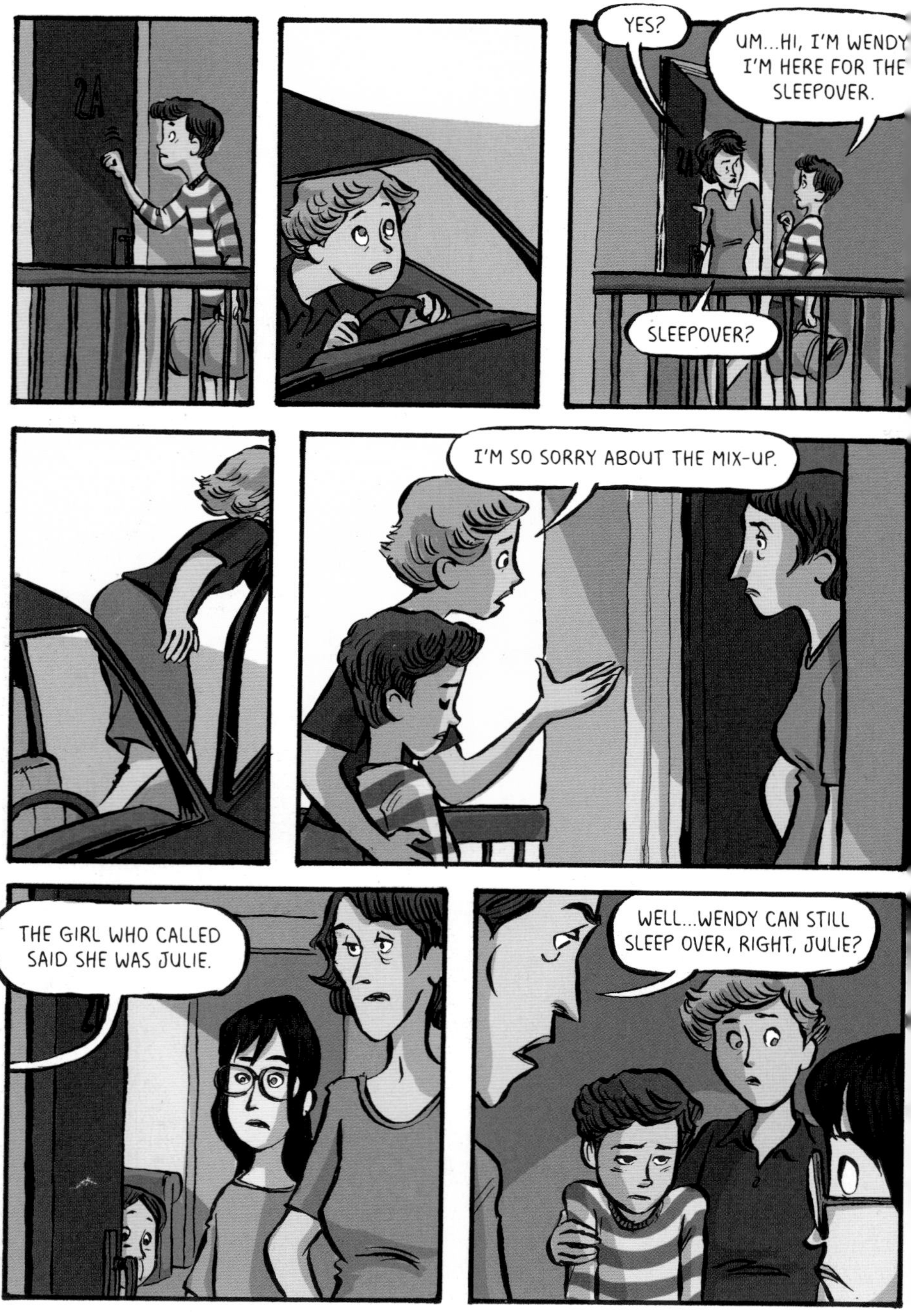
YES?
UM...HI, I'M WENDY. I'M HERE FOR THE SLEEPOVER.
SLEEPOVER?
I'M SO SORRY ABOUT THE MIX-UP.
THE GIRL WHO CALLED SAID SHE WAS JULIE.
WELL...WENDY CAN STILL SLEEP OVER, RIGHT, JULIE?

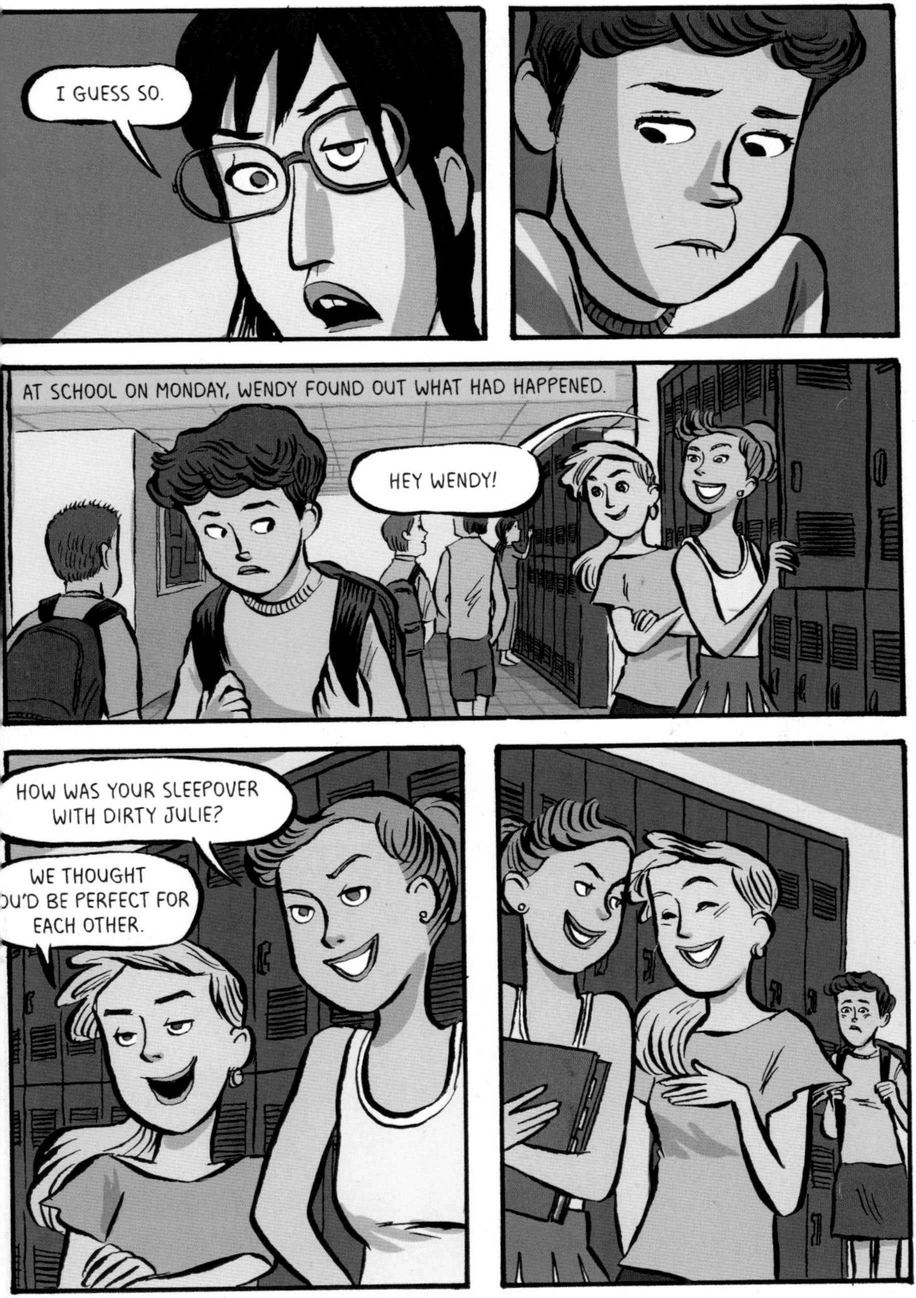
I GUESS SO.
AT SCHOOL ON MONDAY, WENDY FOUND OUT WHAT HAD HAPPENED.
HEY WENDY!
HOW WAS YOUR SLEEPOVER WITH DIRTY JULIE?
WE THOUGHT OU'D BE PERFECT FOR EACH OTHER.

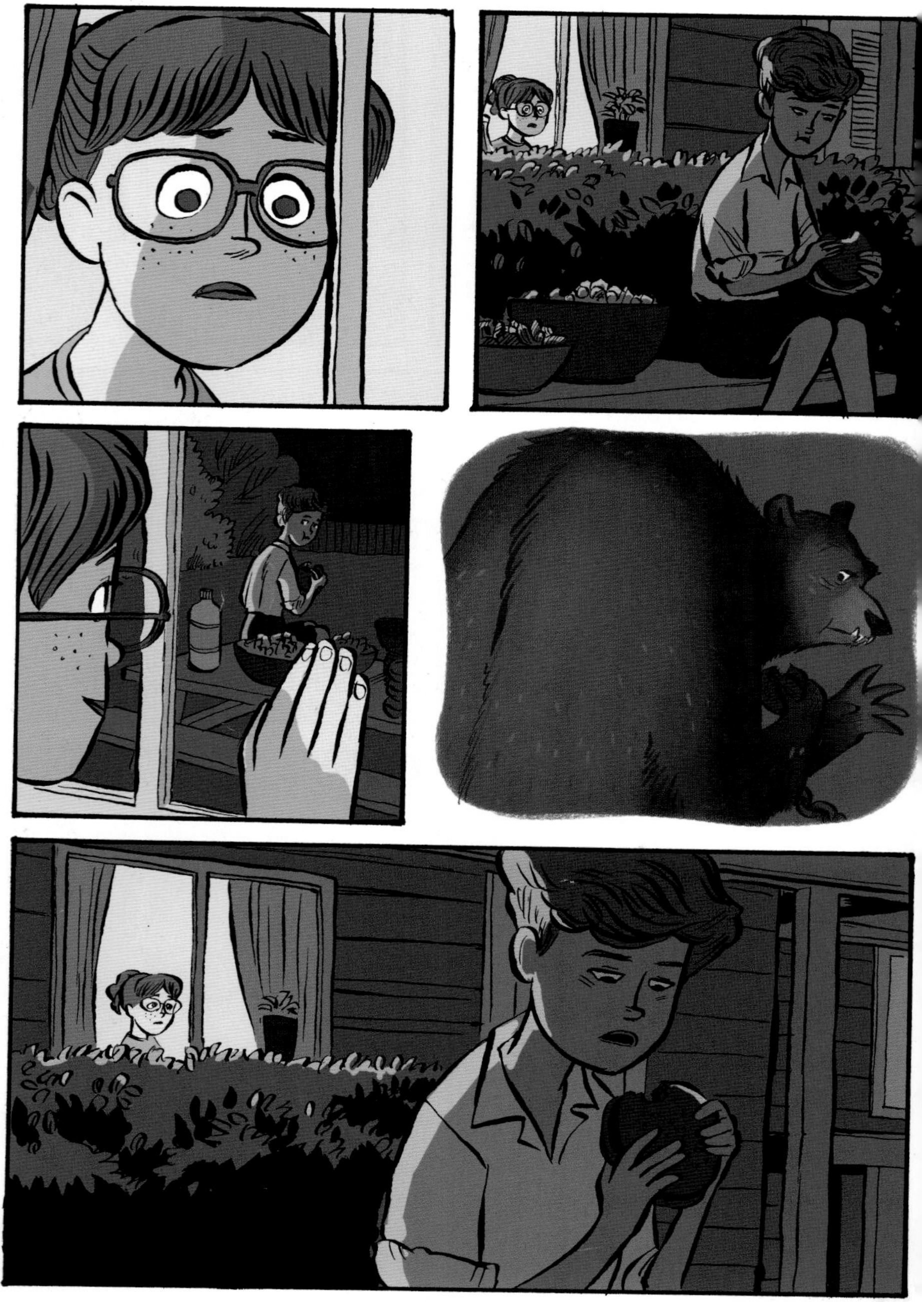

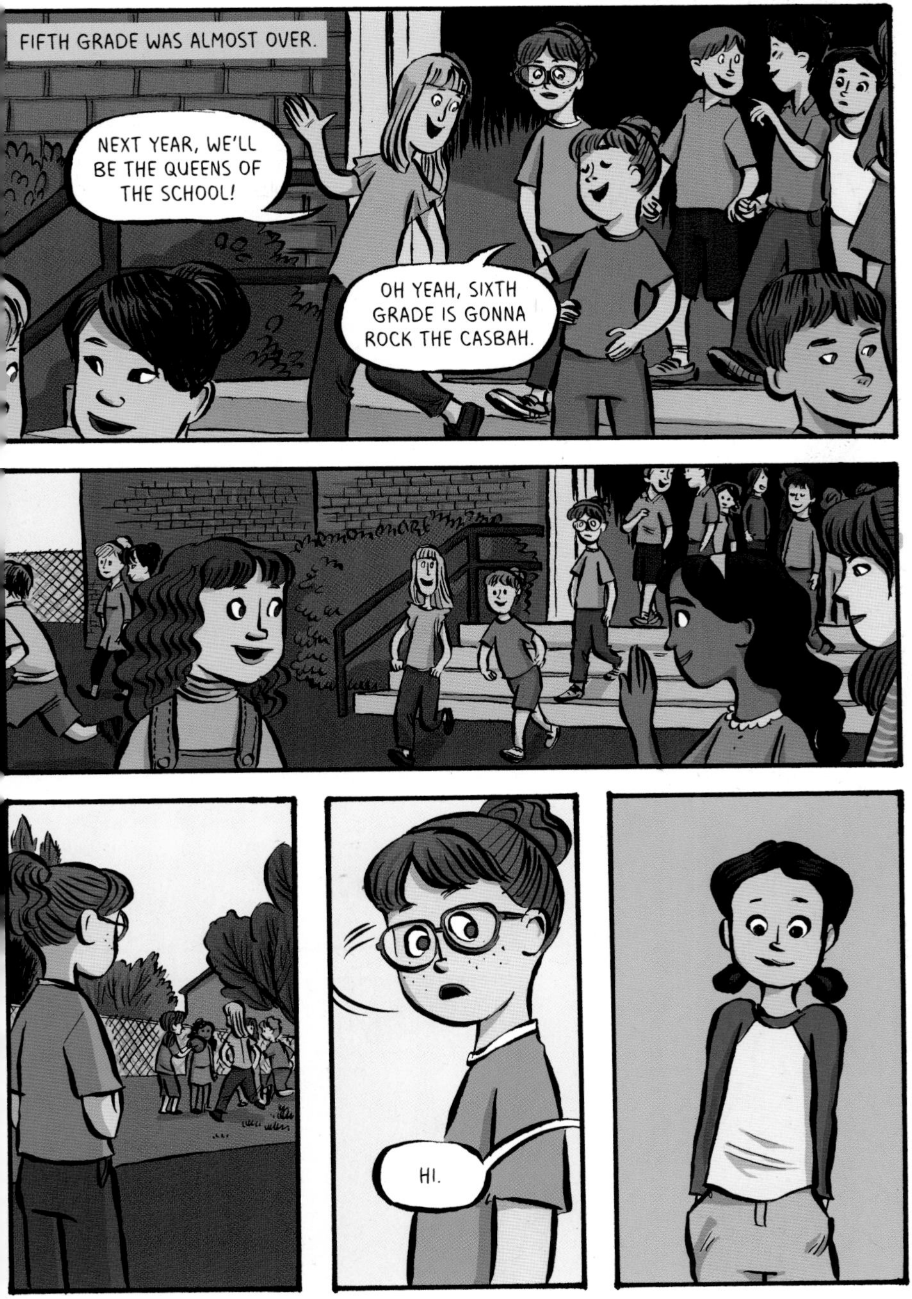
FIFTH GRADE WAS ALMOST OVER.
NEXT YEAR, WE'LL BE THE QUEENS OF THE SCHOOL!
OH YEAH, SIXTH GRADE IS GONNA ROCK THE CASBAH.
HI.

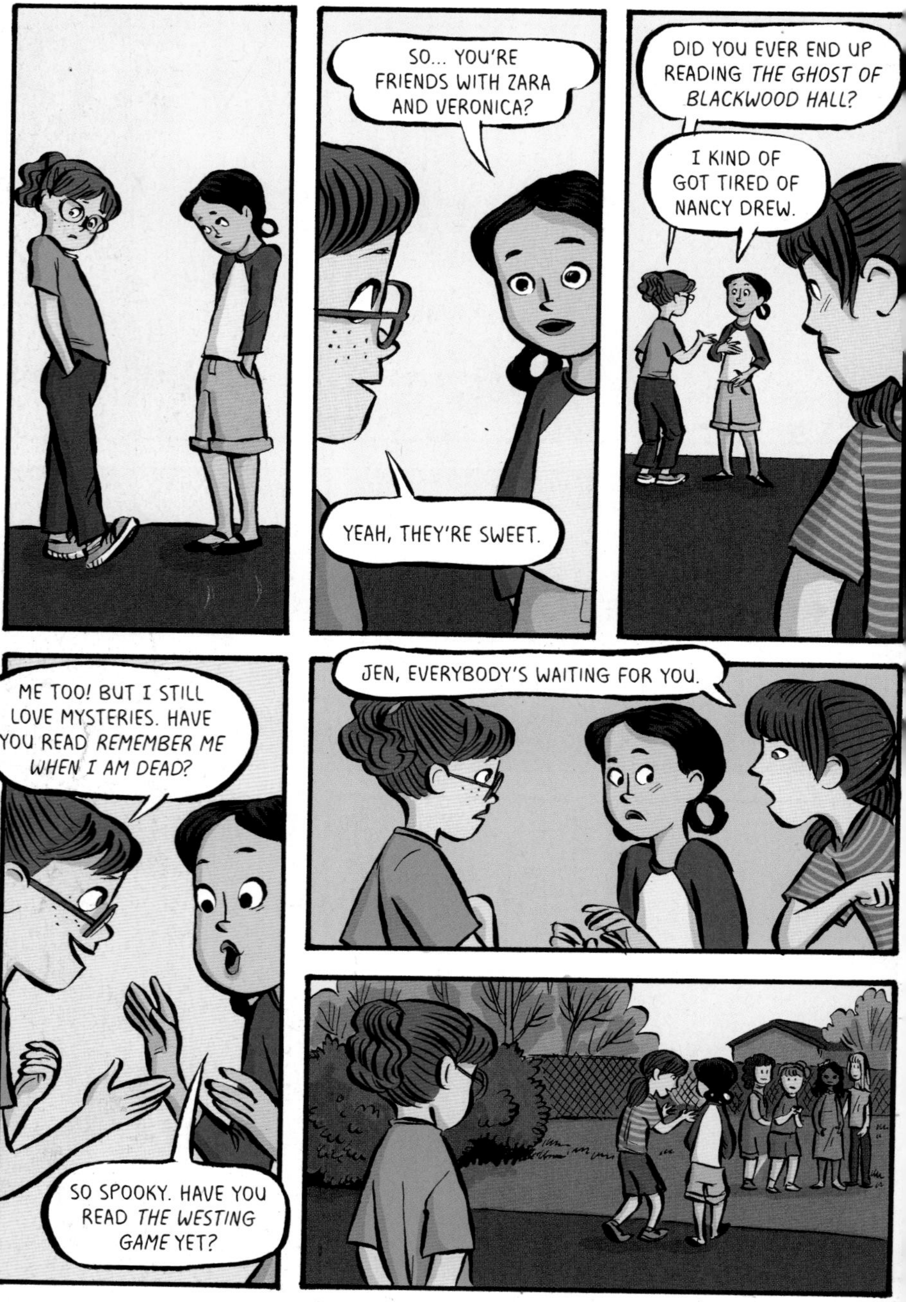
SO... YOU'RE FRIENDS WITH ZARA AND VERONICA?
YEAH, THEY'RE SWEET.
DID YOU EVER END UP READING *THE GHOST OF BLACKWOOD HALL?*
I KIND OF GOT TIRED OF NANCY DREW.
ME TOO! BUT I STILL LOVE MYSTERIES. HAVE YOU READ *REMEMBER ME WHEN I AM DEAD?*
SO SPOOKY. HAVE YOU READ *THE WESTING GAME* YET?
JEN, EVERYBODY'S WAITING FOR YOU.

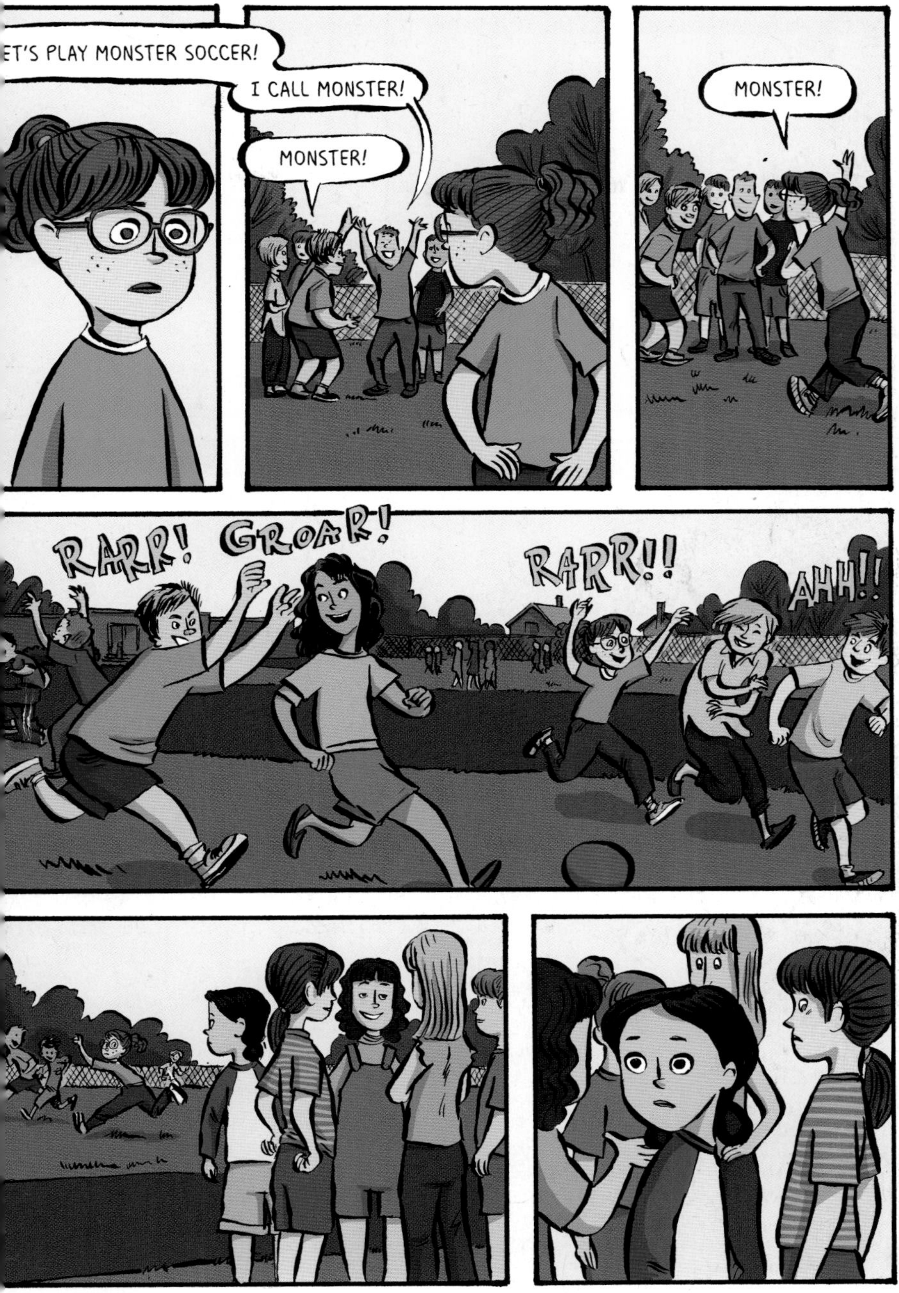

ET'S PLAY MONSTER SOCCER!
I CALL MONSTER!
MONSTER!
MONSTER!
RARR!
GROAR!
RARR!!
AHH!!

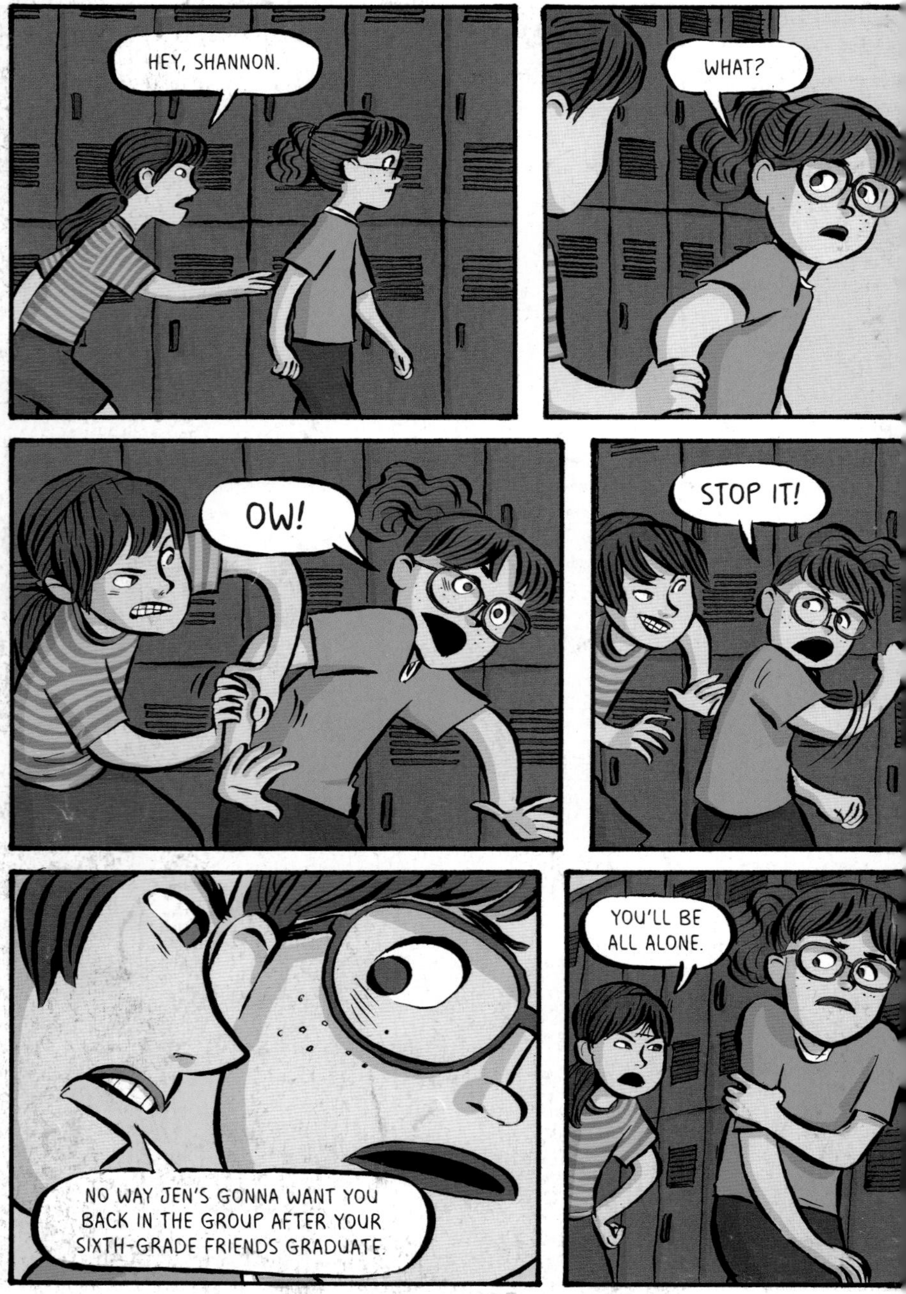
HEY, SHANNON.
WHAT?
OW!
STOP IT!
NO WAY JEN'S GONNA WANT YOU BACK IN THE GROUP AFTER YOUR SIXTH-GRADE FRIENDS GRADUATE.
YOU'LL BE ALL ALONE.

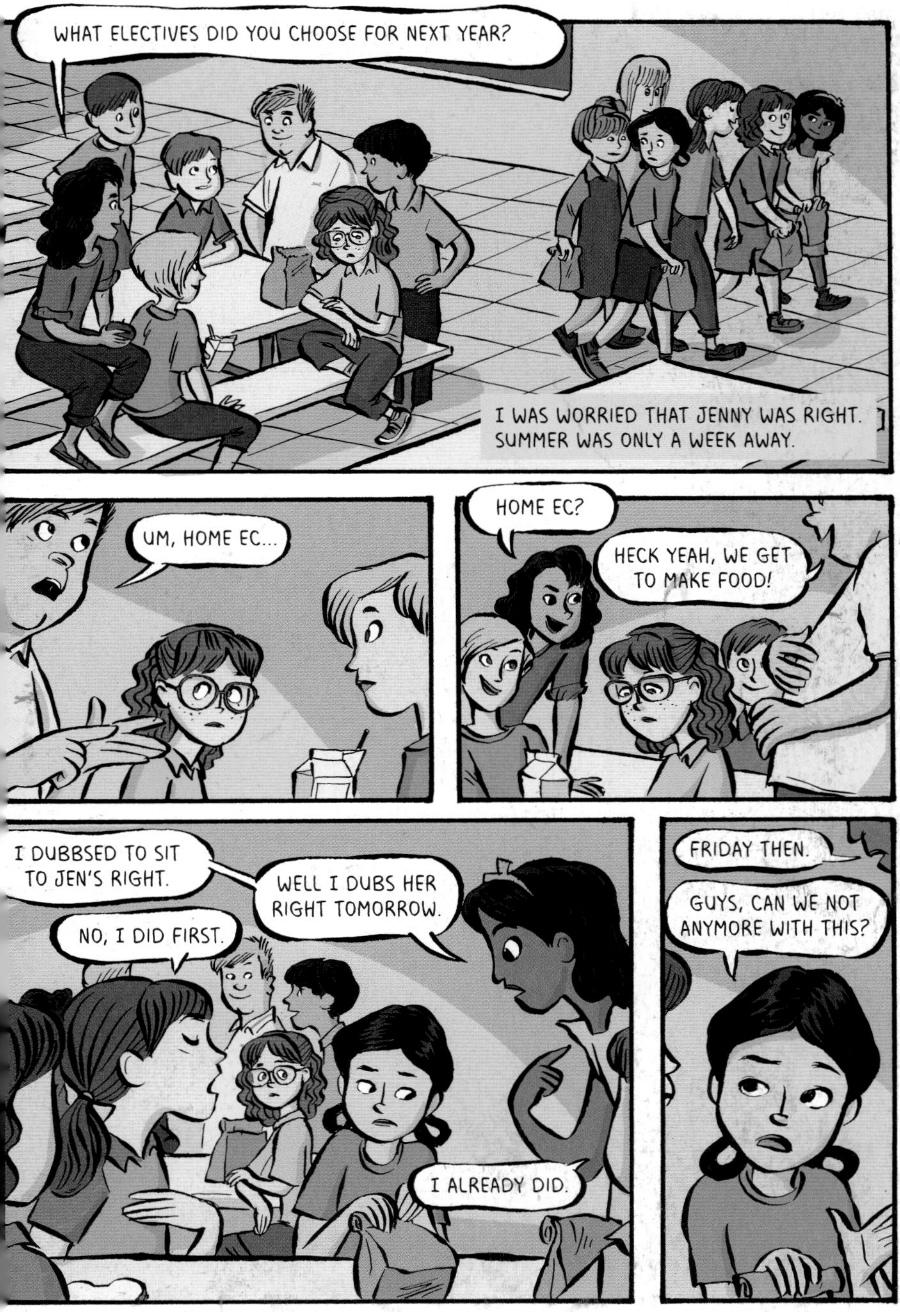

WHAT ELECTIVES DID YOU CHOOSE FOR NEXT YEAR?
I WAS WORRIED THAT JENNY WAS RIGHT. SUMMER WAS ONLY A WEEK AWAY.
UM, HOME EC...
HOME EC?
HECK YEAH, WE GET TO MAKE FOOD!
I DUBBSED TO SIT TO JEN'S RIGHT.
NO, I DID FIRST.
WELL I DUBS HER RIGHT TOMORROW.
I ALREADY DID.
FRIDAY THEN.
GUYS, CAN WE NOT ANYMORE WITH THIS?

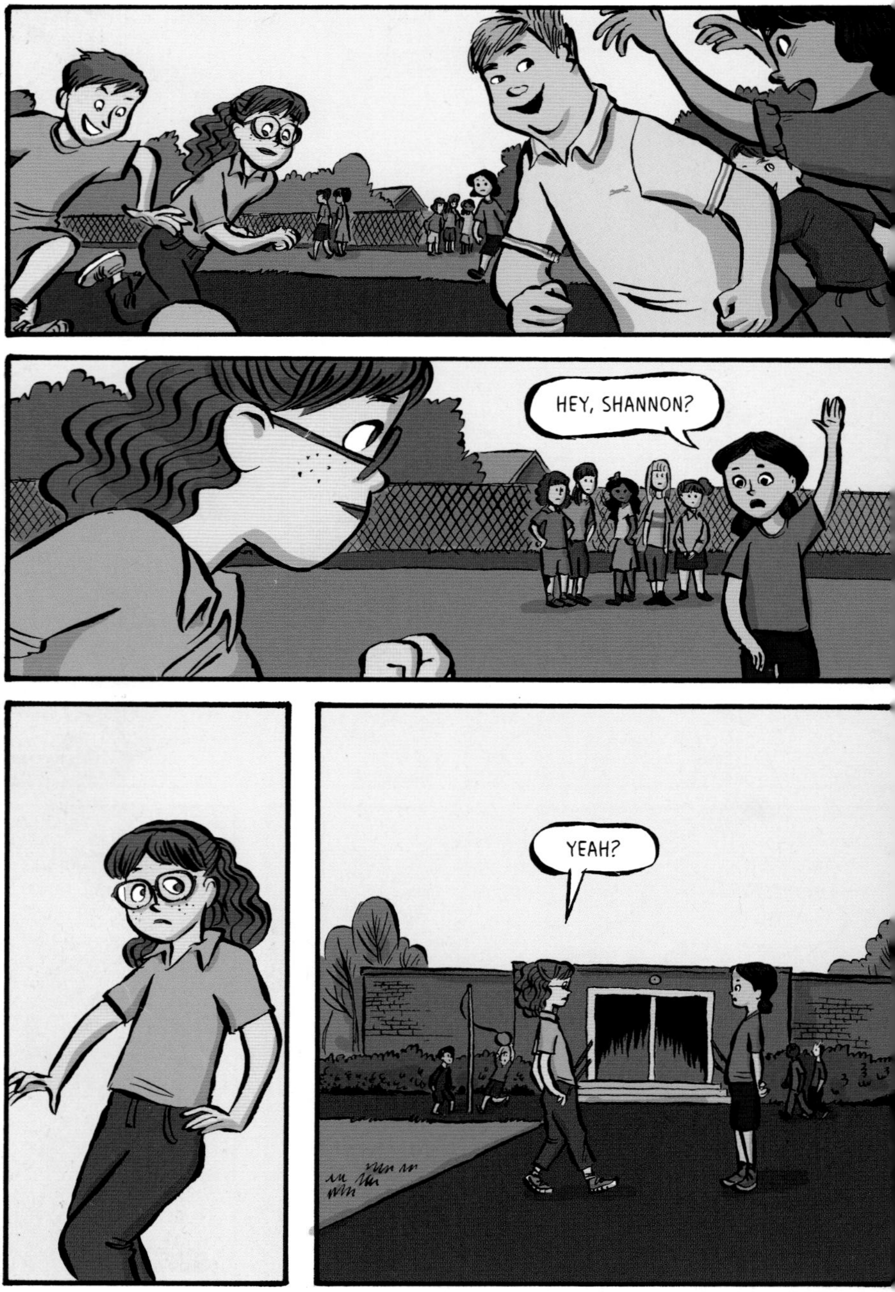
HEY, SHANNON?
YEAH?

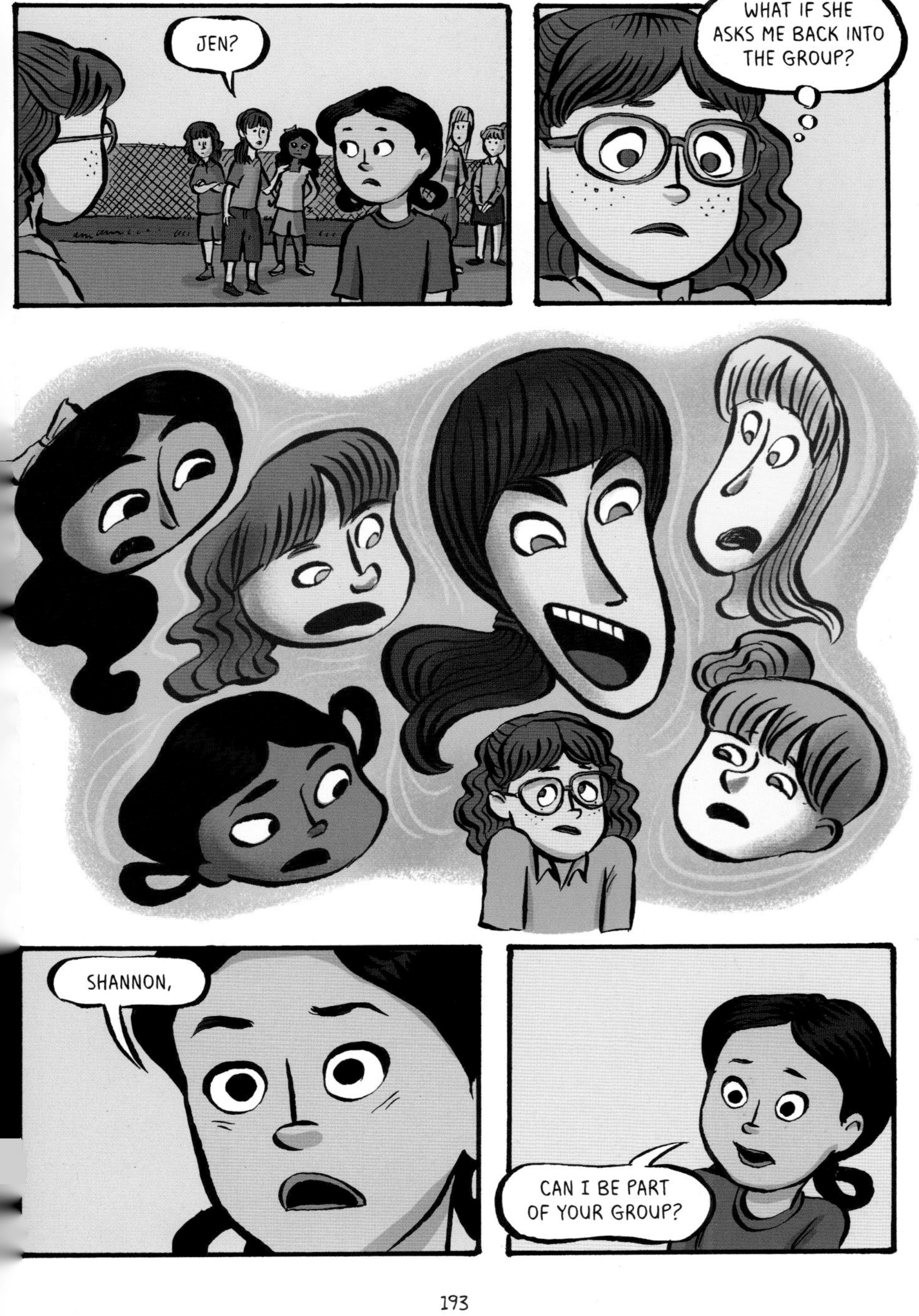
JEN?
WHAT IF SHE ASKS ME BACK INTO THE GROUP?
SHANNON,
CAN I BE PART OF YOUR GROUP?

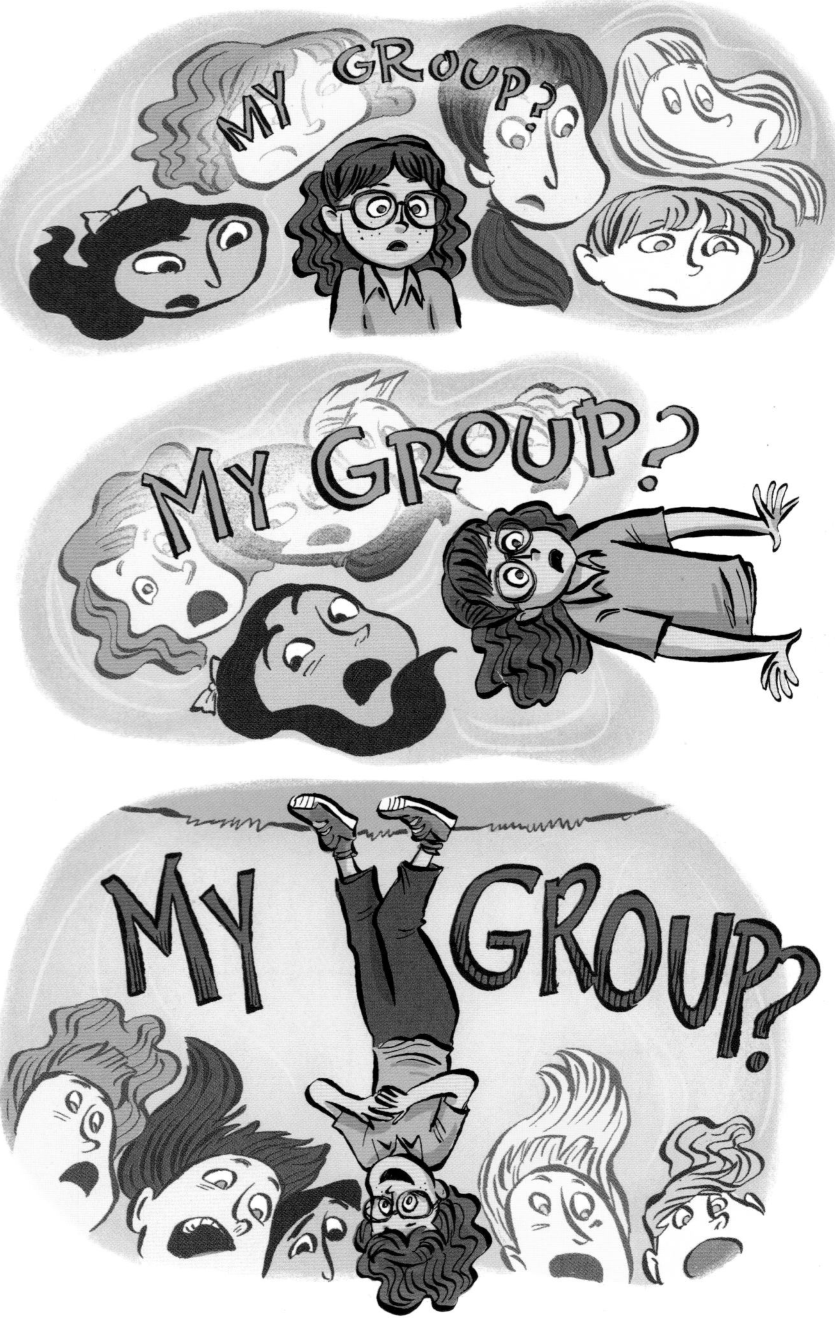
MY GROUP?
MY GROUP?
MY GROUP?

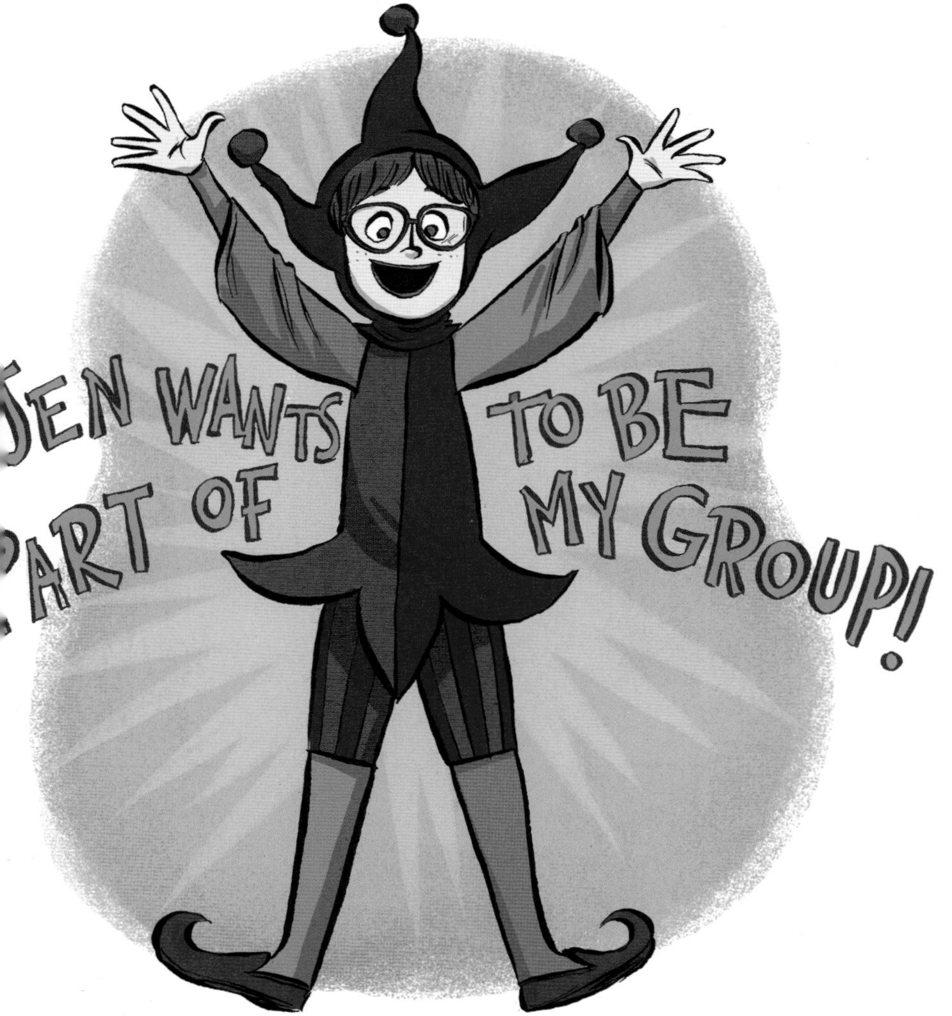
JEN WANTS TO BE PART OF MY GROUP!

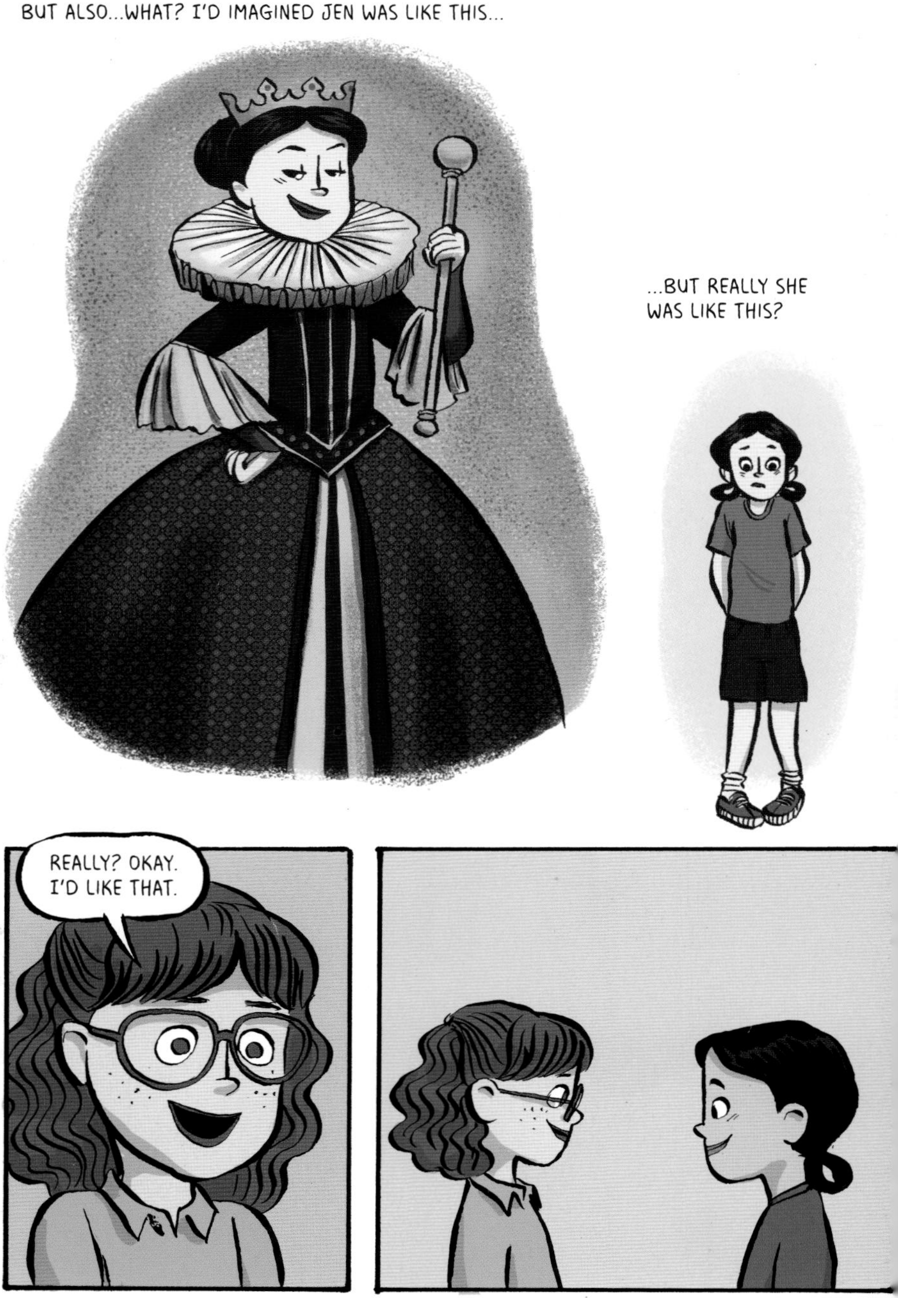
BUT ALSO...WHAT? I'D IMAGINED JEN WAS LIKE THIS...
...BUT REALLY SHE WAS LIKE THIS?
REALLY? OKAY. I'D LIKE THAT.

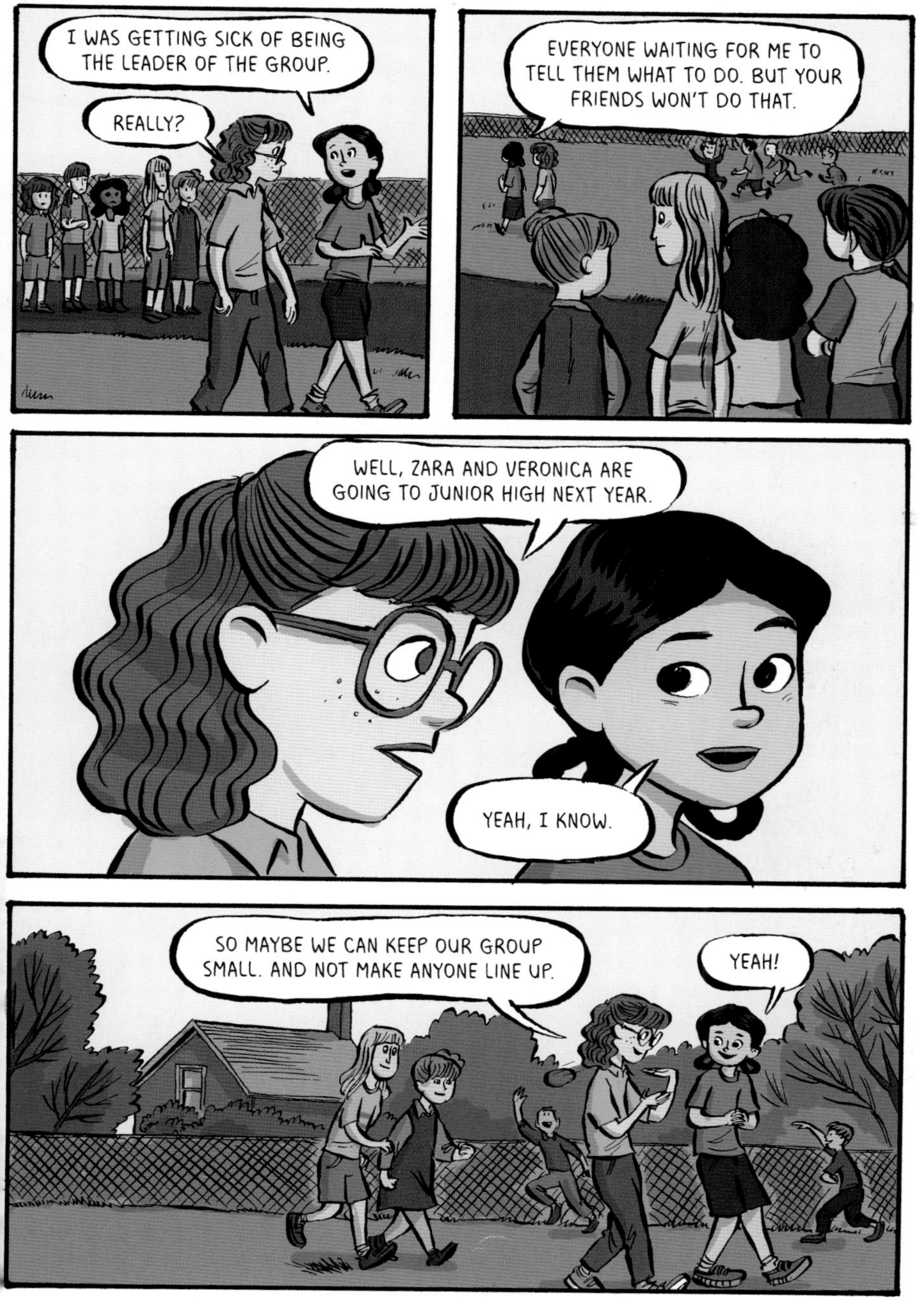
I WAS GETTING SICK OF BEING THE LEADER OF THE GROUP.
REALLY?
EVERYONE WAITING FOR ME TO TELL THEM WHAT TO DO. BUT YOUR FRIENDS WON'T DO THAT.
WELL, ZARA AND VERONICA ARE GOING TO JUNIOR HIGH NEXT YEAR.
YEAH, I KNOW.
SO MAYBE WE CAN KEEP OUR GROUP SMALL. AND NOT MAKE ANYONE LINE UP.
YEAH!

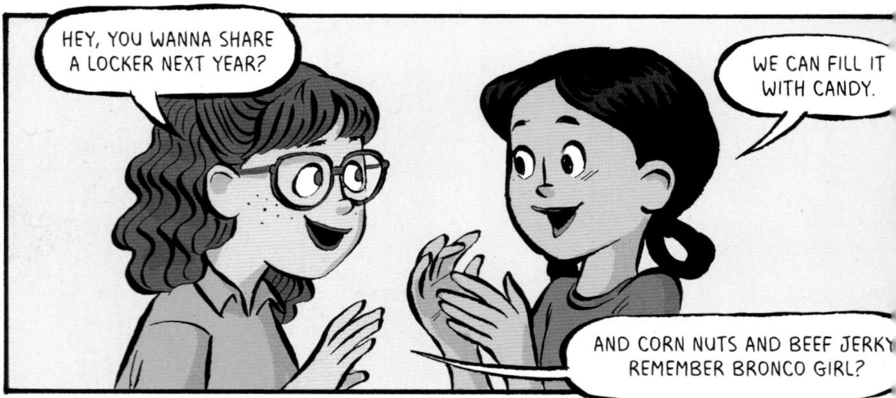
HEY, YOU WANNA SHARE A LOCKER NEXT YEAR?
WE CAN FILL IT WITH CANDY.
AND CORN NUTS AND BEEF JERKY
REMEMBER BRONCO GIRL?

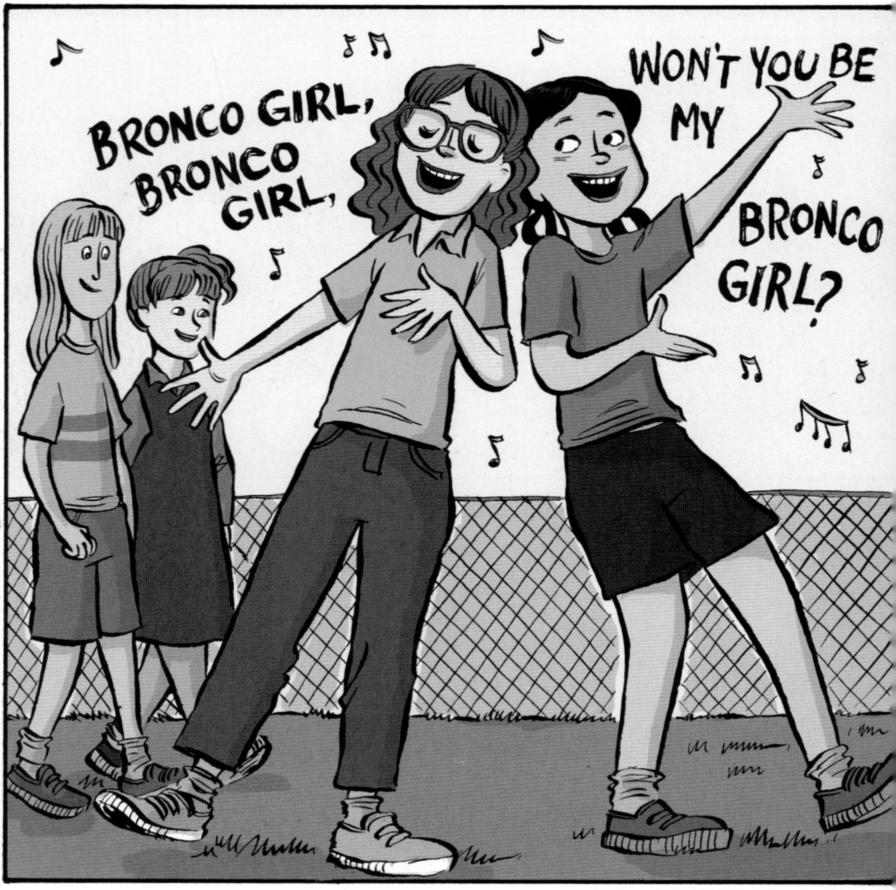
BRONCO GIRL, BRONCO GIRL,
WON'T YOU BE MY BRONCO GIRL?

FOR FIELD DAY, OUR NEW GROUP WENT SHOPPING FOR OUTFITS IN THE LATEST STYLES.

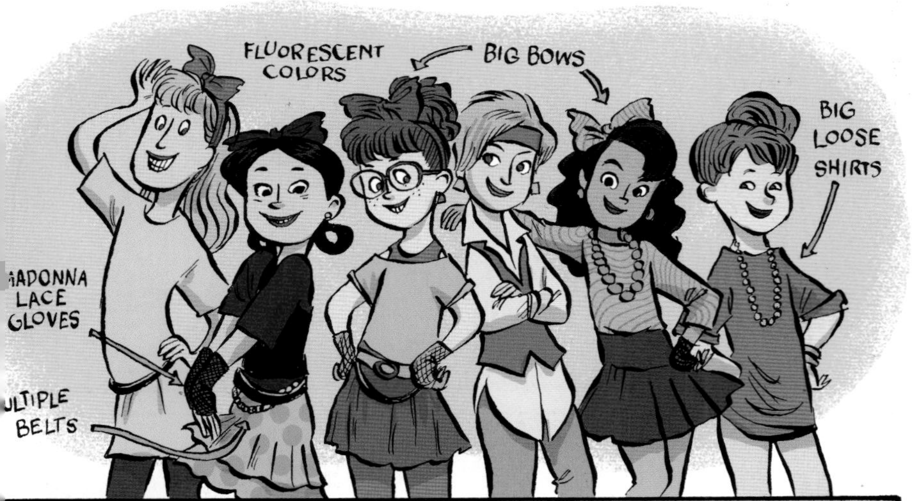
FLUORESCENT COLORS
BIG BOWS
BIG LOOSE SHIRTS
ADONNA LACE GLOVES
ULTIPLE BELTS

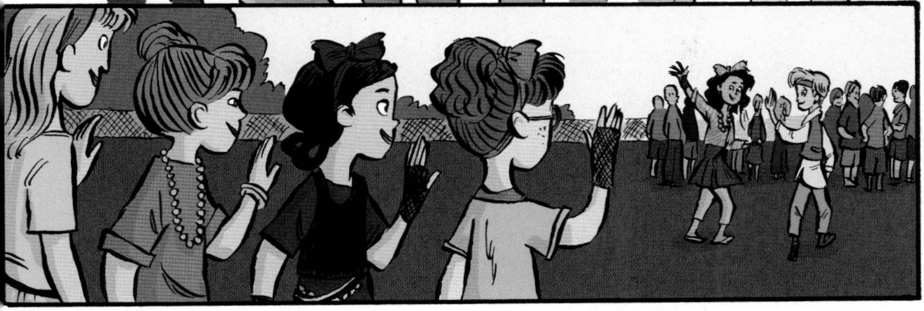

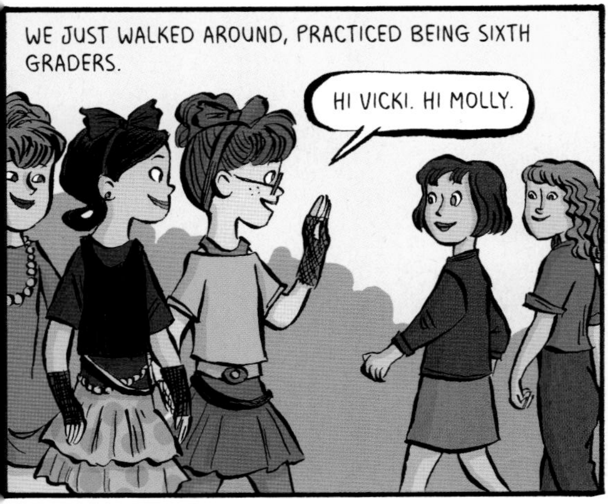
WE JUST WALKED AROUND, PRACTICED BEING SIXTH GRADERS.
HI VICKI. HI MOLLY.

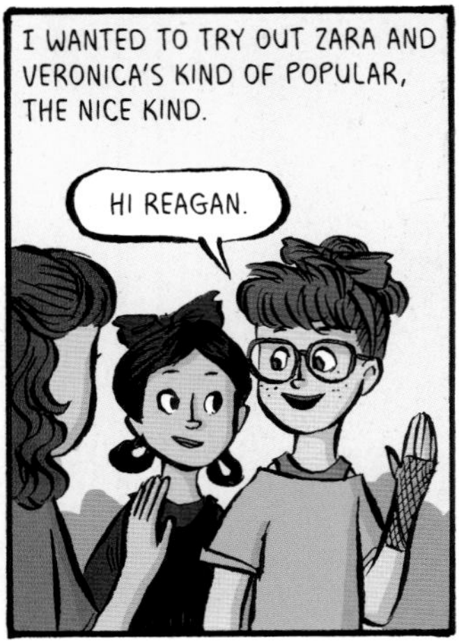
I WANTED TO TRY OUT ZARA AND VERONICA'S KIND OF POPULAR, THE NICE KIND.
HI REAGAN.

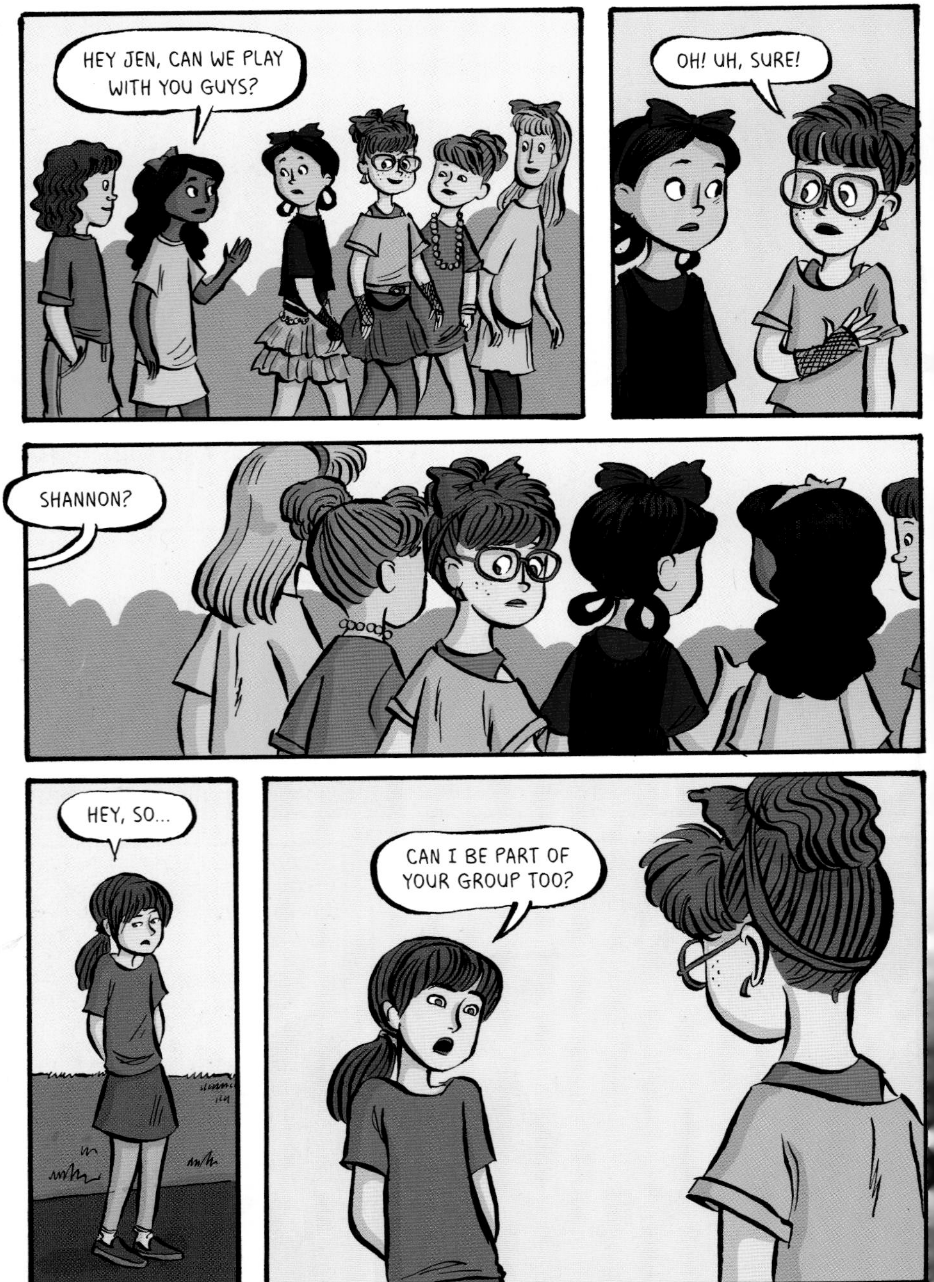
HEY JEN, CAN WE PLAY WITH YOU GUYS?
OH! UH, SURE!
SHANNON?
HEY, SO...
CAN I BE PART OF YOUR GROUP TOO?

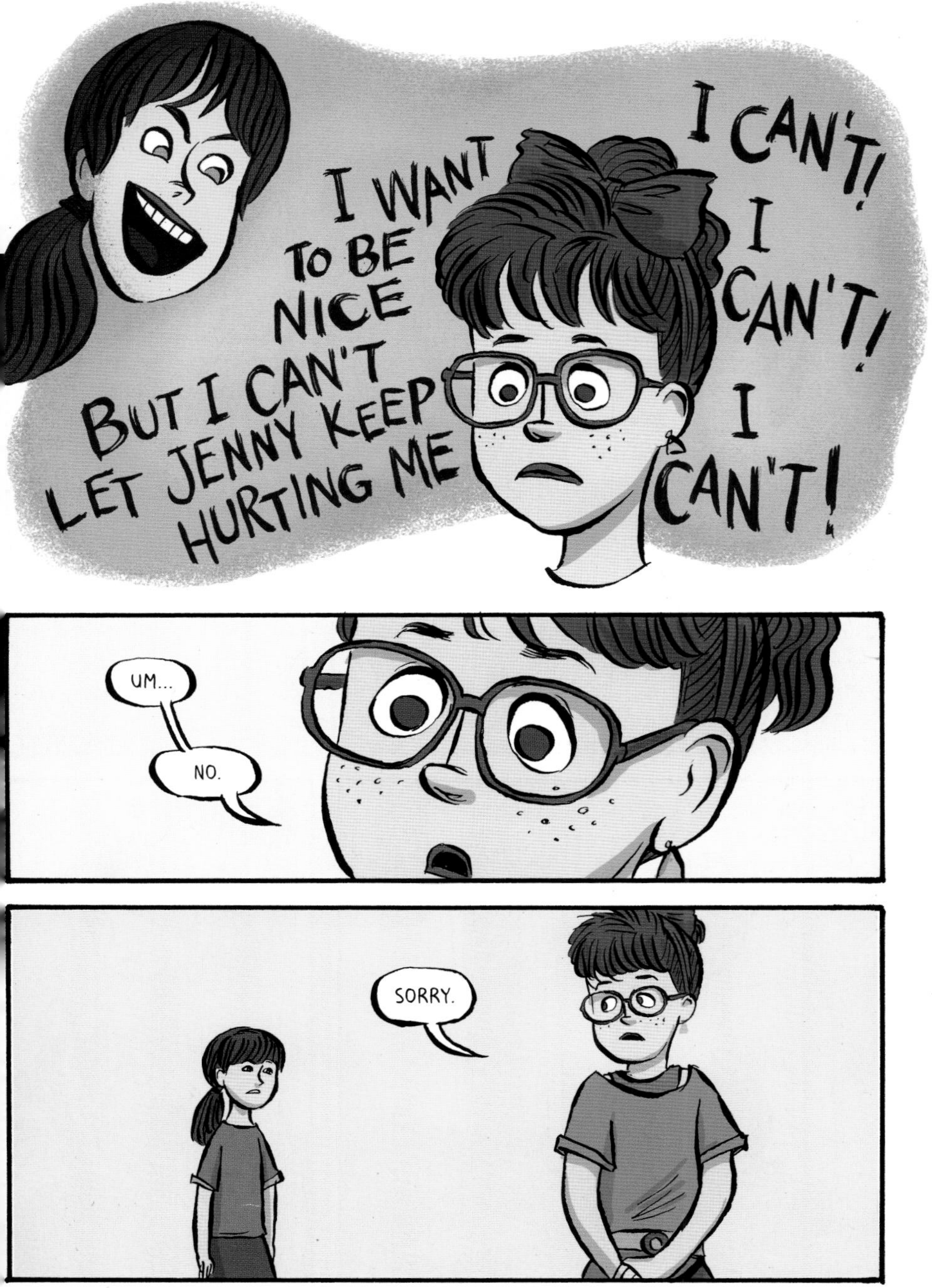
I WANT TO BE NICE BUT I CAN'T LET JENNY KEEP HURTING ME
I CAN'T! I CAN'T! I CAN'T!
UM...
NO.
SORRY.

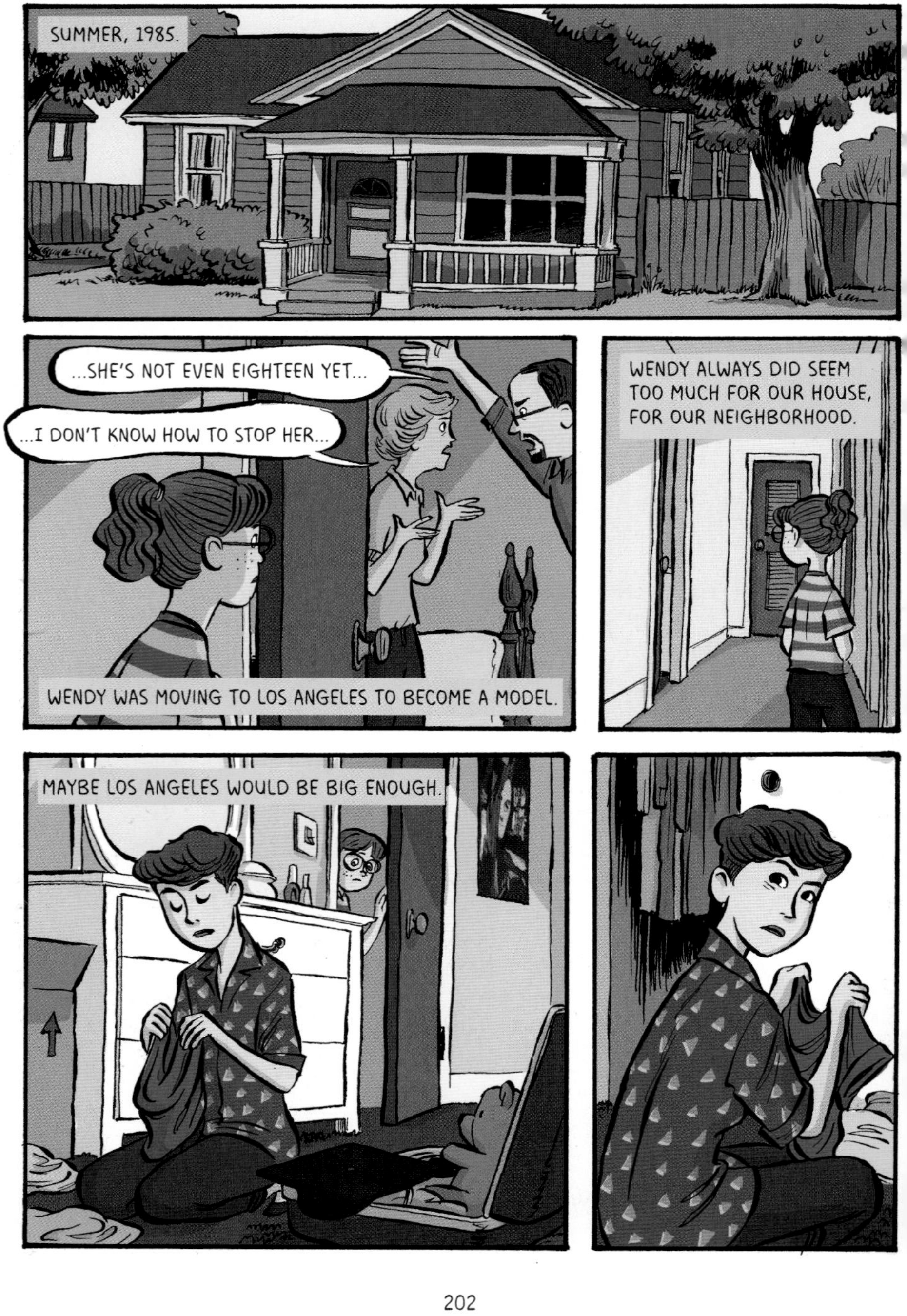
SUMMER, 1985.
...SHE'S NOT EVEN EIGHTEEN YET...
...I DON'T KNOW HOW TO STOP HER...
WENDY WAS MOVING TO LOS ANGELES TO BECOME A MODEL.
WENDY ALWAYS DID SEEM TOO MUCH FOR OUR HOUSE, FOR OUR NEIGHBORHOOD.
MAYBE LOS ANGELES WOULD BE BIG ENOUGH.

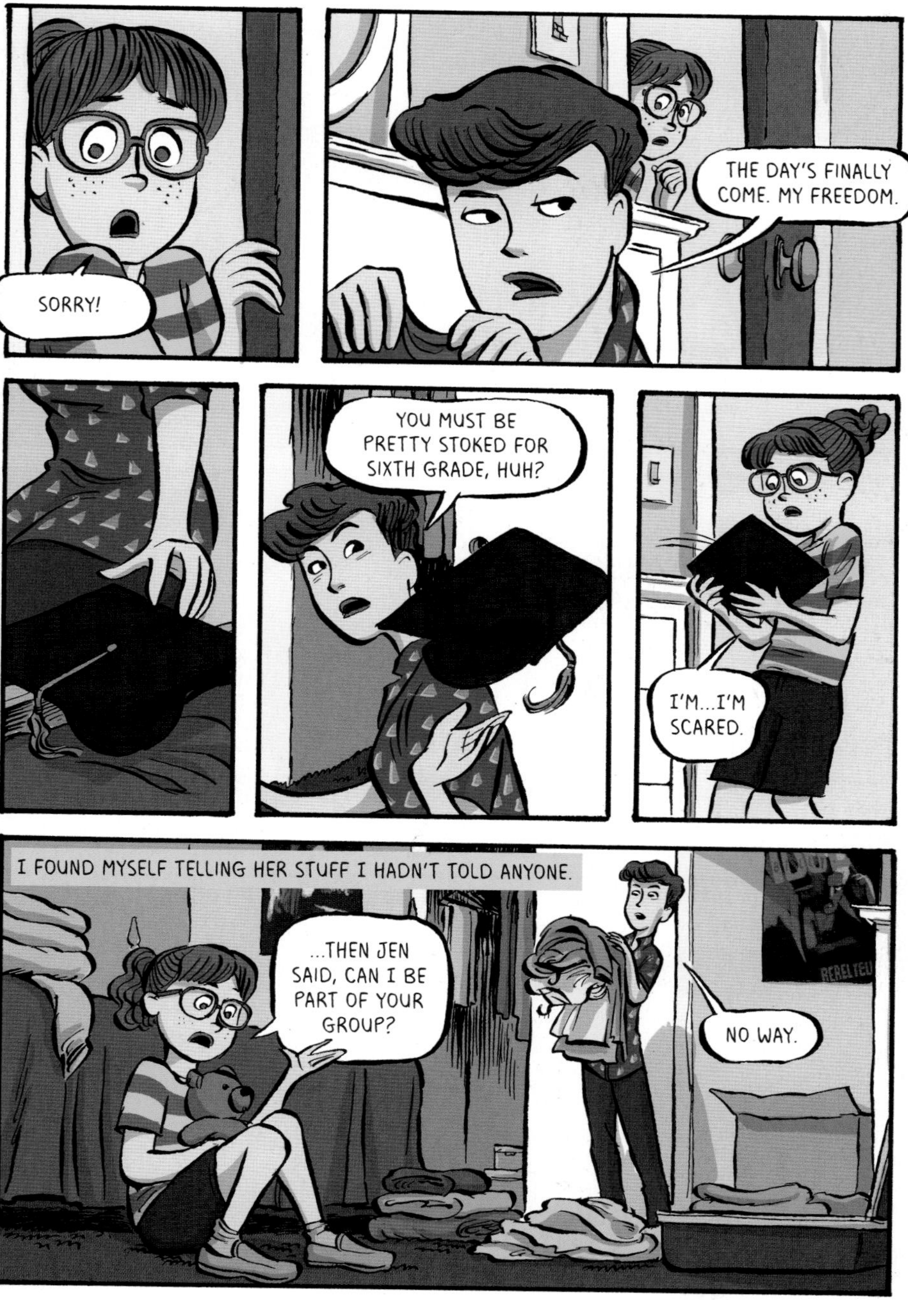
SORRY!
THE DAY'S FINALLY COME. MY FREEDOM.
YOU MUST BE PRETTY STOKED FOR SIXTH GRADE, HUH?
I'M...I'M SCARED.
I FOUND MYSELF TELLING HER STUFF I HADN'T TOLD ANYONE.
...THEN JEN SAID, CAN I BE PART OF YOUR GROUP?
NO WAY.

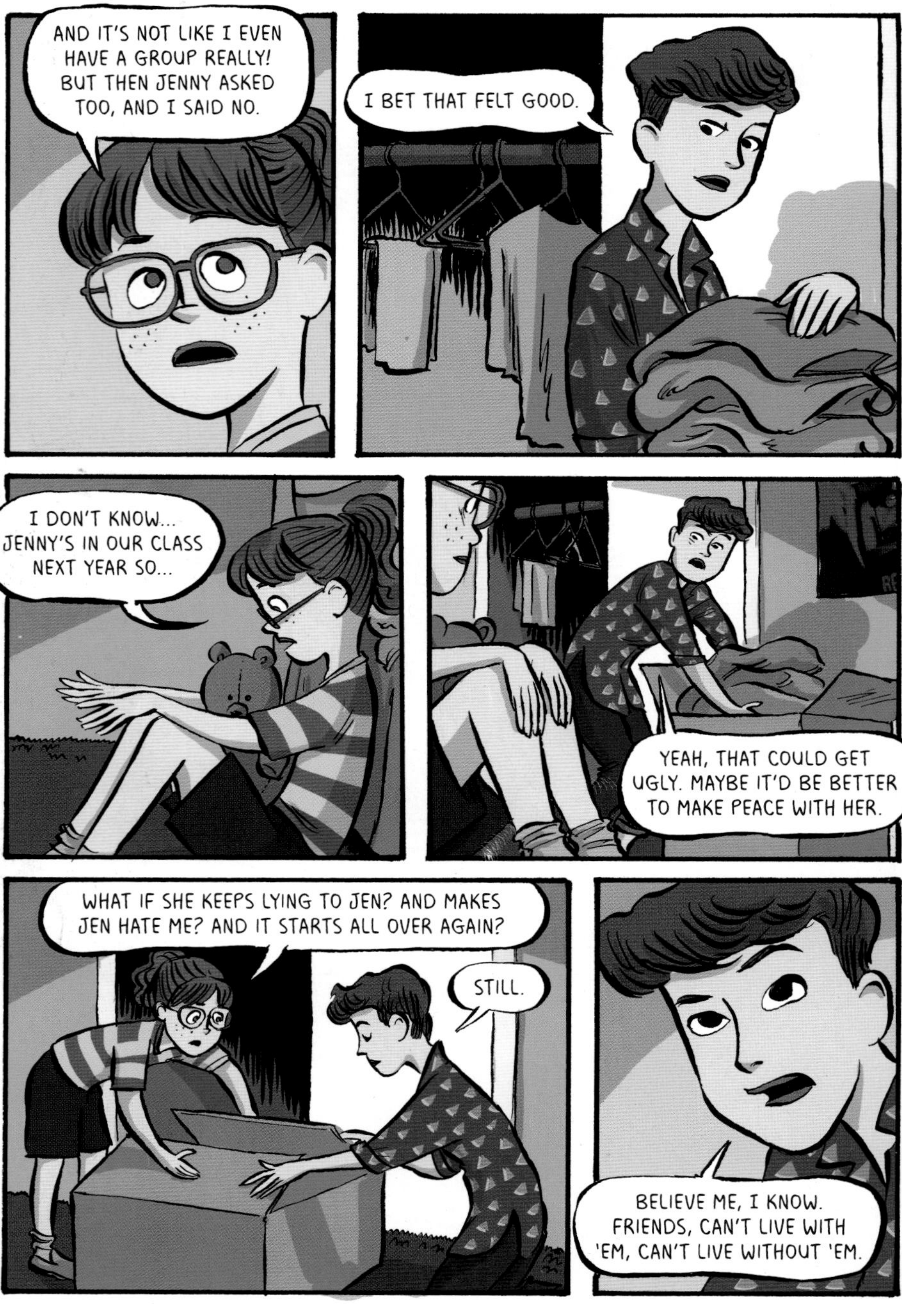
AND IT'S NOT LIKE I EVEN HAVE A GROUP REALLY! BUT THEN JENNY ASKED TOO, AND I SAID NO.
I BET THAT FELT GOOD.
I DON'T KNOW... JENNY'S IN OUR CLASS NEXT YEAR SO...
YEAH, THAT COULD GET UGLY. MAYBE IT'D BE BETTER TO MAKE PEACE WITH HER.
WHAT IF SHE KEEPS LYING TO JEN? AND MAKES JEN HATE ME? AND IT STARTS ALL OVER AGAIN?
STILL.
BELIEVE ME, I KNOW. FRIENDS, CAN'T LIVE WITH 'EM, CAN'T LIVE WITHOUT 'EM.

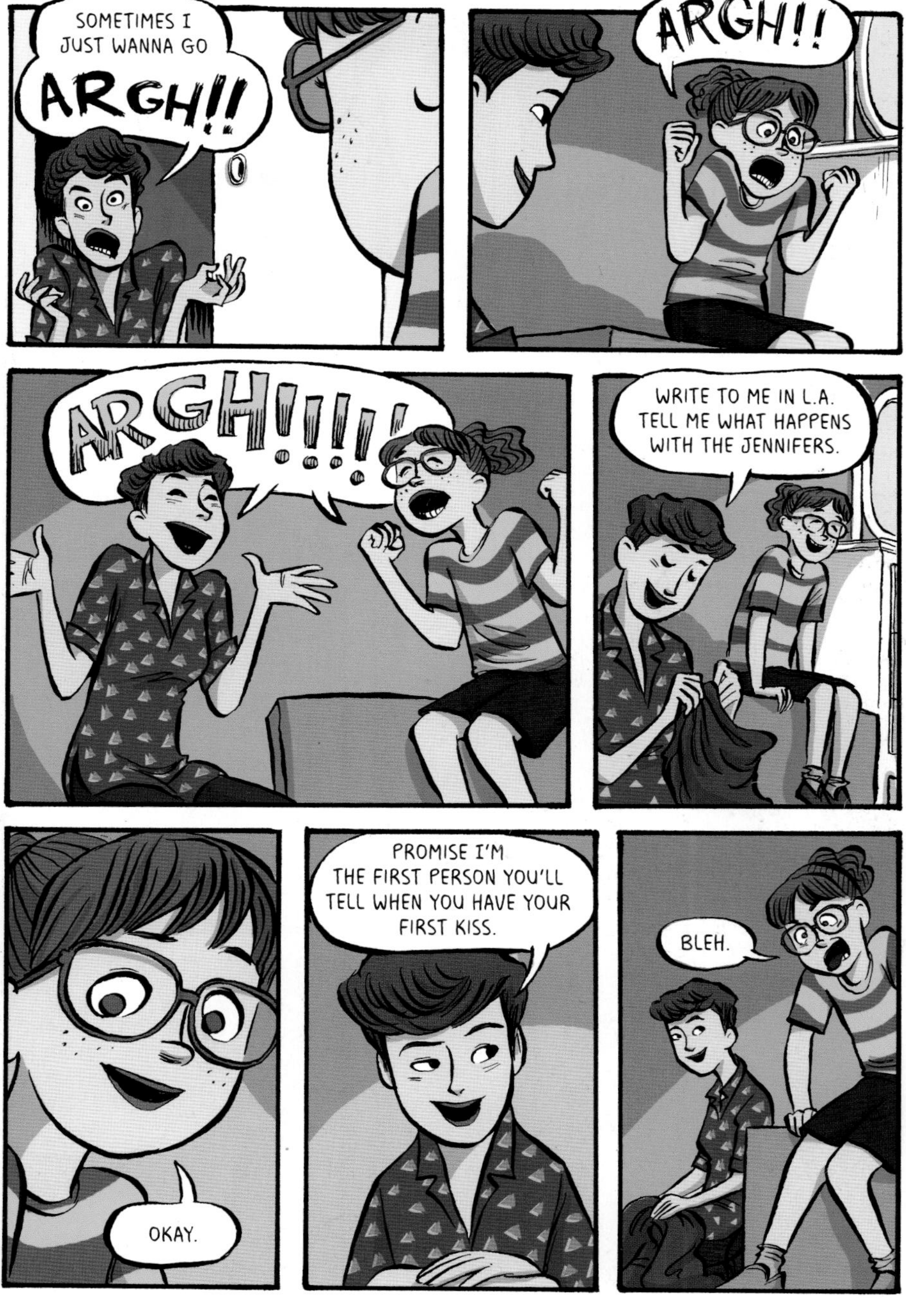
SOMETIMES I JUST WANNA GO
ARGH!!
ARGH!!
ARGH!!!!!
WRITE TO ME IN L.A. TELL ME WHAT HAPPENS WITH THE JENNIFERS.
OKAY.
PROMISE I'M THE FIRST PERSON YOU'LL TELL WHEN YOU HAVE YOUR FIRST KISS.
BLEH.

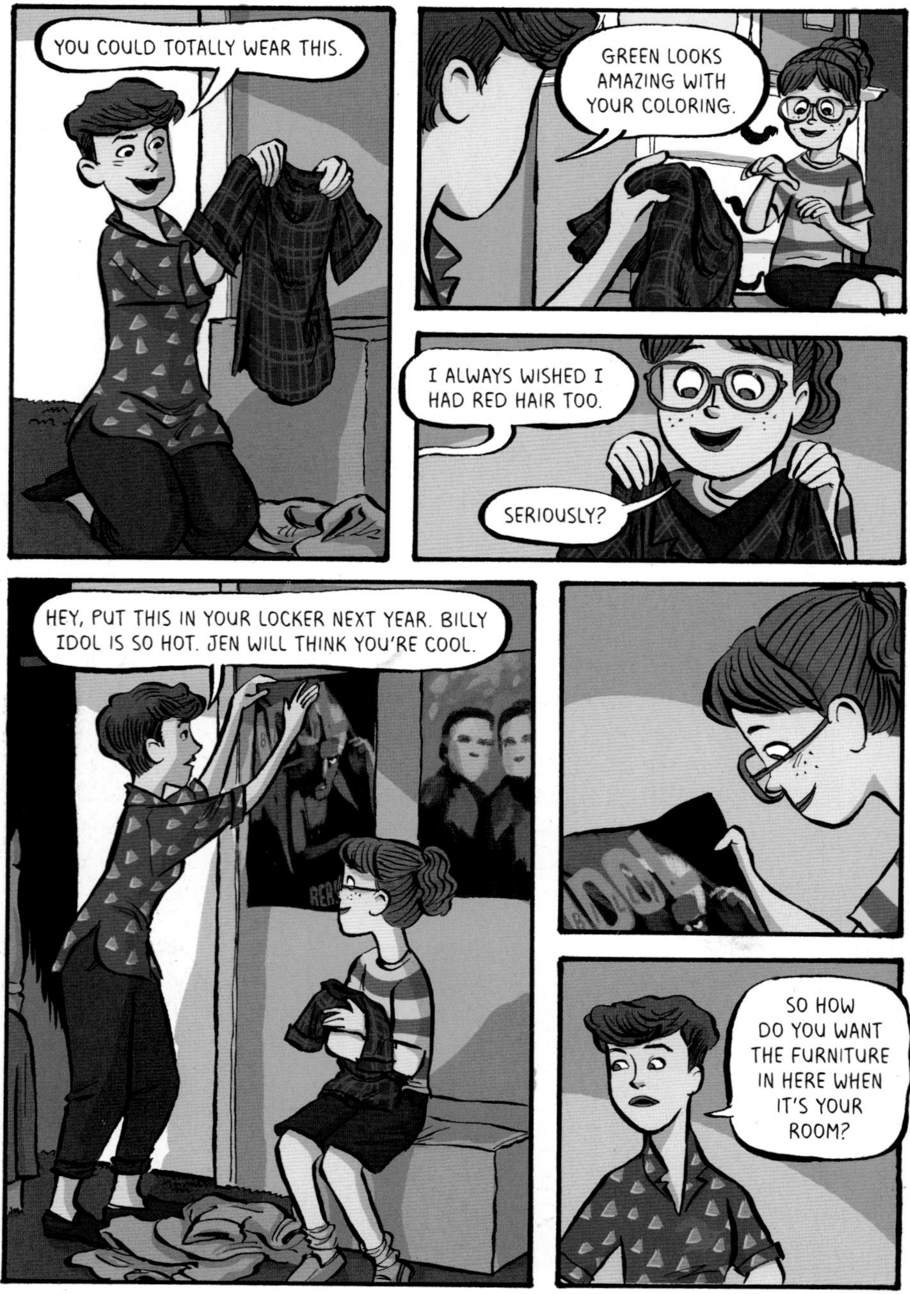
YOU COULD TOTALLY WEAR THIS.
GREEN LOOKS AMAZING WITH YOUR COLORING.
I ALWAYS WISHED I HAD RED HAIR TOO.
SERIOUSLY?
HEY, PUT THIS IN YOUR LOCKER NEXT YEAR. BILLY IDOL IS SO HOT. JEN WILL THINK YOU'RE COOL.
SO HOW DO YOU WANT THE FURNITURE IN HERE WHEN IT'S YOUR ROOM?

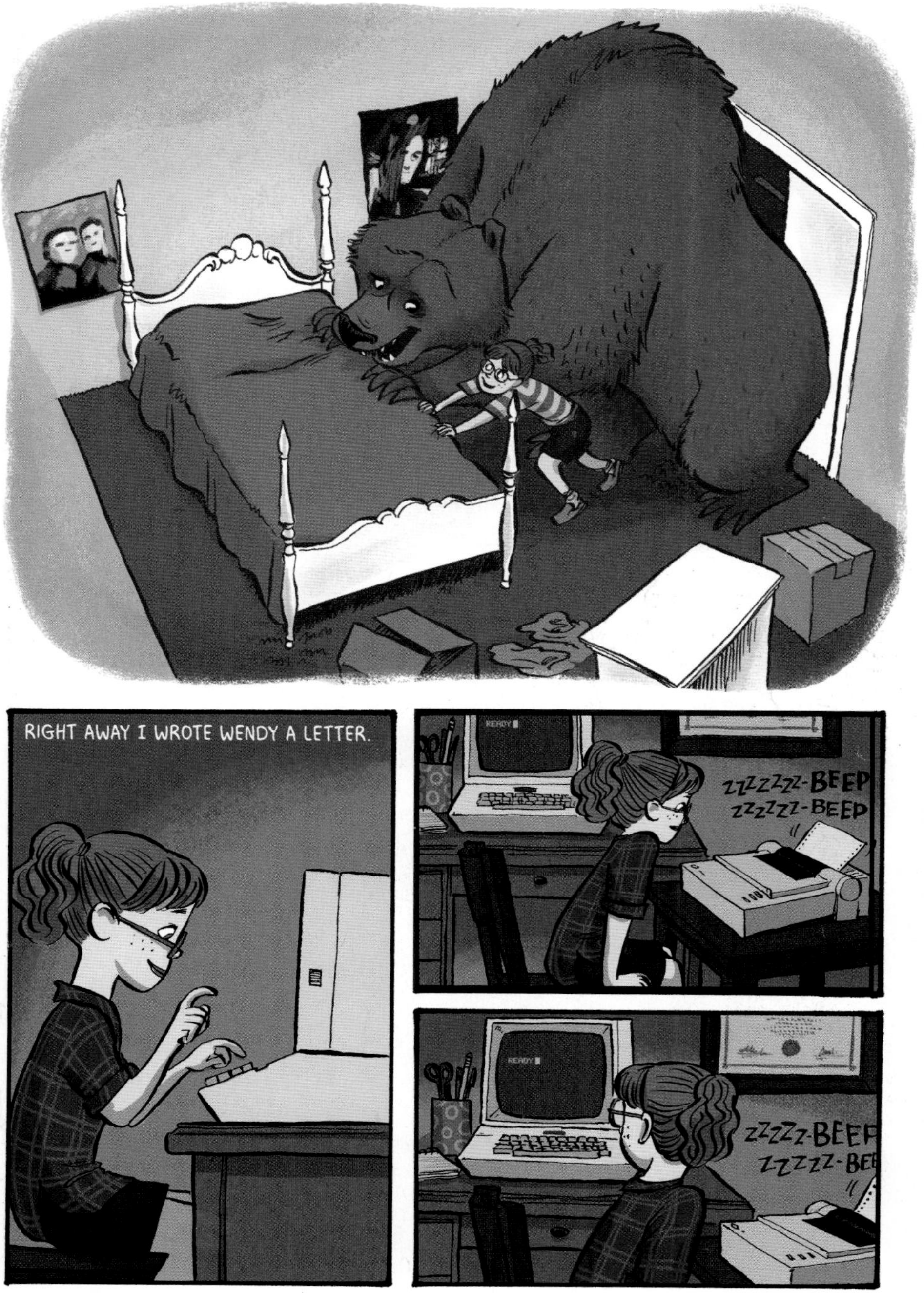
RIGHT AWAY I WROTE WENDY A LETTER.
READY
ZZZZZZZ-BEEP
ZZZZZZZ-BEEP
READY
ZZZZZ-BEEP
ZZZZZ-BE

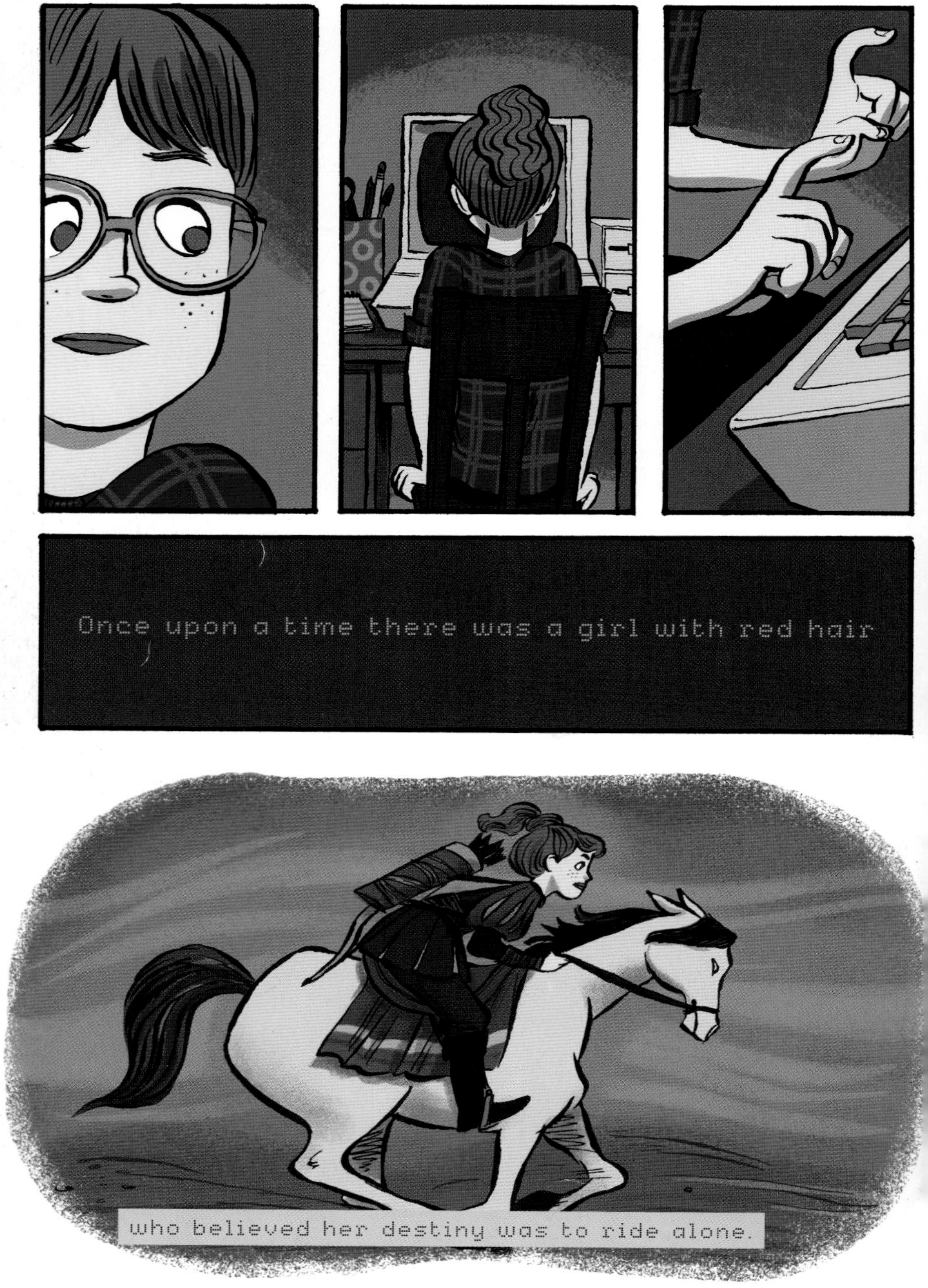
Once upon a time there was a girl with red hair
who believed her destiny was to ride alone.

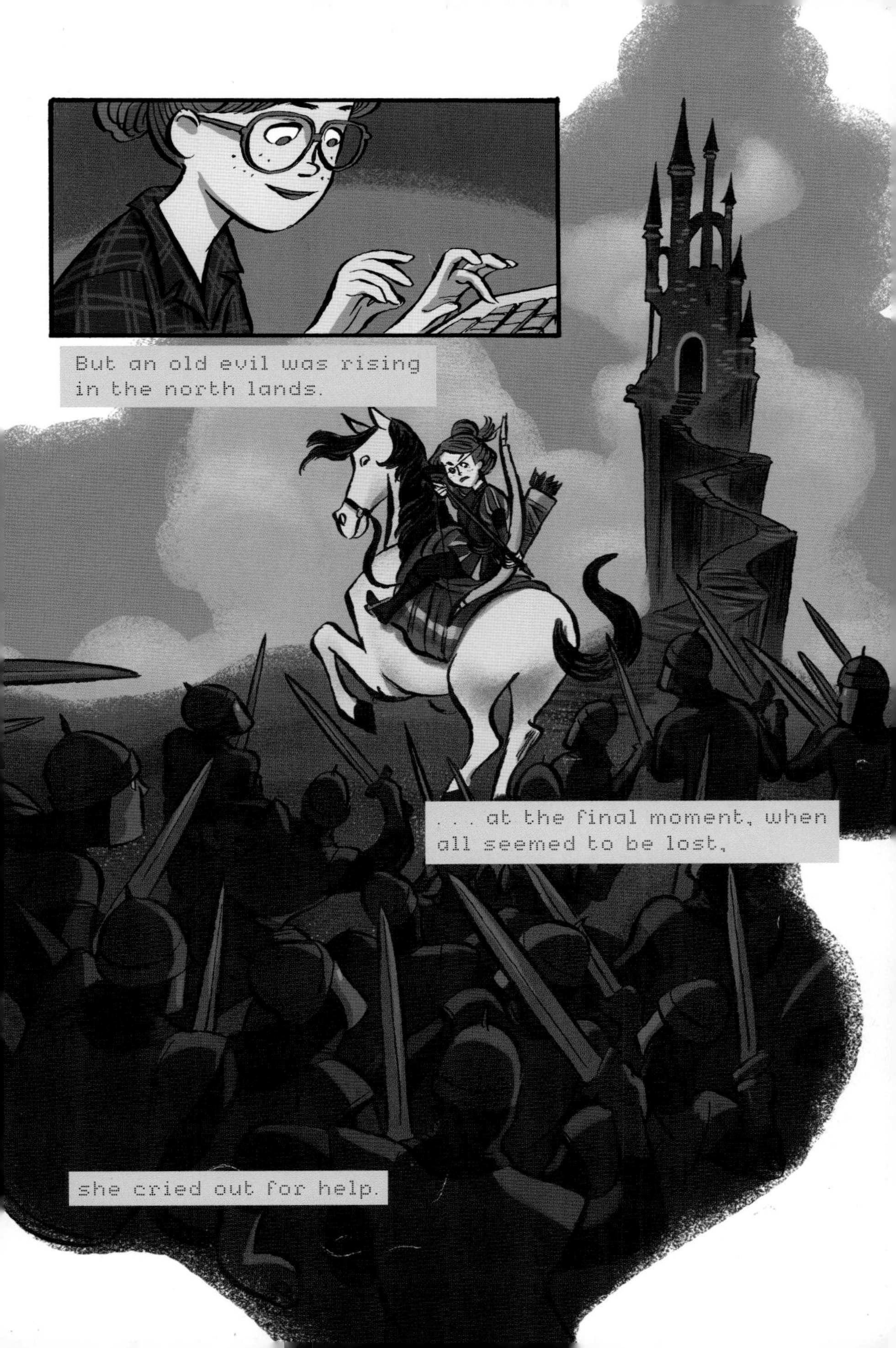

But an old evil was rising in the north lands.
. . . at the final moment, when all seemed to be lost,
she cried out for help.

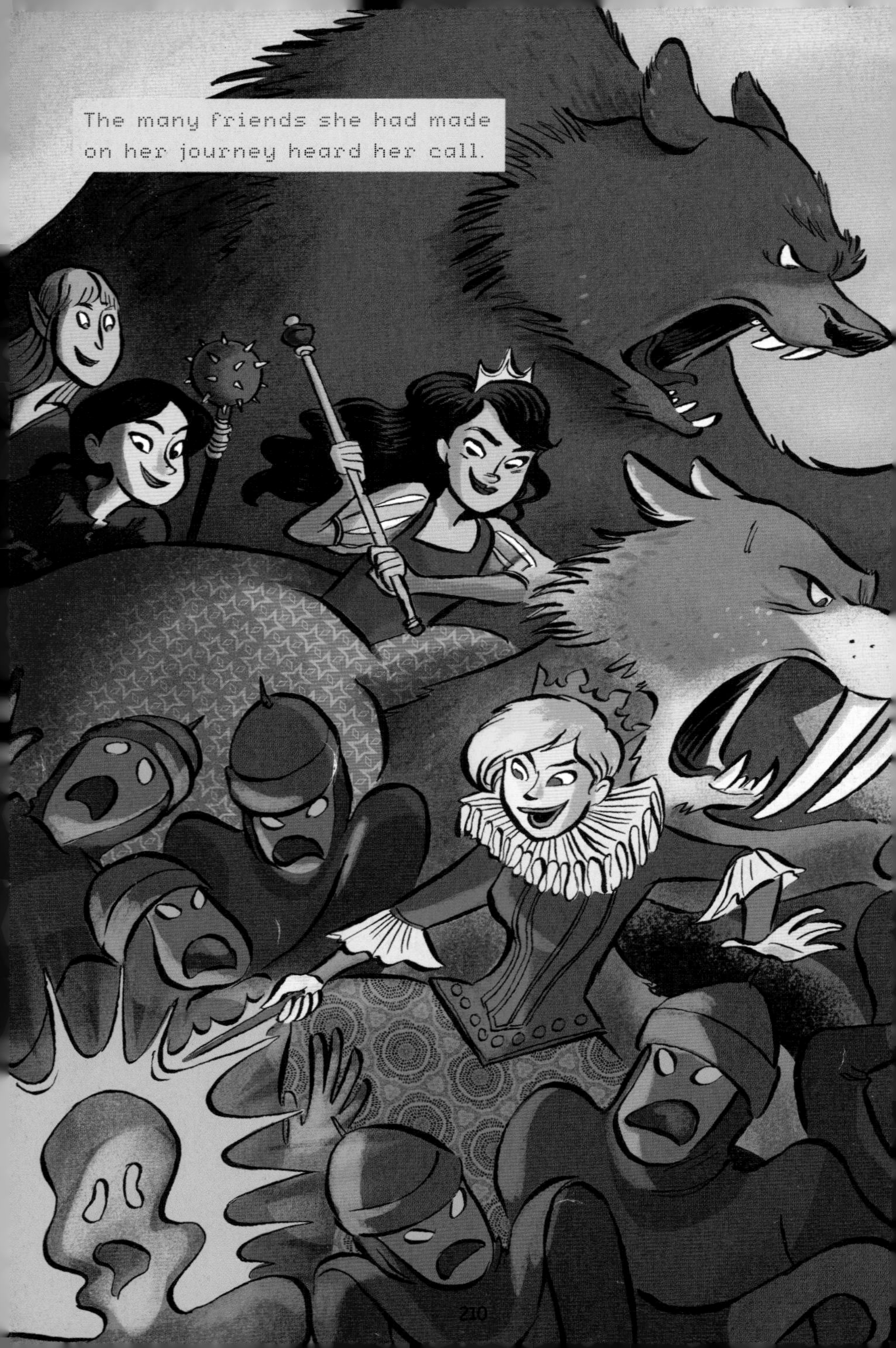
The many friends she had made on her journey heard her call.

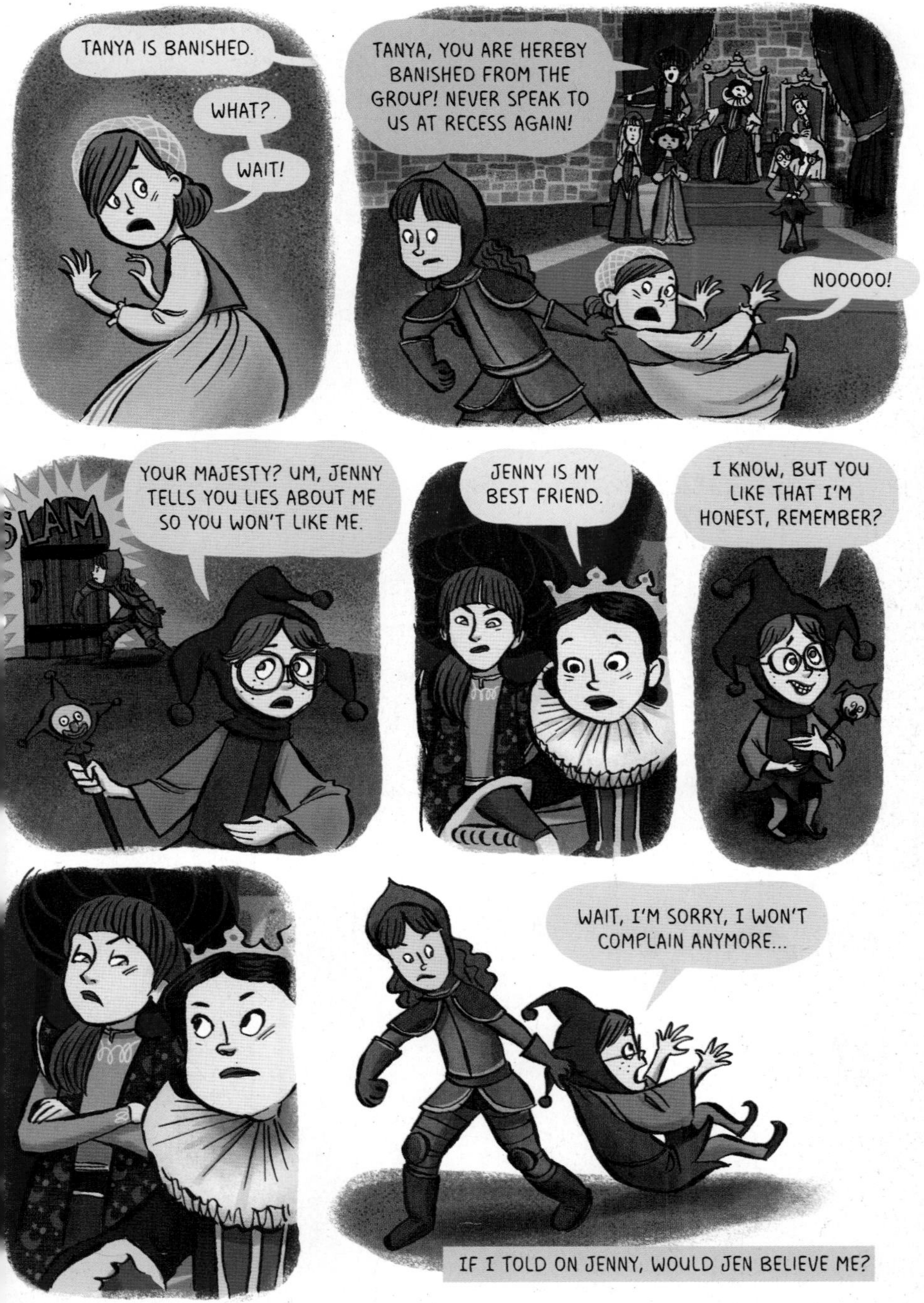
TANYA IS BANISHED.
WHAT?
WAIT!
TANYA, YOU ARE HEREBY BANISHED FROM THE GROUP! NEVER SPEAK TO US AT RECESS AGAIN!
NOOOOO!
SLAM
YOUR MAJESTY? UM, JENNY TELLS YOU LIES ABOUT ME SO YOU WON'T LIKE ME.
JENNY IS MY BEST FRIEND.
I KNOW, BUT YOU LIKE THAT I'M HONEST, REMEMBER?
WAIT, I'M SORRY, I WON'T COMPLAIN ANYMORE...
IF I TOLD ON JENNY, WOULD JEN BELIEVE ME?

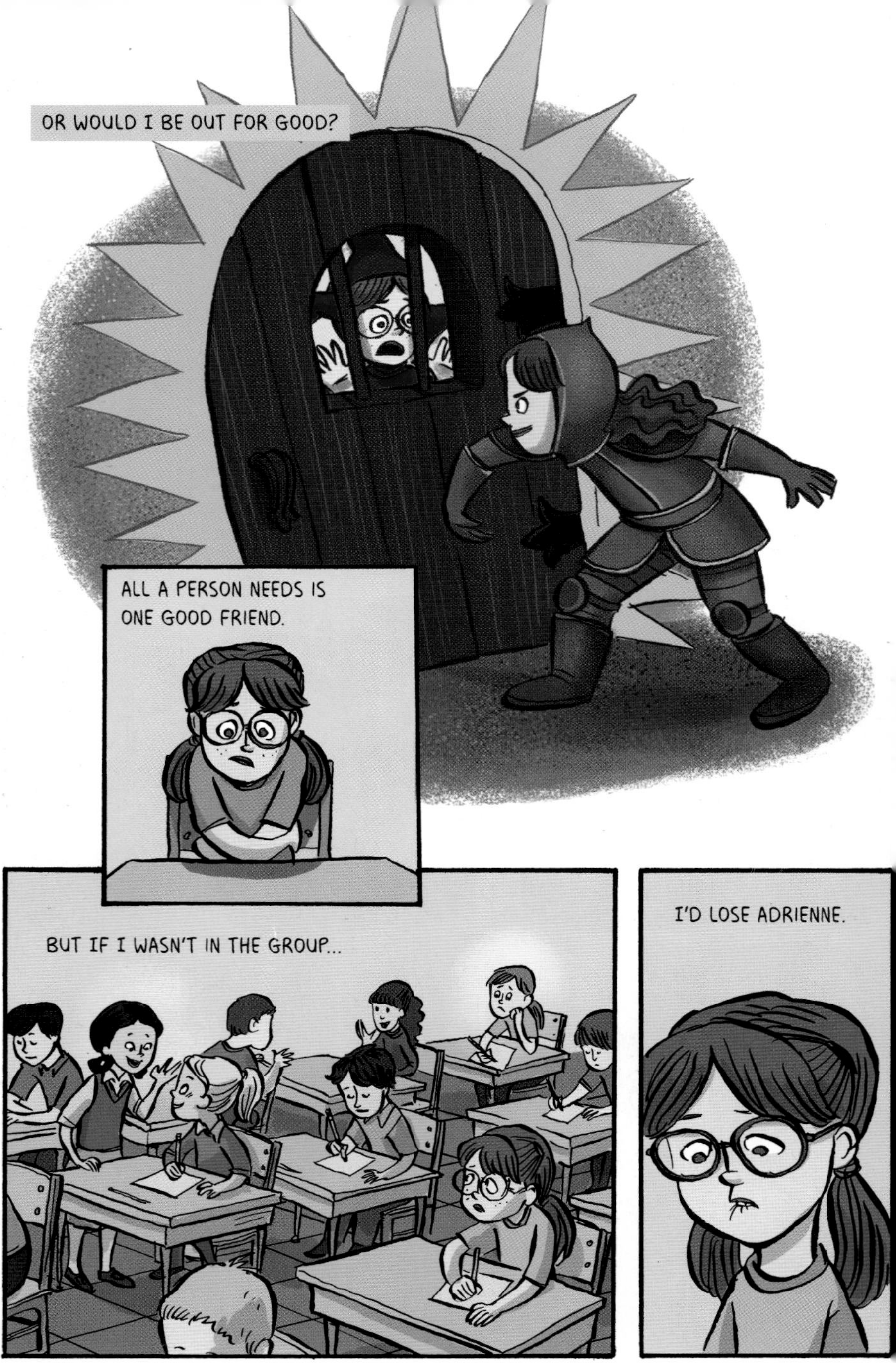
OR WOULD I BE OUT FOR GOOD?
ALL A PERSON NEEDS IS ONE GOOD FRIEND.
BUT IF I WASN'T IN THE GROUP...
I'D LOSE ADRIENNE.

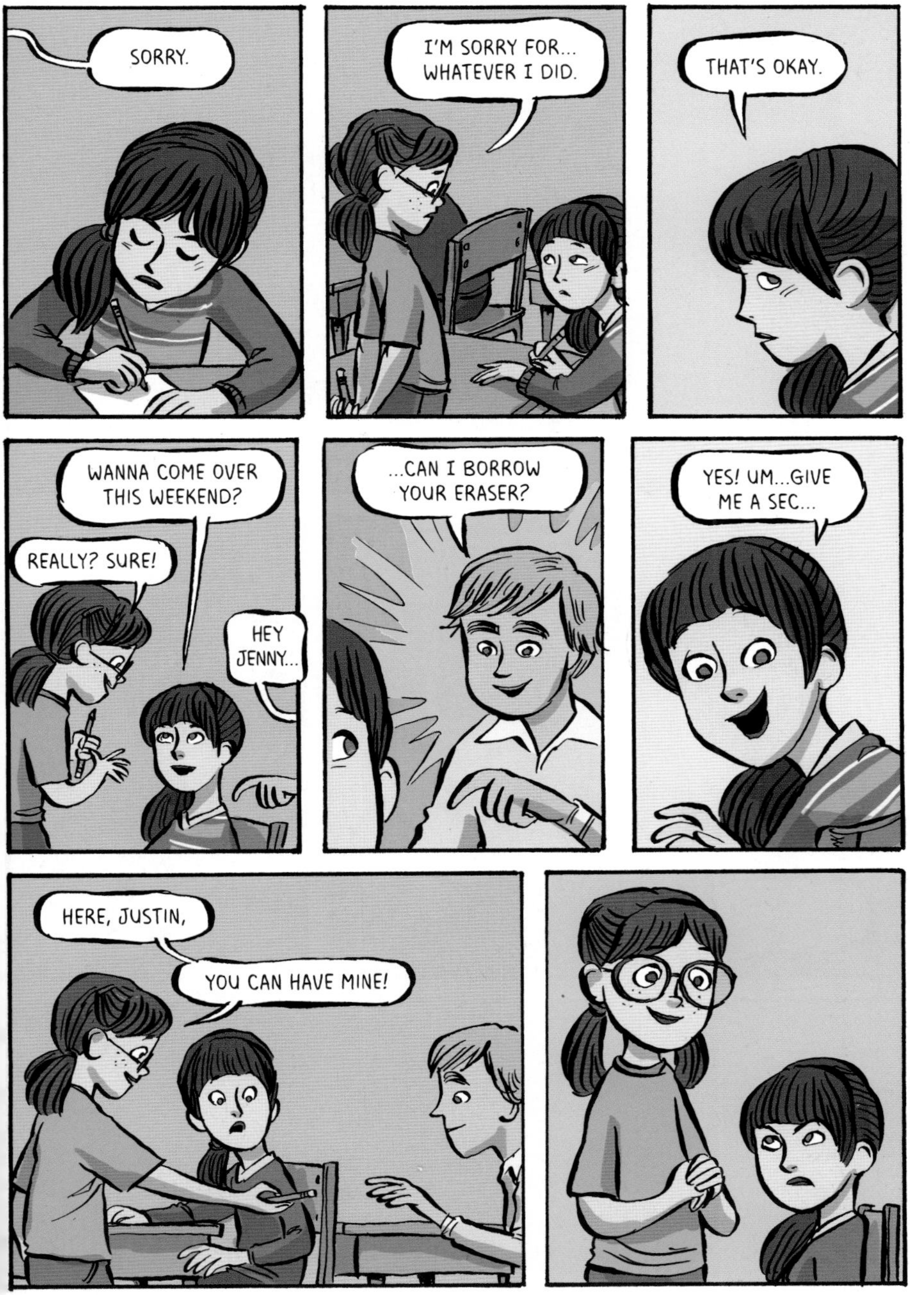
SORRY.
I'M SORRY FOR... WHATEVER I DID.
THAT'S OKAY.
WANNA COME OVER THIS WEEKEND?
REALLY? SURE!
HEY JENNY...
...CAN I BORROW YOUR ERASER?
YES! UM...GIVE ME A SEC...
HERE, JUSTIN,
YOU CAN HAVE MINE!

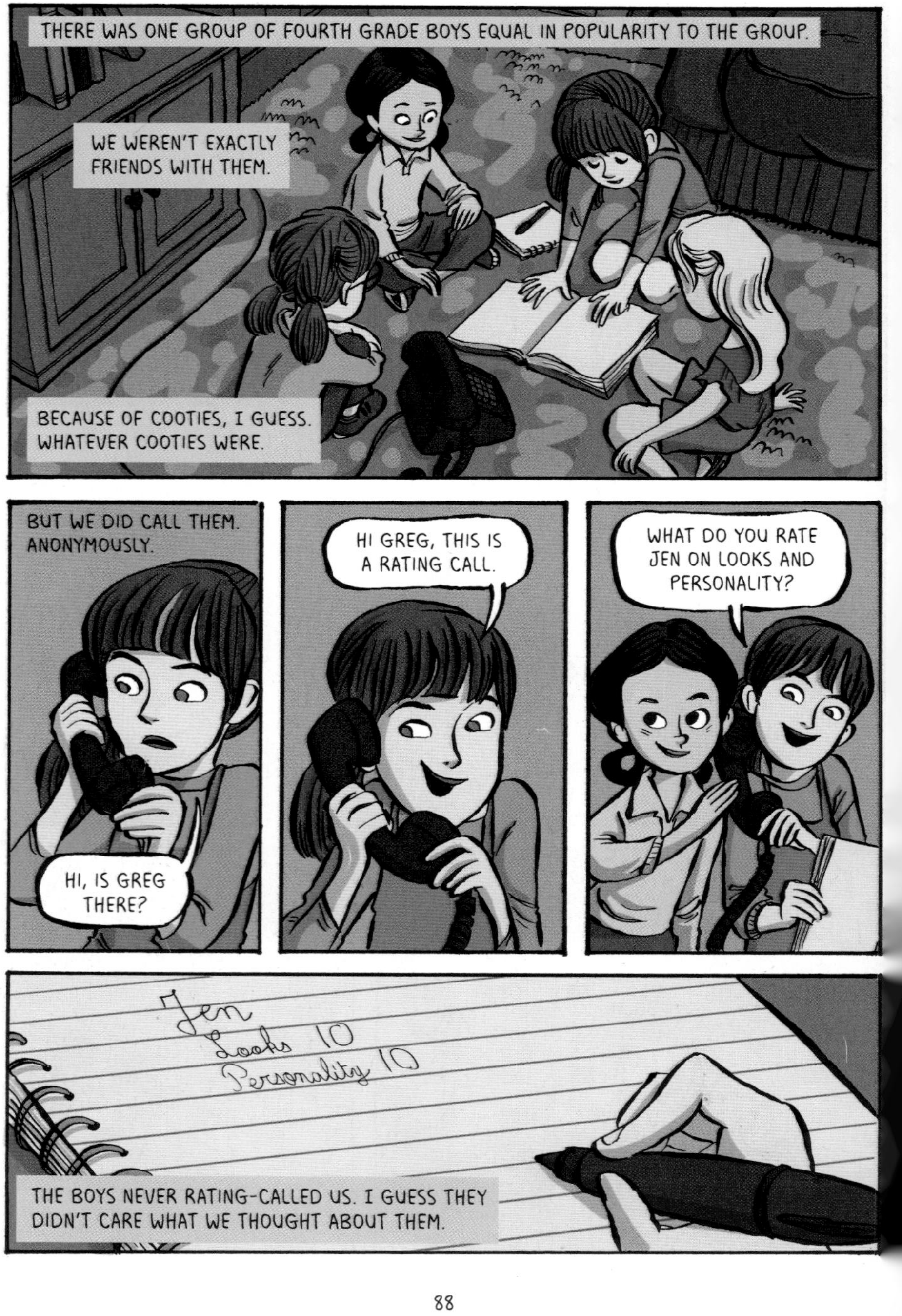

THERE WAS ONE GROUP OF FOURTH GRADE BOYS EQUAL IN POPULARITY TO THE GROUP.
WE WEREN'T EXACTLY FRIENDS WITH THEM.
BECAUSE OF COOTIES, I GUESS. WHATEVER COOTIES WERE.
BUT WE DID CALL THEM. ANONYMOUSLY.
HI, IS GREG THERE?
HI GREG, THIS IS A RATING CALL.
WHAT DO YOU RATE JEN ON LOOKS AND PERSONALITY?
Jen
Looks 10
Personality 10
THE BOYS NEVER RATING-CALLED US. I GUESS THEY DIDN'T CARE WHAT WE THOUGHT ABOUT THEM.

WHAT DO YOU RATE ADRIENNE ON LOOKS AND PERSONALITY?

Jen
Looks 10
Personality 10

Adrienne
Looks 10
Personality 8

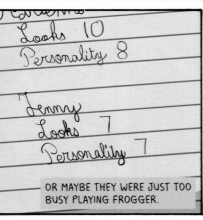

Looks 10
Personality 8

Jenny
Looks 7
Personality 7

OR MAYBE THEY WERE JUST TOO BUSY PLAYING FROGGER.

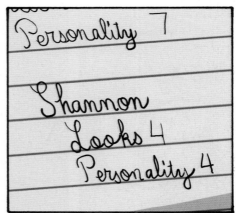

Personality 7

Shannon
Looks 4
Personality 4

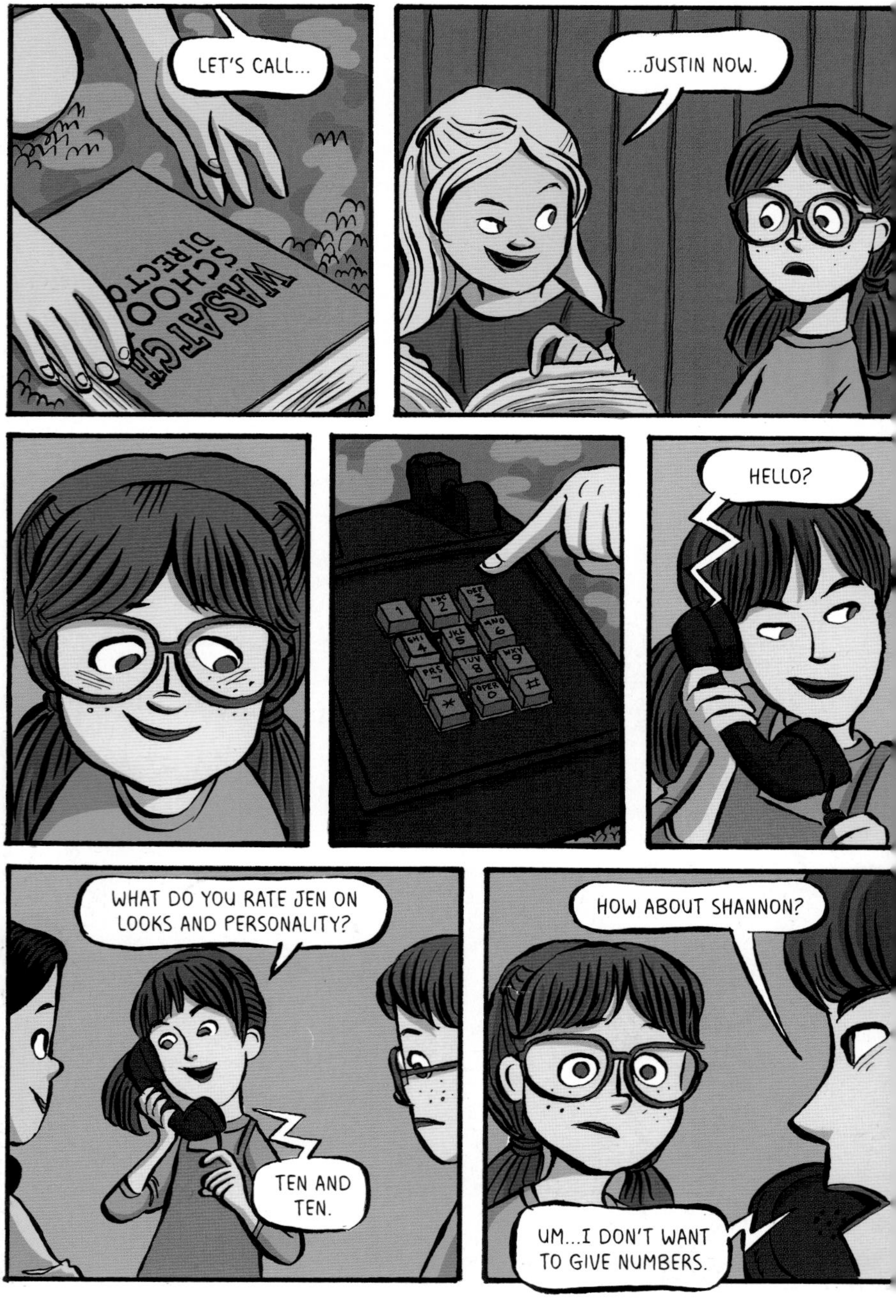
LET'S CALL...
WASATCH SCHOOL DIRECTO
...JUSTIN NOW.
HELLO?
WHAT DO YOU RATE JEN ON LOOKS AND PERSONALITY?
TEN AND TEN.
HOW ABOUT SHANNON?
UM...I DON'T WANT TO GIVE NUMBERS.

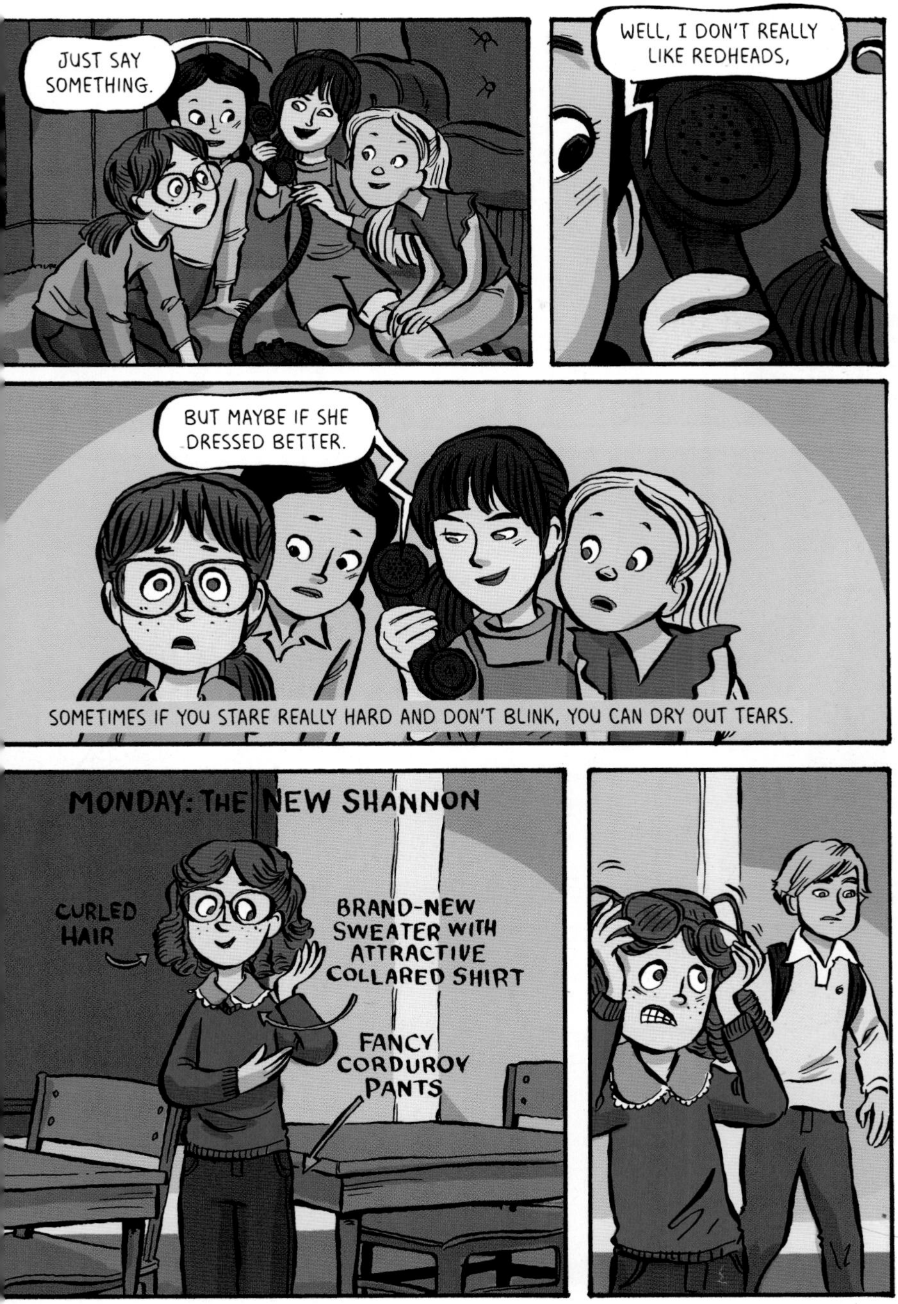

JUST SAY SOMETHING.
WELL, I DON'T REALLY LIKE REDHEADS,
BUT MAYBE IF SHE DRESSED BETTER.
SOMETIMES IF YOU STARE REALLY HARD AND DON'T BLINK, YOU CAN DRY OUT TEARS.
MONDAY: THE NEW SHANNON
CURLED HAIR
BRAND-NEW SWEATER WITH ATTRACTIVE COLLARED SHIRT
FANCY CORDUROY PANTS

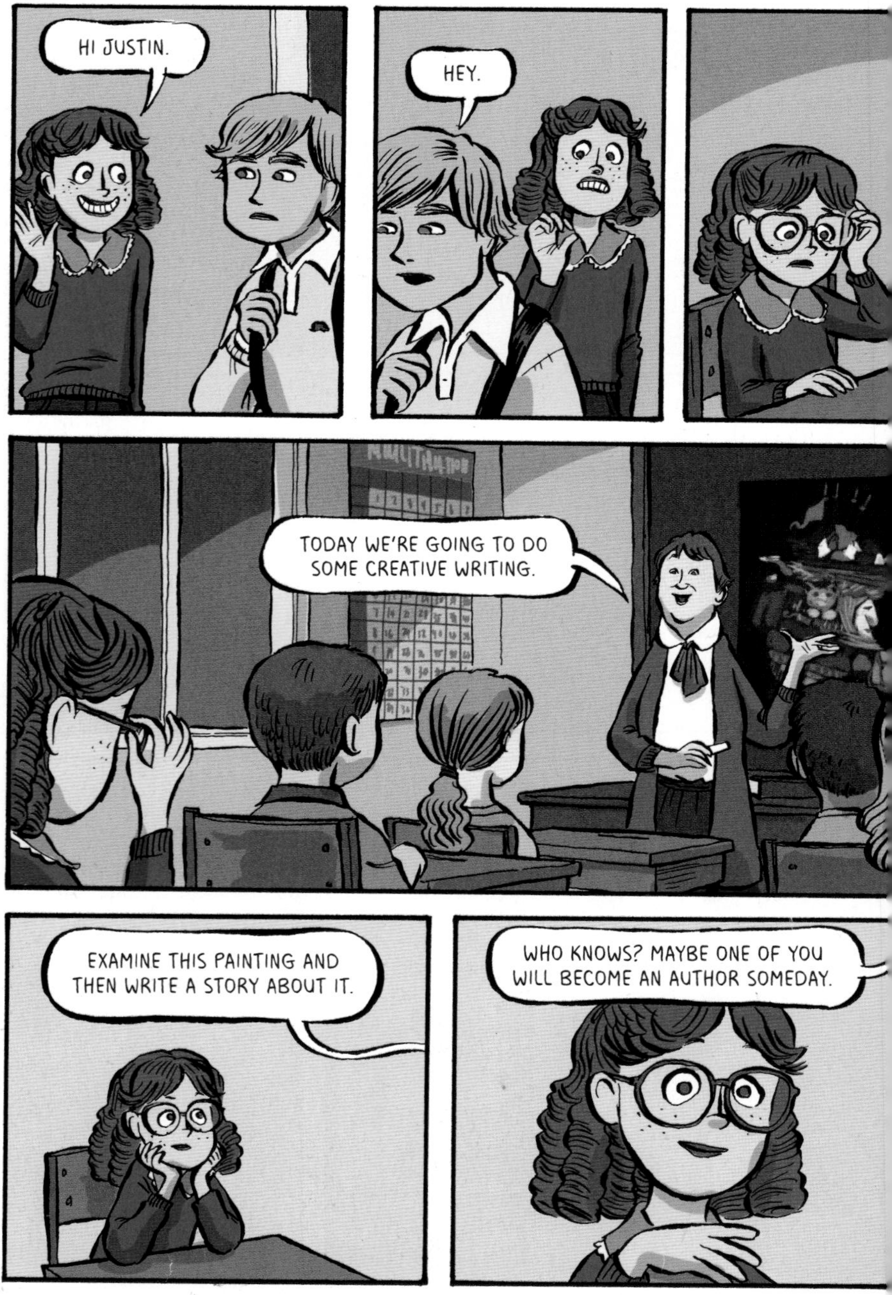
HI JUSTIN.
HEY.
TODAY WE'RE GOING TO DO SOME CREATIVE WRITING.
EXAMINE THIS PAINTING AND THEN WRITE A STORY ABOUT IT.
WHO KNOWS? MAYBE ONE OF YOU WILL BECOME AN AUTHOR SOMEDAY.

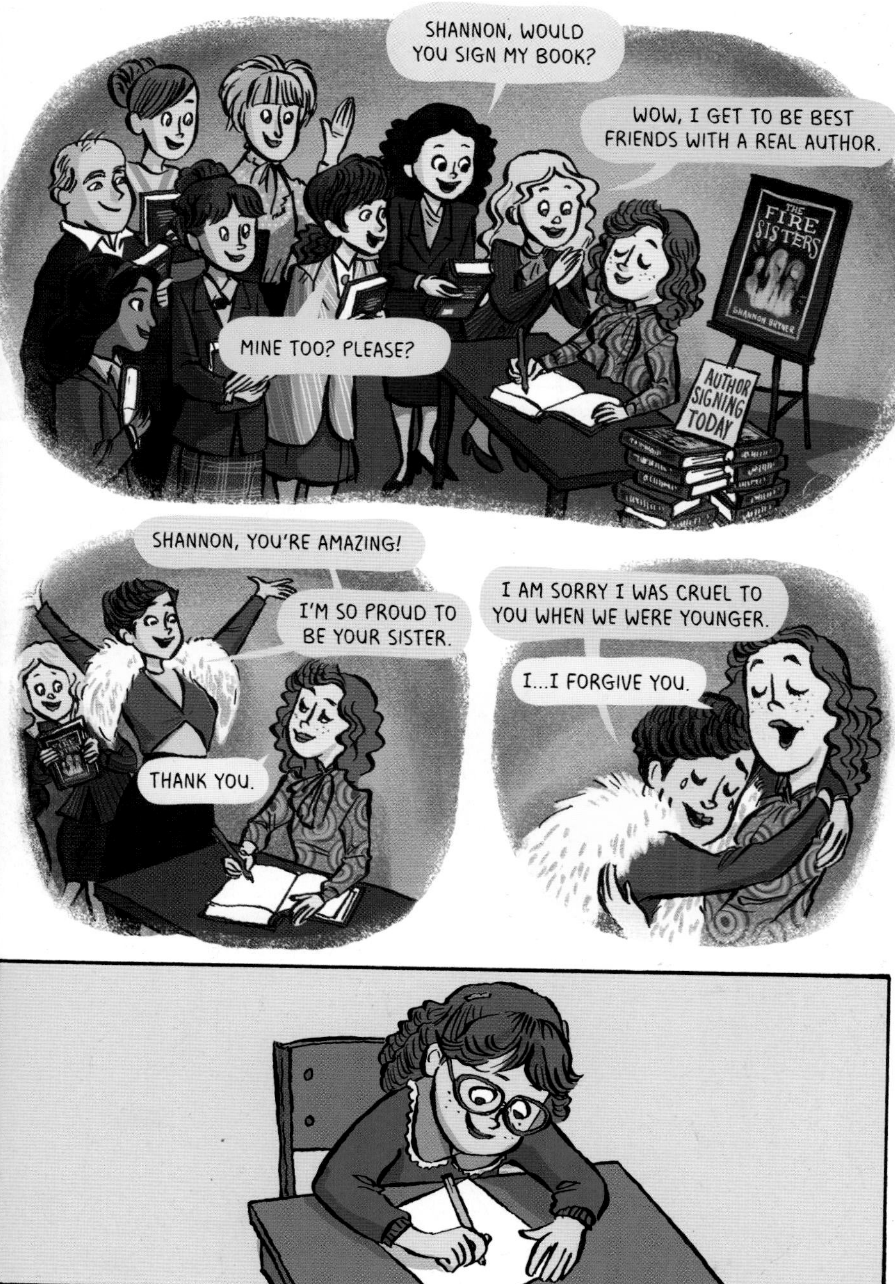
SHANNON, WOULD YOU SIGN MY BOOK?
WOW, I GET TO BE BEST FRIENDS WITH A REAL AUTHOR.
THE FIRE SISTERS
SHANNON BRYNER
MINE TOO? PLEASE?
AUTHOR SIGNING TODAY
SHANNON, YOU'RE AMAZING!
I'M SO PROUD TO BE YOUR SISTER.
THANK YOU.
I AM SORRY I WAS CRUEL TO YOU WHEN WE WERE YOUNGER.
I...I FORGIVE YOU.

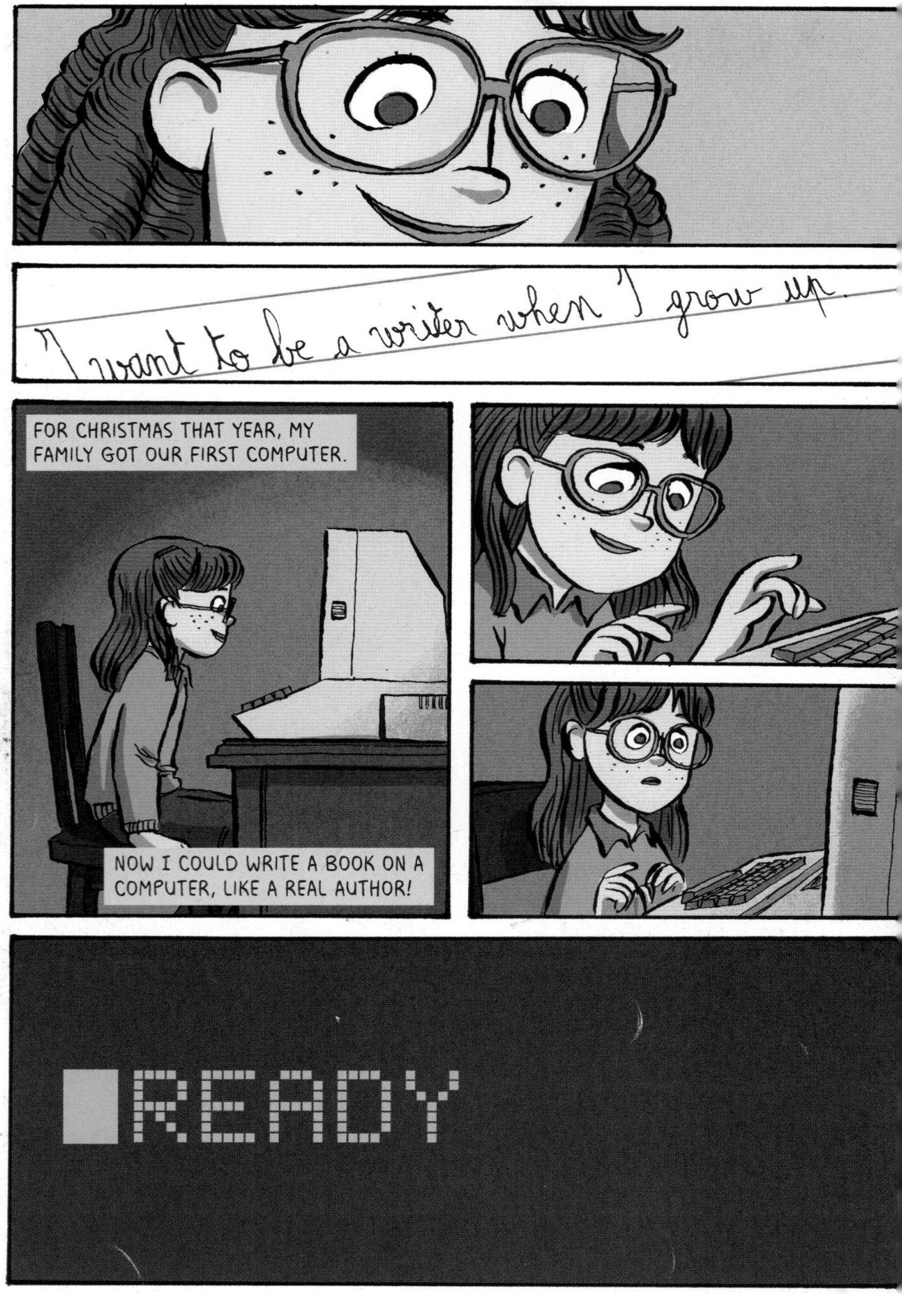
I want to be a writer when I grow up.
FOR CHRISTMAS THAT YEAR, MY FAMILY GOT OUR FIRST COMPUTER.
NOW I COULD WRITE A BOOK ON A COMPUTER, LIKE A REAL AUTHOR!
READY

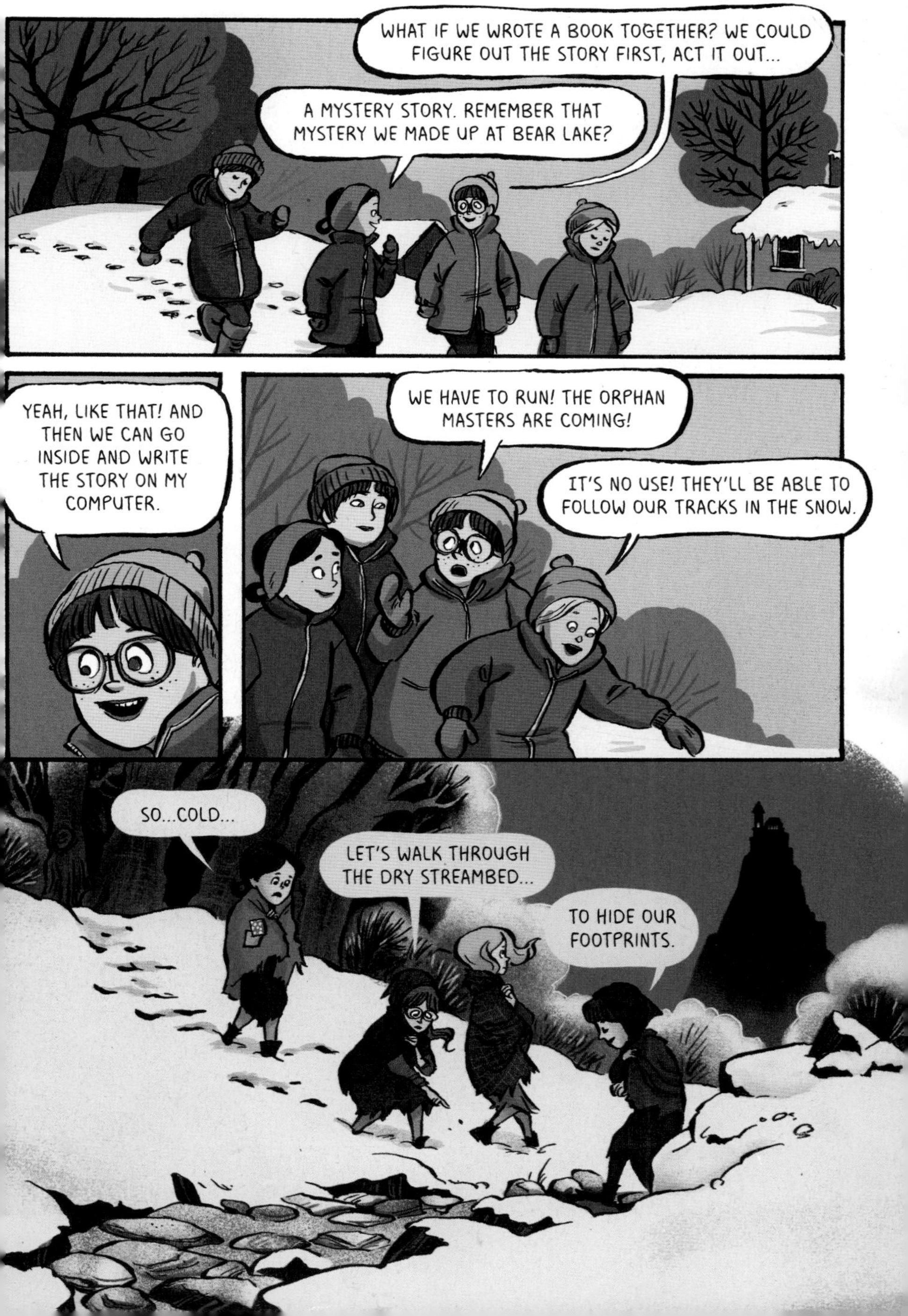

WHAT IF WE WROTE A BOOK TOGETHER? WE COULD FIGURE OUT THE STORY FIRST, ACT IT OUT...
A MYSTERY STORY. REMEMBER THAT MYSTERY WE MADE UP AT BEAR LAKE?
YEAH, LIKE THAT! AND THEN WE CAN GO INSIDE AND WRITE THE STORY ON MY COMPUTER.
WE HAVE TO RUN! THE ORPHAN MASTERS ARE COMING!
IT'S NO USE! THEY'LL BE ABLE TO FOLLOW OUR TRACKS IN THE SNOW.
SO...COLD...
LET'S WALK THROUGH THE DRY STREAMBED...
TO HIDE OUR FOOTPRINTS.

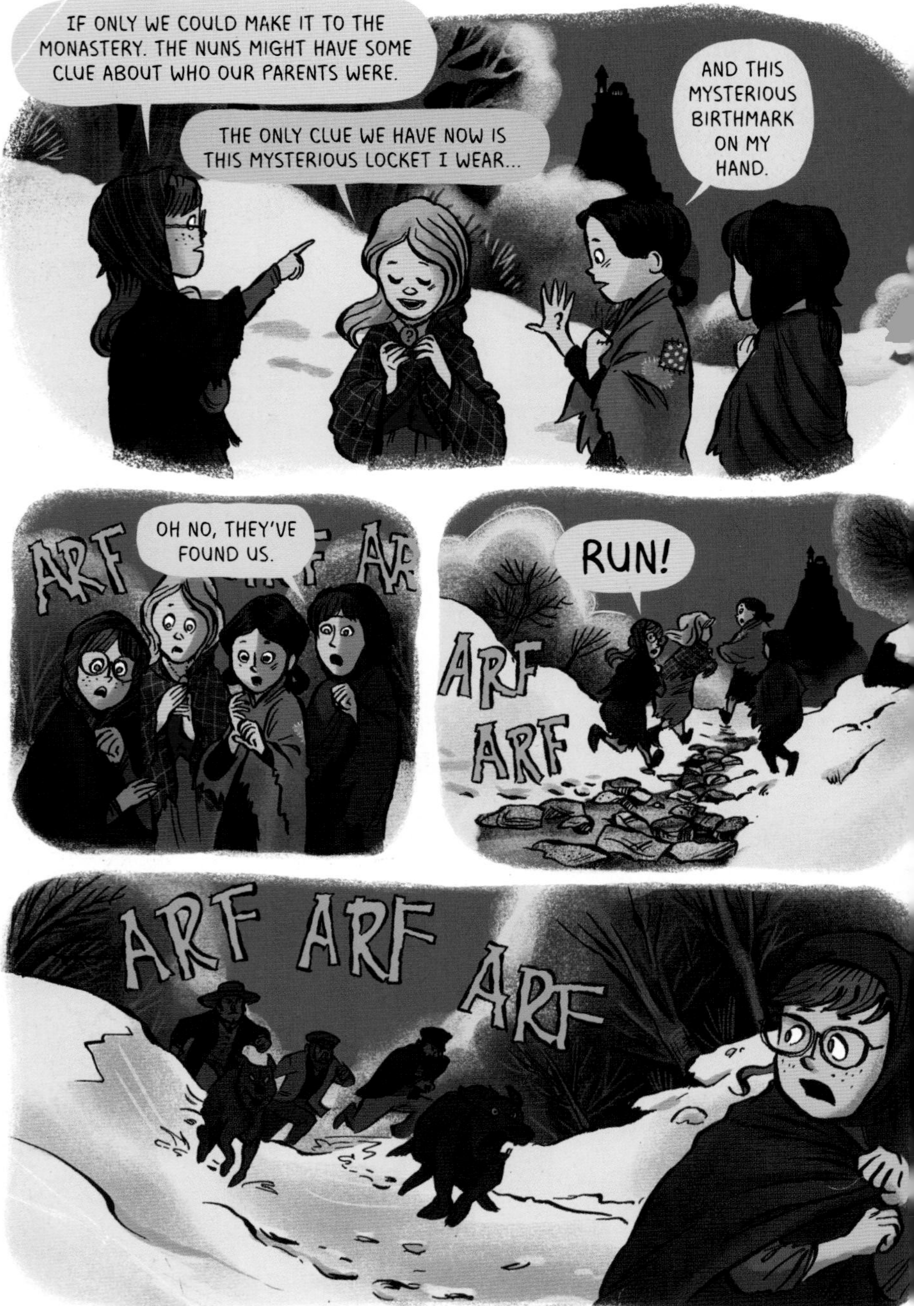
IF ONLY WE COULD MAKE IT TO THE MONASTERY. THE NUNS MIGHT HAVE SOME CLUE ABOUT WHO OUR PARENTS WERE.
THE ONLY CLUE WE HAVE NOW IS THIS MYSTERIOUS LOCKET I WEAR...
AND THIS MYSTERIOUS BIRTHMARK ON MY HAND.
ARF
OH NO, THEY'VE FOUND US.
RUN!
ARF
ARF
ARF ARF
ARF

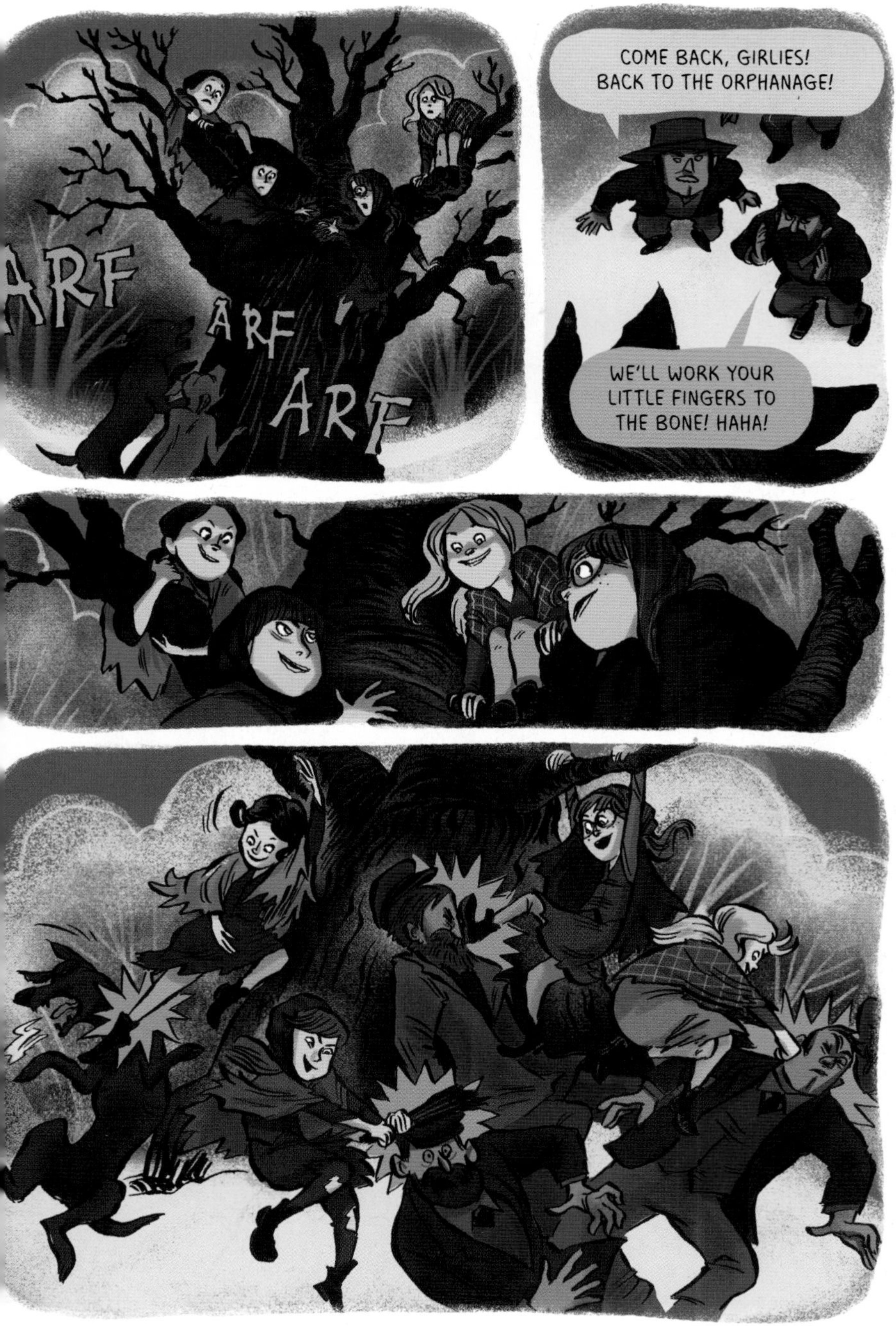
ARF
ARF
ARF
COME BACK, GIRLIES! BACK TO THE ORPHANAGE!
WE'LL WORK YOUR LITTLE FINGERS TO THE BONE! HAHA!

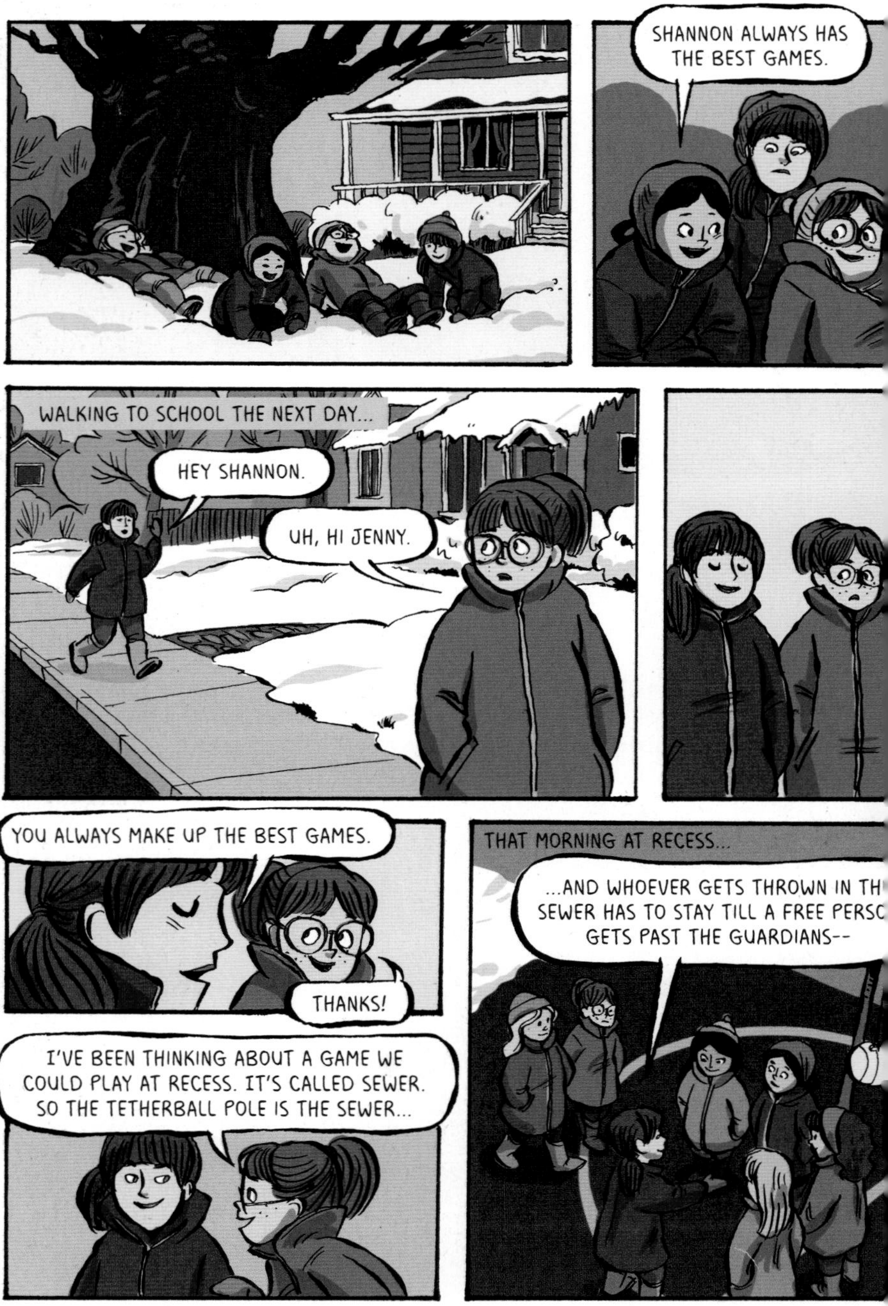
SHANNON ALWAYS HAS THE BEST GAMES.
WALKING TO SCHOOL THE NEXT DAY...
HEY SHANNON.
UH, HI JENNY.
YOU ALWAYS MAKE UP THE BEST GAMES.
THANKS!
I'VE BEEN THINKING ABOUT A GAME WE COULD PLAY AT RECESS. IT'S CALLED SEWER. SO THE TETHERBALL POLE IS THE SEWER...
THAT MORNING AT RECESS...
...AND WHOEVER GETS THROWN IN TH
SEWER HAS TO STAY TILL A FREE PERSC
GETS PAST THE GUARDIANS--

BUT THAT'S MY GAME.

NO IT'S NOT.

YOU STOLE THE IDEA FROM ME.

LIAR.

SHANNON, YOU DON'T HAVE TO BE THE ONLY ONE WHO MAKES UP GAMES.

YEAH, LET JENNY HAVE A TURN.

I'M NOT A BABY.

YOU'RE A SULKY BABY-WABY.

STICKS AND STONES MAY BREAK MY BONES,

SHANNY GONNA GO SULK LIKE A BABY?

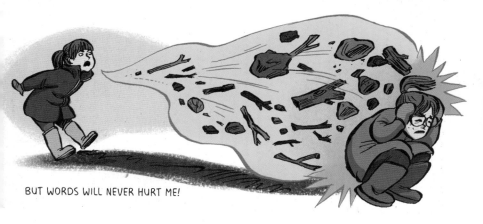

BUT WORDS WILL NEVER HURT ME!

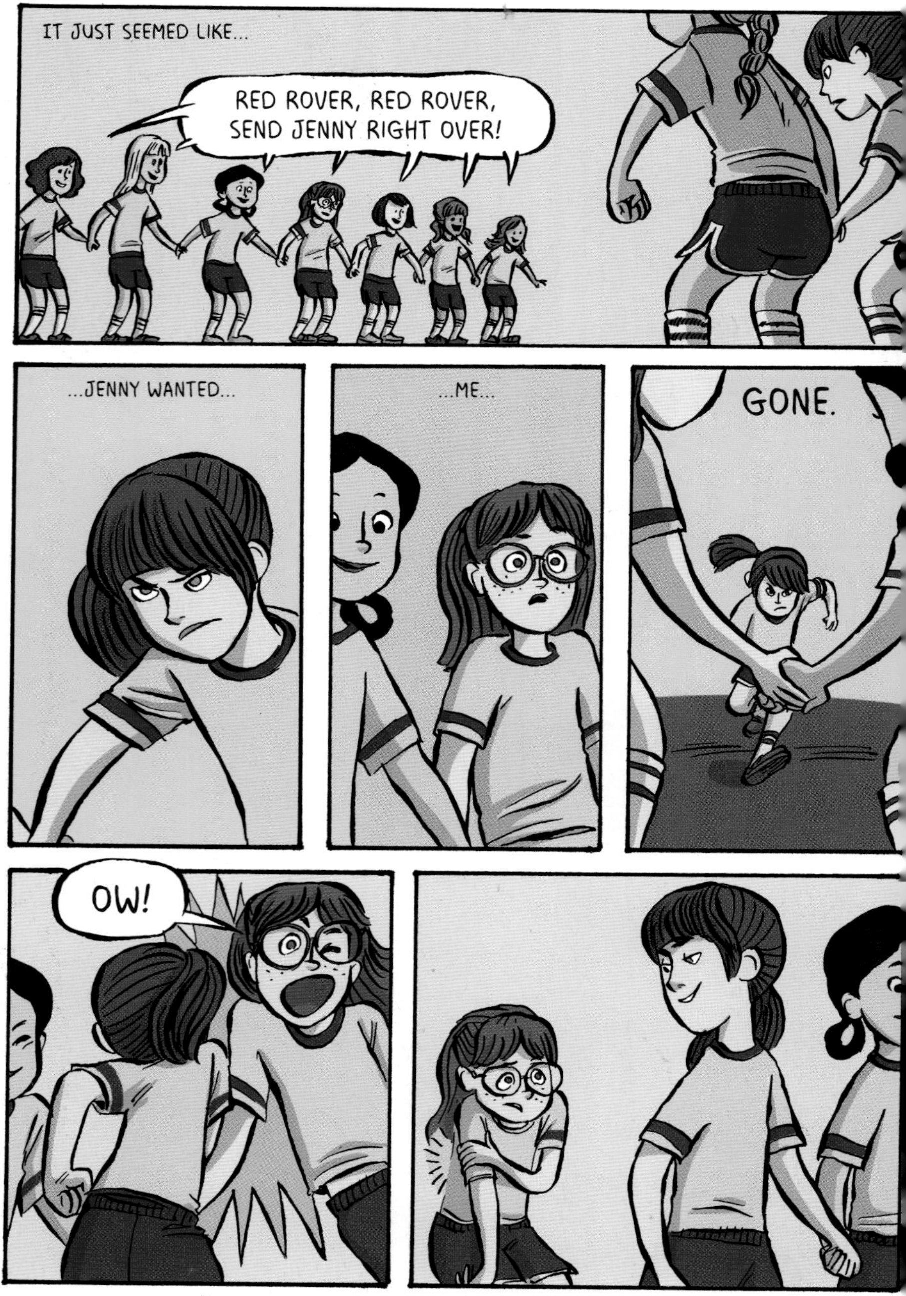
IT JUST SEEMED LIKE...
RED ROVER, RED ROVER, SEND JENNY RIGHT OVER!
...JENNY WANTED...
...ME...
GONE.
OW!

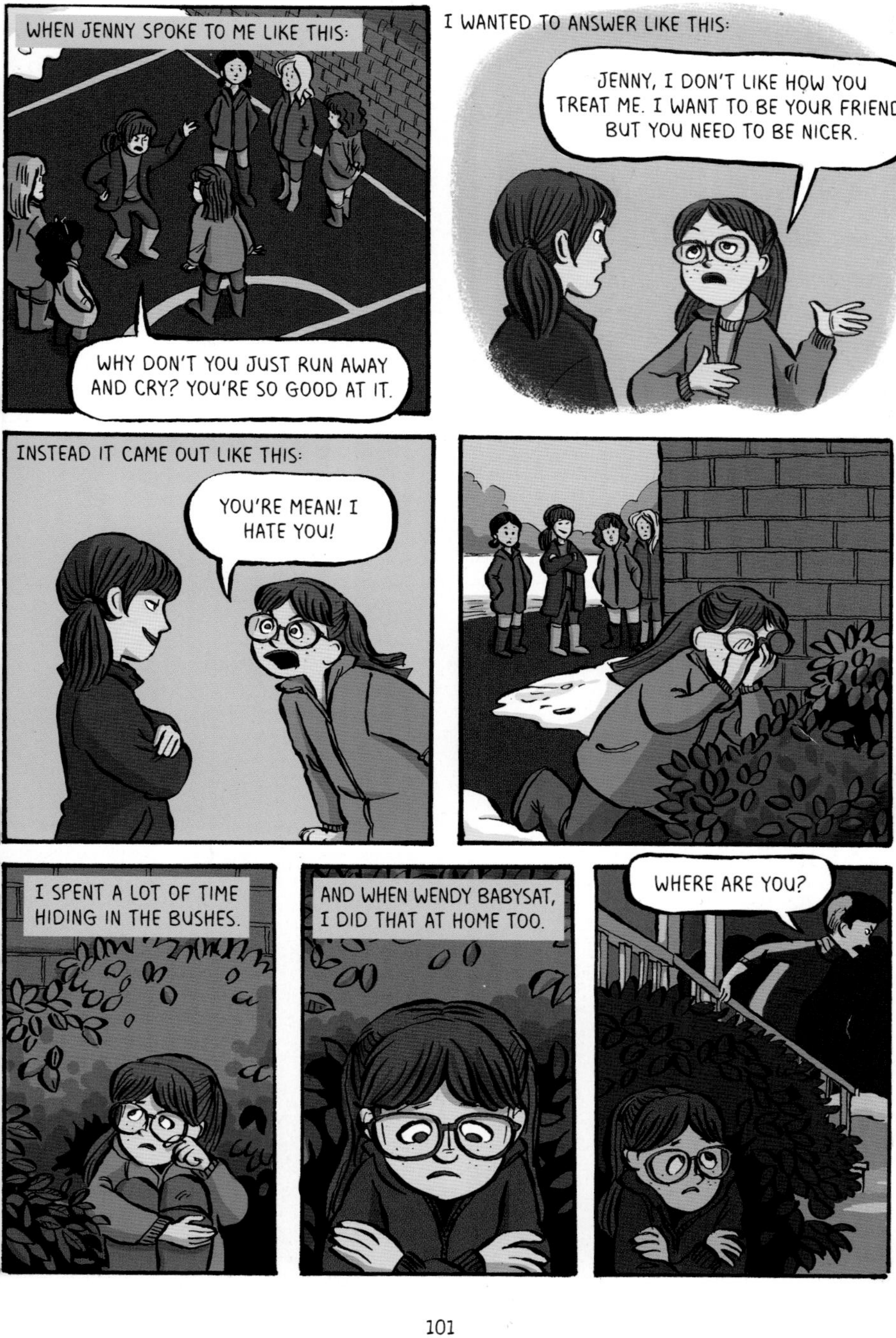

WHEN JENNY SPOKE TO ME LIKE THIS:
WHY DON'T YOU JUST RUN AWAY AND CRY? YOU'RE SO GOOD AT IT.
I WANTED TO ANSWER LIKE THIS:
JENNY, I DON'T LIKE HOW YOU TREAT ME. I WANT TO BE YOUR FRIEND, BUT YOU NEED TO BE NICER.
INSTEAD IT CAME OUT LIKE THIS:
YOU'RE MEAN! I HATE YOU!
I SPENT A LOT OF TIME HIDING IN THE BUSHES.
AND WHEN WENDY BABYSAT, I DID THAT AT HOME TOO.
WHERE ARE YOU?

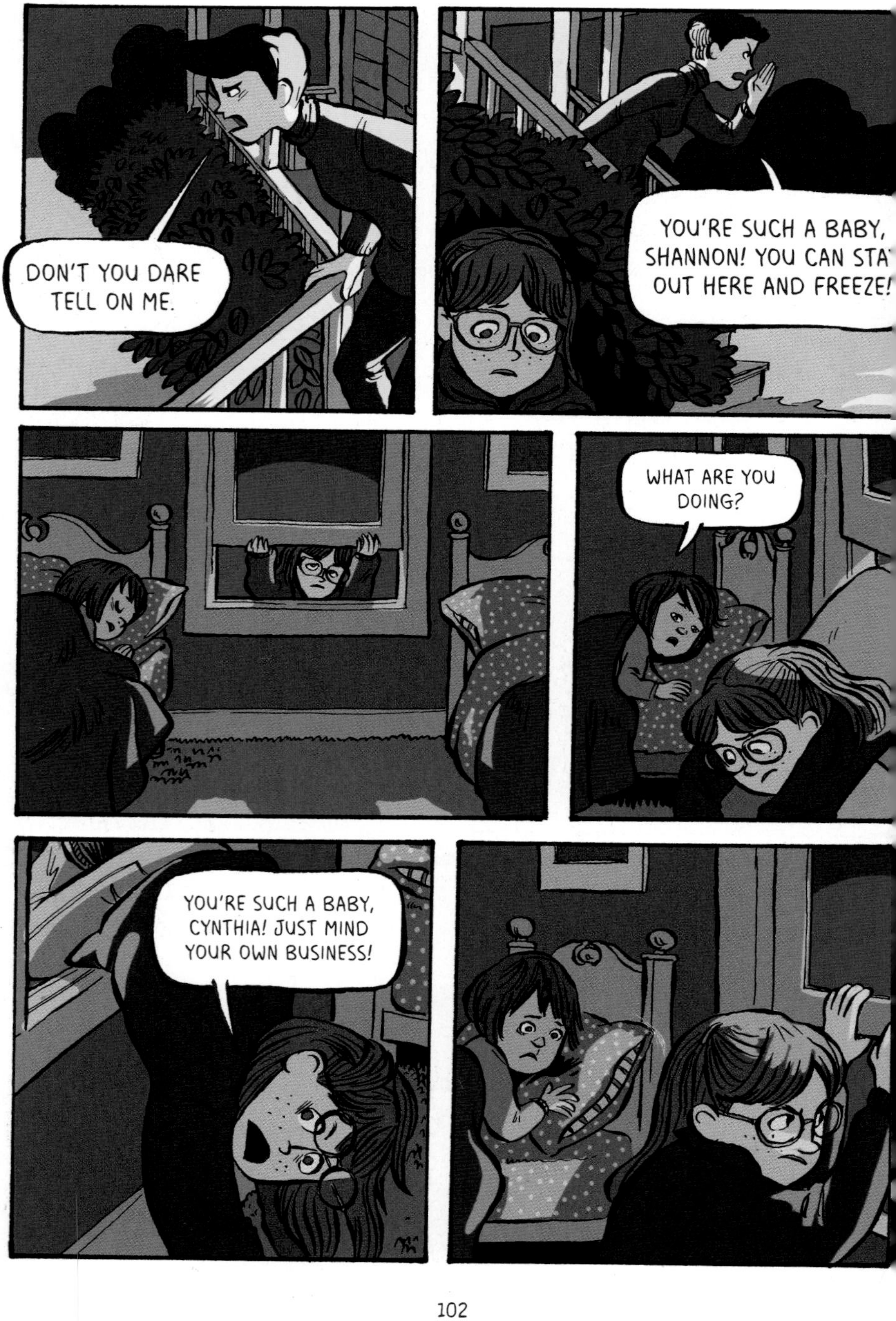
DON'T YOU DARE TELL ON ME.
YOU'RE SUCH A BABY, SHANNON! YOU CAN STA OUT HERE AND FREEZE!
WHAT ARE YOU DOING?
YOU'RE SUCH A BABY, CYNTHIA! JUST MIND YOUR OWN BUSINESS!

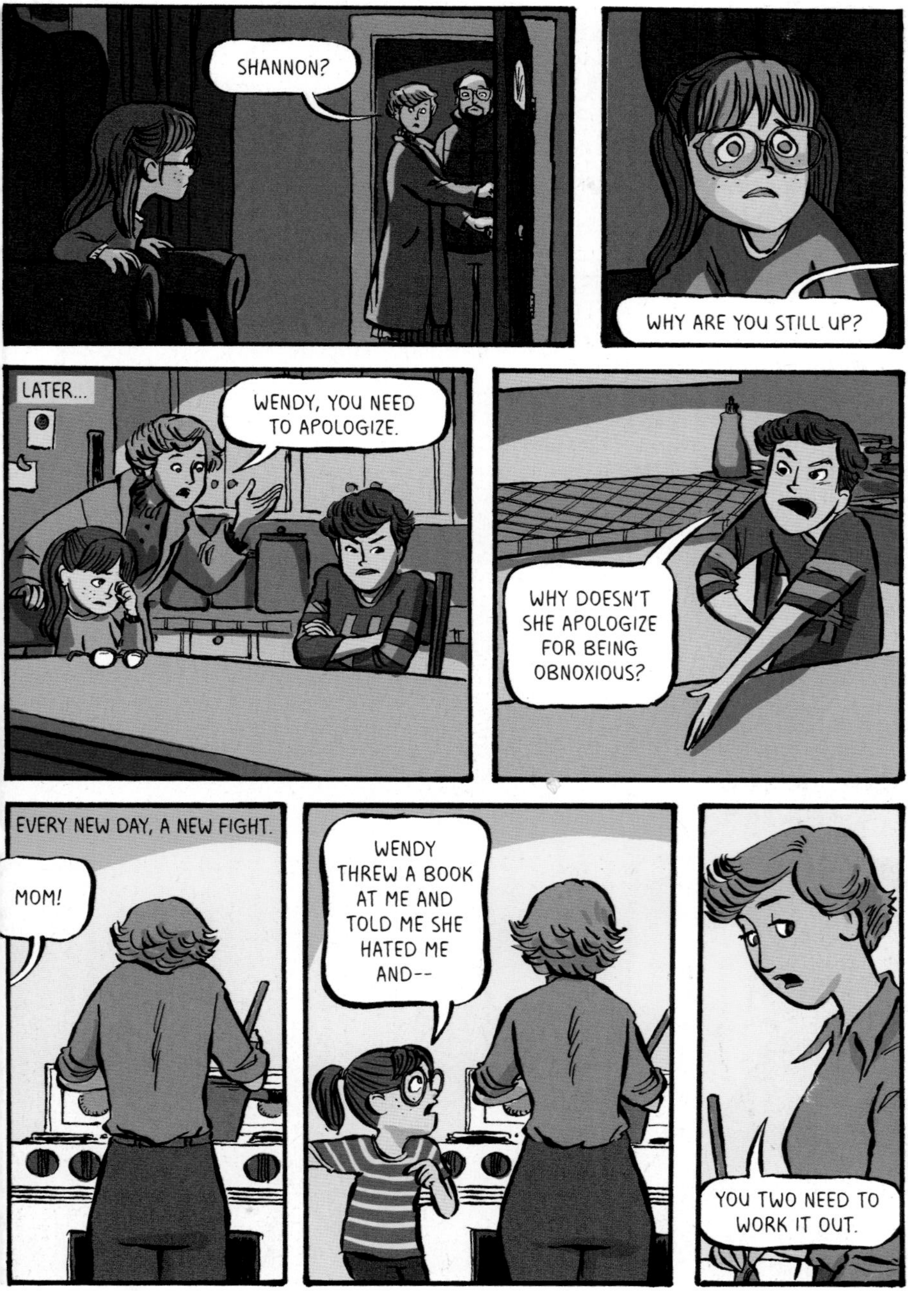
SHANNON?
WHY ARE YOU STILL UP?
LATER...
WENDY, YOU NEED TO APOLOGIZE.
WHY DOESN'T SHE APOLOGIZE FOR BEING OBNOXIOUS?
EVERY NEW DAY, A NEW FIGHT.
MOM!
WENDY THREW A BOOK AT ME AND TOLD ME SHE HATED ME AND--
YOU TWO NEED TO WORK IT OUT.

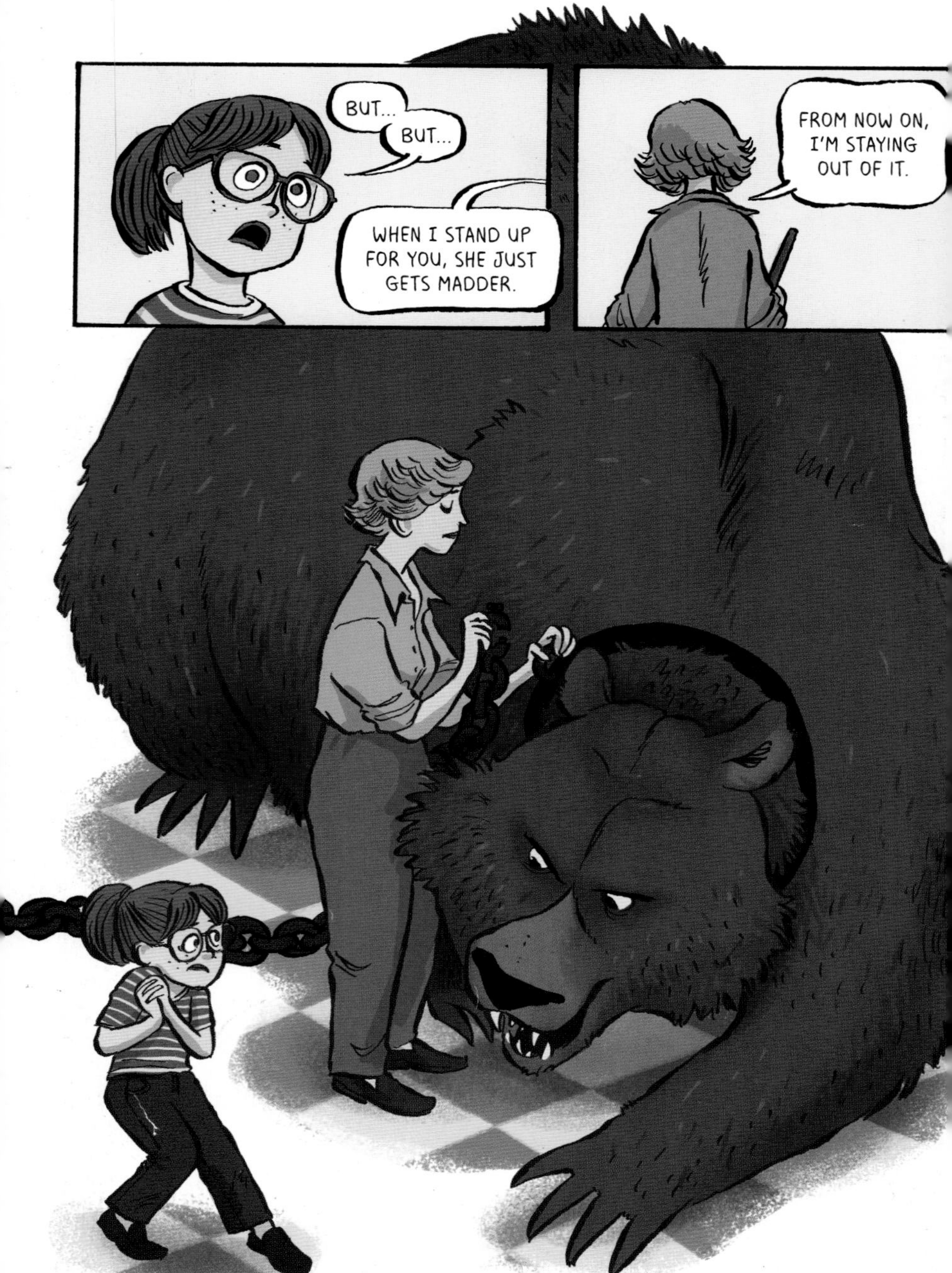
BUT...
BUT...
WHEN I STAND UP FOR YOU, SHE JUST GETS MADDER.
FROM NOW ON, I'M STAYING OUT OF IT.

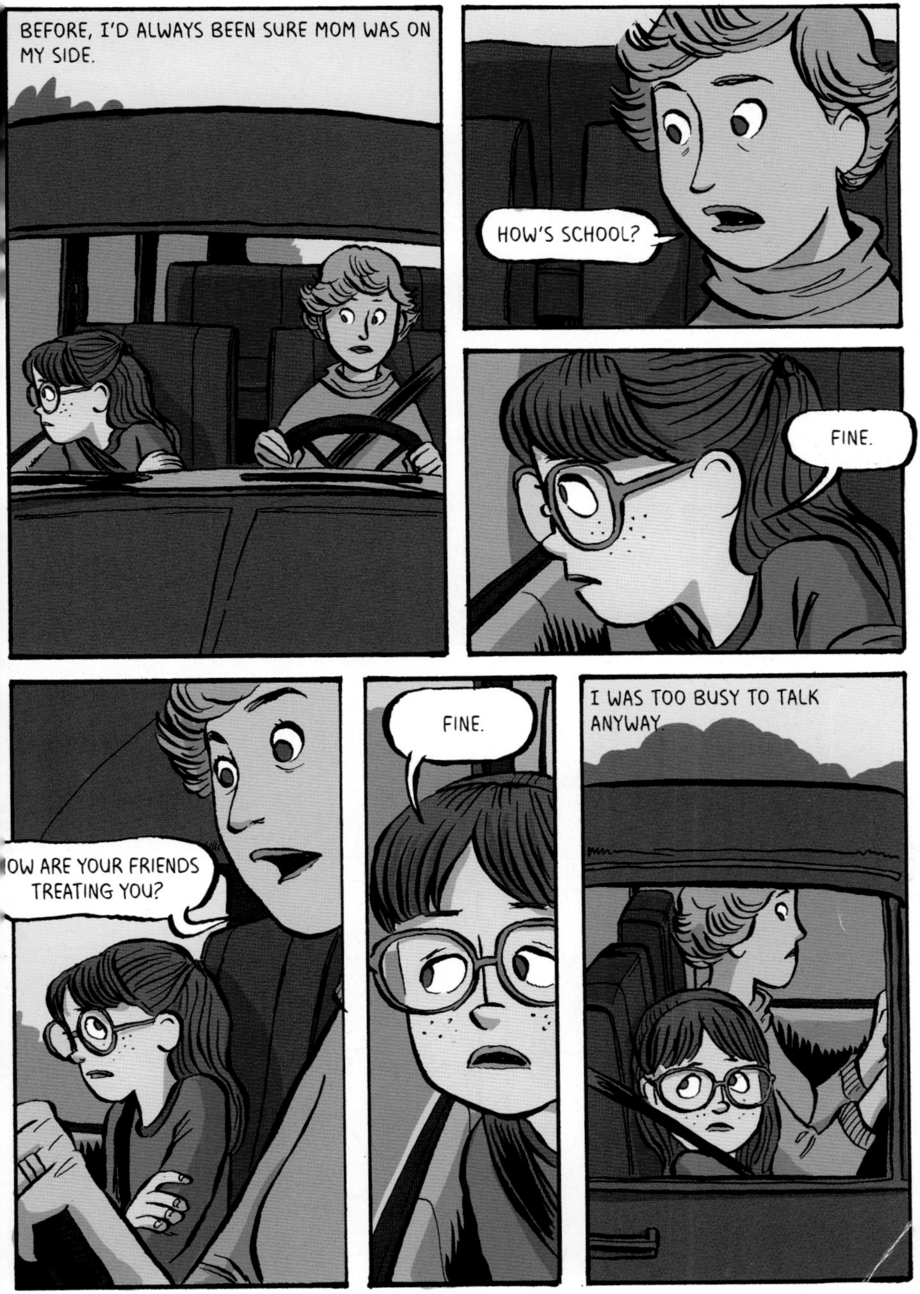
BEFORE, I'D ALWAYS BEEN SURE MOM WAS ON MY SIDE.
HOW'S SCHOOL?
FINE.
OW ARE YOUR FRIENDS TREATING YOU?
FINE.
I WAS TOO BUSY TO TALK ANYWAY.

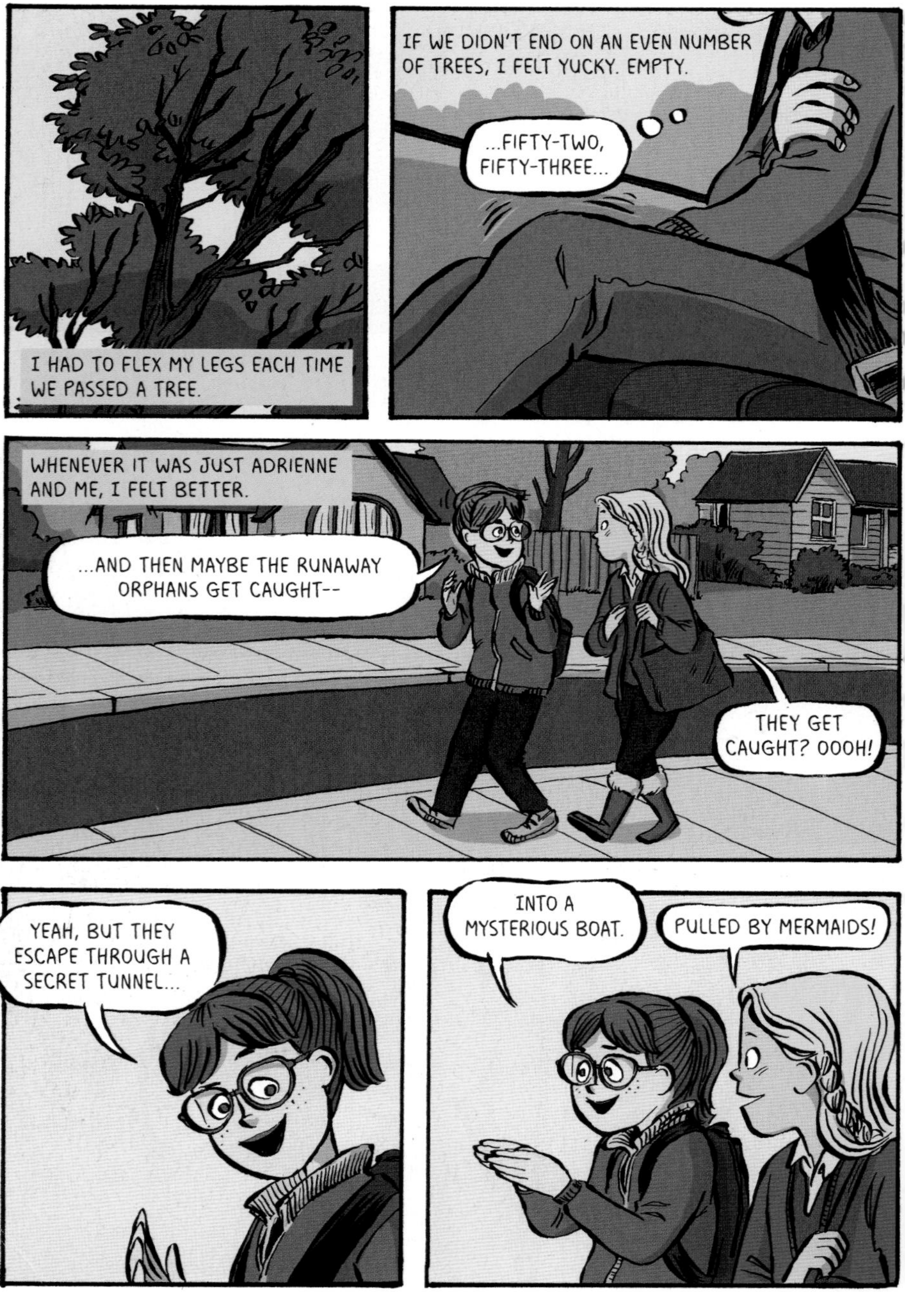
I HAD TO FLEX MY LEGS EACH TIME WE PASSED A TREE.
IF WE DIDN'T END ON AN EVEN NUMBER OF TREES, I FELT YUCKY. EMPTY.
...FIFTY-TWO, FIFTY-THREE...
WHENEVER IT WAS JUST ADRIENNE AND ME, I FELT BETTER.
...AND THEN MAYBE THE RUNAWAY ORPHANS GET CAUGHT--
THEY GET CAUGHT? OOOH!
YEAH, BUT THEY ESCAPE THROUGH A SECRET TUNNEL...
INTO A MYSTERIOUS BOAT.
PULLED BY MERMAIDS!

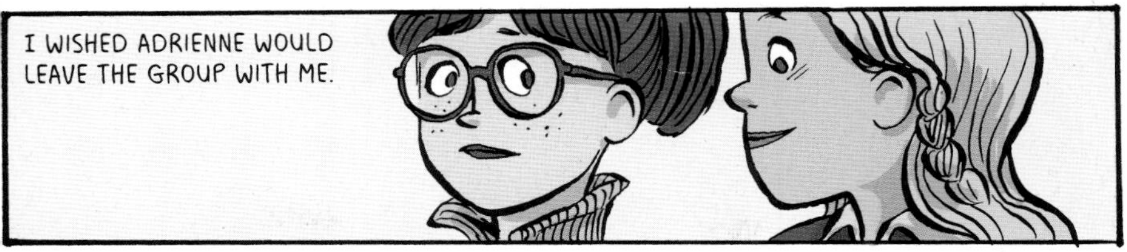
I WISHED ADRIENNE WOULD LEAVE THE GROUP WITH ME.

IT WAS ONE OF MY FAVORITE DAYDREAMS.

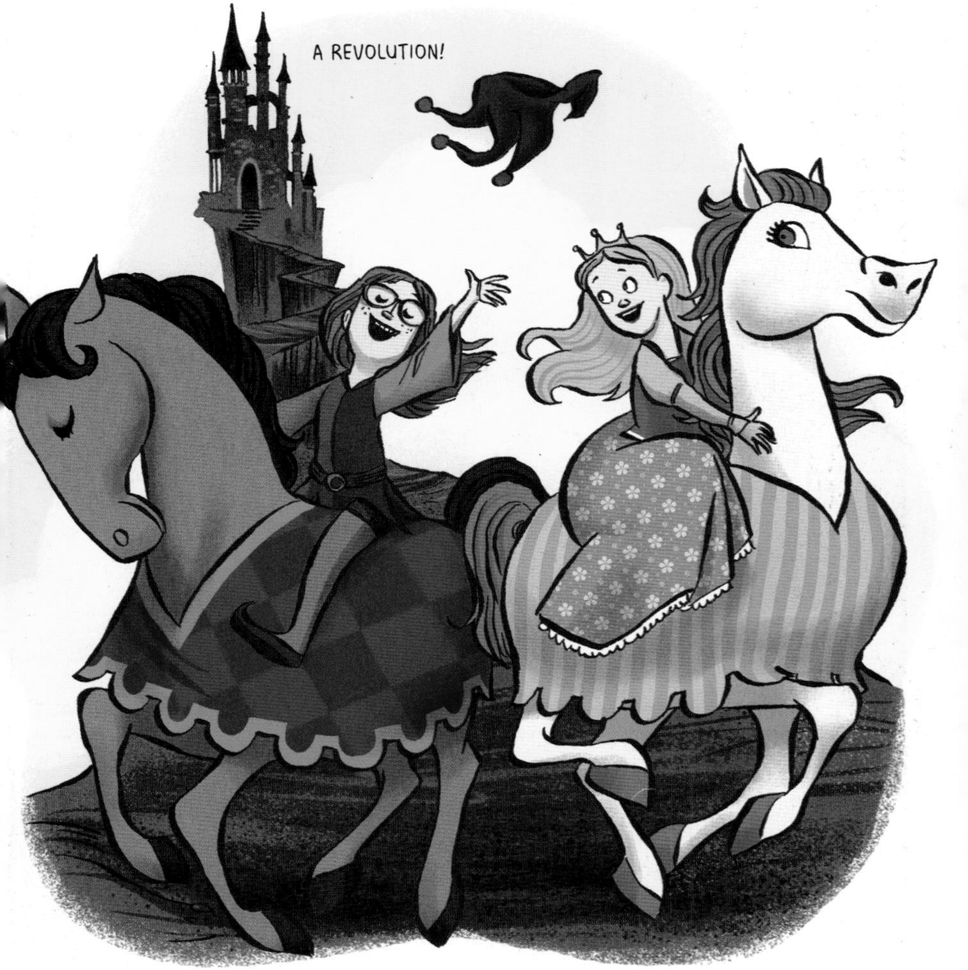
A REVOLUTION!

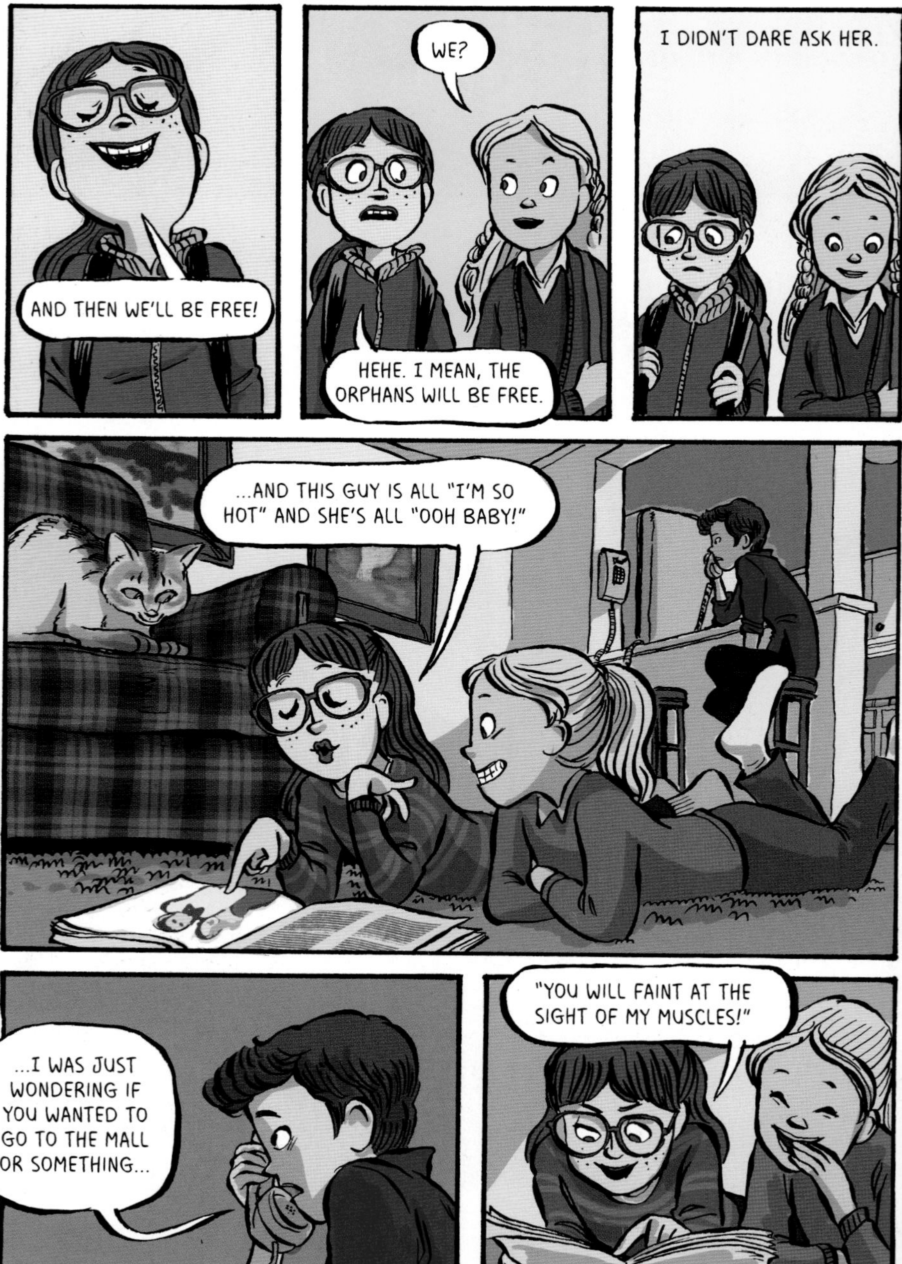
AND THEN WE'LL BE FREE!
WE?
HEHE. I MEAN, THE ORPHANS WILL BE FREE.
I DIDN'T DARE ASK HER.
...AND THIS GUY IS ALL "I'M SO HOT" AND SHE'S ALL "OOH BABY!"
...I WAS JUST WONDERING IF YOU WANTED TO GO TO THE MALL OR SOMETHING...
"YOU WILL FAINT AT THE SIGHT OF MY MUSCLES!"

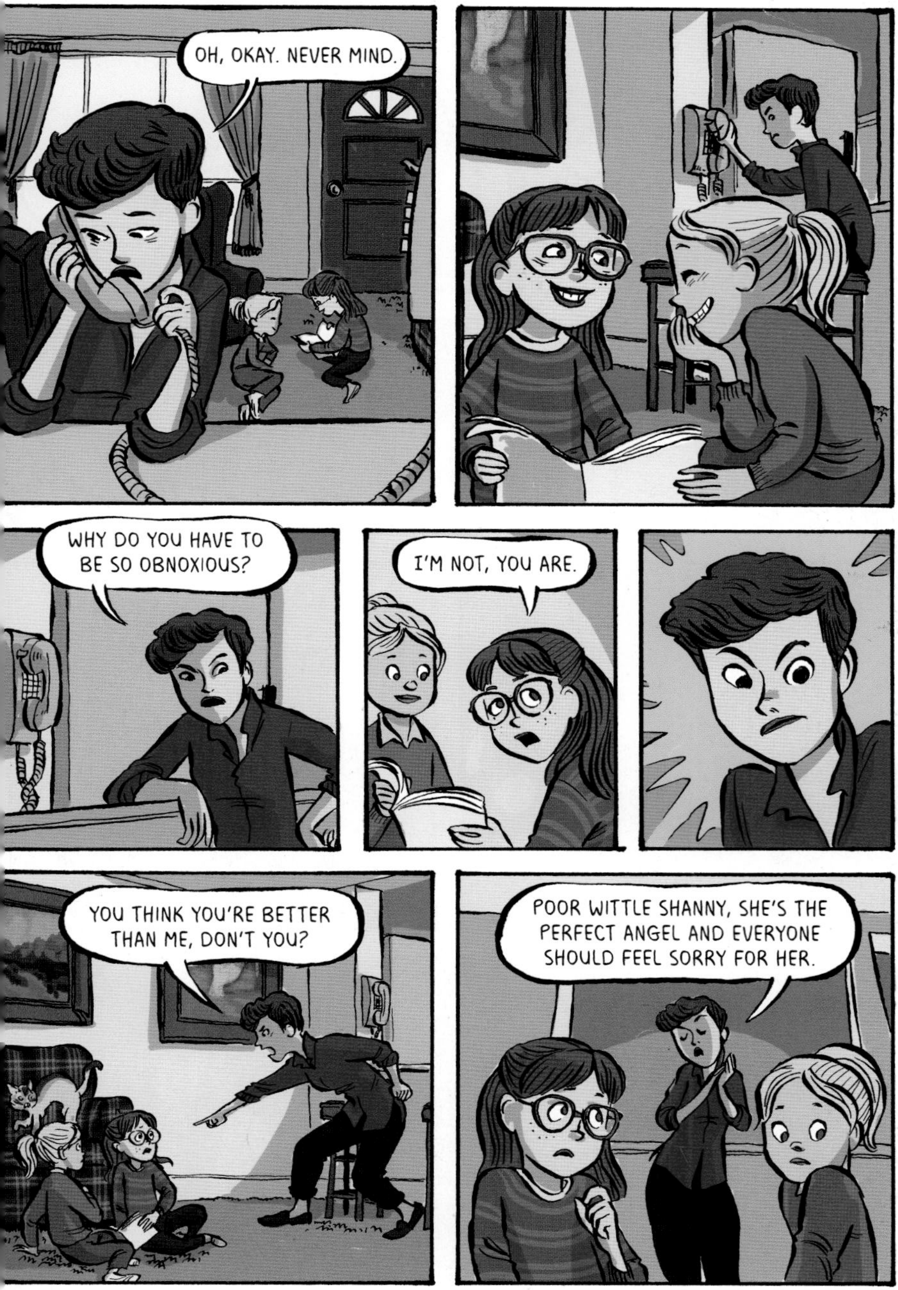
OH, OKAY. NEVER MIND.
WHY DO YOU HAVE TO BE SO OBNOXIOUS?
I'M NOT, YOU ARE.
YOU THINK YOU'RE BETTER THAN ME, DON'T YOU?
POOR WITTLE SHANNY, SHE'S THE PERFECT ANGEL AND EVERYONE SHOULD FEEL SORRY FOR HER.

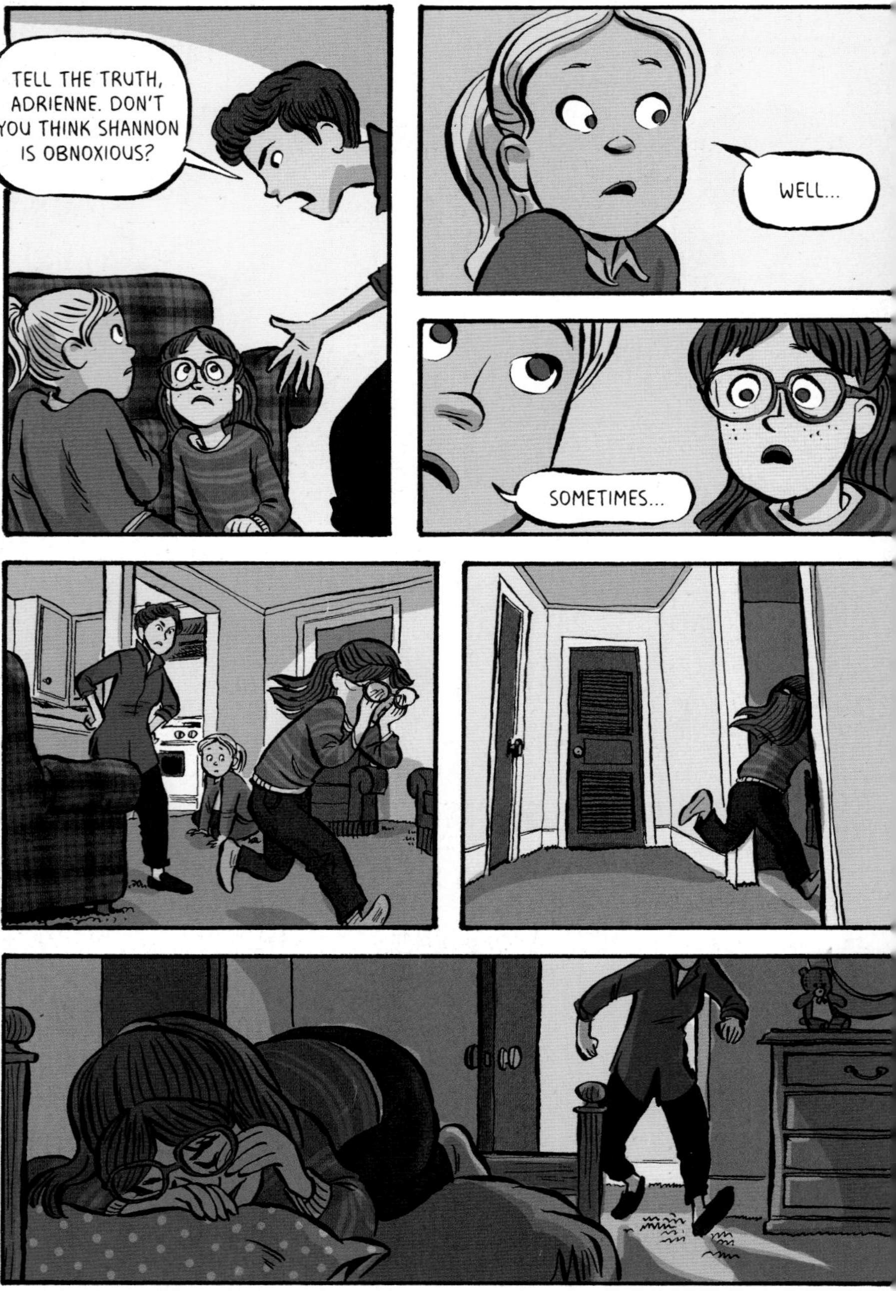
TELL THE TRUTH, ADRIENNE. DON'T YOU THINK SHANNON IS OBNOXIOUS?
WELL...
SOMETIMES...

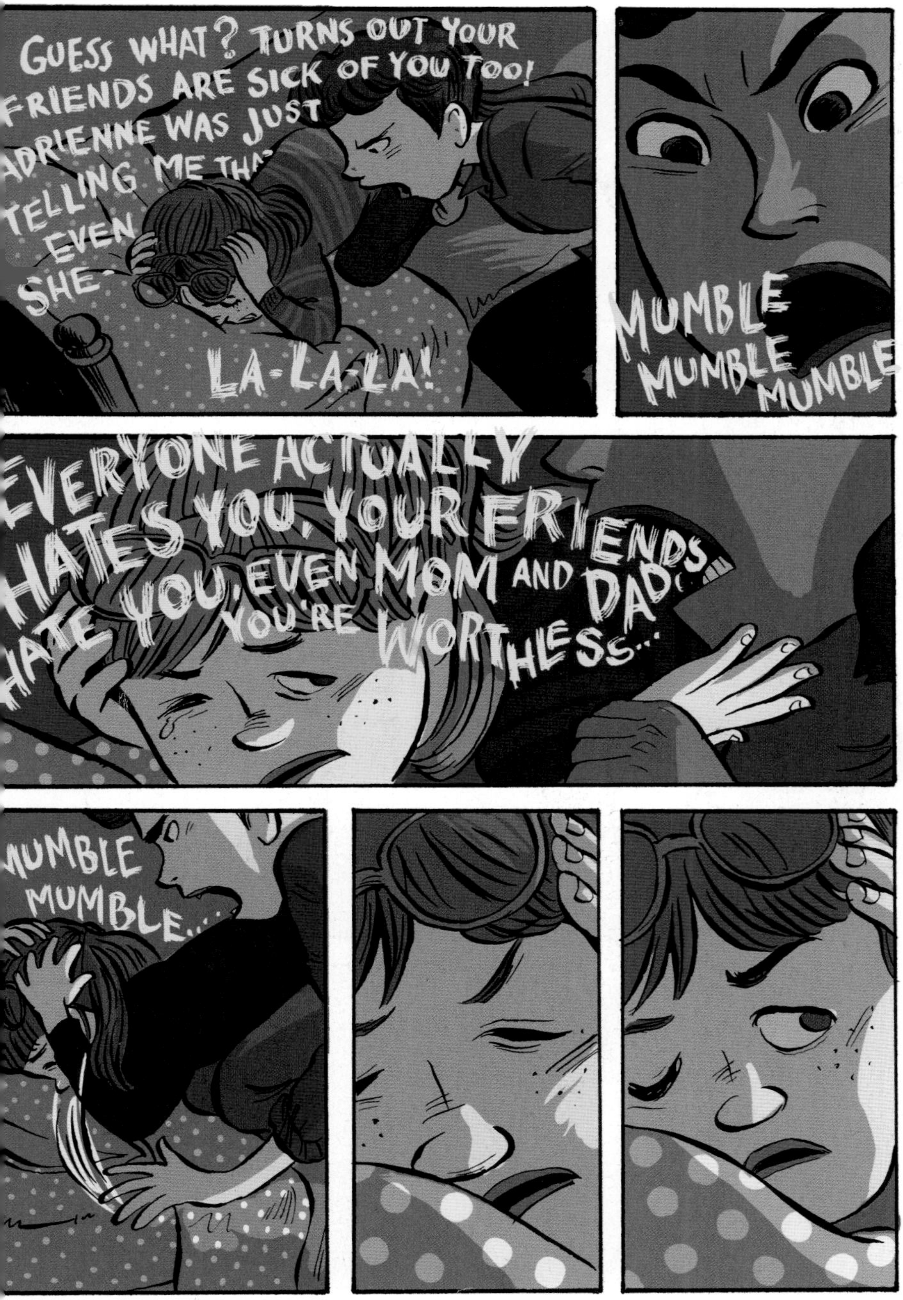
GUESS WHAT? TURNS OUT YOUR FRIENDS ARE SICK OF YOU TOO! ADRIENNE WAS JUST TELLING ME THA EVEN SHE-
LA-LA-LA!
MUMBLE MUMBLE MUMBLE
EVERYONE ACTUALLY HATES YOU. YOUR FRIENDS HATE YOU. EVEN MOM AND DAD. YOU'RE WORTHLESS...
MUMBLE MUMBLE...

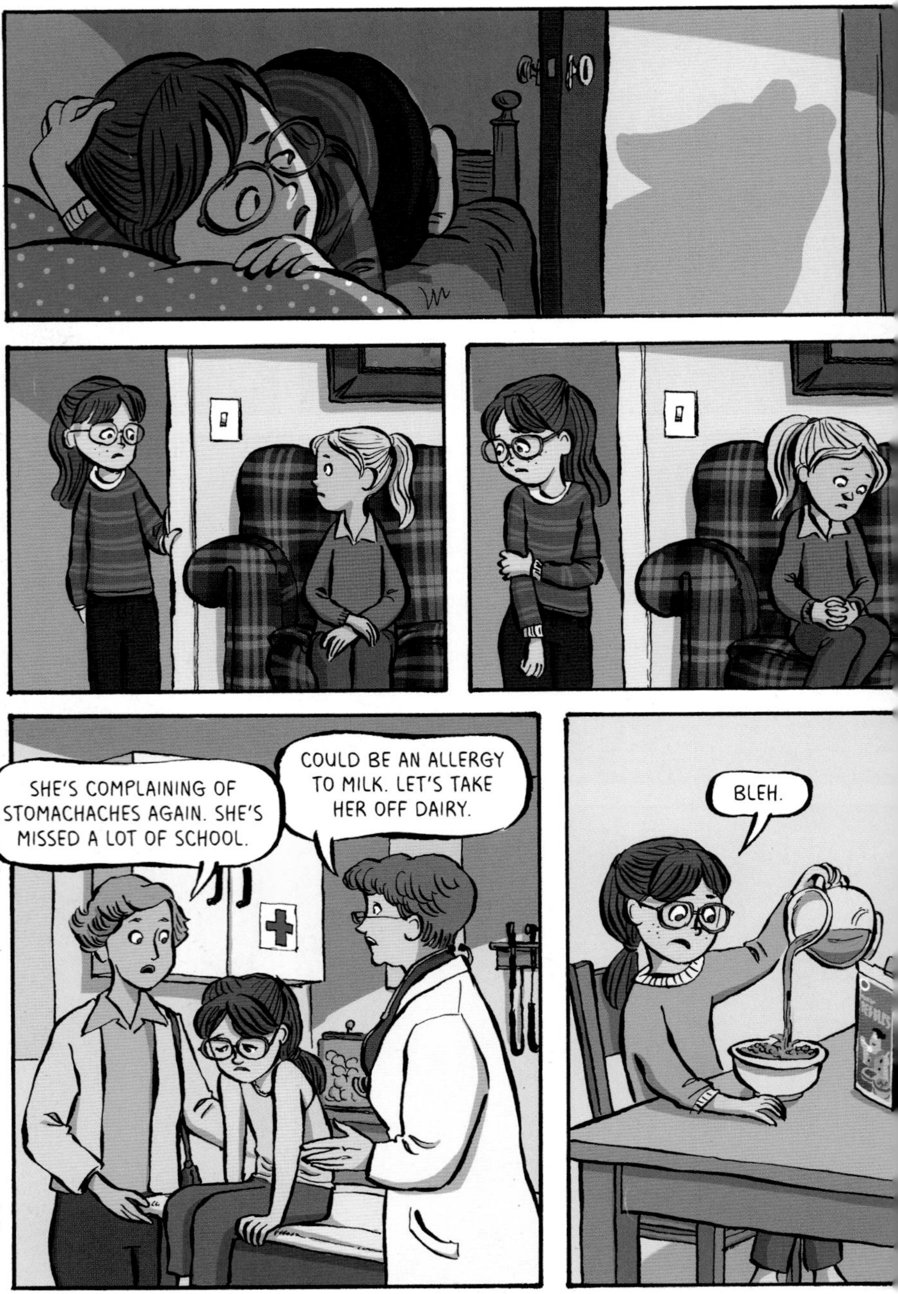
SHE'S COMPLAINING OF STOMACHACHES AGAIN. SHE'S MISSED A LOT OF SCHOOL.
COULD BE AN ALLERGY TO MILK. LET'S TAKE HER OFF DAIRY.
BLEH.

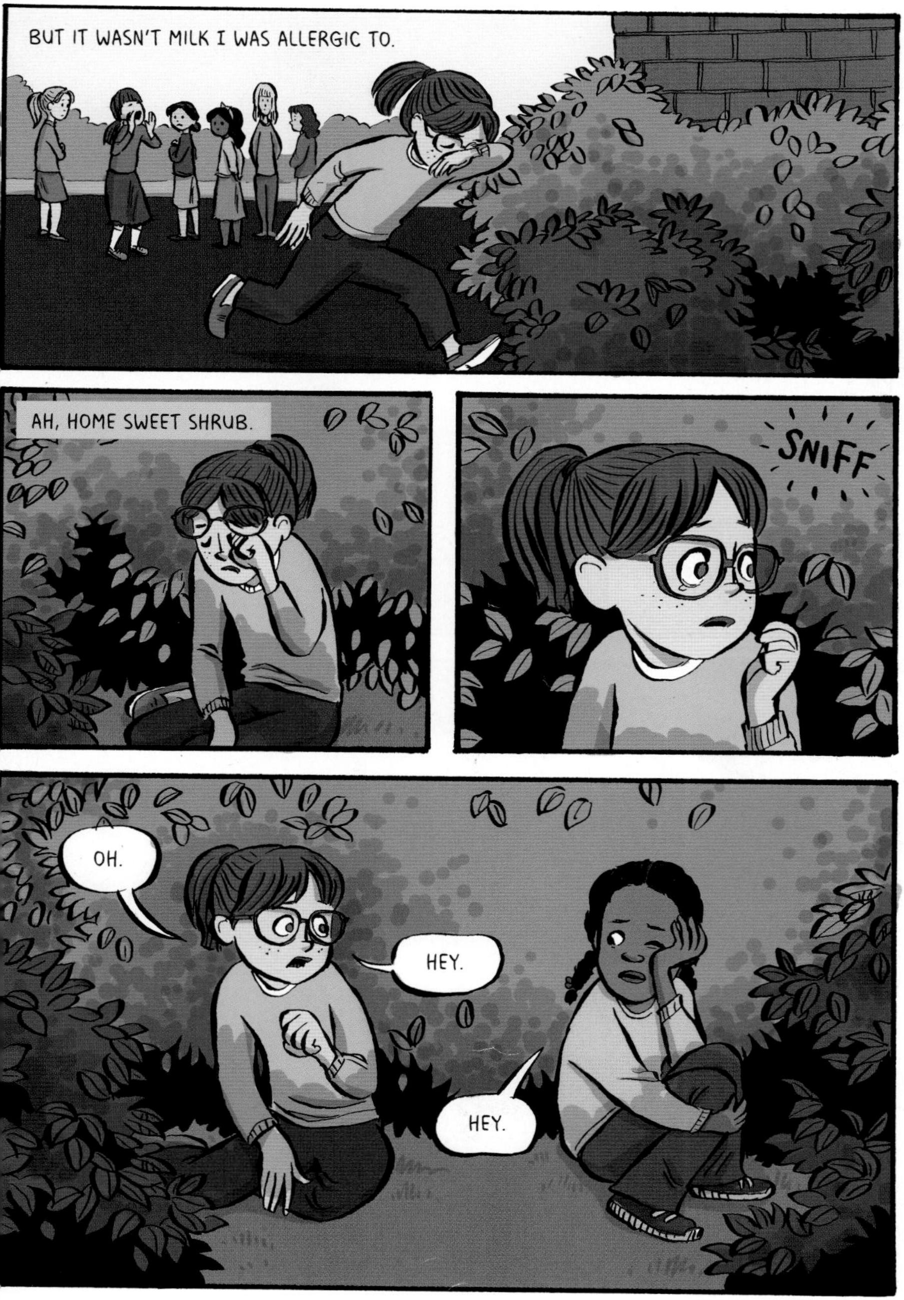
BUT IT WASN'T MILK I WAS ALLERGIC TO.
AH, HOME SWEET SHRUB.
SNIFF
OH.
HEY.
HEY.

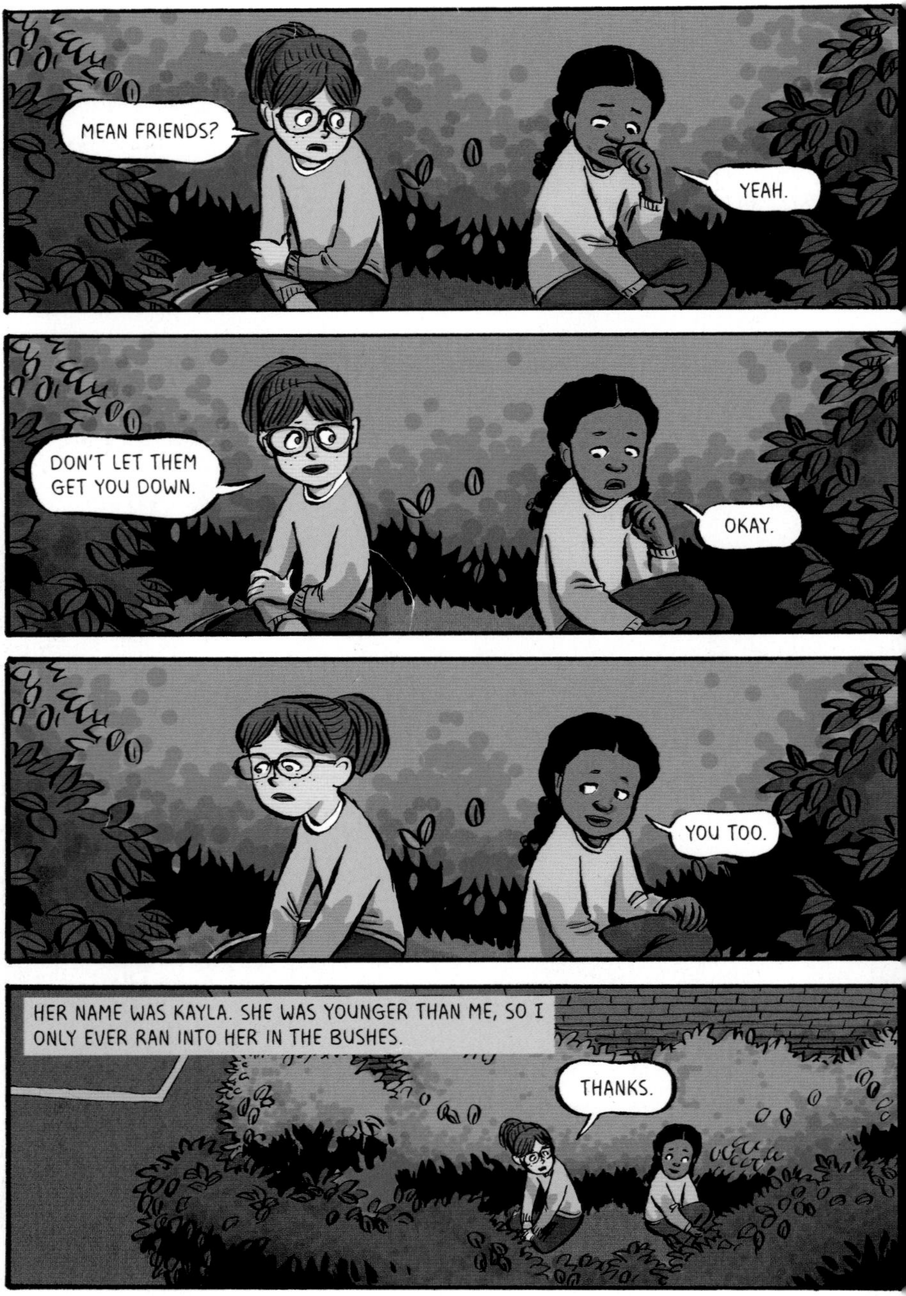
MEAN FRIENDS?
YEAH.
DON'T LET THEM GET YOU DOWN.
OKAY.
YOU TOO.
HER NAME WAS KAYLA. SHE WAS YOUNGER THAN ME, SO I ONLY EVER RAN INTO HER IN THE BUSHES.
THANKS.

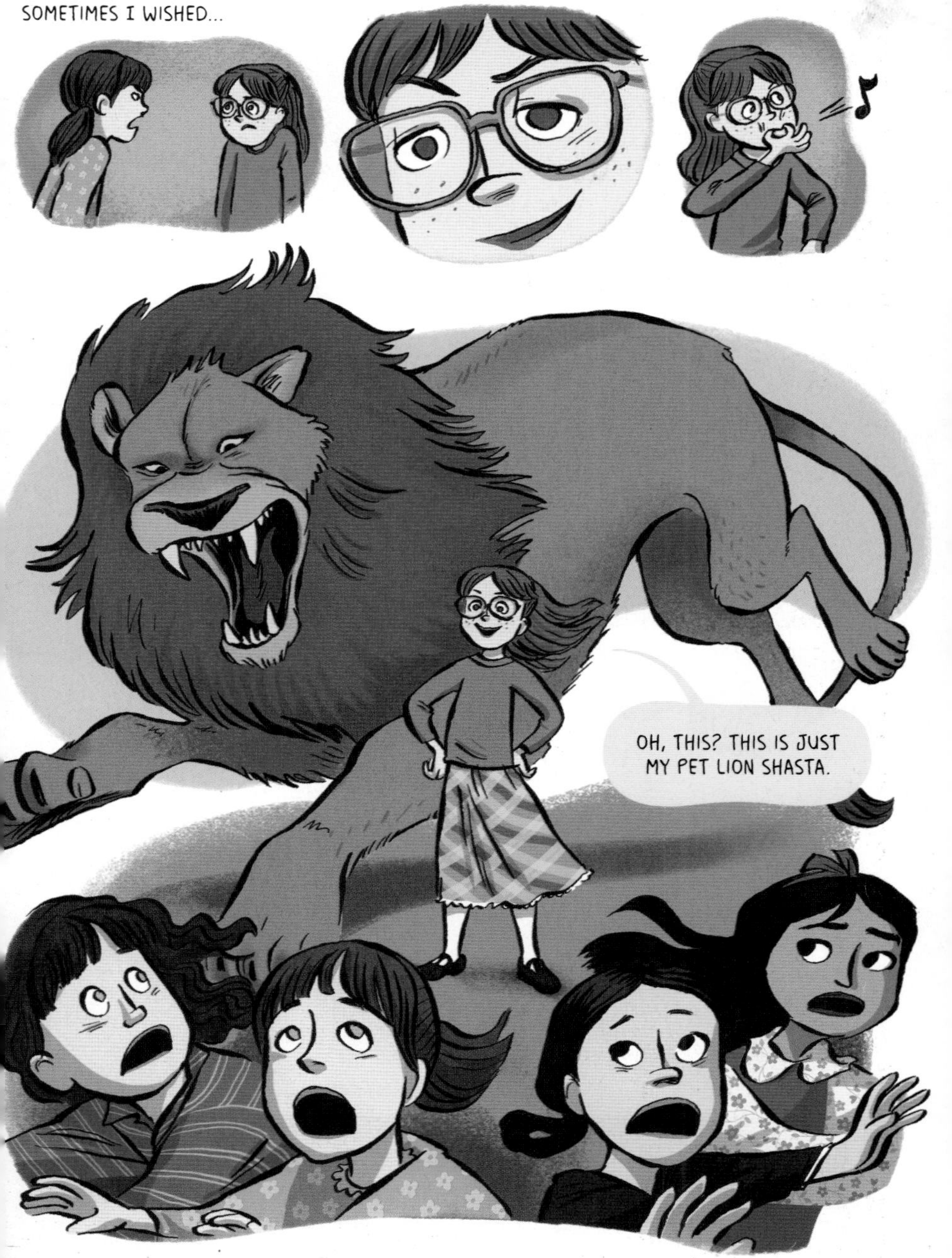
SOMETIMES I WISHED...
OH, THIS? THIS IS JUST MY PET LION SHASTA.

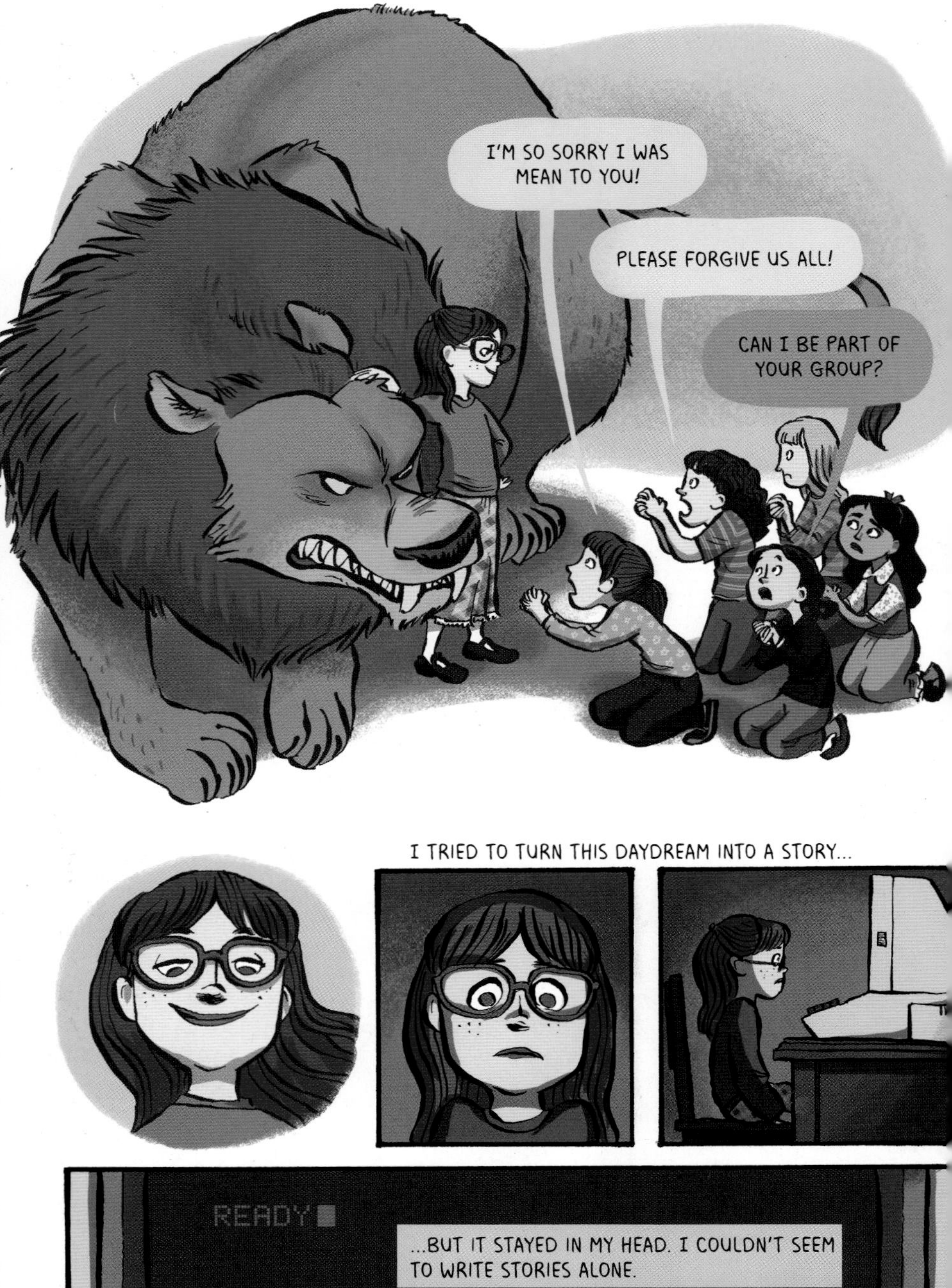
I'M SO SORRY I WAS MEAN TO YOU!
PLEASE FORGIVE US ALL!
CAN I BE PART OF YOUR GROUP?
I TRIED TO TURN THIS DAYDREAM INTO A STORY...
READY
...BUT IT STAYED IN MY HEAD. I COULDN'T SEEM TO WRITE STORIES ALONE.

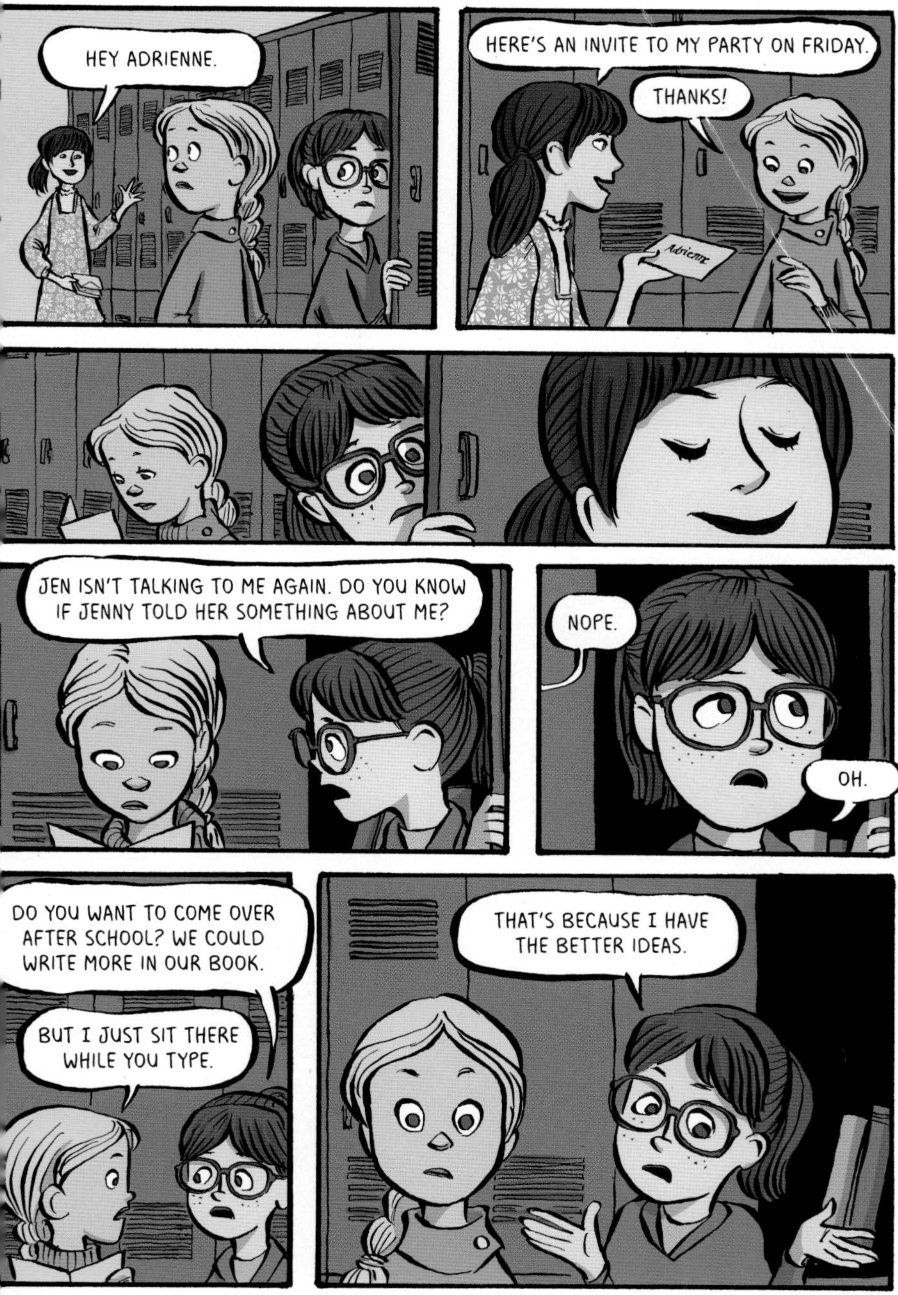
HEY ADRIENNE.
HERE'S AN INVITE TO MY PARTY ON FRIDAY.
THANKS!
Adrienne
JEN ISN'T TALKING TO ME AGAIN. DO YOU KNOW IF JENNY TOLD HER SOMETHING ABOUT ME?
NOPE.
OH.
DO YOU WANT TO COME OVER AFTER SCHOOL? WE COULD WRITE MORE IN OUR BOOK.
BUT I JUST SIT THERE WHILE YOU TYPE.
THAT'S BECAUSE I HAVE THE BETTER IDEAS.

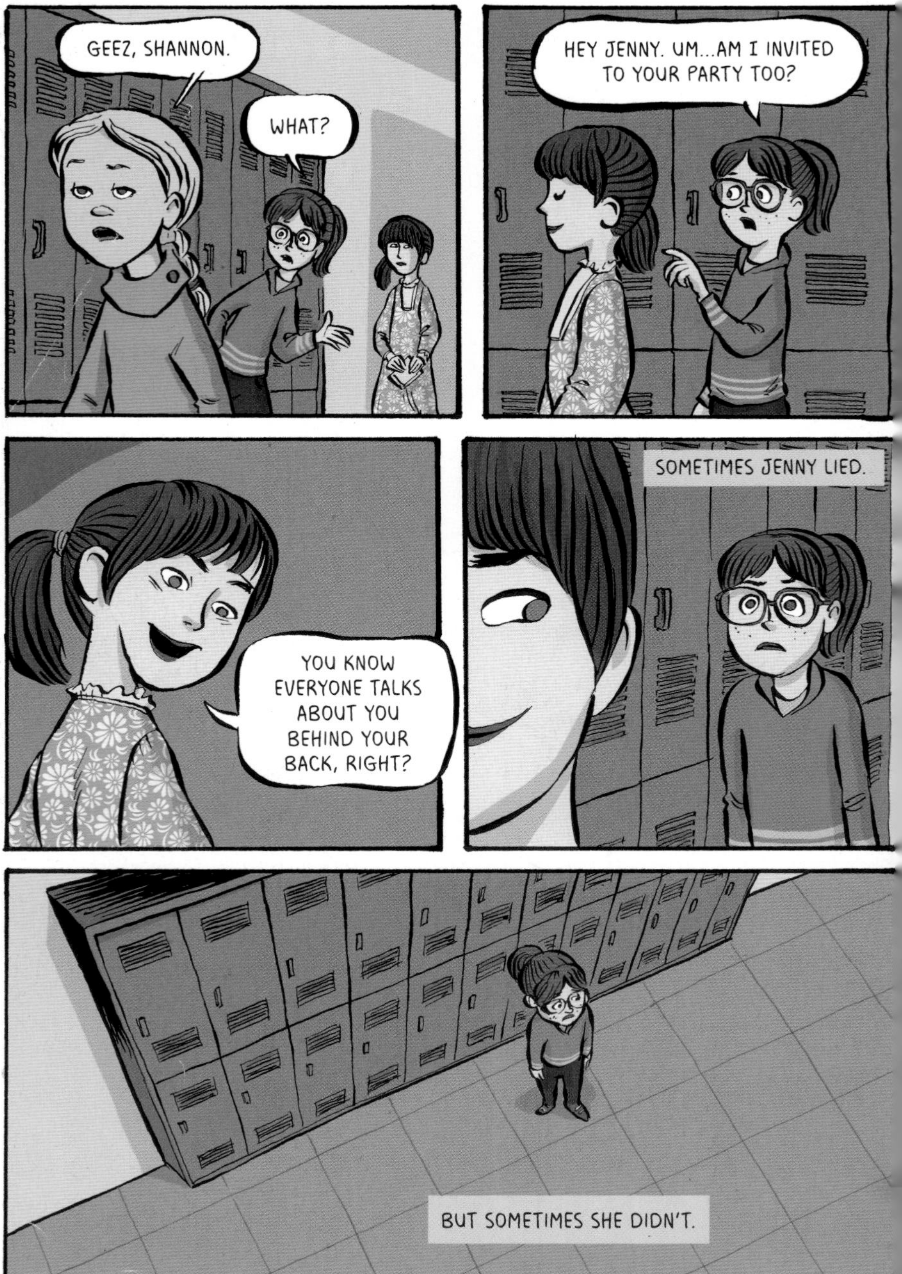
GEEZ, SHANNON.
WHAT?
HEY JENNY. UM...AM I INVITED TO YOUR PARTY TOO?
YOU KNOW EVERYONE TALKS ABOUT YOU BEHIND YOUR BACK, RIGHT?
SOMETIMES JENNY LIED.
BUT SOMETIMES SHE DIDN'T.

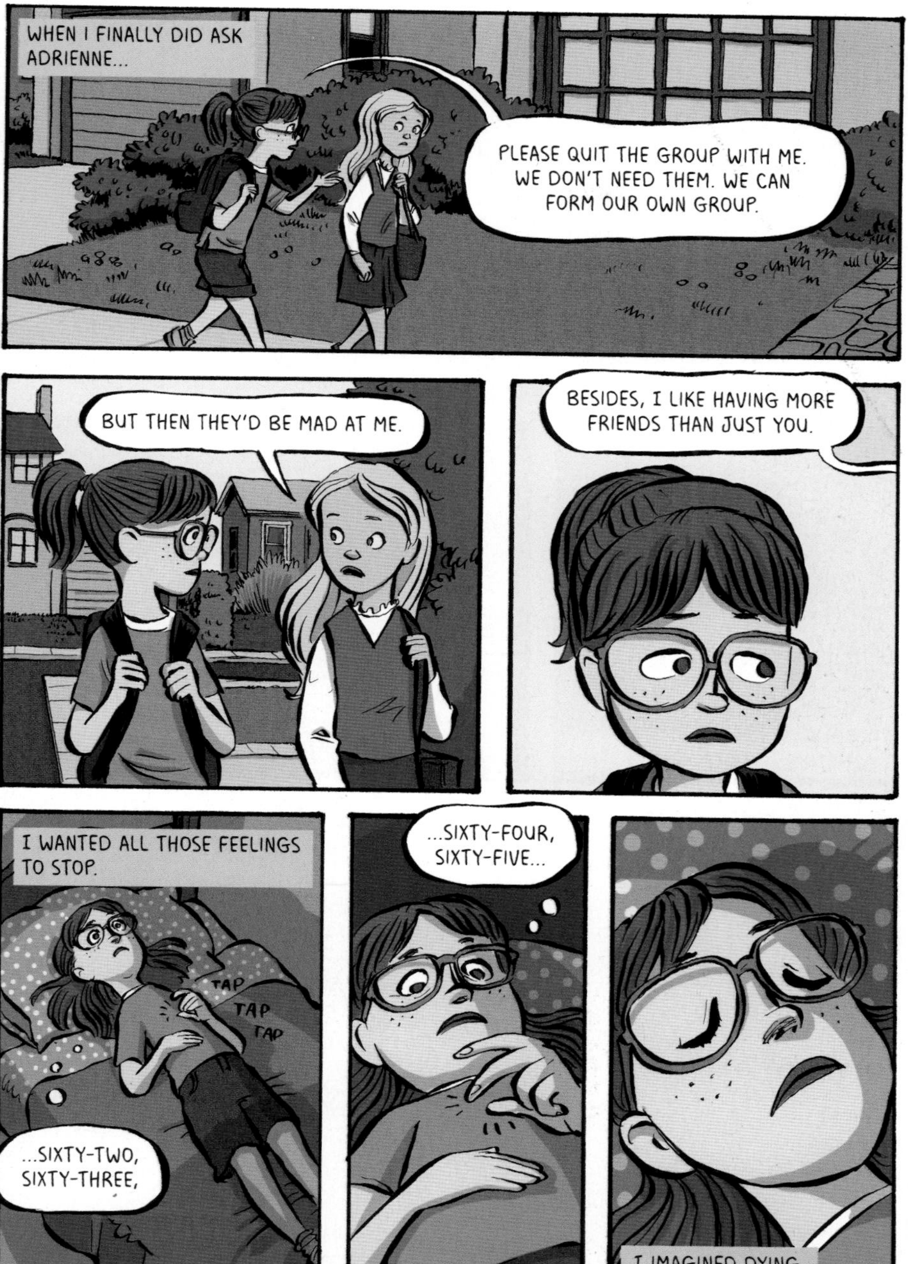
WHEN I FINALLY DID ASK ADRIENNE...
PLEASE QUIT THE GROUP WITH ME. WE DON'T NEED THEM. WE CAN FORM OUR OWN GROUP.
BUT THEN THEY'D BE MAD AT ME.
BESIDES, I LIKE HAVING MORE FRIENDS THAN JUST YOU.
I WANTED ALL THOSE FEELINGS TO STOP.
TAP
TAP
TAP
...SIXTY-TWO, SIXTY-THREE,
...SIXTY-FOUR, SIXTY-FIVE...
I IMAGINED DYING.

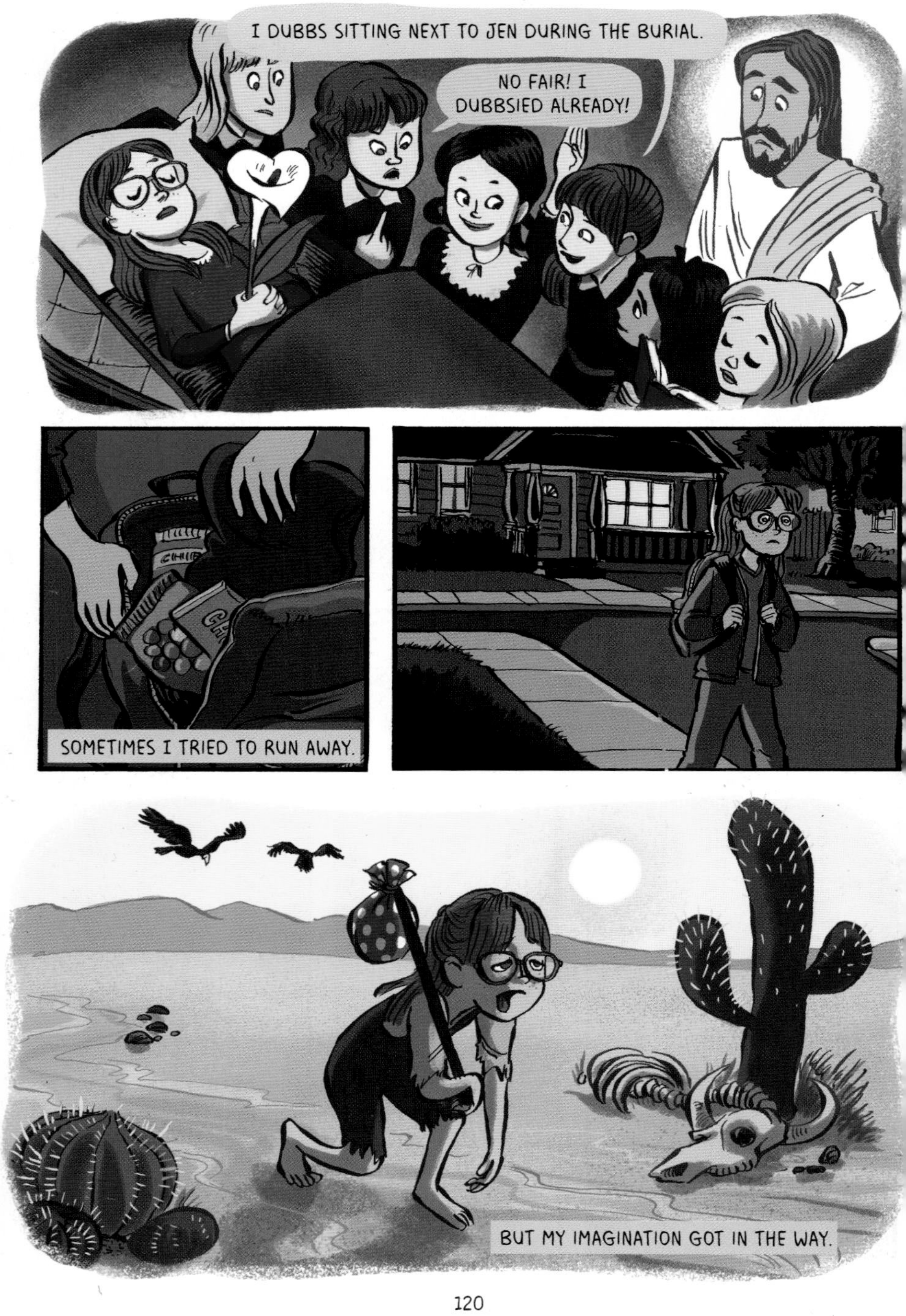
I DUBBS SITTING NEXT TO JEN DURING THE BURIAL.
NO FAIR! I DUBBSIED ALREADY!
SOMETIMES I TRIED TO RUN AWAY.
BUT MY IMAGINATION GOT IN THE WAY.

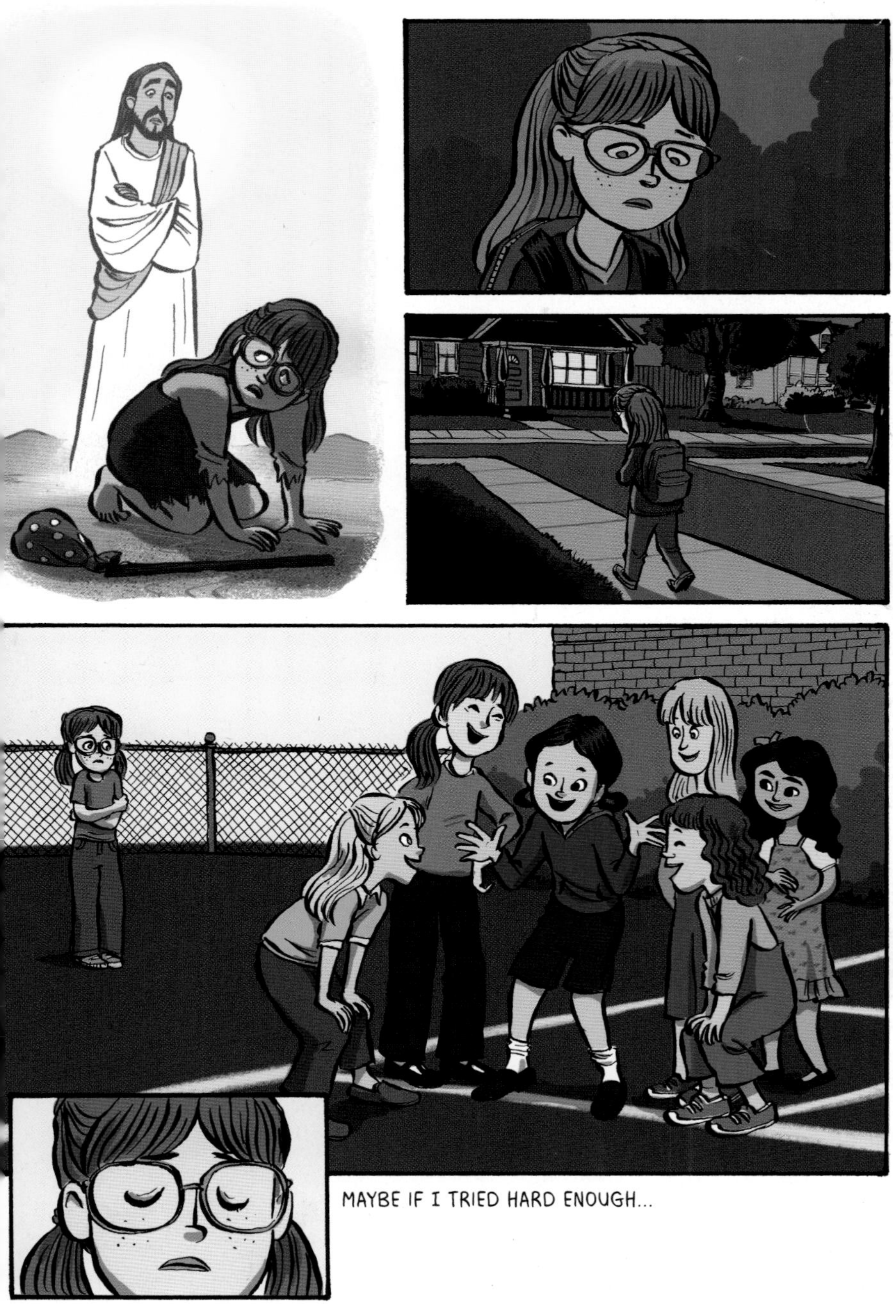
MAYBE IF I TRIED HARD ENOUGH...

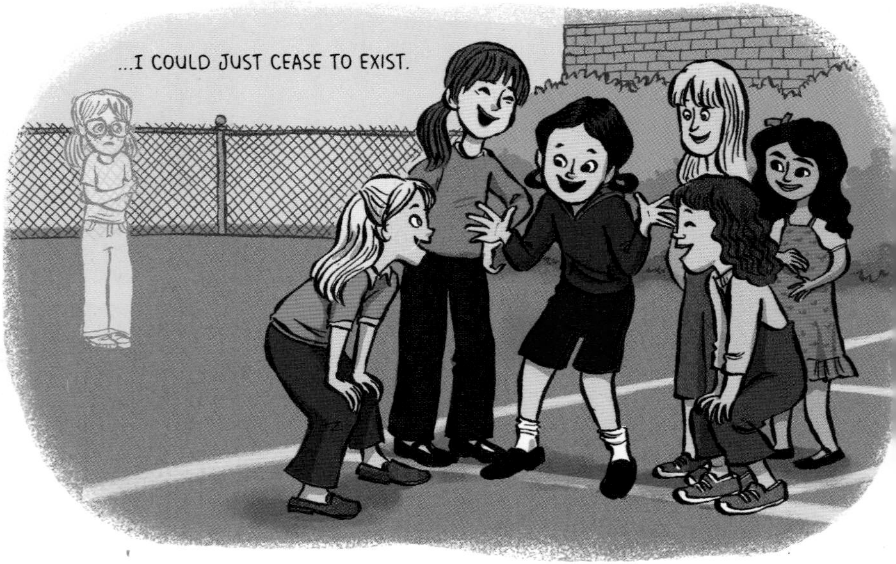
...I COULD JUST CEASE TO EXIST.

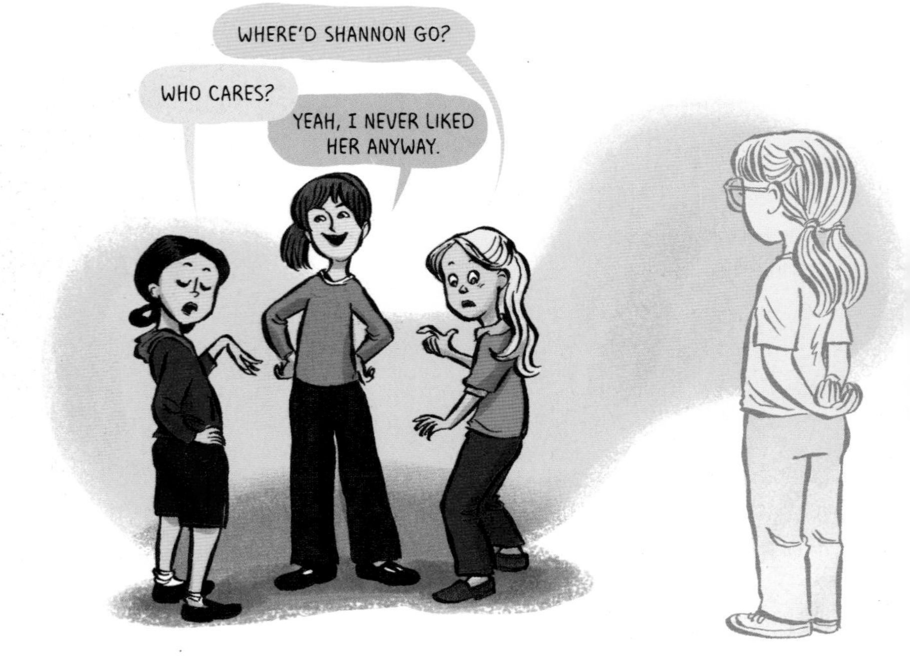
WHERE'D SHANNON GO?
WHO CARES?
YEAH, I NEVER LIKED HER ANYWAY.

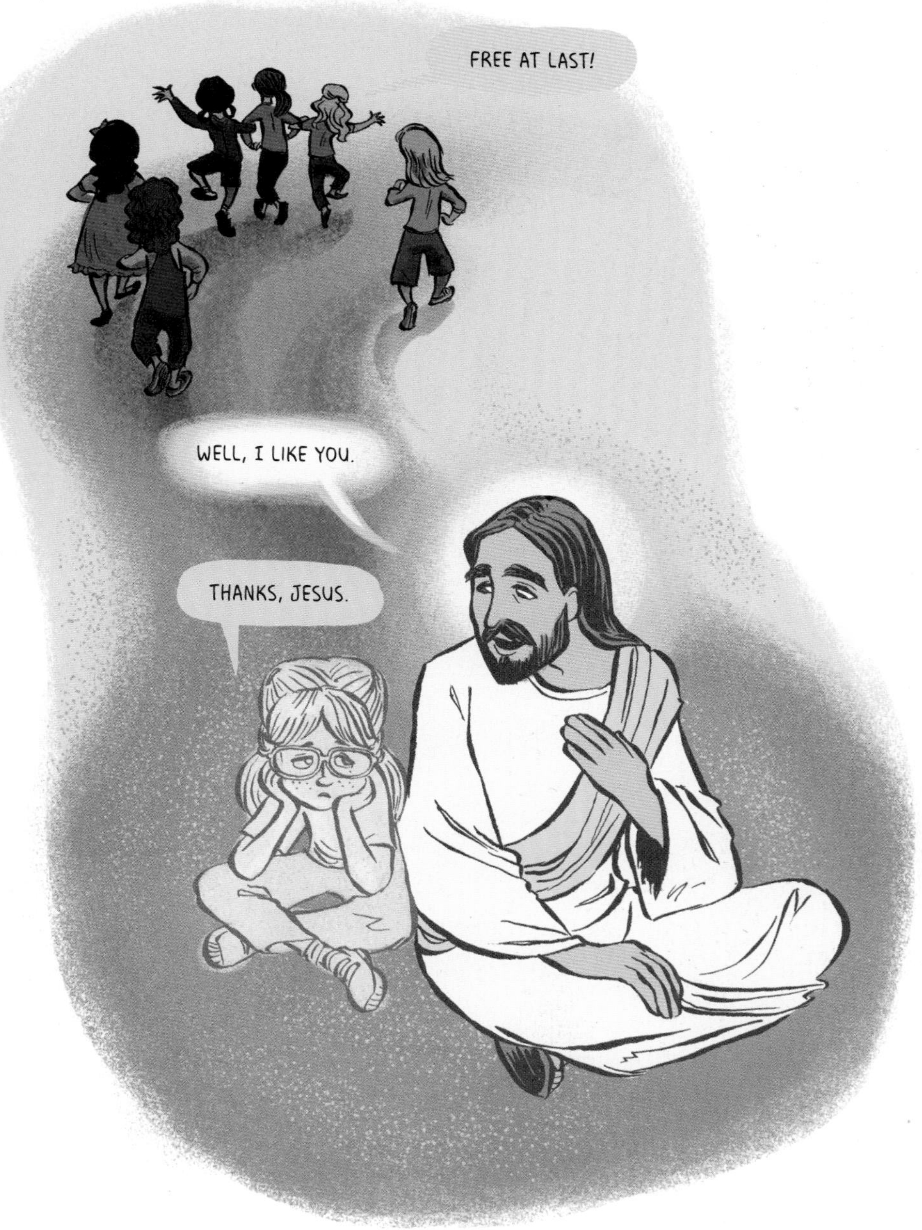
FREE AT LAST!
WELL, I LIKE YOU.
THANKS, JESUS.

ADRIENNE

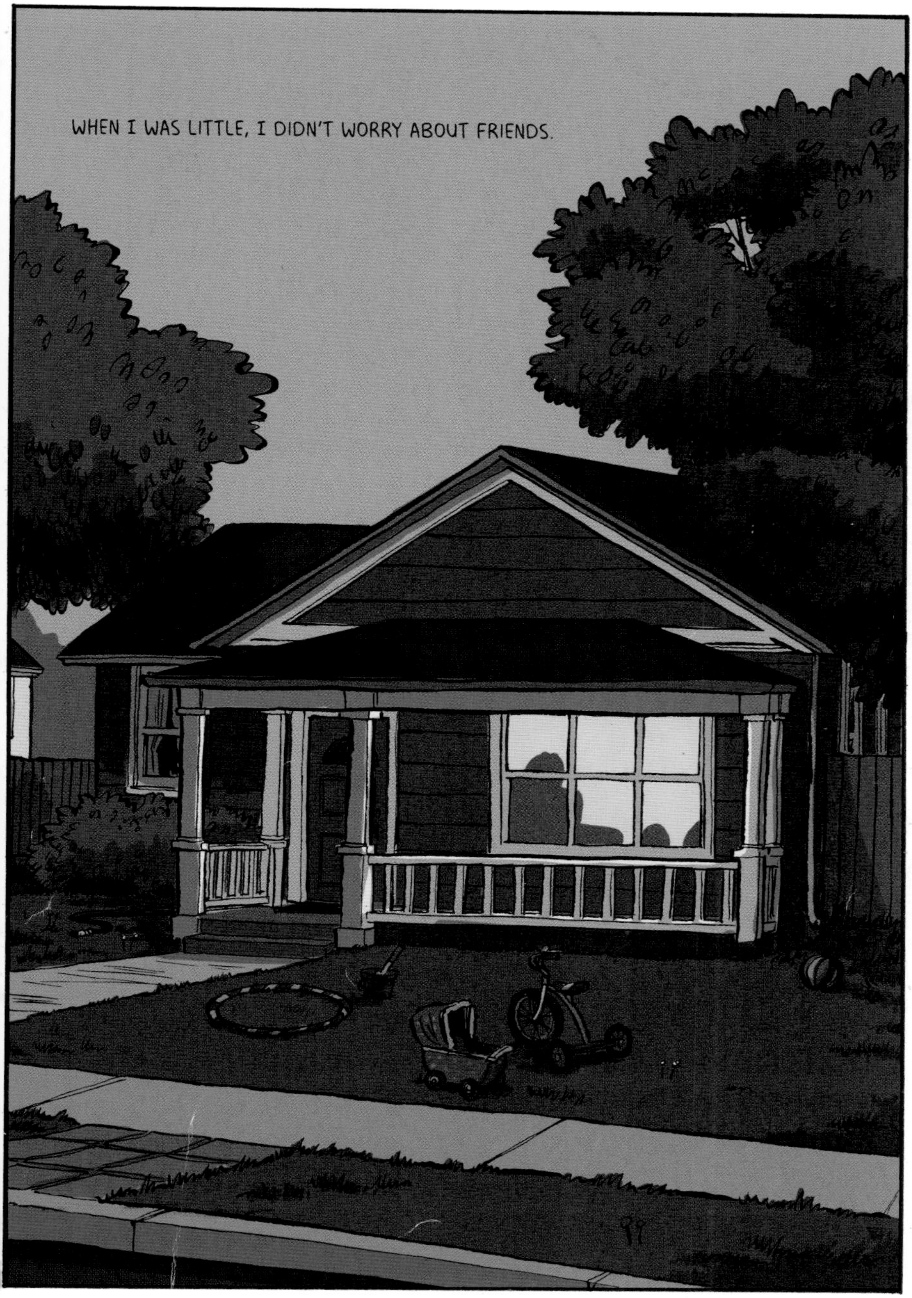
WHEN I WAS LITTLE, I DIDN'T WORRY ABOUT FRIENDS.

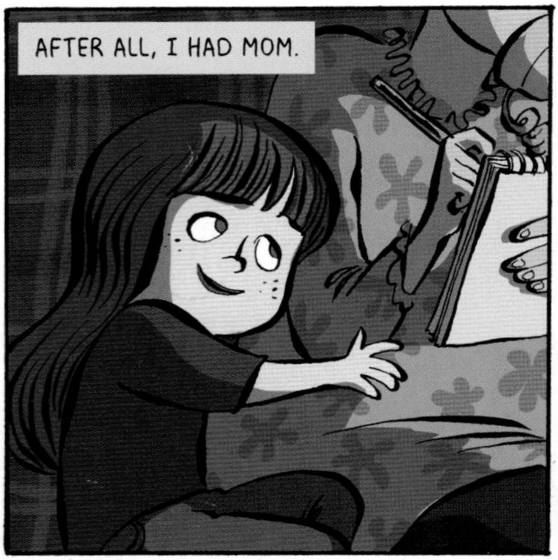
AFTER ALL, I HAD MOM.

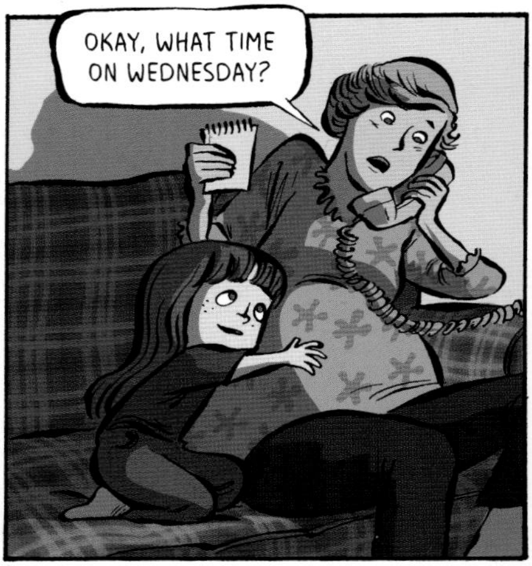
OKAY, WHAT TIME ON WEDNESDAY?

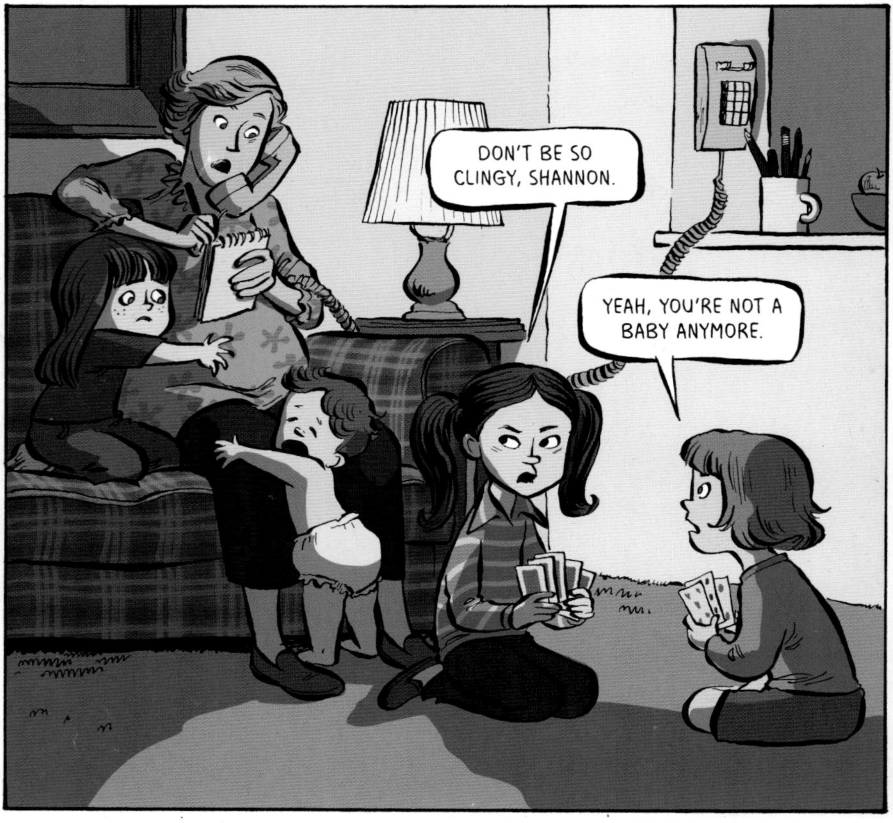
DON'T BE SO CLINGY, SHANNON.
YEAH, YOU'RE NOT A BABY ANYMORE.

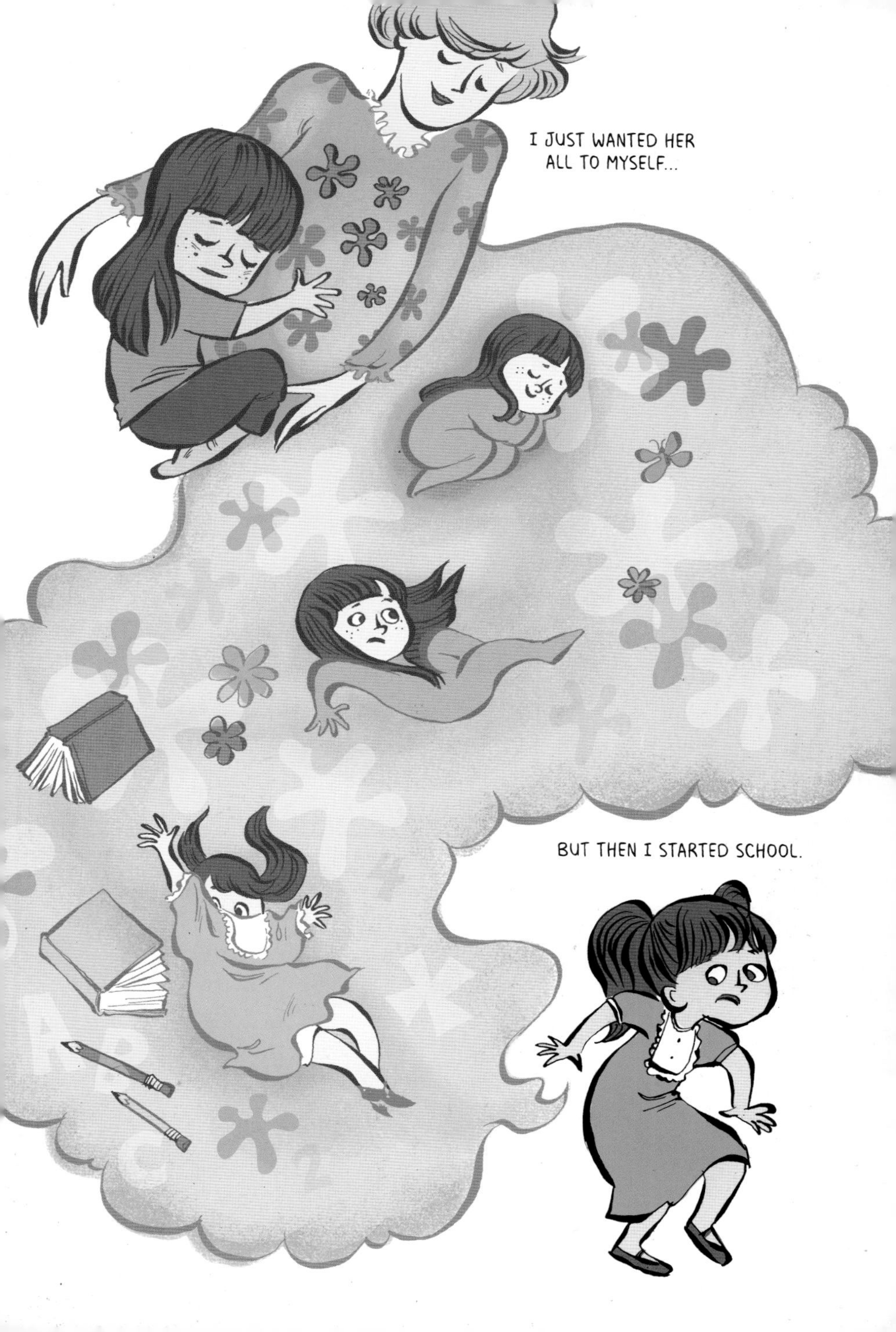
I JUST WANTED HER ALL TO MYSELF...
BUT THEN I STARTED SCHOOL.

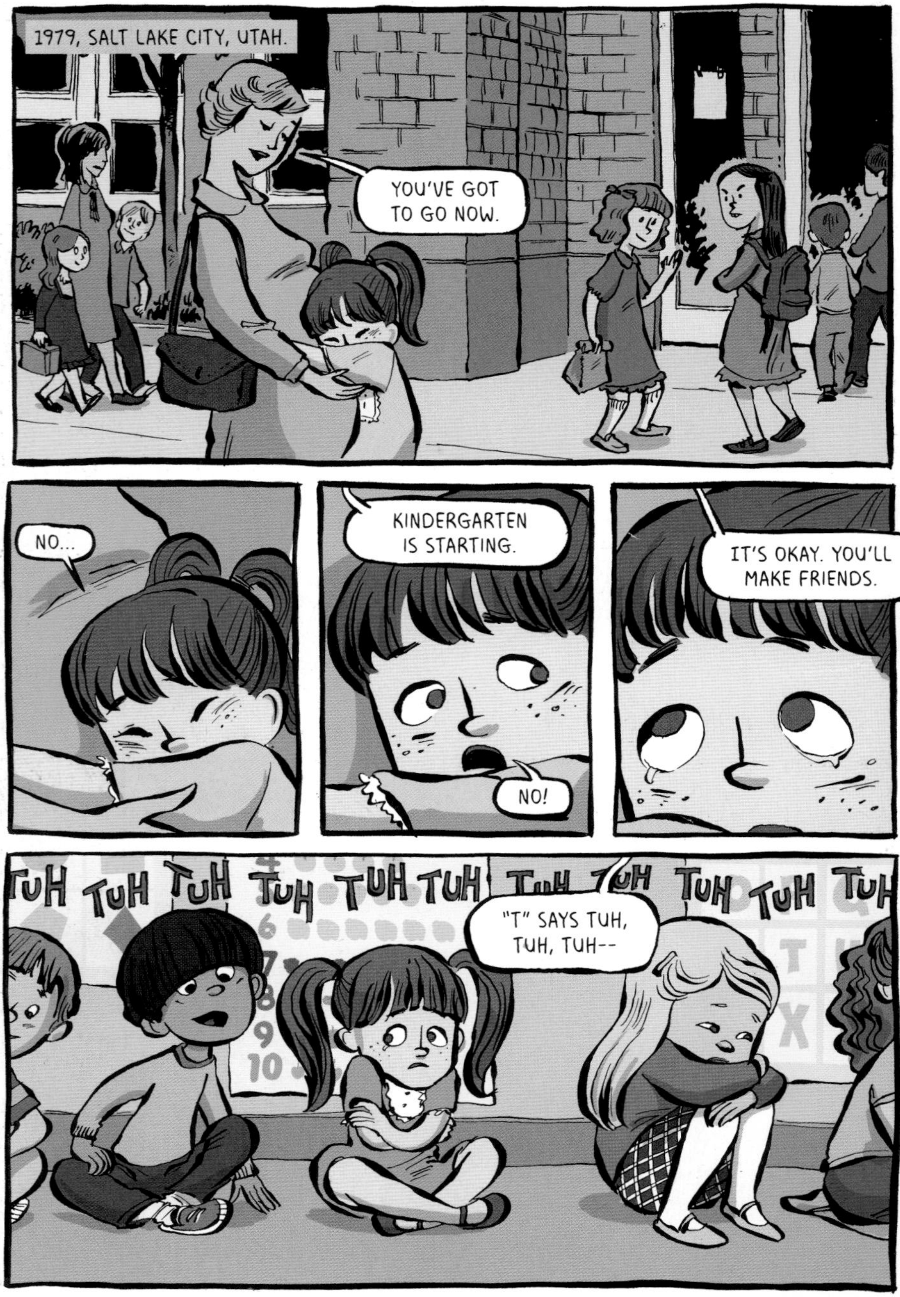
1979, SALT LAKE CITY, UTAH.
YOU'VE GOT TO GO NOW.
NO...
KINDERGARTEN IS STARTING.
NO!
IT'S OKAY. YOU'LL MAKE FRIENDS.
TUH TUH TUH TUH TUH TUH TUH TUH TUH TUH TUH TUH
"T" SAYS TUH, TUH, TUH--

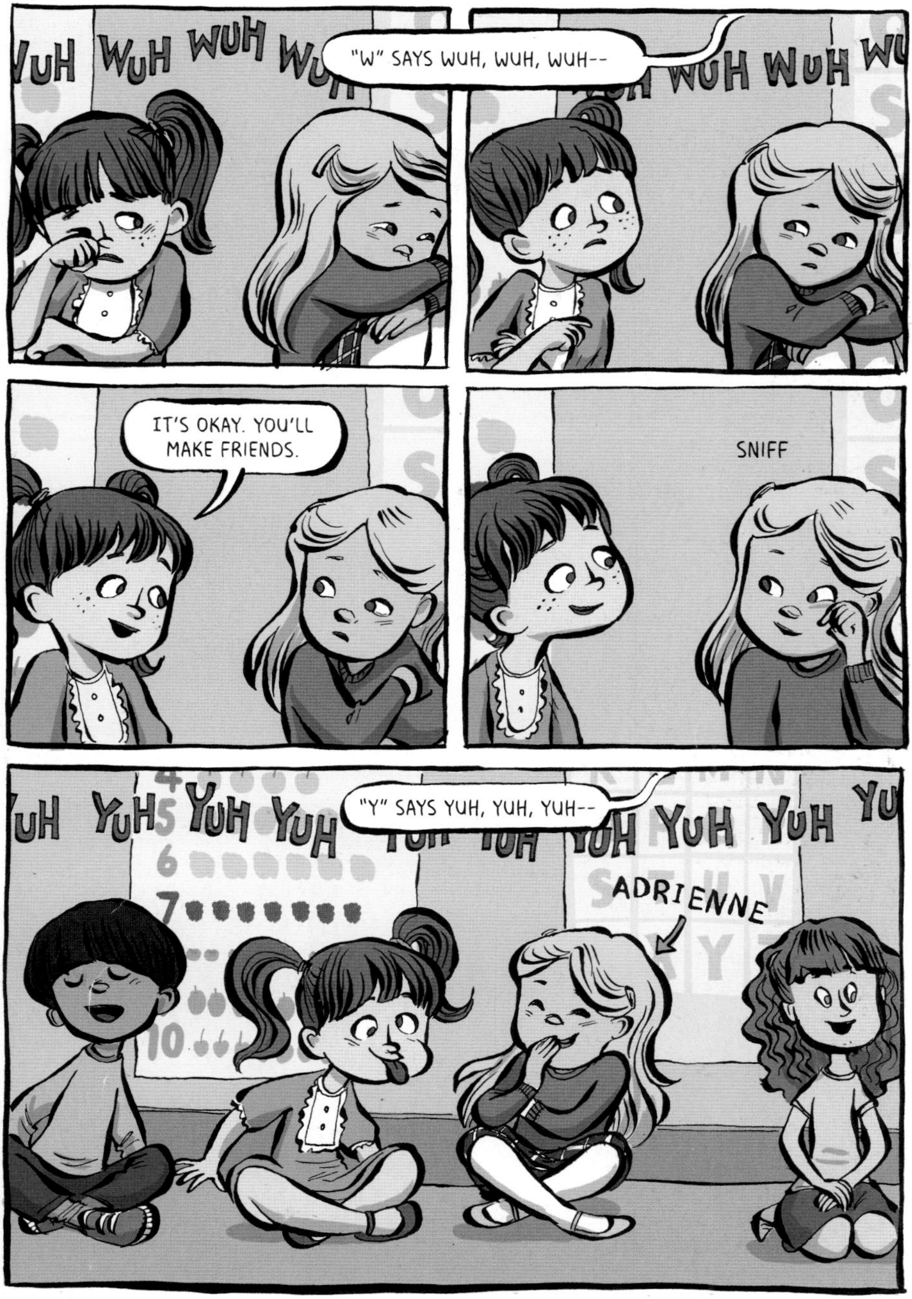
WUH WUH WUH WUH
"W" SAYS WUH, WUH, WUH--
WUH WUH WUH WU
IT'S OKAY. YOU'LL MAKE FRIENDS.
SNIFF
YUH YUH YUH YUH
"Y" SAYS YUH, YUH, YUH--
YUH YUH YUH YU
ADRIENNE

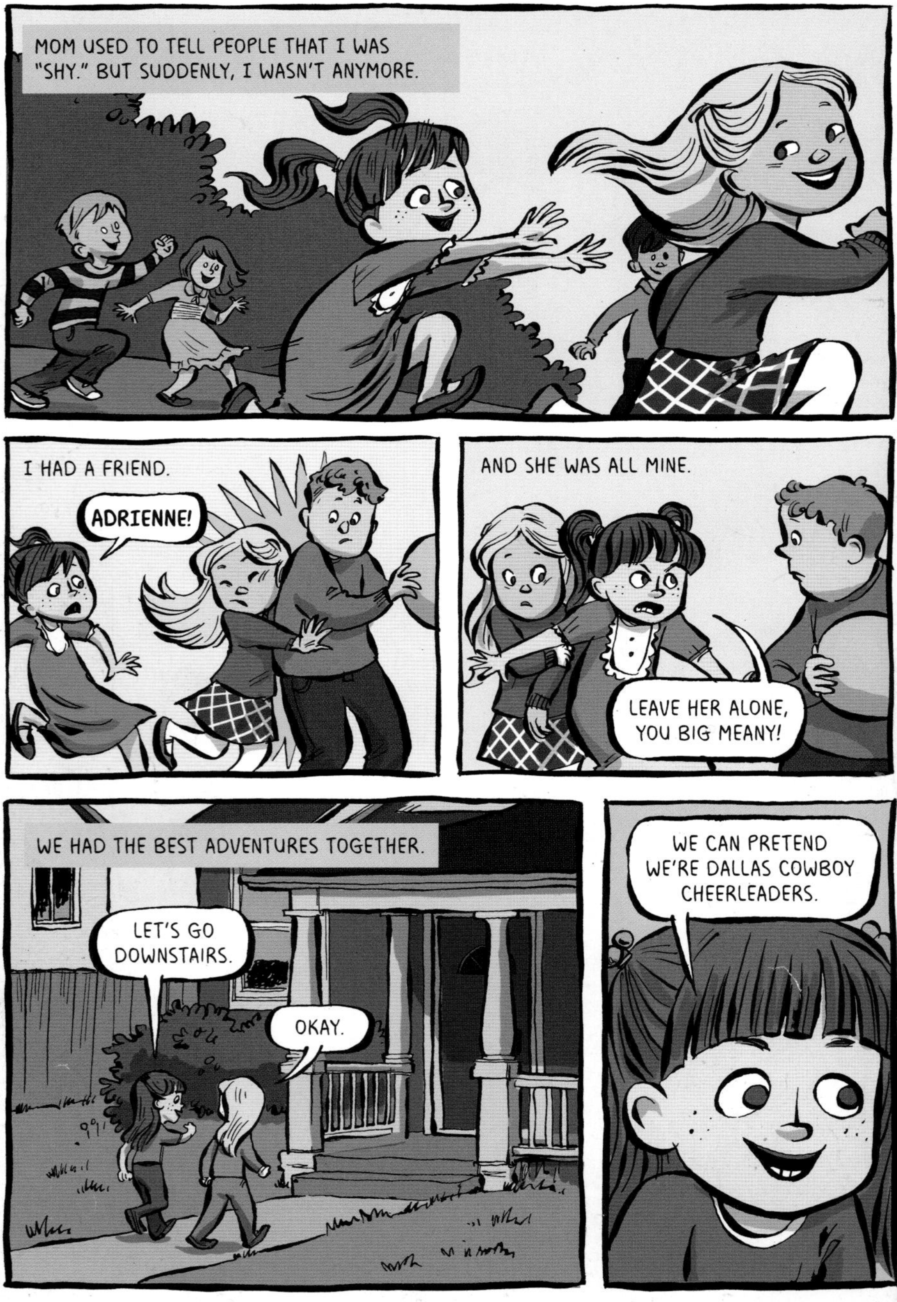

MOM USED TO TELL PEOPLE THAT I WAS "SHY." BUT SUDDENLY, I WASN'T ANYMORE.
I HAD A FRIEND.
ADRIENNE!
AND SHE WAS ALL MINE.
LEAVE HER ALONE, YOU BIG MEANY!
WE HAD THE BEST ADVENTURES TOGETHER.
LET'S GO DOWNSTAIRS.
OKAY.
WE CAN PRETEND WE'RE DALLAS COWBOY CHEERLEADERS.

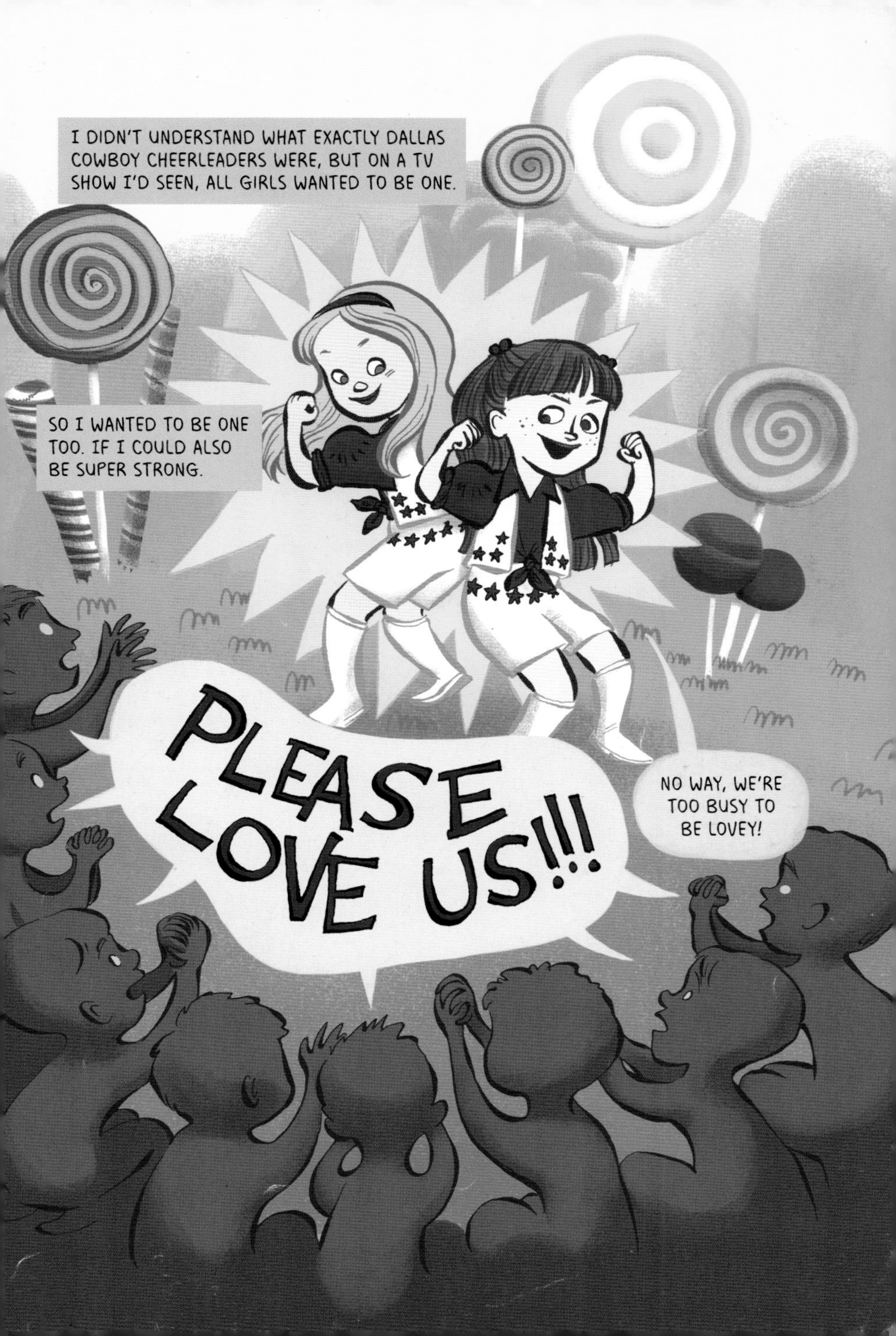
I DIDN'T UNDERSTAND WHAT EXACTLY DALLAS COWBOY CHEERLEADERS WERE, BUT ON A TV SHOW I'D SEEN, ALL GIRLS WANTED TO BE ONE.
SO I WANTED TO BE ONE TOO. IF I COULD ALSO BE SUPER STRONG.
PLEASE LOVE US!!!
NO WAY, WE'RE TOO BUSY TO BE LOVEY!

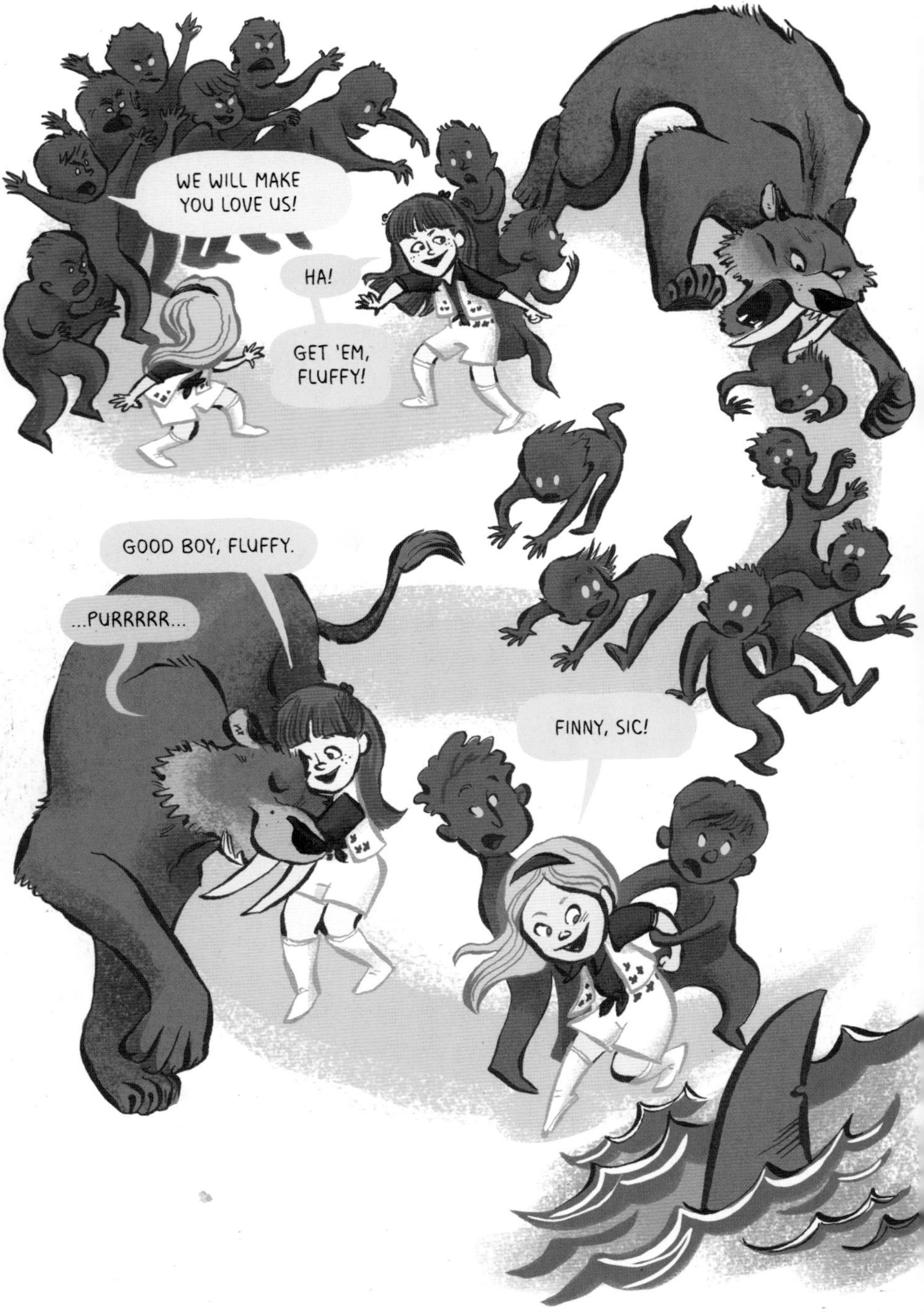
WE WILL MAKE YOU LOVE US!
HA!
GET 'EM, FLUFFY!
GOOD BOY, FLUFFY.
...PURRRRR...
FINNY, SIC!

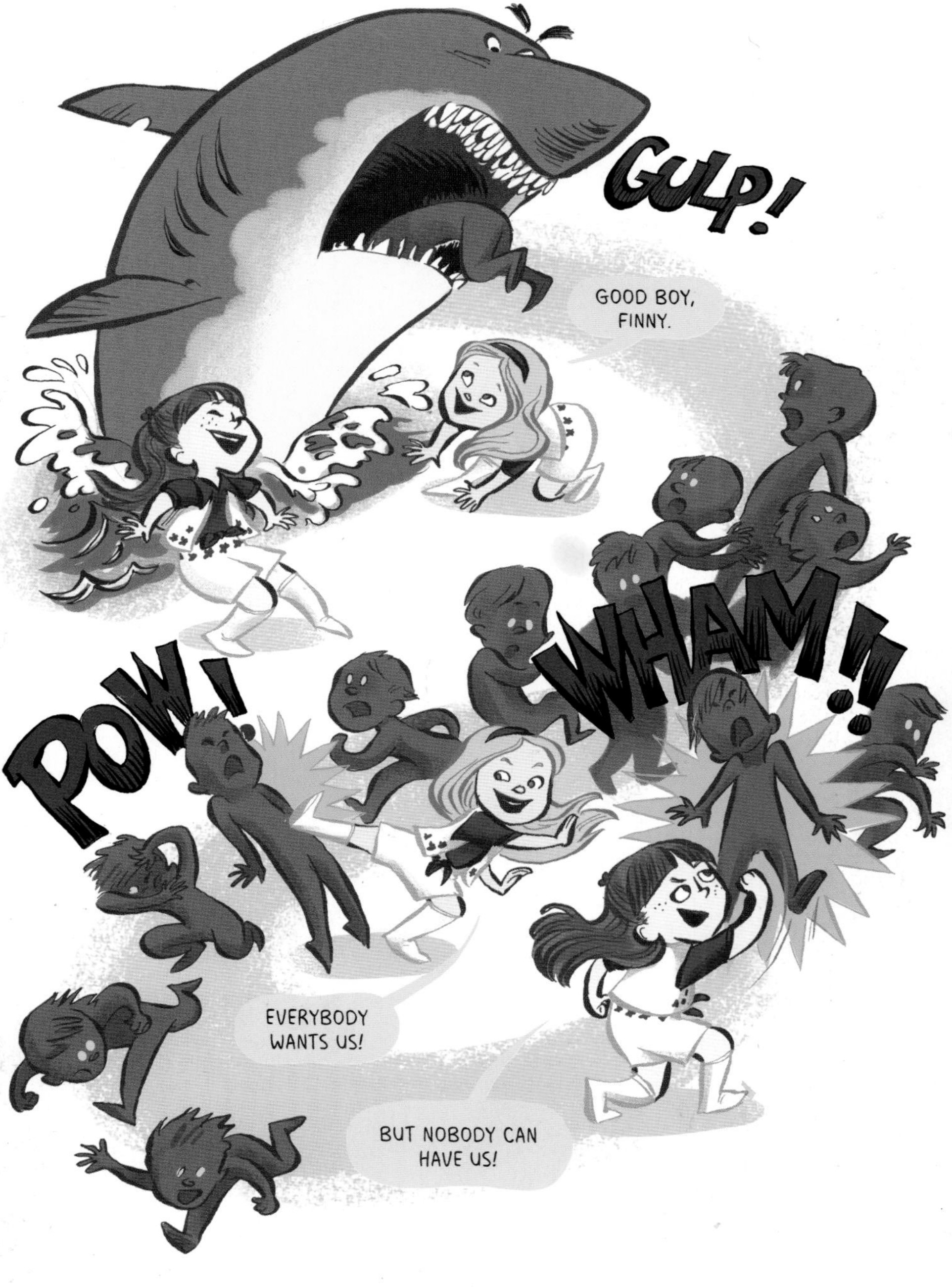
GULP!
GOOD BOY, FINNY.
POW!
WHAM!!
EVERYBODY WANTS US!
BUT NOBODY CAN HAVE US!

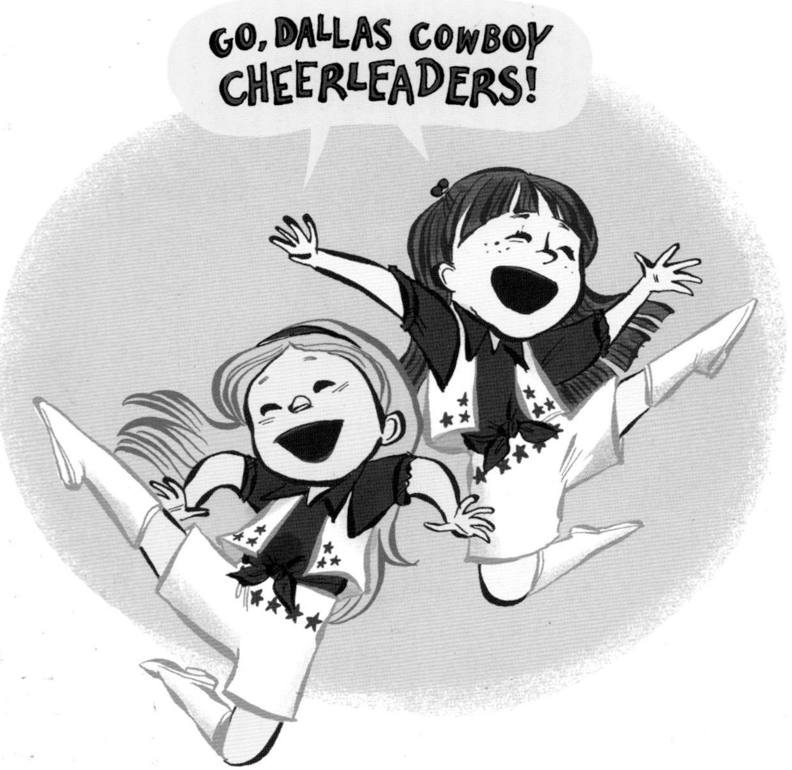
GO, DALLAS COWBOY CHEERLEADERS!

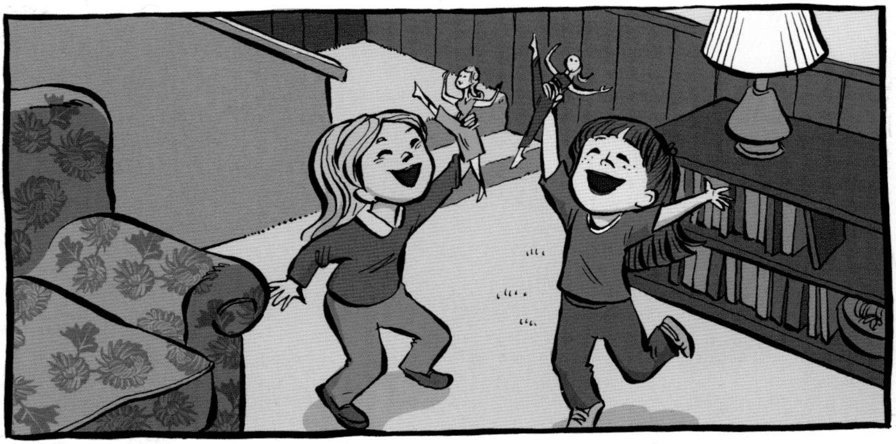

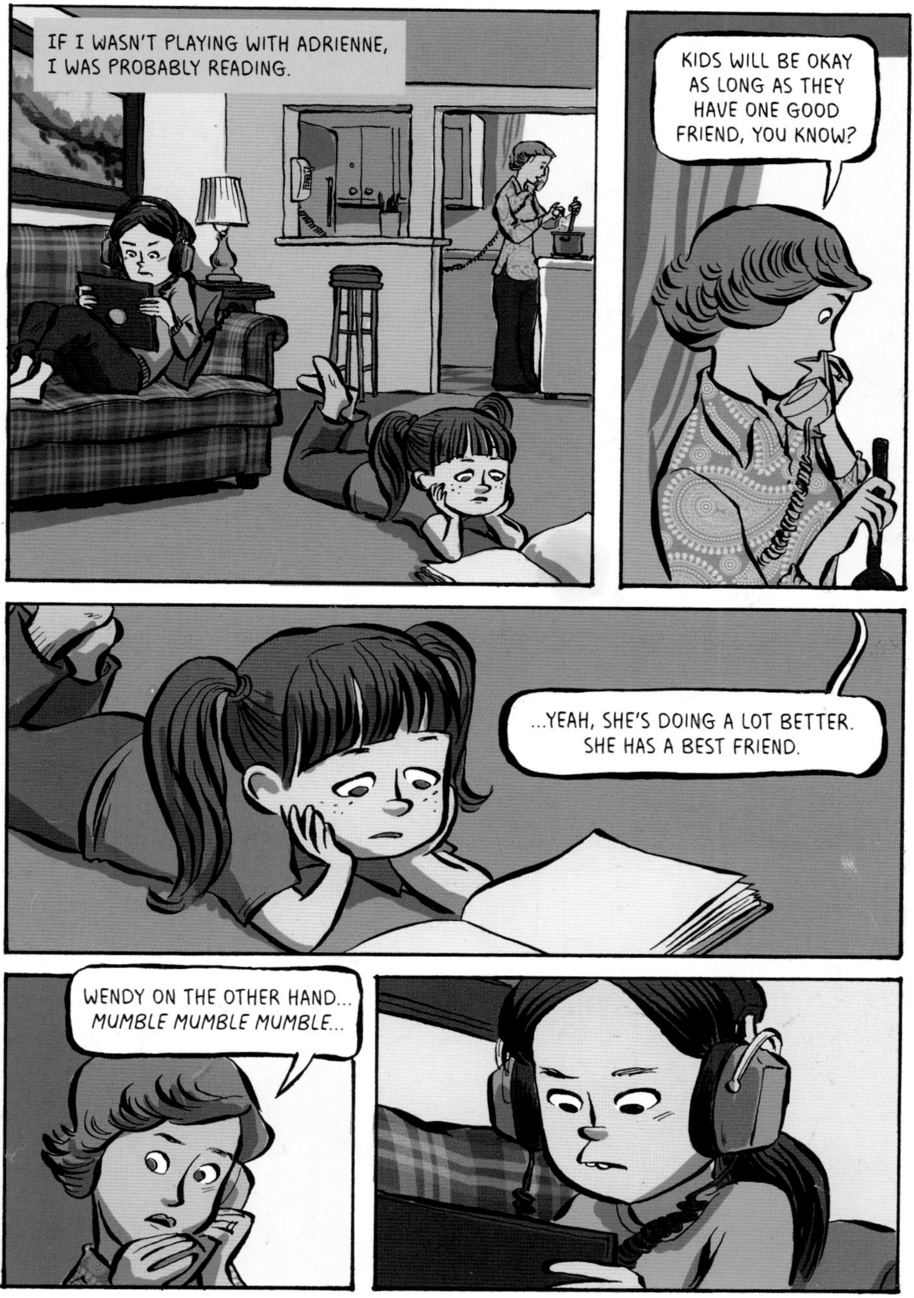
IF I WASN'T PLAYING WITH ADRIENNE, I WAS PROBABLY READING.
KIDS WILL BE OKAY AS LONG AS THEY HAVE ONE GOOD FRIEND, YOU KNOW?
...YEAH, SHE'S DOING A LOT BETTER. SHE HAS A BEST FRIEND.
WENDY ON THE OTHER HAND... *MUMBLE MUMBLE MUMBLE...*

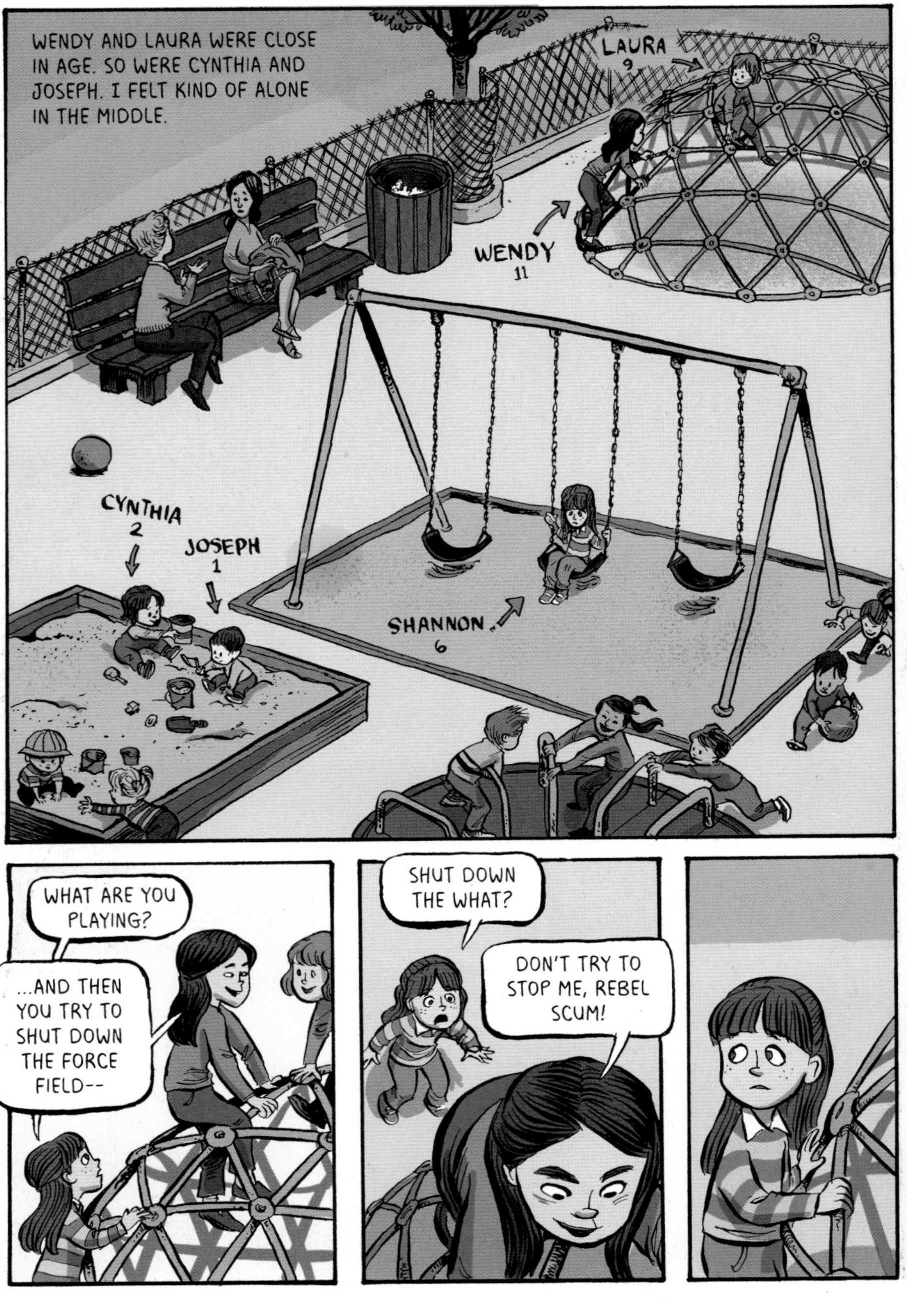
WENDY AND LAURA WERE CLOSE IN AGE. SO WERE CYNTHIA AND JOSEPH. I FELT KIND OF ALONE IN THE MIDDLE.
LAURA 9
WENDY 11
CYNTHIA 2
JOSEPH 1
SHANNON 6
WHAT ARE YOU PLAYING?
...AND THEN YOU TRY TO SHUT DOWN THE FORCE FIELD--
SHUT DOWN THE WHAT?
DON'T TRY TO STOP ME, REBEL SCUM!

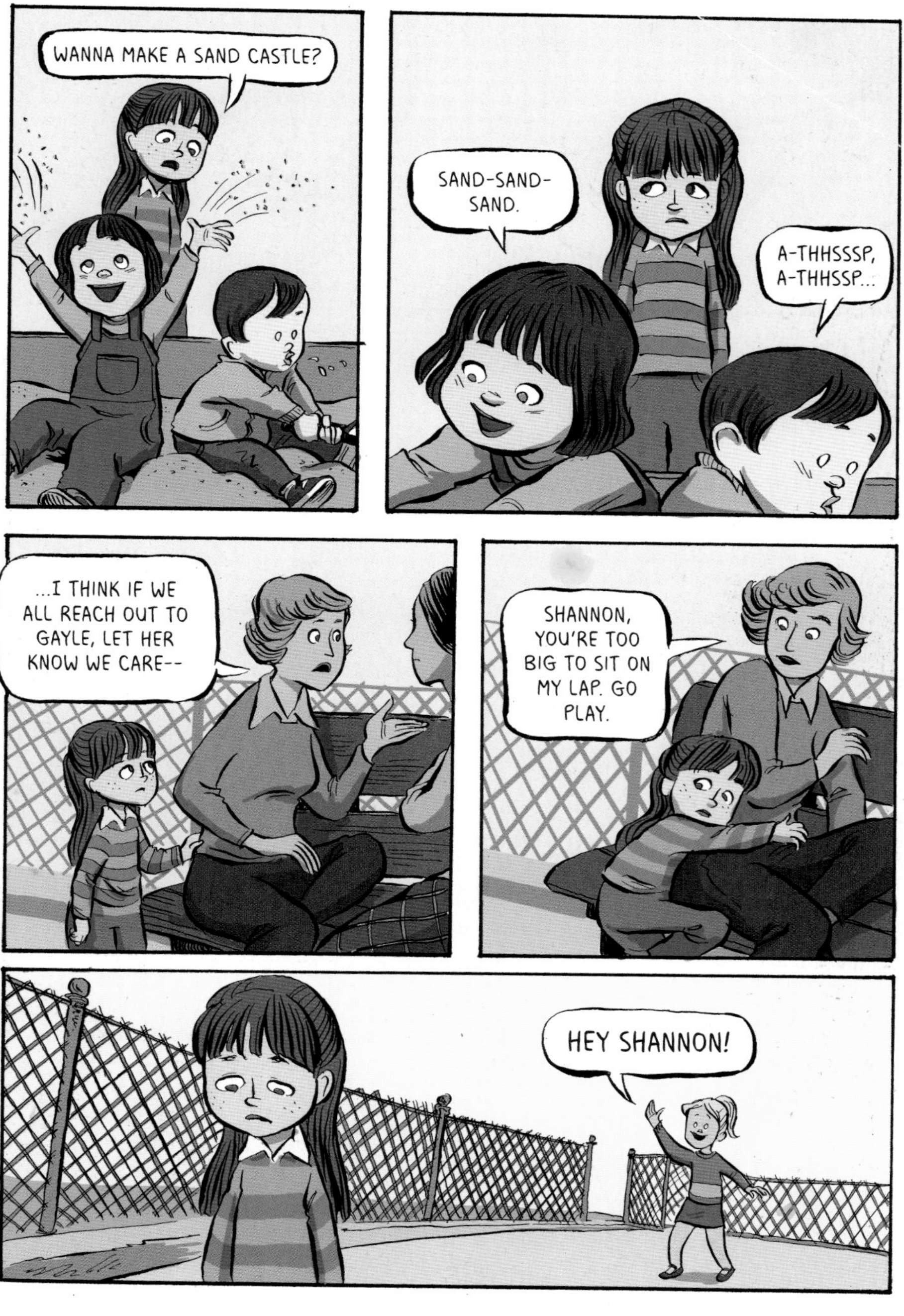

WANNA MAKE A SAND CASTLE?
SAND-SAND-SAND.
A-THHSSSP, A-THHSSP...
...I THINK IF WE ALL REACH OUT TO GAYLE, LET HER KNOW WE CARE--
SHANNON, YOU'RE TOO BIG TO SIT ON MY LAP. GO PLAY.
HEY SHANNON!

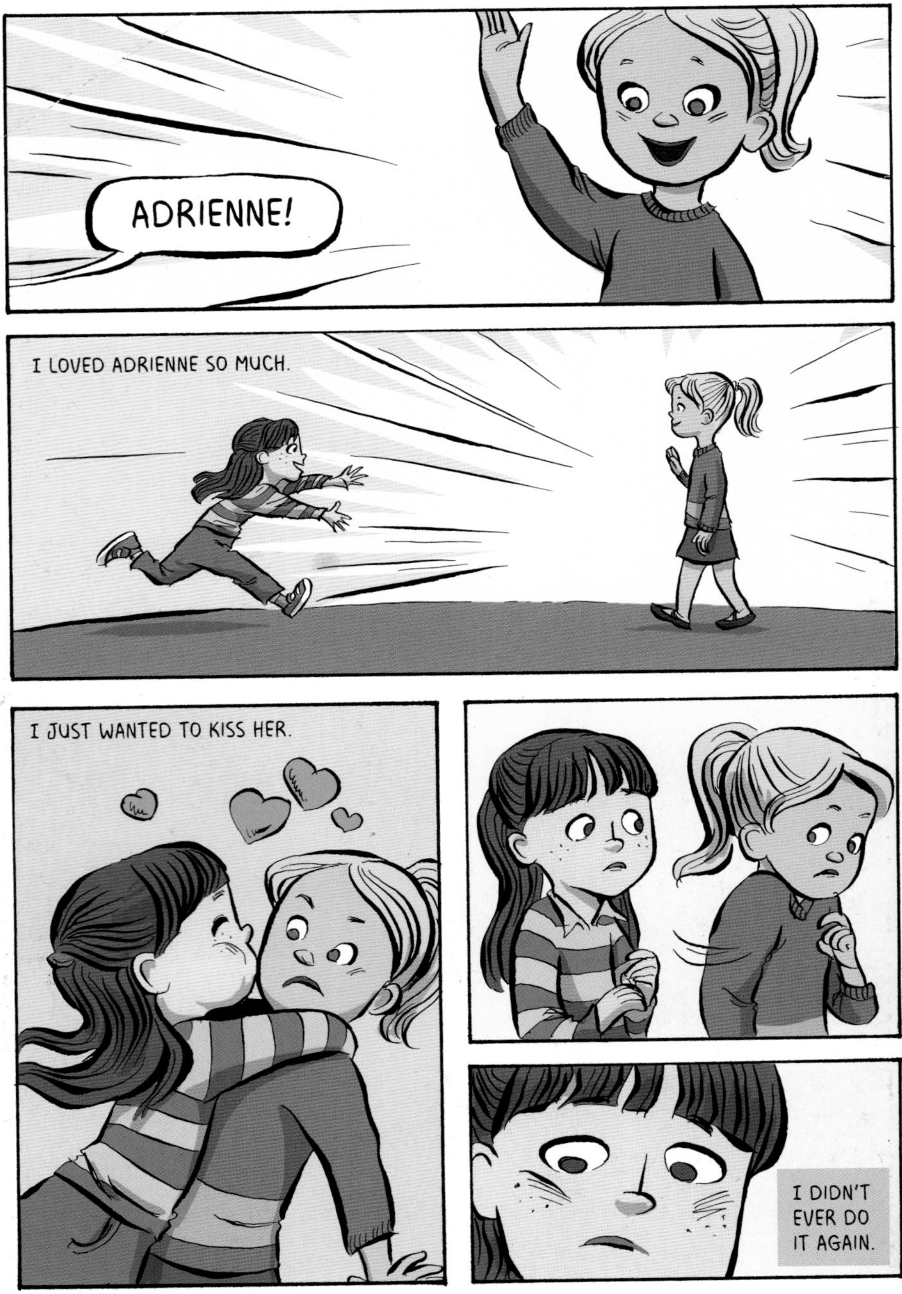
ADRIENNE!
I LOVED ADRIENNE SO MUCH.
I JUST WANTED TO KISS HER.
I DIDN'T EVER DO IT AGAIN.

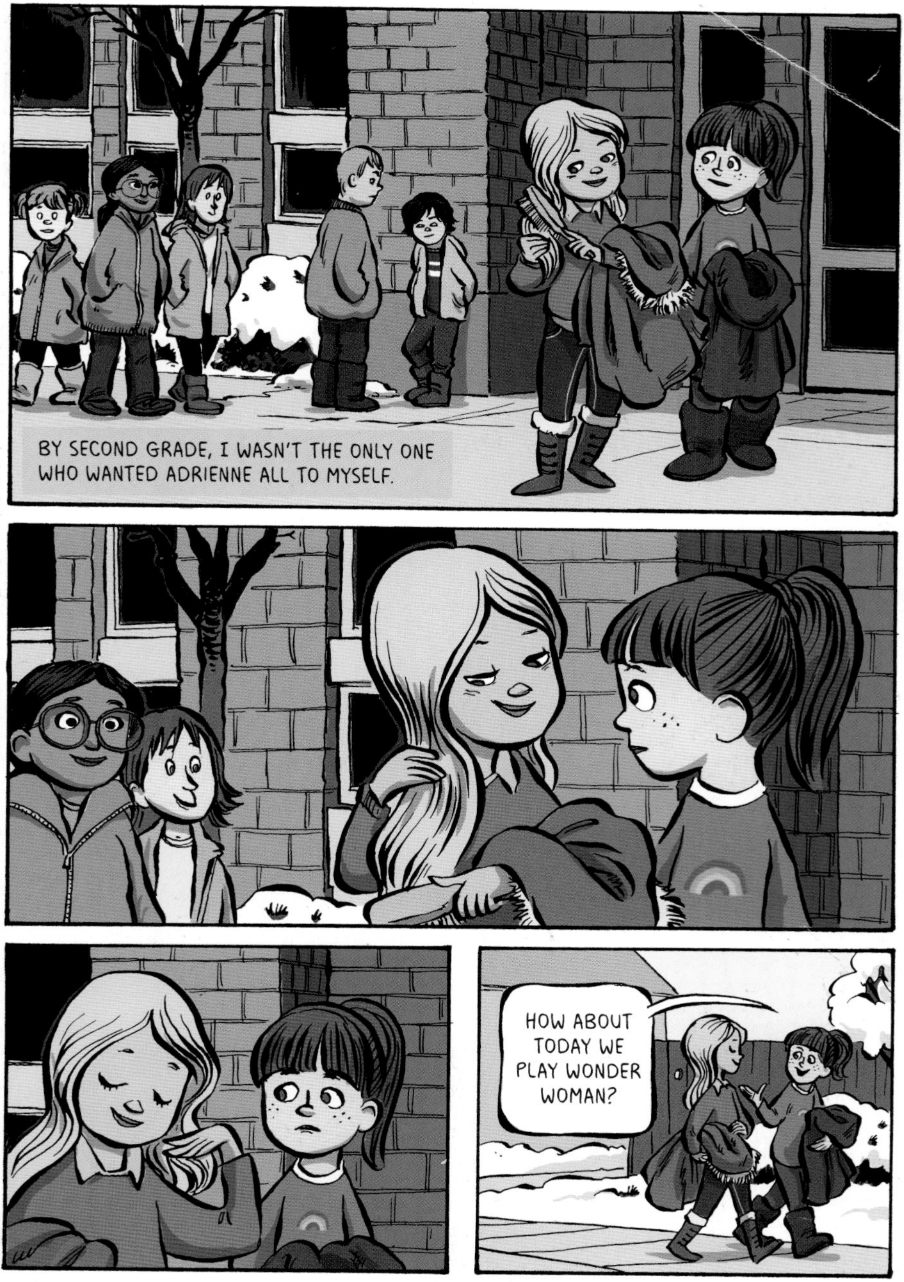
BY SECOND GRADE, I WASN'T THE ONLY ONE WHO WANTED ADRIENNE ALL TO MYSELF.
HOW ABOUT TODAY WE PLAY WONDER WOMAN?

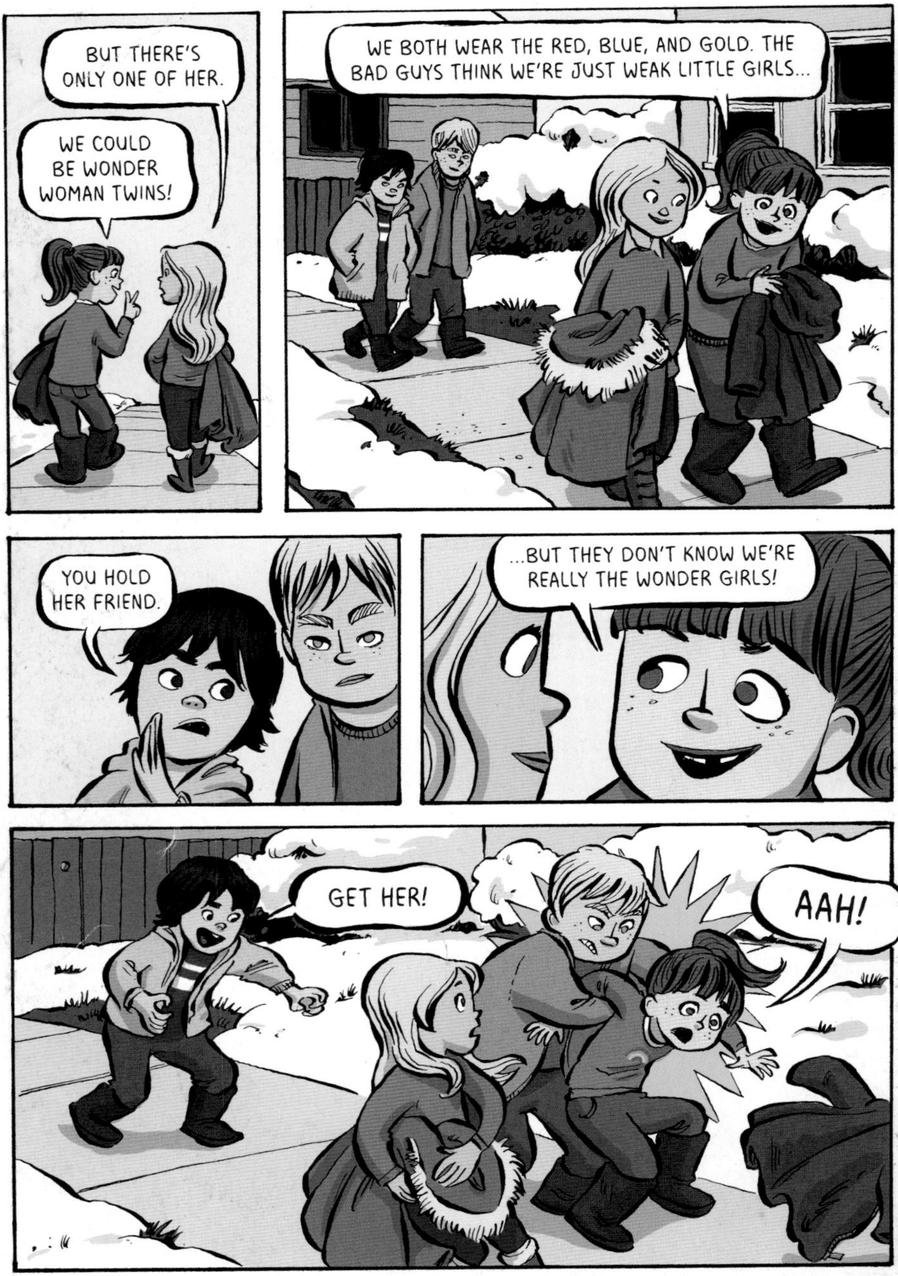
BUT THERE'S ONLY ONE OF HER.
WE COULD BE WONDER WOMAN TWINS!
WE BOTH WEAR THE RED, BLUE, AND GOLD. THE BAD GUYS THINK WE'RE JUST WEAK LITTLE GIRLS...
YOU HOLD HER FRIEND.
...BUT THEY DON'T KNOW WE'RE REALLY THE WONDER GIRLS!
GET HER!
AAH!

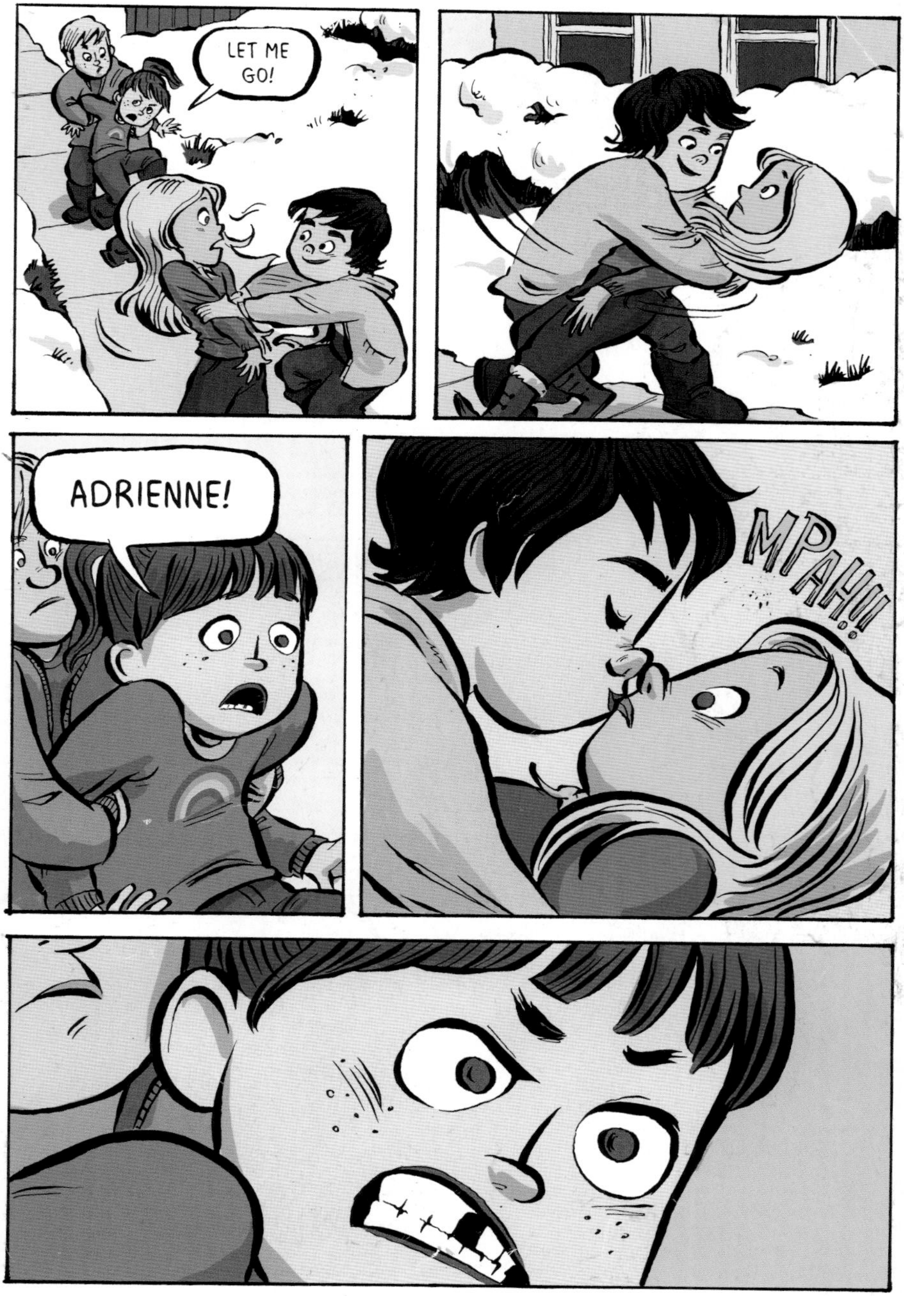
LET ME GO!
ADRIENNE!
MPAH!!!

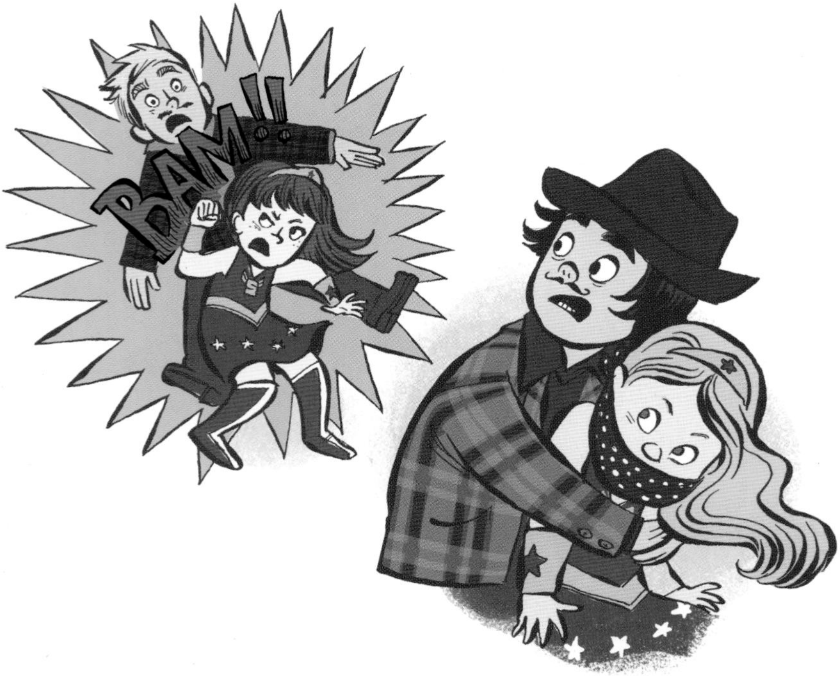
BAM!!
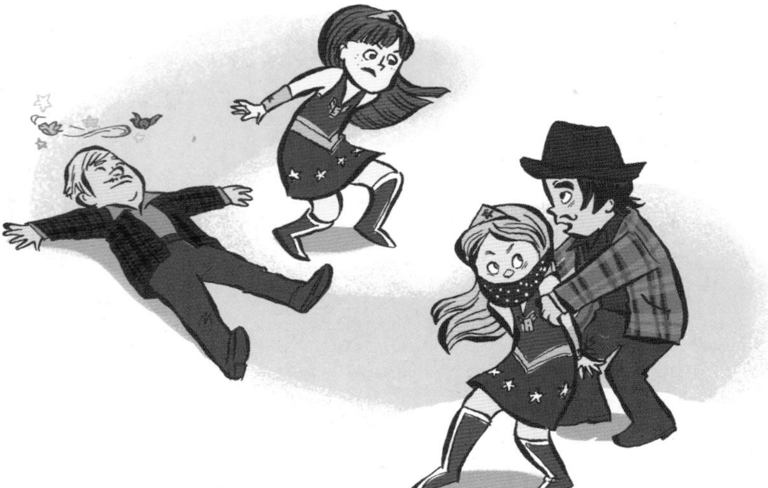

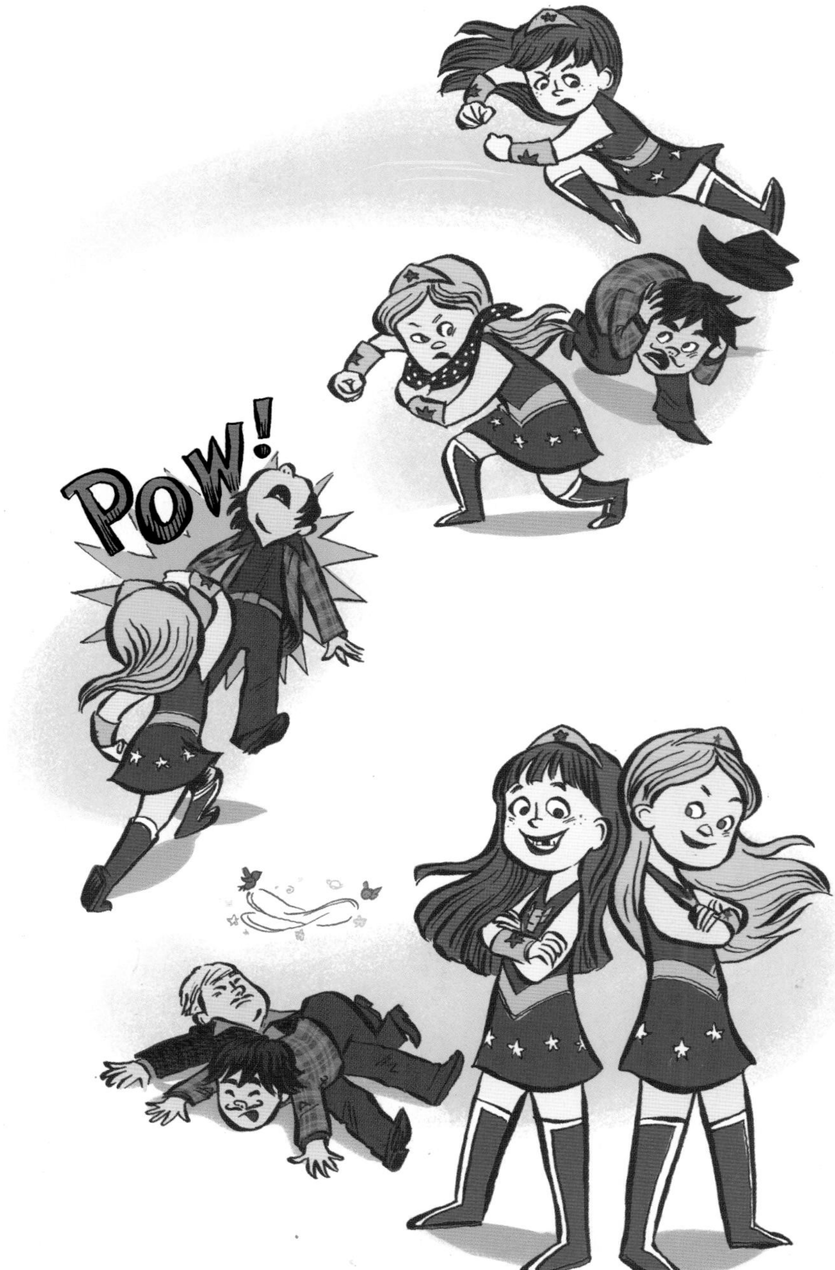
POW!

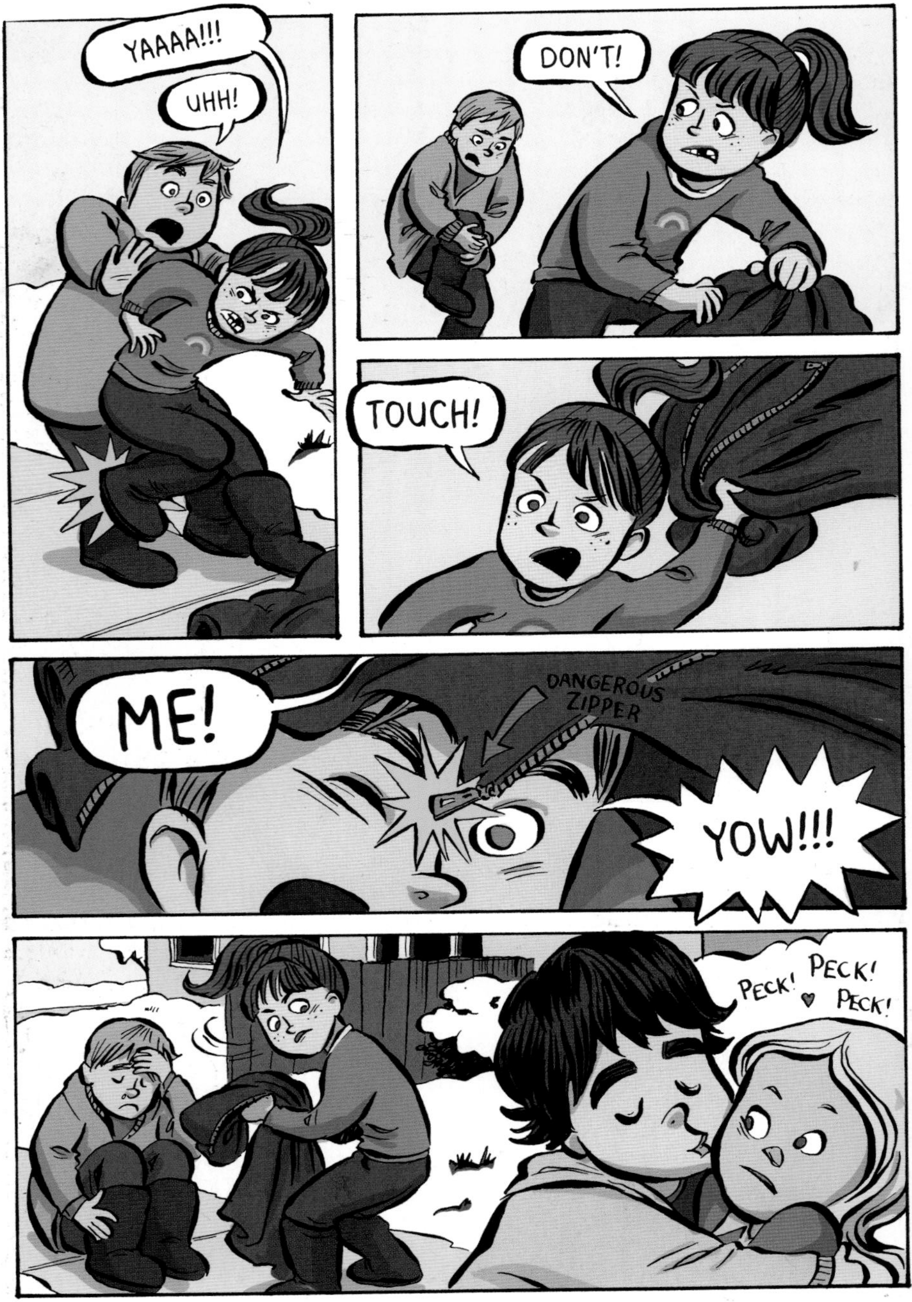
YAAAA!!!
UHH!
DON'T!
TOUCH!
ME!
DANGEROUS ZIPPER
YOW!!!
PECK!
PECK!
PECK!

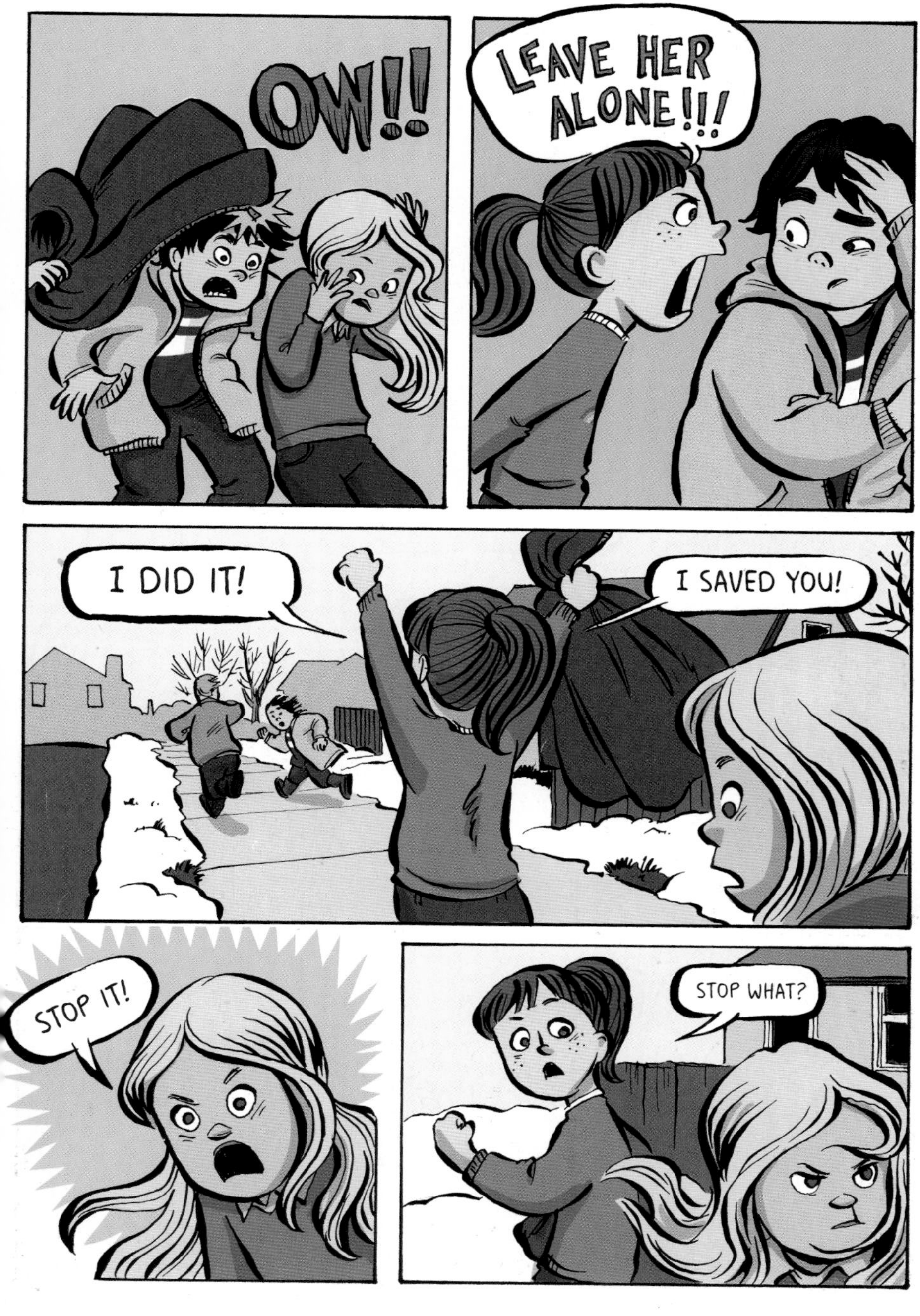
OW!!
LEAVE HER ALONE!!!
I DID IT!
I SAVED YOU!
STOP IT!
STOP WHAT?

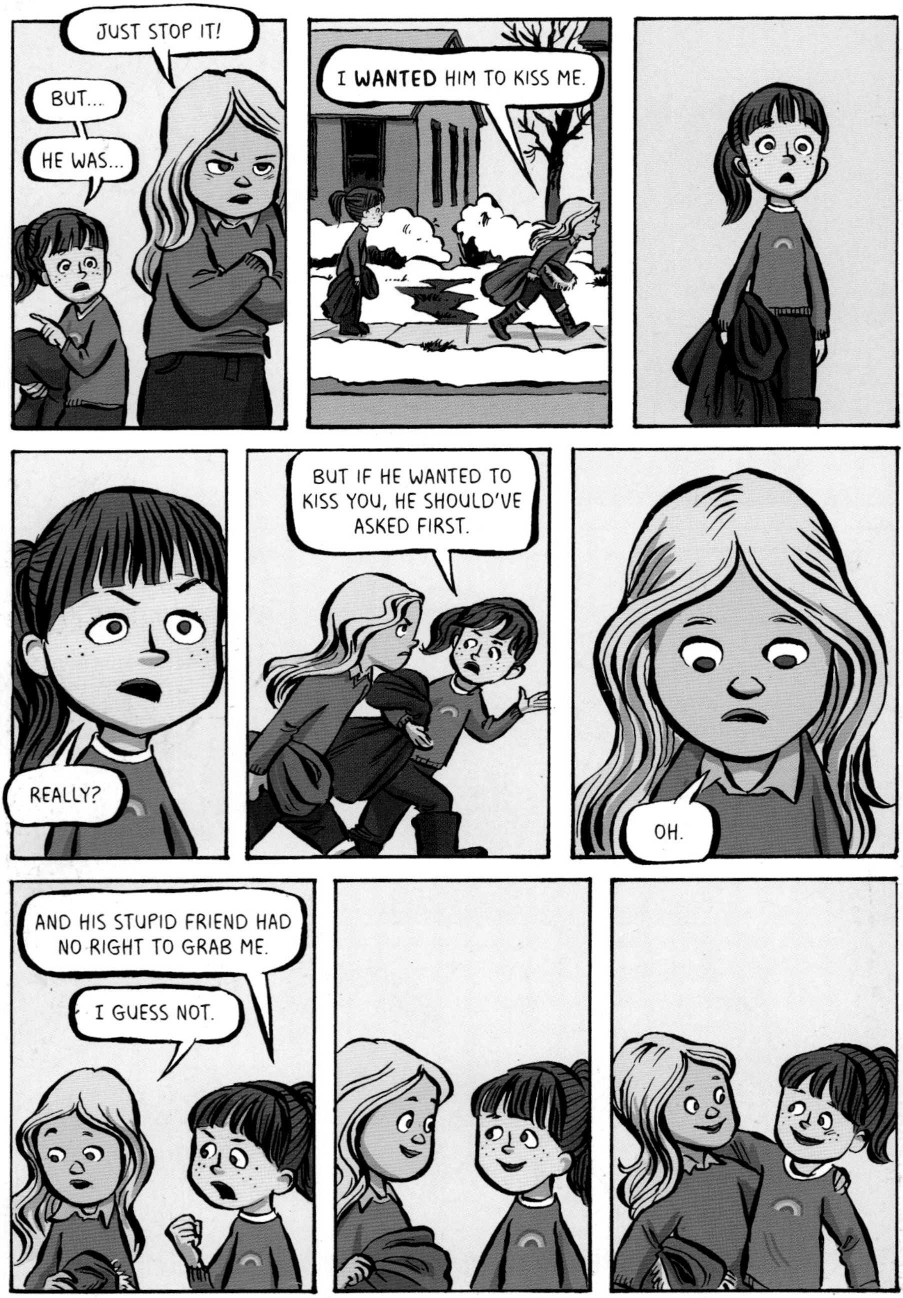
JUST STOP IT!
BUT....
HE WAS...
I WANTED HIM TO KISS ME.
REALLY?
BUT IF HE WANTED TO KISS YOU, HE SHOULD'VE ASKED FIRST.
OH.
AND HIS STUPID FRIEND HAD NO RIGHT TO GRAB ME.
I GUESS NOT.

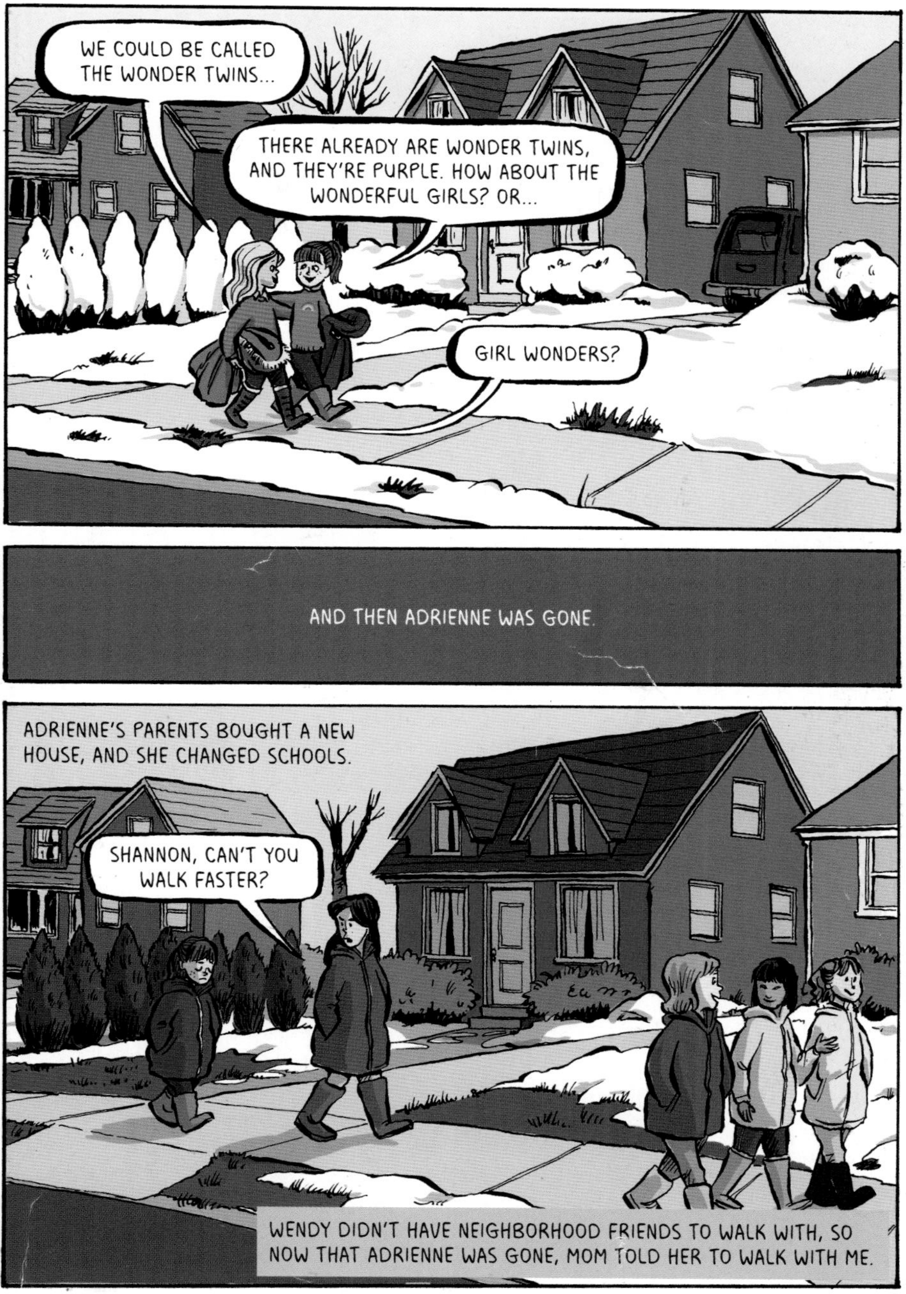
WE COULD BE CALLED THE WONDER TWINS...
THERE ALREADY ARE WONDER TWINS, AND THEY'RE PURPLE. HOW ABOUT THE WONDERFUL GIRLS? OR...
GIRL WONDERS?
AND THEN ADRIENNE WAS GONE.
ADRIENNE'S PARENTS BOUGHT A NEW HOUSE, AND SHE CHANGED SCHOOLS.
SHANNON, CAN'T YOU WALK FASTER?
WENDY DIDN'T HAVE NEIGHBORHOOD FRIENDS TO WALK WITH, SO NOW THAT ADRIENNE WAS GONE, MOM TOLD HER TO WALK WITH ME.

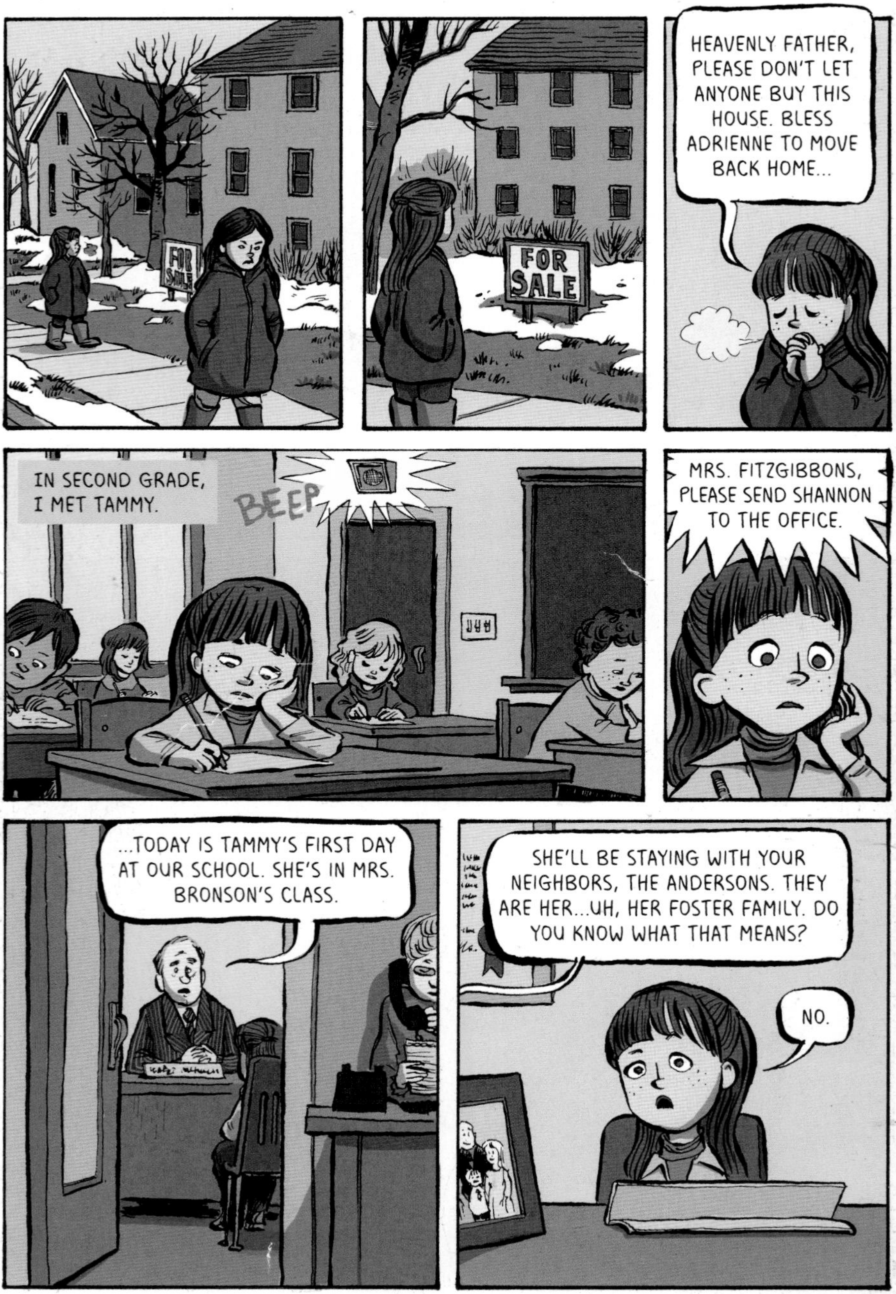
HEAVENLY FATHER, PLEASE DON'T LET ANYONE BUY THIS HOUSE. BLESS ADRIENNE TO MOVE BACK HOME...
FOR SALE
IN SECOND GRADE, I MET TAMMY.
BEEP
MRS. FITZGIBBONS, PLEASE SEND SHANNON TO THE OFFICE.
...TODAY IS TAMMY'S FIRST DAY AT OUR SCHOOL. SHE'S IN MRS. BRONSON'S CLASS.
SHE'LL BE STAYING WITH YOUR NEIGHBORS, THE ANDERSONS. THEY ARE HER...UH, HER FOSTER FAMILY. DO YOU KNOW WHAT THAT MEANS?
NO.

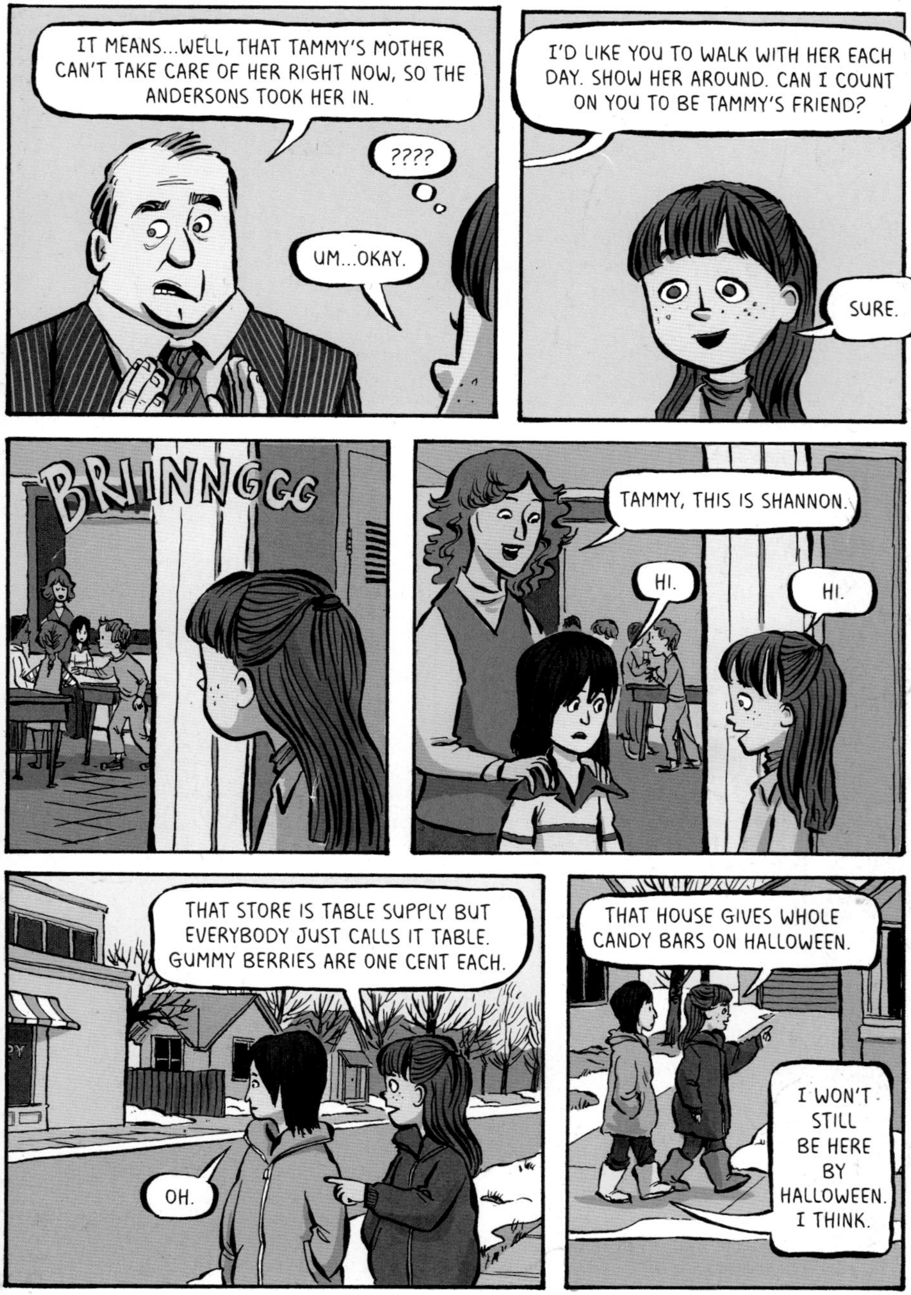
IT MEANS...WELL, THAT TAMMY'S MOTHER CAN'T TAKE CARE OF HER RIGHT NOW, SO THE ANDERSONS TOOK HER IN.
????
UM...OKAY.
I'D LIKE YOU TO WALK WITH HER EACH DAY. SHOW HER AROUND. CAN I COUNT ON YOU TO BE TAMMY'S FRIEND?
SURE.
BRINNGGG
TAMMY, THIS IS SHANNON.
HI.
HI.
THAT STORE IS TABLE SUPPLY BUT EVERYBODY JUST CALLS IT TABLE. GUMMY BERRIES ARE ONE CENT EACH.
OH.
THAT HOUSE GIVES WHOLE CANDY BARS ON HALLOWEEN.
I WON'T STILL BE HERE BY HALLOWEEN. I THINK.

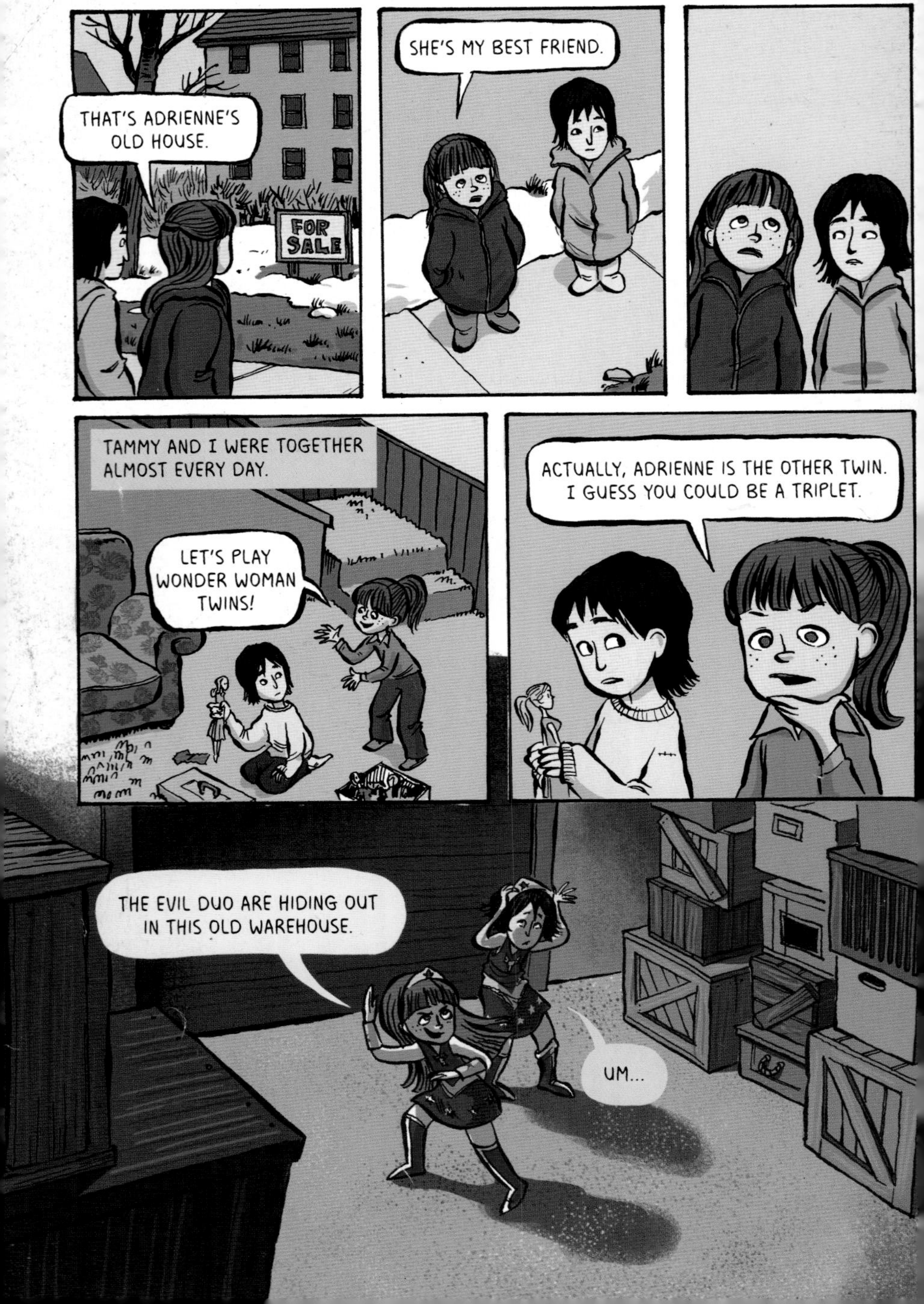
THAT'S ADRIENNE'S OLD HOUSE.
FOR SALE
SHE'S MY BEST FRIEND.
TAMMY AND I WERE TOGETHER ALMOST EVERY DAY.
LET'S PLAY WONDER WOMAN TWINS!
ACTUALLY, ADRIENNE IS THE OTHER TWIN. I GUESS YOU COULD BE A TRIPLET.
THE EVIL DUO ARE HIDING OUT IN THIS OLD WAREHOUSE.
UM...

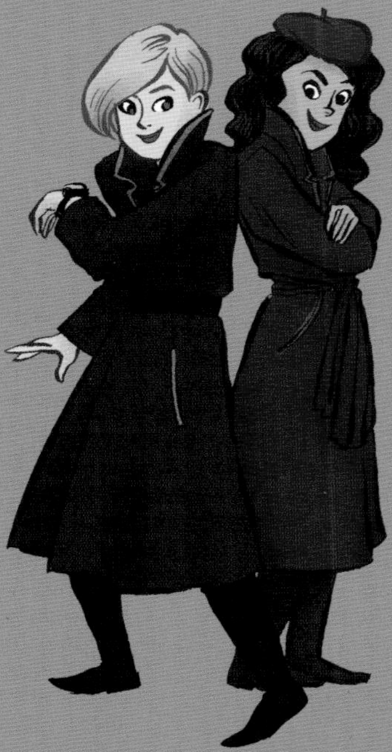

# ZARA & VERONICA

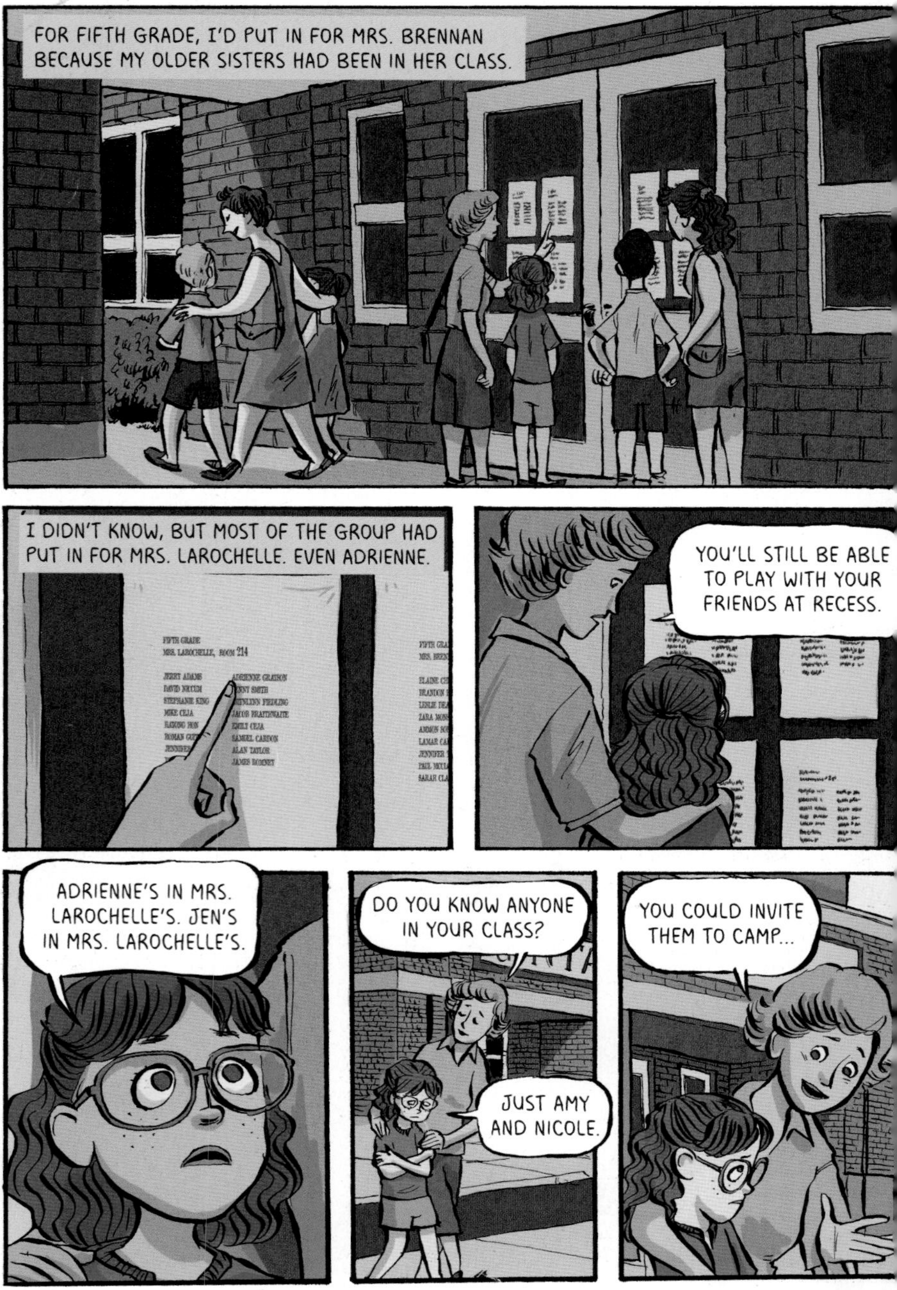
FOR FIFTH GRADE, I'D PUT IN FOR MRS. BRENNAN BECAUSE MY OLDER SISTERS HAD BEEN IN HER CLASS.
I DIDN'T KNOW, BUT MOST OF THE GROUP HAD PUT IN FOR MRS. LAROCHELLE. EVEN ADRIENNE.
FIFTH GRADE
MRS. LAROCHELLE, ROOM 214
YOU'LL STILL BE ABLE TO PLAY WITH YOUR FRIENDS AT RECESS.
ADRIENNE'S IN MRS. LAROCHELLE'S. JEN'S IN MRS. LAROCHELLE'S.
DO YOU KNOW ANYONE IN YOUR CLASS?
JUST AMY AND NICOLE.
YOU COULD INVITE THEM TO CAMP...

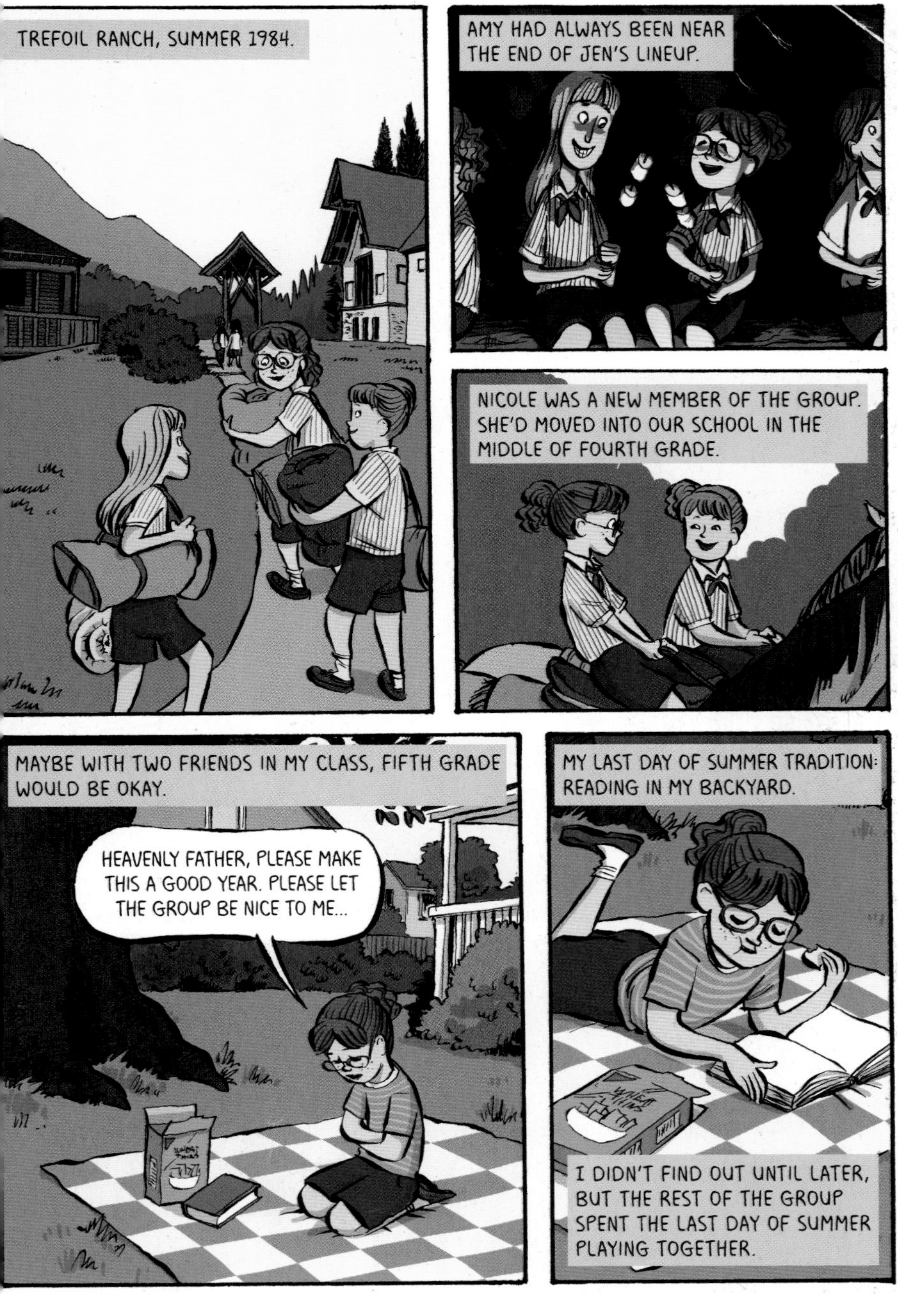
TREFOIL RANCH, SUMMER 1984.
AMY HAD ALWAYS BEEN NEAR THE END OF JEN'S LINEUP.
NICOLE WAS A NEW MEMBER OF THE GROUP. SHE'D MOVED INTO OUR SCHOOL IN THE MIDDLE OF FOURTH GRADE.
MAYBE WITH TWO FRIENDS IN MY CLASS, FIFTH GRADE WOULD BE OKAY.
HEAVENLY FATHER, PLEASE MAKE THIS A GOOD YEAR. PLEASE LET THE GROUP BE NICE TO ME...
MY LAST DAY OF SUMMER TRADITION: READING IN MY BACKYARD.
I DIDN'T FIND OUT UNTIL LATER, BUT THE REST OF THE GROUP SPENT THE LAST DAY OF SUMMER PLAYING TOGETHER.

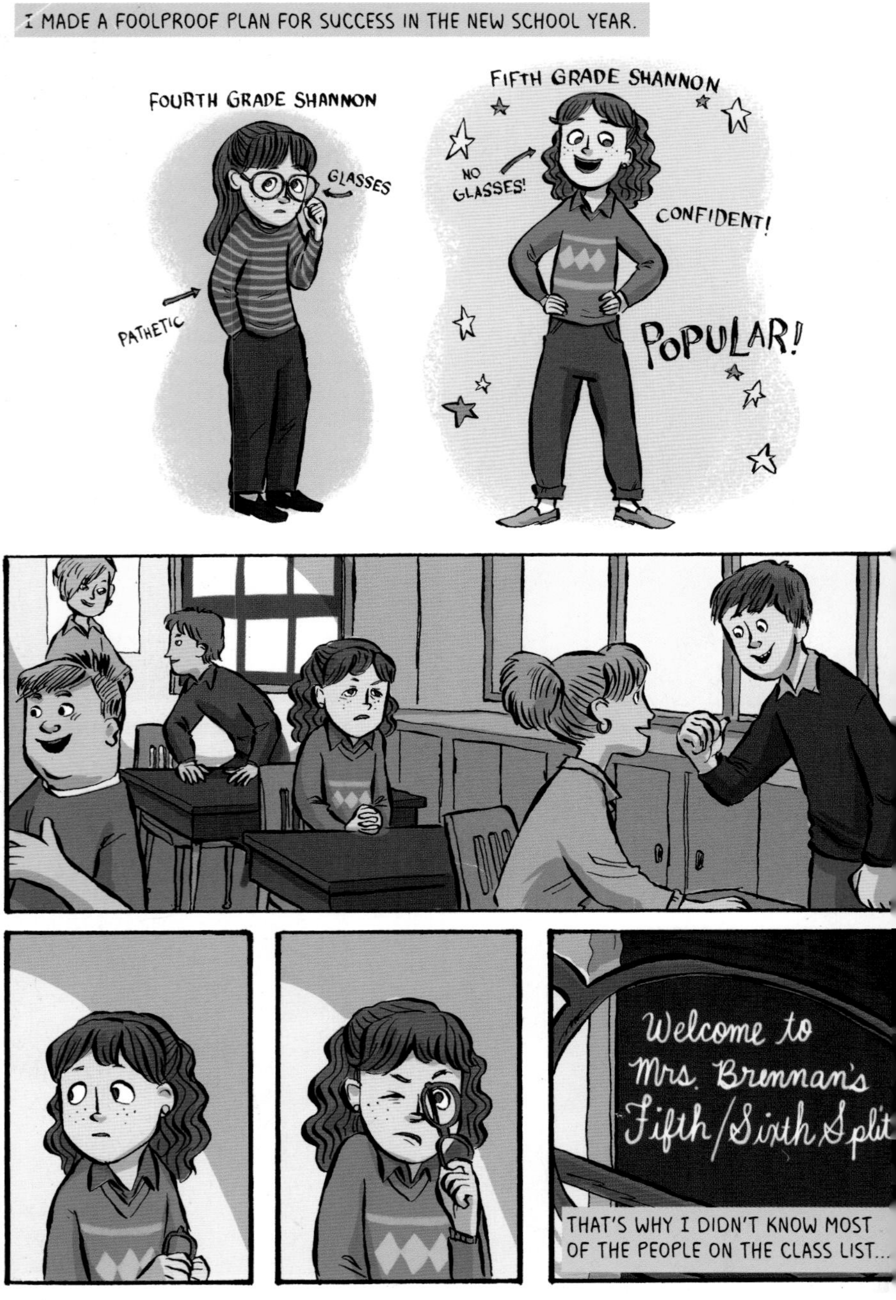
I MADE A FOOLPROOF PLAN FOR SUCCESS IN THE NEW SCHOOL YEAR.
FOURTH GRADE SHANNON
GLASSES
PATHETIC
FIFTH GRADE SHANNON
NO GLASSES!
CONFIDENT!
POPULAR!
Welcome to Mrs. Brennan's Fifth/Sixth Split
THAT'S WHY I DIDN'T KNOW MOST OF THE PEOPLE ON THE CLASS LIST...

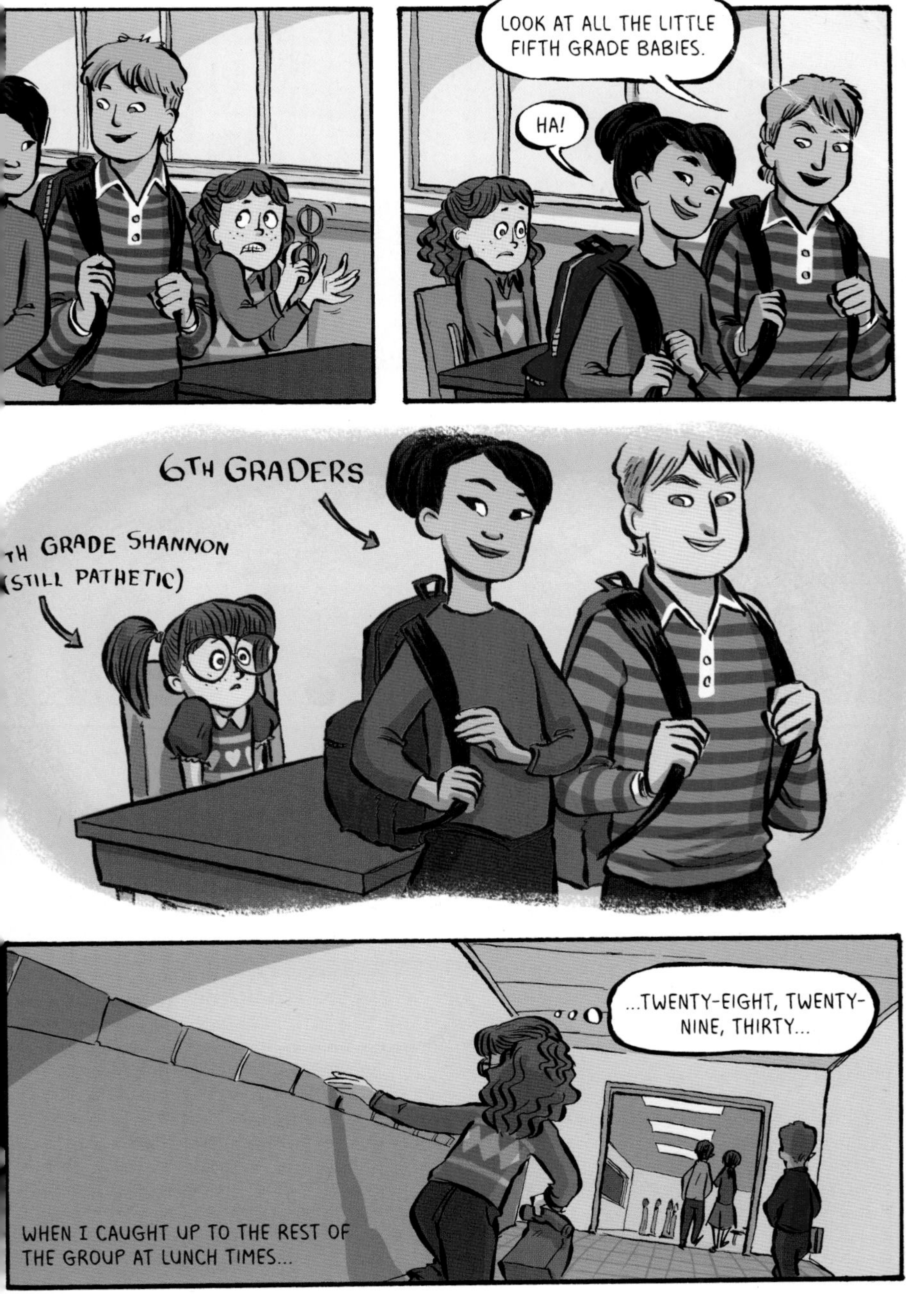

LOOK AT ALL THE LITTLE FIFTH GRADE BABIES.
HA!
6TH GRADERS
TH GRADE SHANNON (STILL PATHETIC)
...TWENTY-EIGHT, TWENTY-NINE, THIRTY...
WHEN I CAUGHT UP TO THE REST OF THE GROUP AT LUNCH TIMES...

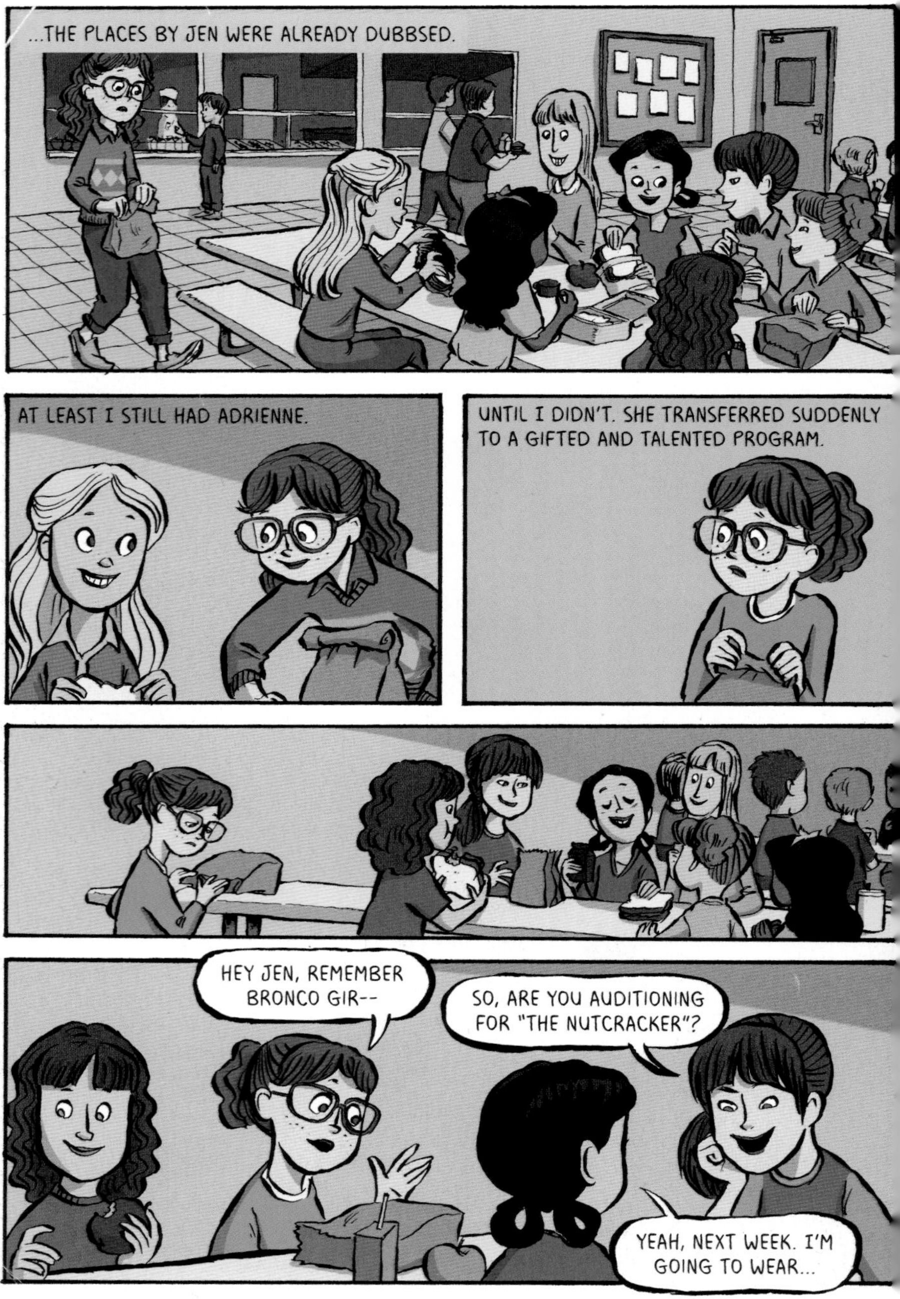
...THE PLACES BY JEN WERE ALREADY DUBBSED.
AT LEAST I STILL HAD ADRIENNE.
UNTIL I DIDN'T. SHE TRANSFERRED SUDDENLY TO A GIFTED AND TALENTED PROGRAM.
HEY JEN, REMEMBER BRONCO GIR--
SO, ARE YOU AUDITIONING FOR "THE NUTCRACKER"?
YEAH, NEXT WEEK. I'M GOING TO WEAR...

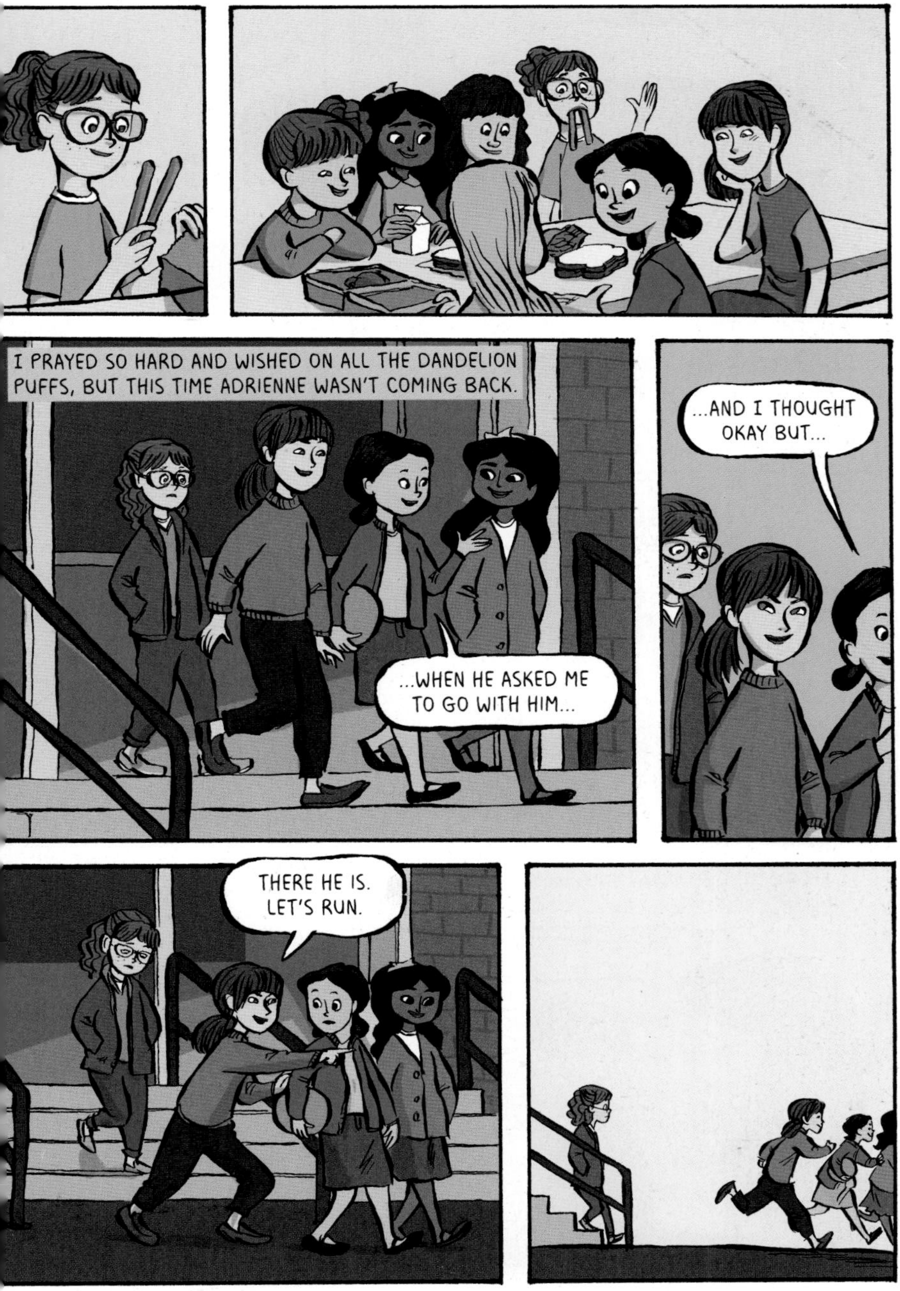
I PRAYED SO HARD AND WISHED ON ALL THE DANDELION PUFFS, BUT THIS TIME ADRIENNE WASN'T COMING BACK.
...WHEN HE ASKED ME TO GO WITH HIM...
...AND I THOUGHT OKAY BUT...
THERE HE IS. LET'S RUN.

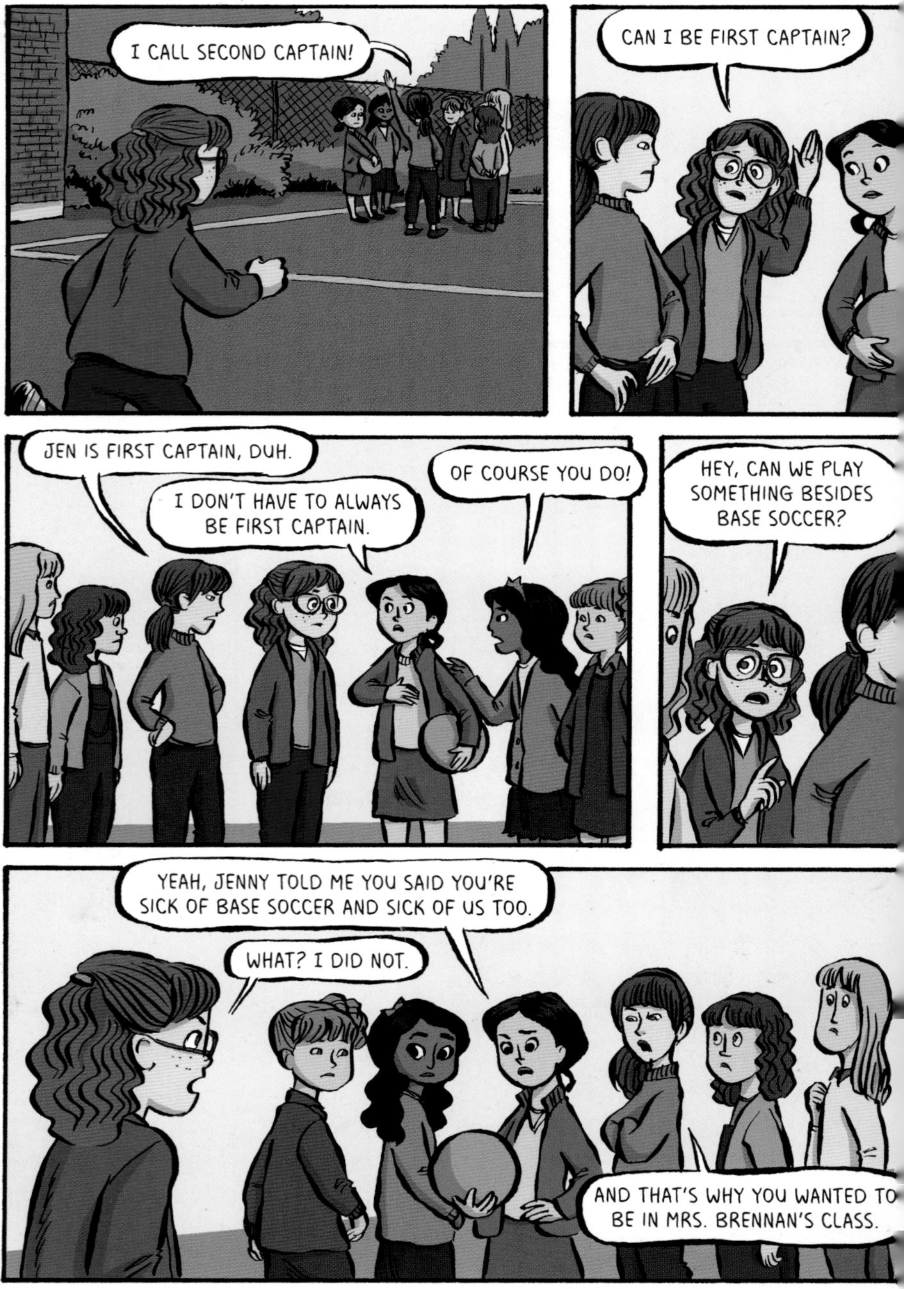
I CALL SECOND CAPTAIN!
CAN I BE FIRST CAPTAIN?
JEN IS FIRST CAPTAIN, DUH.
I DON'T HAVE TO ALWAYS BE FIRST CAPTAIN.
OF COURSE YOU DO!
HEY, CAN WE PLAY SOMETHING BESIDES BASE SOCCER?
YEAH, JENNY TOLD ME YOU SAID YOU'RE SICK OF BASE SOCCER AND SICK OF US TOO.
WHAT? I DID NOT.
AND THAT'S WHY YOU WANTED TO BE IN MRS. BRENNAN'S CLASS.

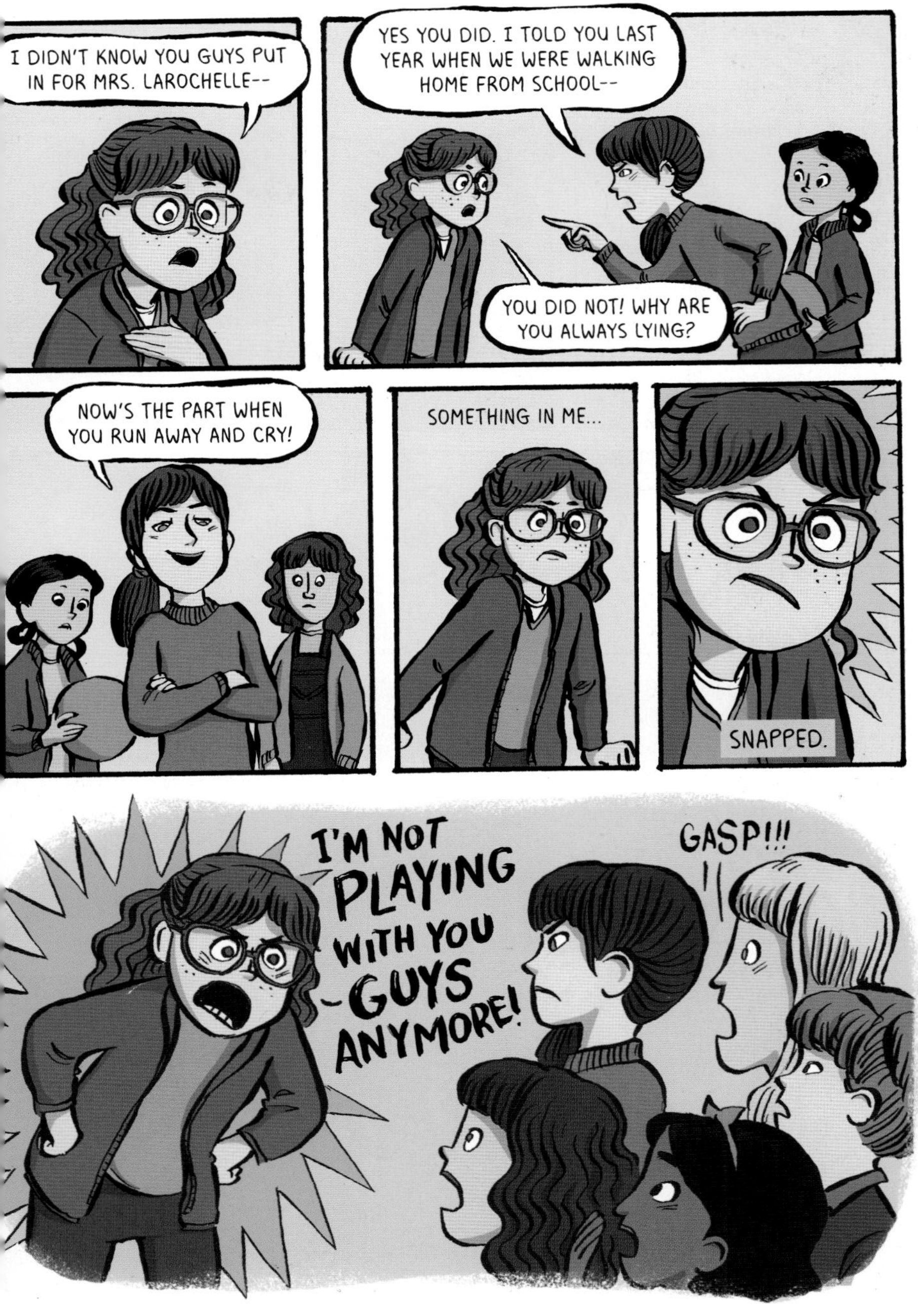
I DIDN'T KNOW YOU GUYS PUT IN FOR MRS. LAROCHELLE--
YES YOU DID. I TOLD YOU LAST YEAR WHEN WE WERE WALKING HOME FROM SCHOOL--
YOU DID NOT! WHY ARE YOU ALWAYS LYING?
NOW'S THE PART WHEN YOU RUN AWAY AND CRY!
SOMETHING IN ME...
SNAPPED.
I'M NOT PLAYING WITH YOU GUYS ANYMORE!
GASP!!!

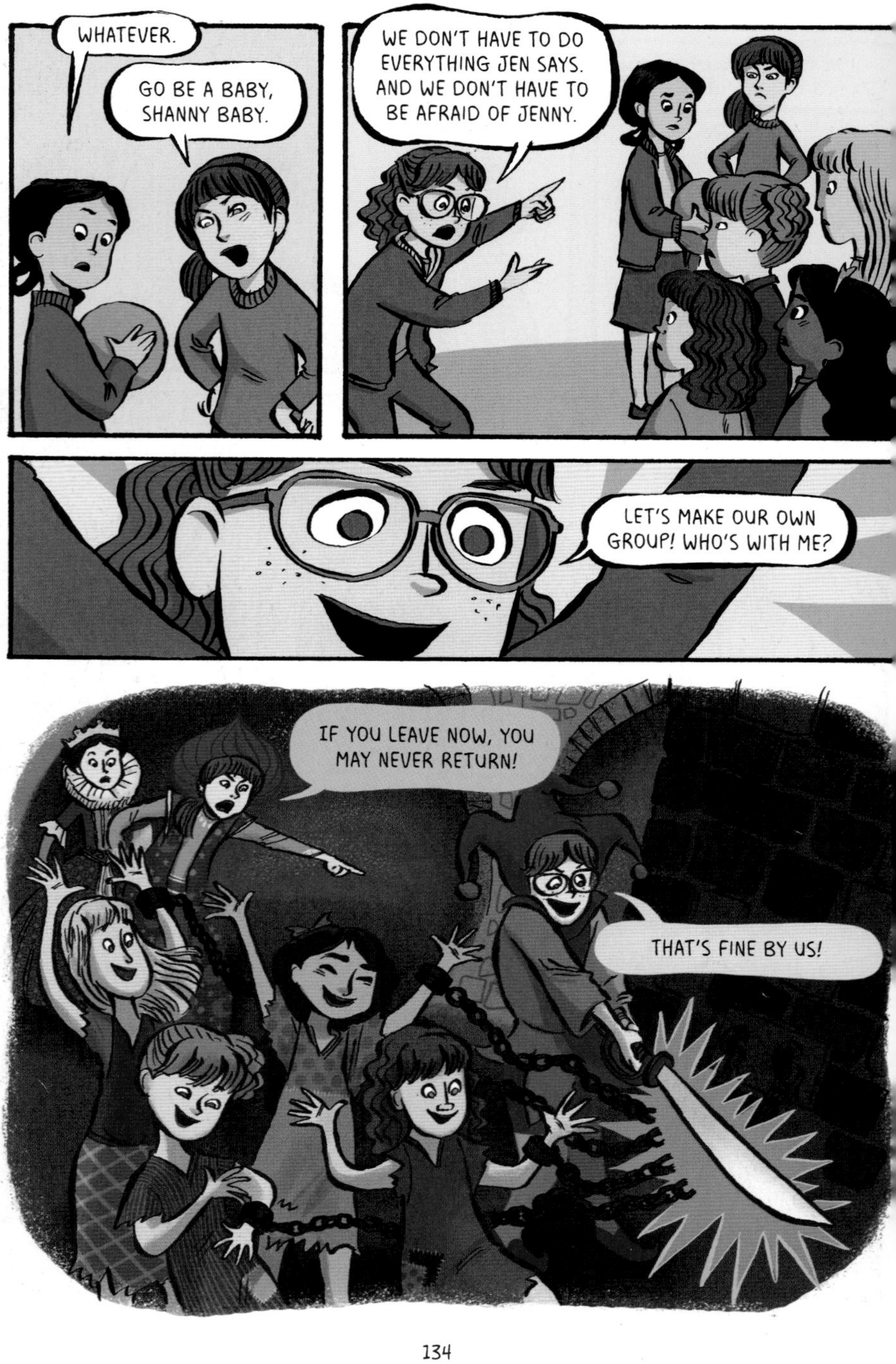
WHATEVER.
GO BE A BABY, SHANNY BABY.
WE DON'T HAVE TO DO EVERYTHING JEN SAYS. AND WE DON'T HAVE TO BE AFRAID OF JENNY.
LET'S MAKE OUR OWN GROUP! WHO'S WITH ME?
IF YOU LEAVE NOW, YOU MAY NEVER RETURN!
THAT'S FINE BY US!

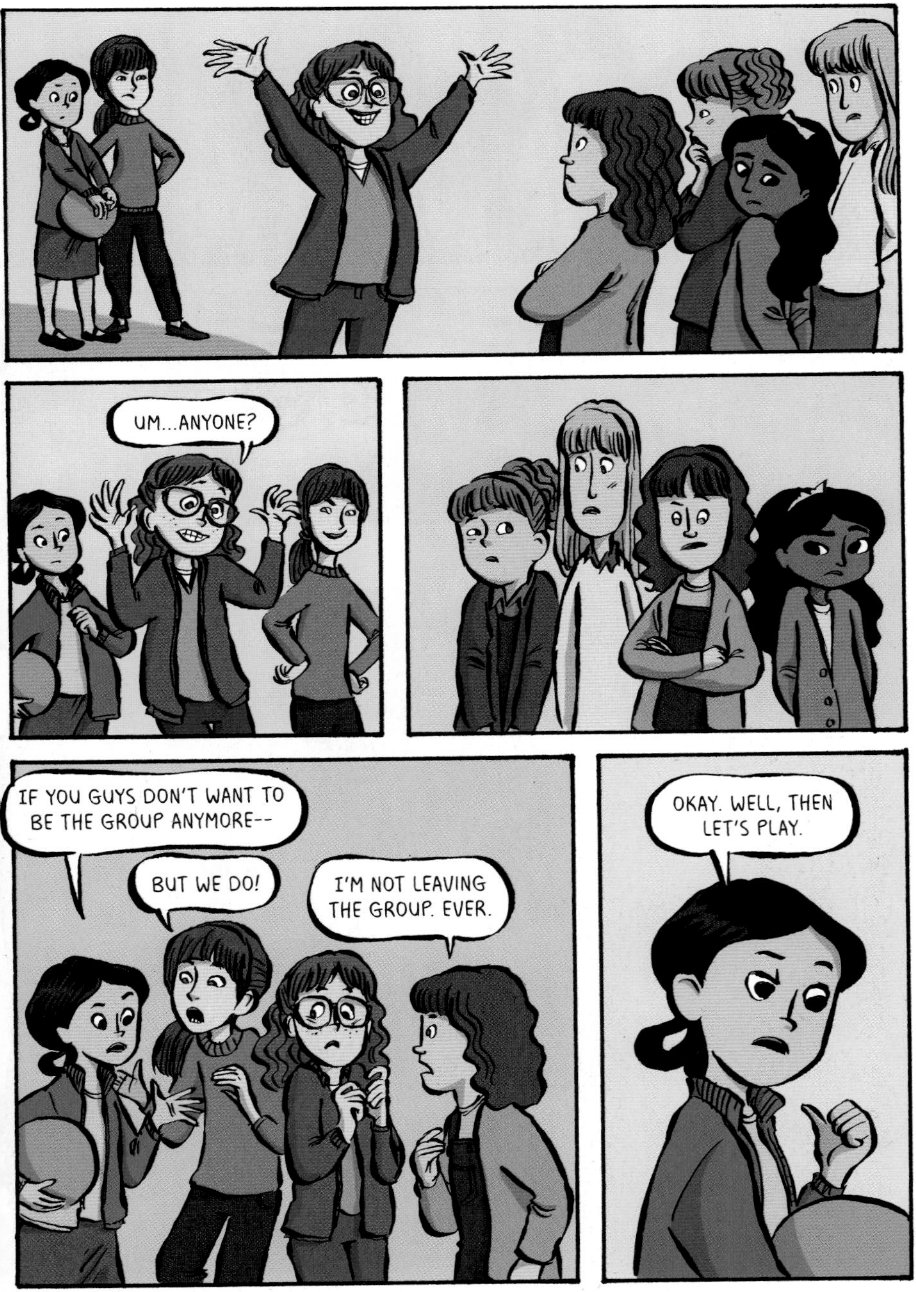
UM...ANYONE?
IF YOU GUYS DON'T WANT TO BE THE GROUP ANYMORE--
BUT WE DO!
I'M NOT LEAVING THE GROUP. EVER.
OKAY. WELL, THEN LET'S PLAY.

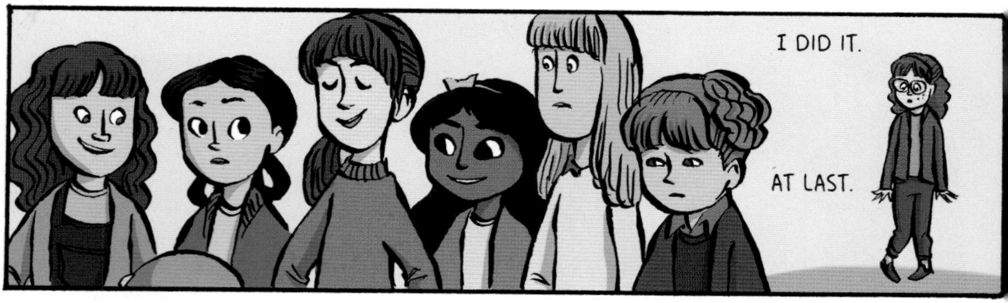
I DID IT.
AT LAST.

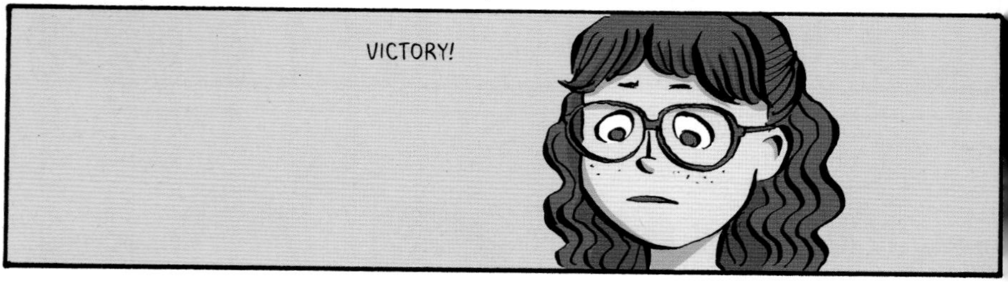
VICTORY!

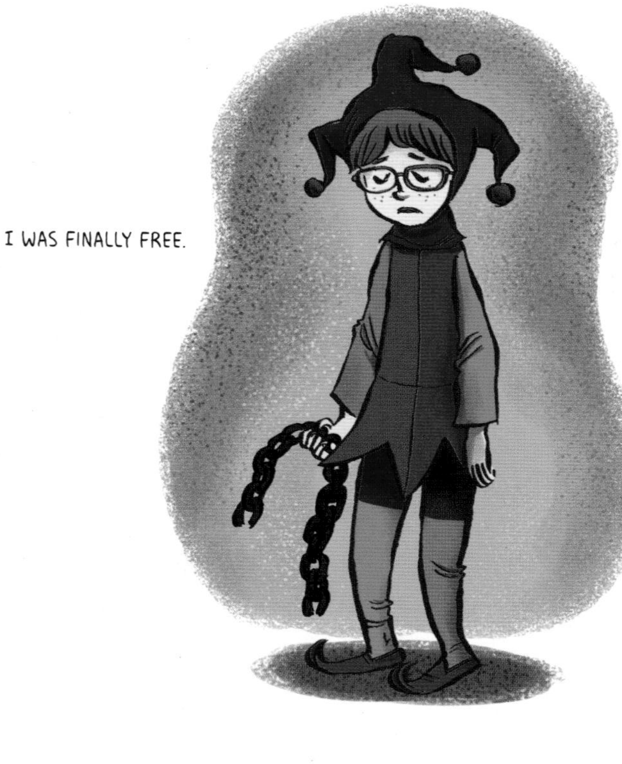
I WAS FINALLY FREE.

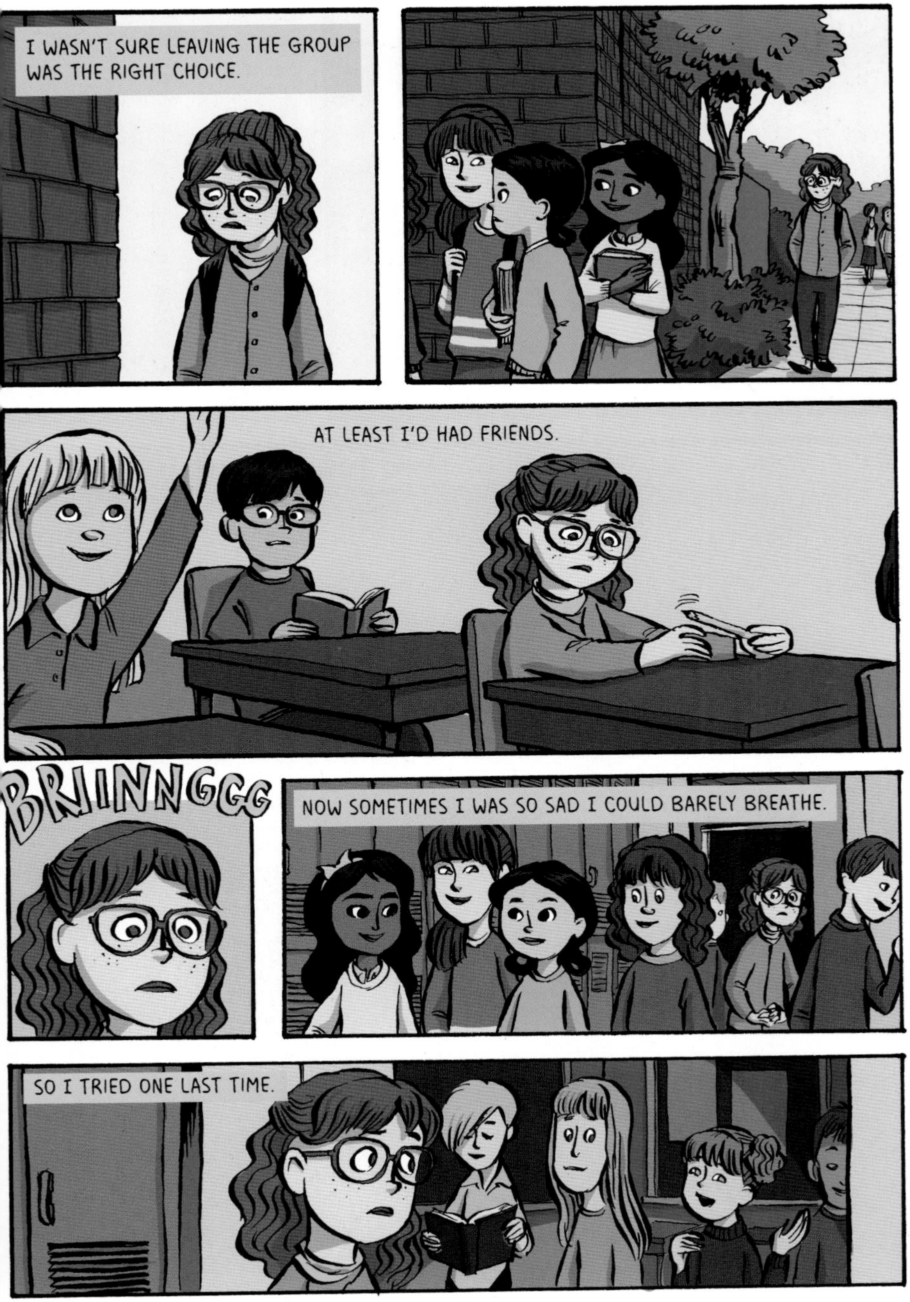

I WASN'T SURE LEAVING THE GROUP WAS THE RIGHT CHOICE.
AT LEAST I'D HAD FRIENDS.
BRINNGGG
NOW SOMETIMES I WAS SO SAD I COULD BARELY BREATHE.
SO I TRIED ONE LAST TIME.

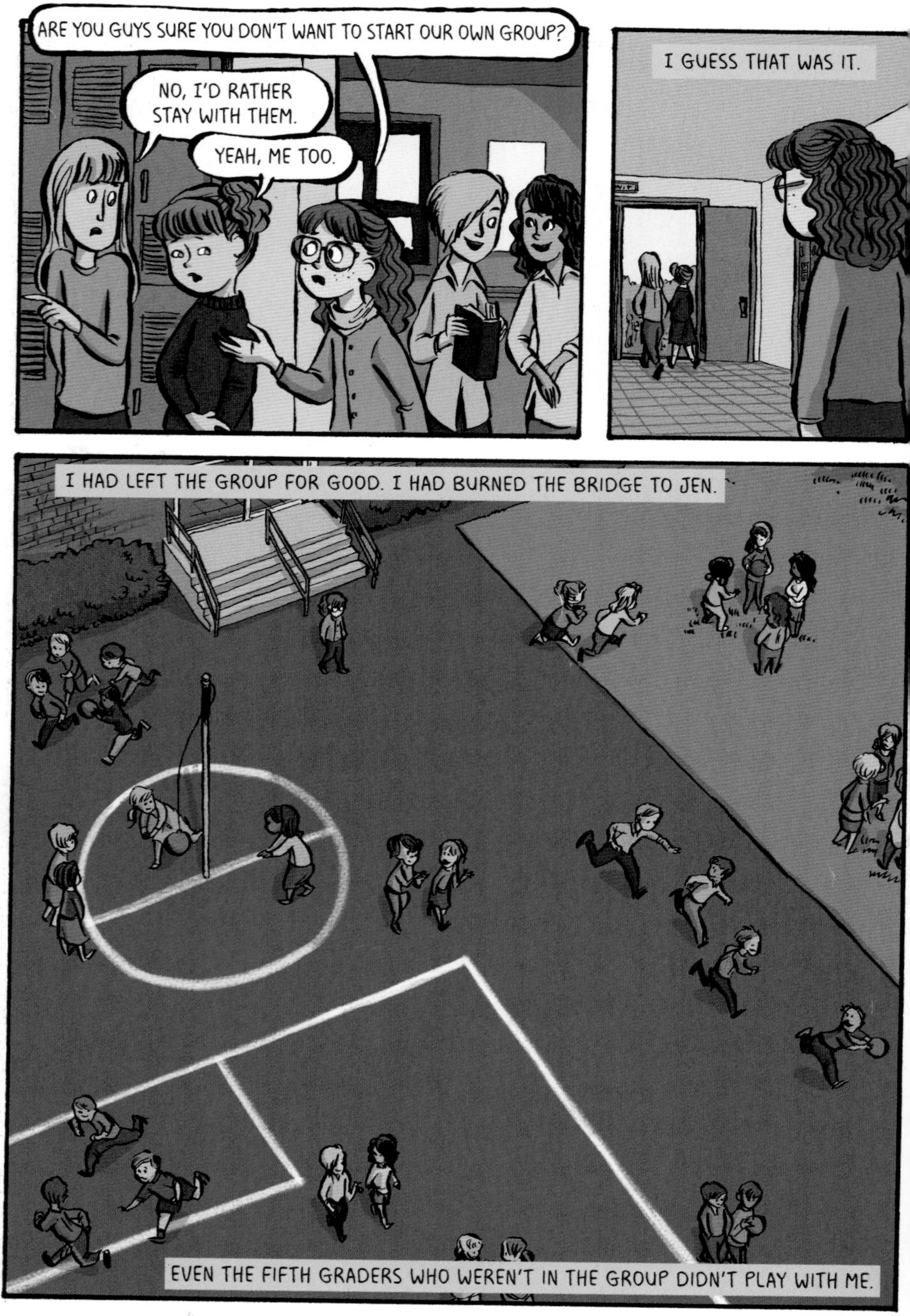
ARE YOU GUYS SURE YOU DON'T WANT TO START OUR OWN GROUP?
NO, I'D RATHER STAY WITH THEM.
YEAH, ME TOO.
I GUESS THAT WAS IT.
I HAD LEFT THE GROUP FOR GOOD. I HAD BURNED THE BRIDGE TO JEN.
EVEN THE FIFTH GRADERS WHO WEREN'T IN THE GROUP DIDN'T PLAY WITH ME.

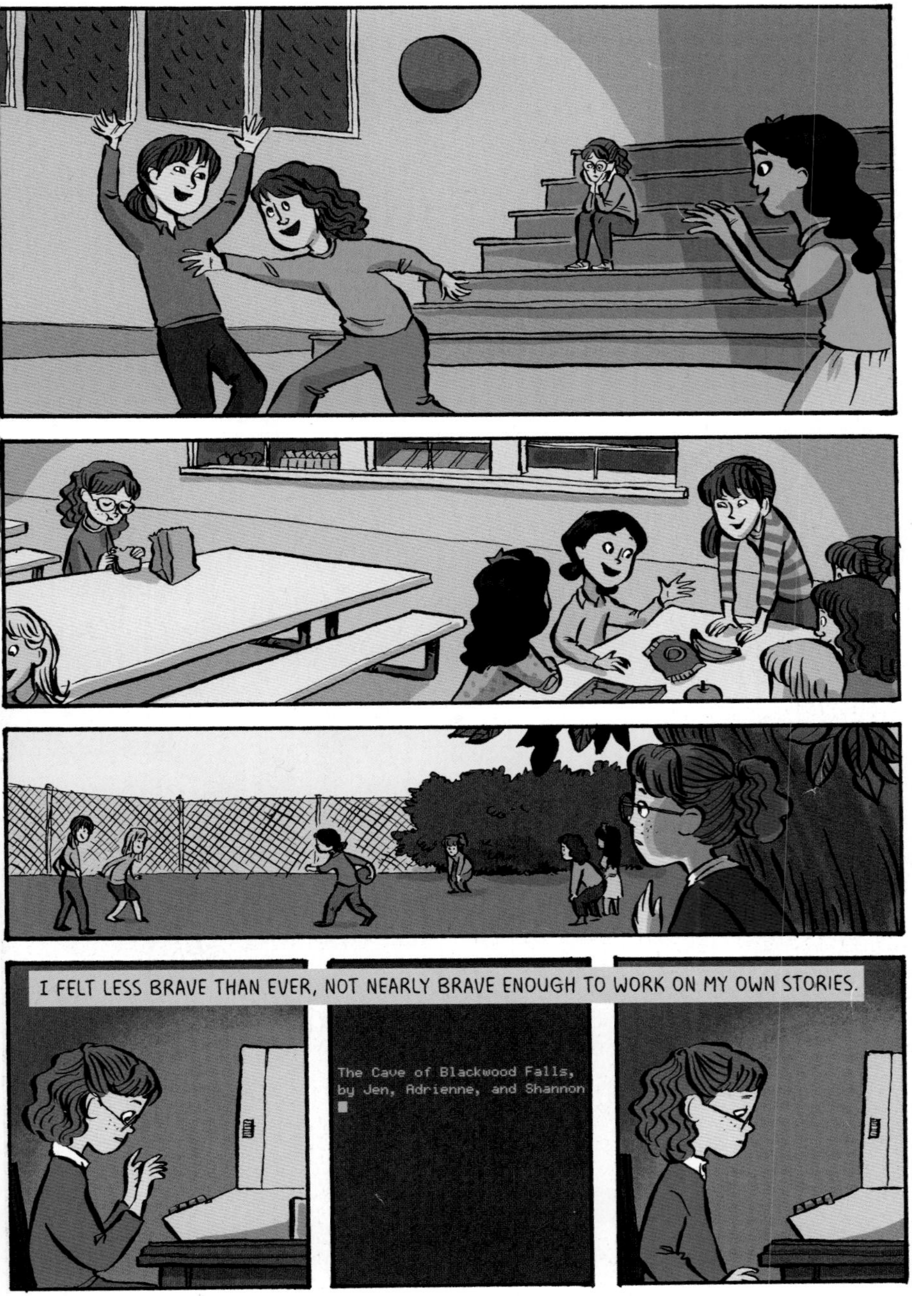
I FELT LESS BRAVE THAN EVER, NOT NEARLY BRAVE ENOUGH TO WORK ON MY OWN STORIES.
The Cave of Blackwood Falls,
by Jen, Adrienne, and Shannon

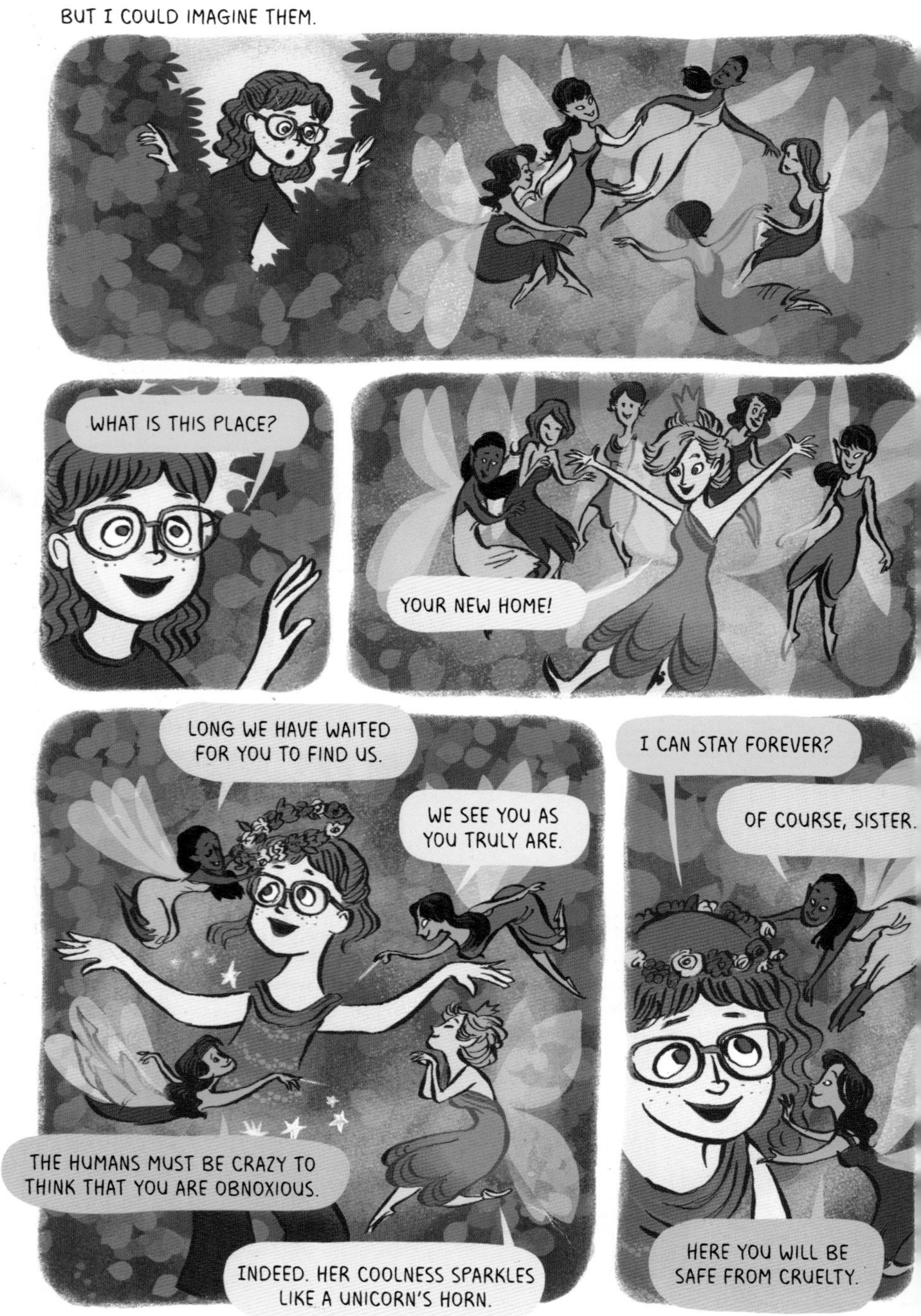
BUT I COULD IMAGINE THEM.
WHAT IS THIS PLACE?
YOUR NEW HOME!
LONG WE HAVE WAITED FOR YOU TO FIND US.
WE SEE YOU AS YOU TRULY ARE.
THE HUMANS MUST BE CRAZY TO THINK THAT YOU ARE OBNOXIOUS.
INDEED. HER COOLNESS SPARKLES LIKE A UNICORN'S HORN.
I CAN STAY FOREVER?
OF COURSE, SISTER.
HERE YOU WILL BE SAFE FROM CRUELTY.

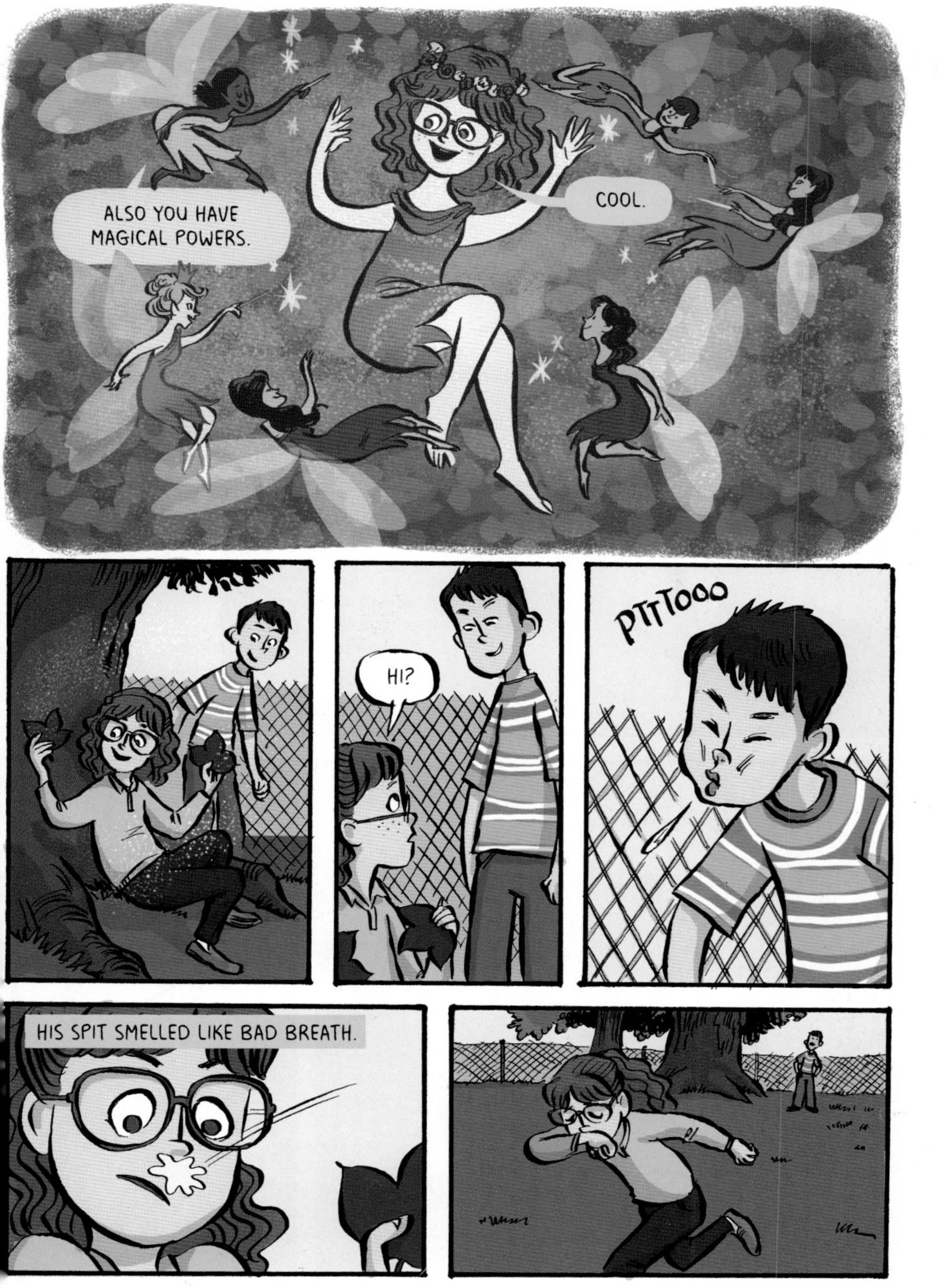
ALSO YOU HAVE MAGICAL POWERS.
COOL.
HI?
PTTTOOO
HIS SPIT SMELLED LIKE BAD BREATH.

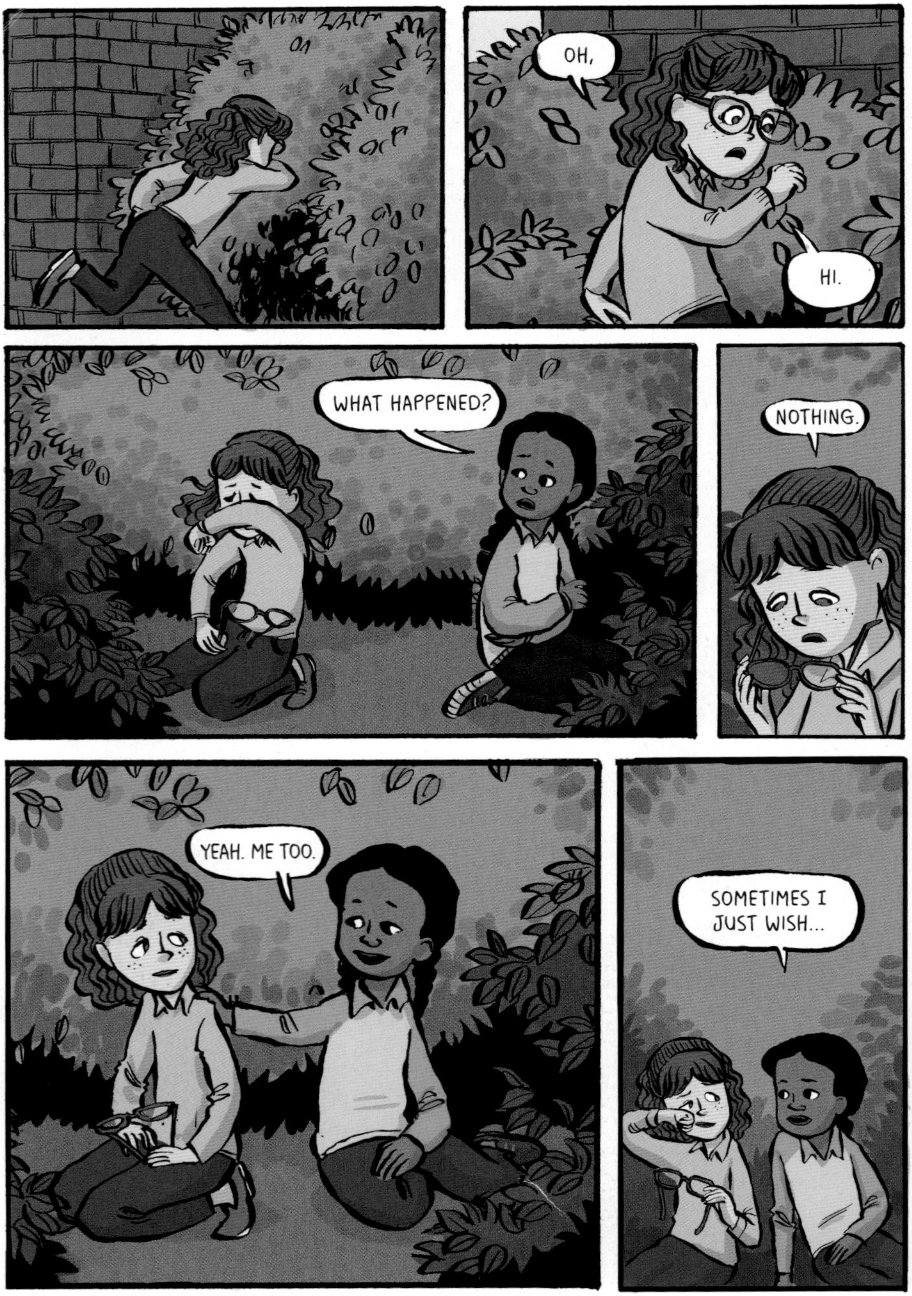
OH,
HI.
WHAT HAPPENED?
NOTHING.
YEAH. ME TOO.
SOMETIMES I JUST WISH...

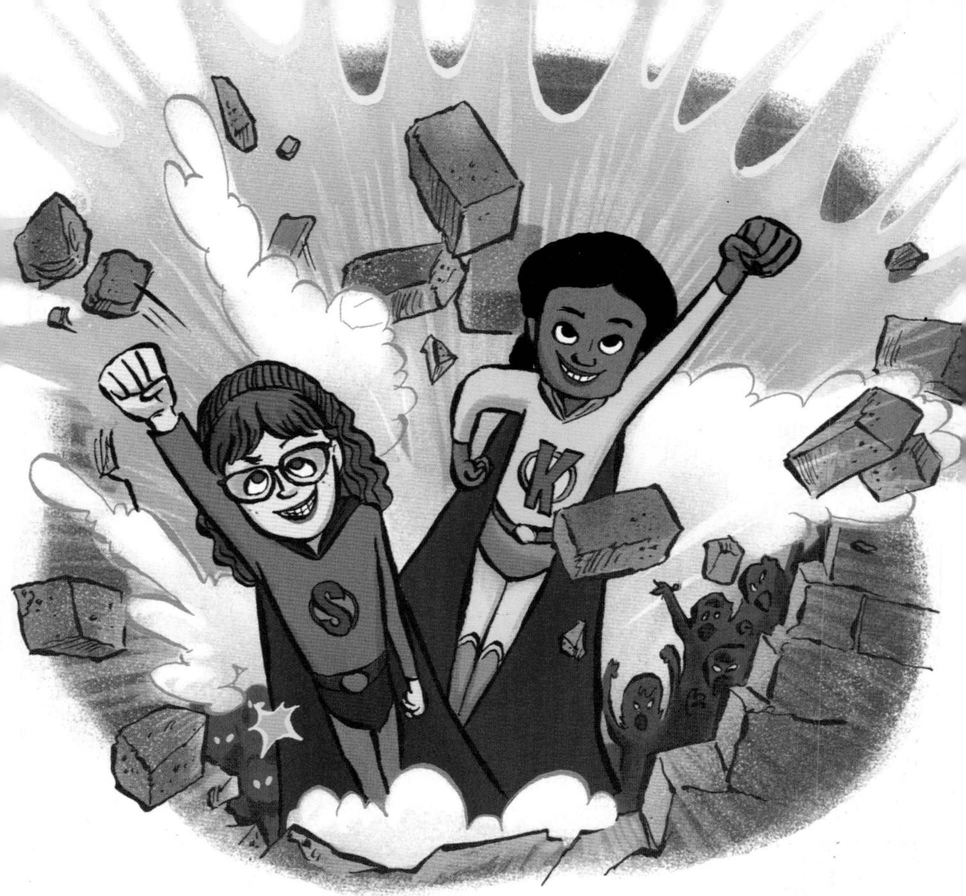

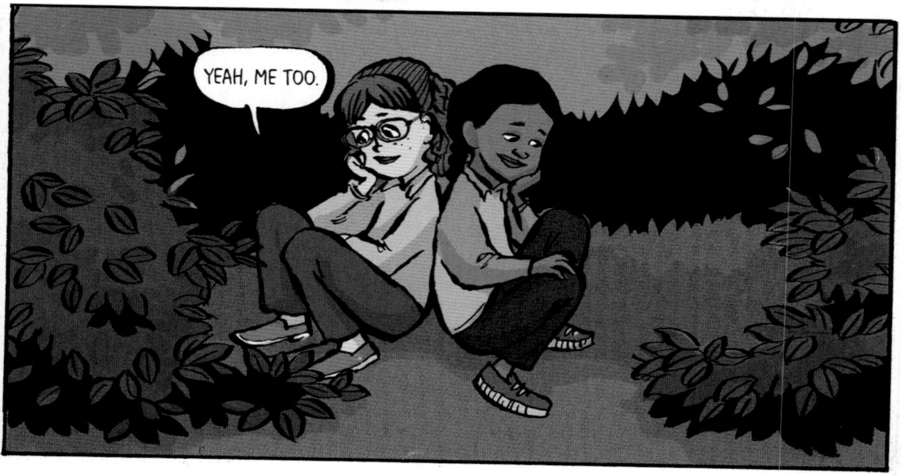
YEAH, ME TOO.

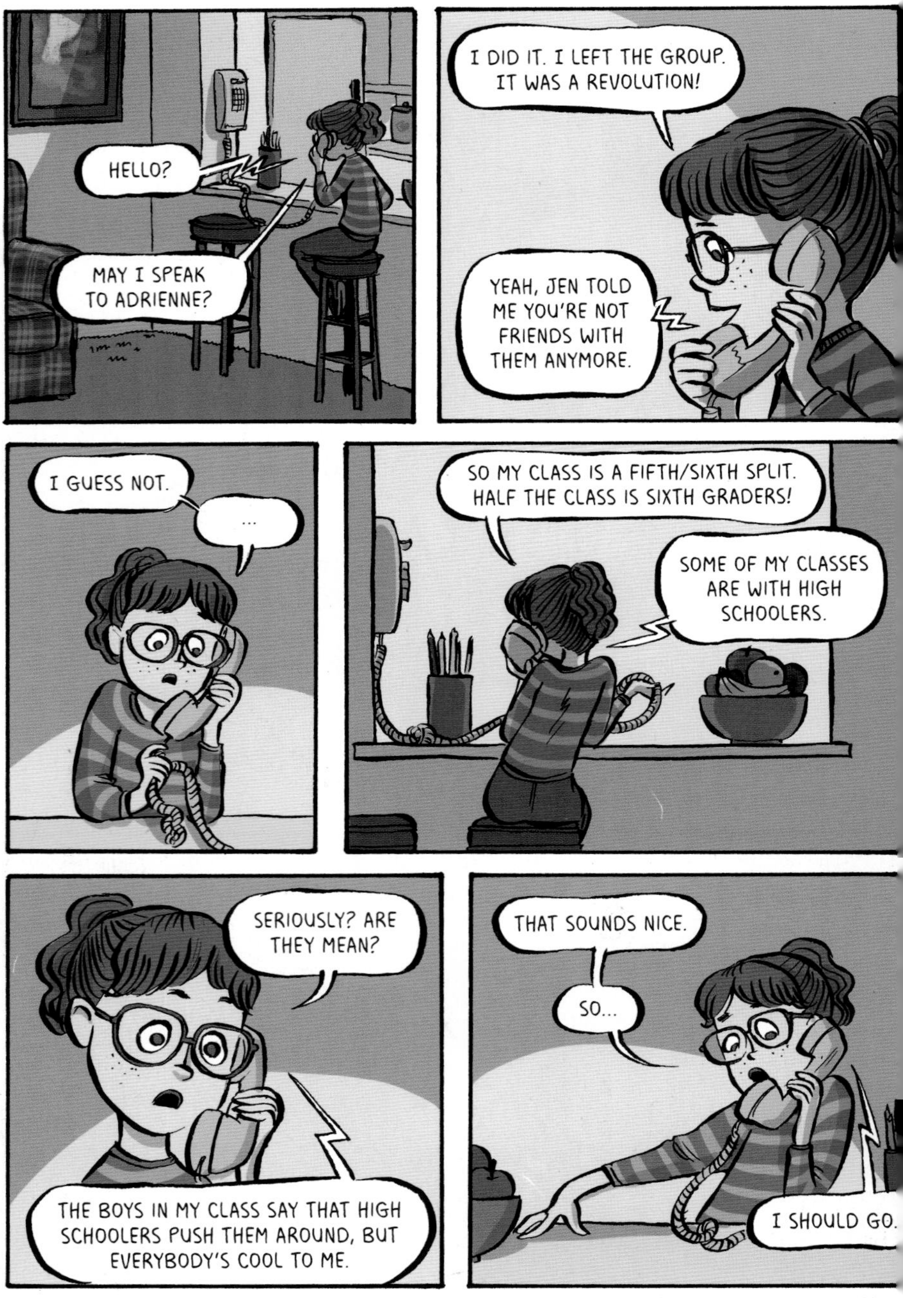
HELLO?
MAY I SPEAK TO ADRIENNE?
I DID IT. I LEFT THE GROUP. IT WAS A REVOLUTION!
YEAH, JEN TOLD ME YOU'RE NOT FRIENDS WITH THEM ANYMORE.
I GUESS NOT.
...
SO MY CLASS IS A FIFTH/SIXTH SPLIT. HALF THE CLASS IS SIXTH GRADERS!
SOME OF MY CLASSES ARE WITH HIGH SCHOOLERS.
SERIOUSLY? ARE THEY MEAN?
THE BOYS IN MY CLASS SAY THAT HIGH SCHOOLERS PUSH THEM AROUND, BUT EVERYBODY'S COOL TO ME.
THAT SOUNDS NICE.
SO...
I SHOULD GO.

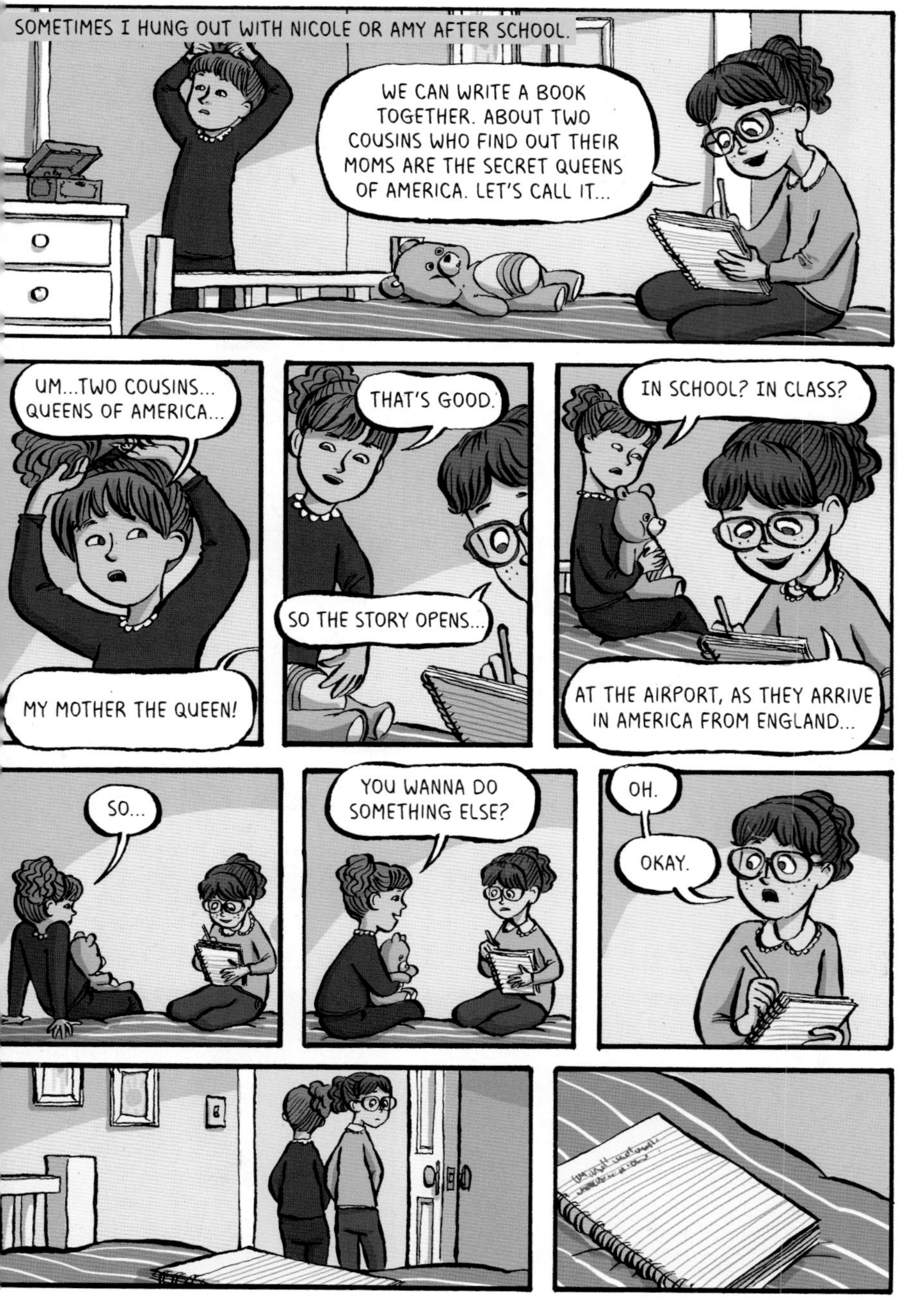
SOMETIMES I HUNG OUT WITH NICOLE OR AMY AFTER SCHOOL.
WE CAN WRITE A BOOK TOGETHER. ABOUT TWO COUSINS WHO FIND OUT THEIR MOMS ARE THE SECRET QUEENS OF AMERICA. LET'S CALL IT...
UM...TWO COUSINS... QUEENS OF AMERICA...
MY MOTHER THE QUEEN!
THAT'S GOOD.
SO THE STORY OPENS...
IN SCHOOL? IN CLASS?
AT THE AIRPORT, AS THEY ARRIVE IN AMERICA FROM ENGLAND...
SO...
YOU WANNA DO SOMETHING ELSE?
OH.
OKAY.

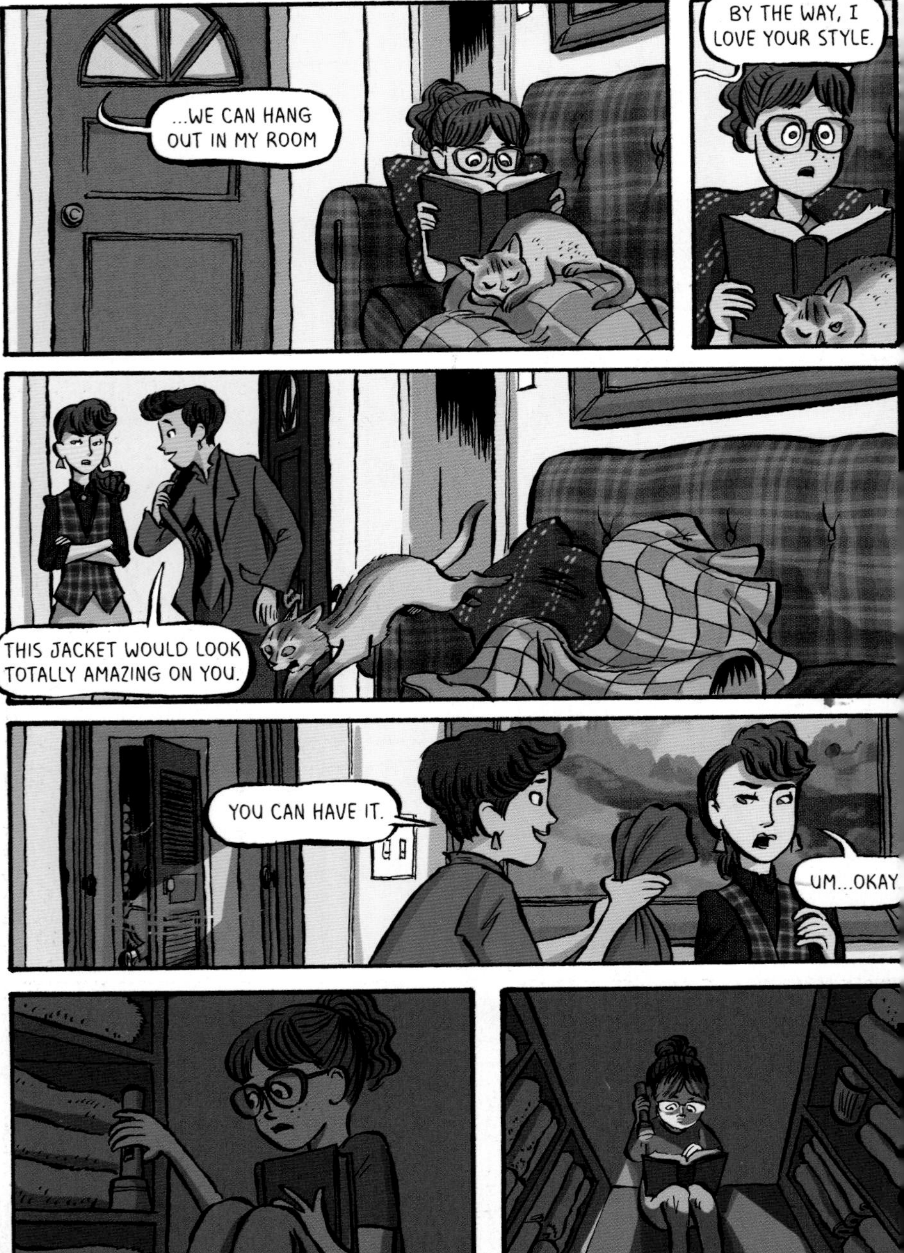
...WE CAN HANG OUT IN MY ROOM
BY THE WAY, I LOVE YOUR STYLE.
THIS JACKET WOULD LOOK TOTALLY AMAZING ON YOU.
YOU CAN HAVE IT.
UM...OKAY

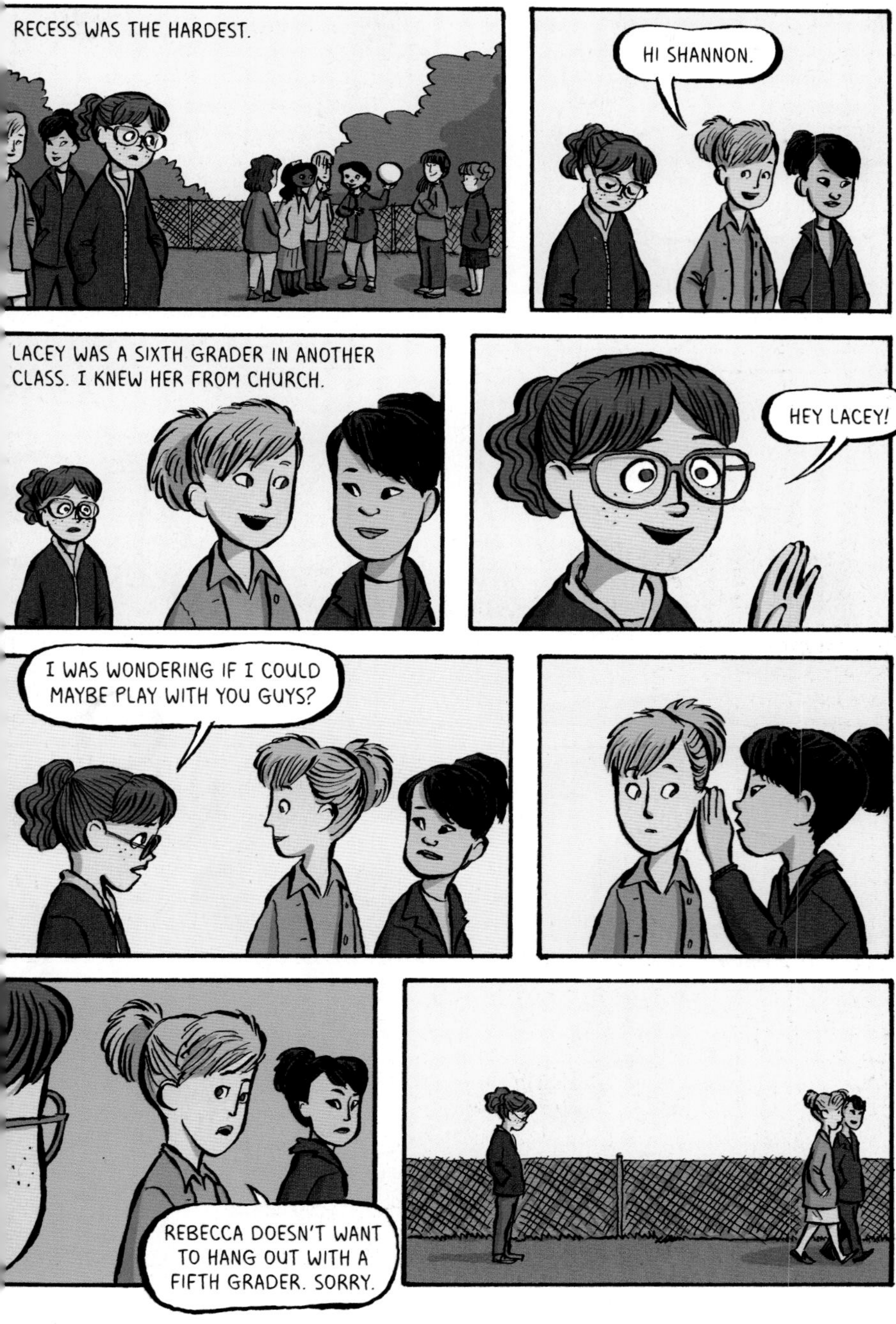
RECESS WAS THE HARDEST.
HI SHANNON.
LACEY WAS A SIXTH GRADER IN ANOTHER CLASS. I KNEW HER FROM CHURCH.
HEY LACEY!
I WAS WONDERING IF I COULD MAYBE PLAY WITH YOU GUYS?
REBECCA DOESN'T WANT TO HANG OUT WITH A FIFTH GRADER. SORRY.

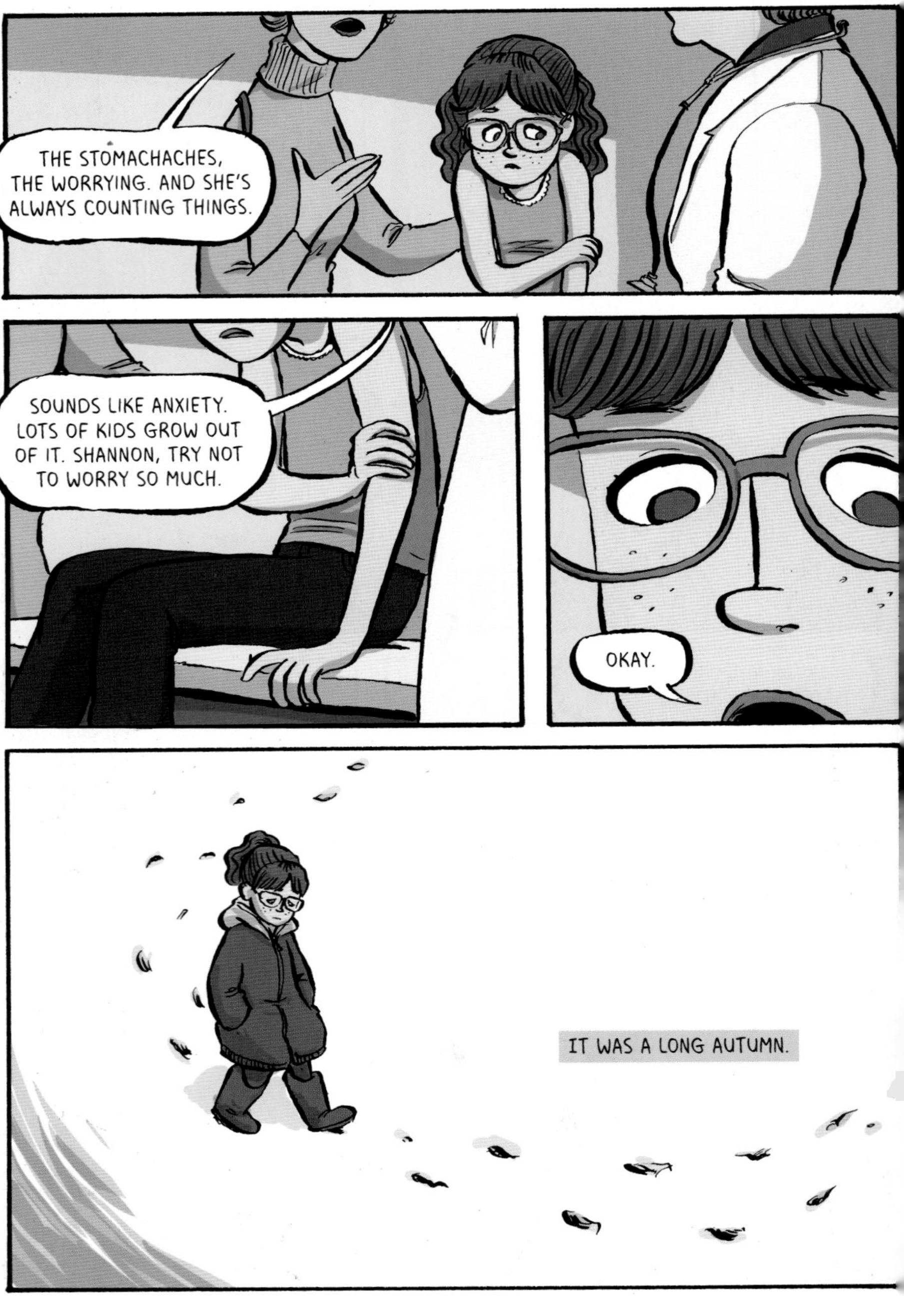
THE STOMACHACHES, THE WORRYING. AND SHE'S ALWAYS COUNTING THINGS.
SOUNDS LIKE ANXIETY. LOTS OF KIDS GROW OUT OF IT. SHANNON, TRY NOT TO WORRY SO MUCH.
OKAY.
IT WAS A LONG AUTUMN.

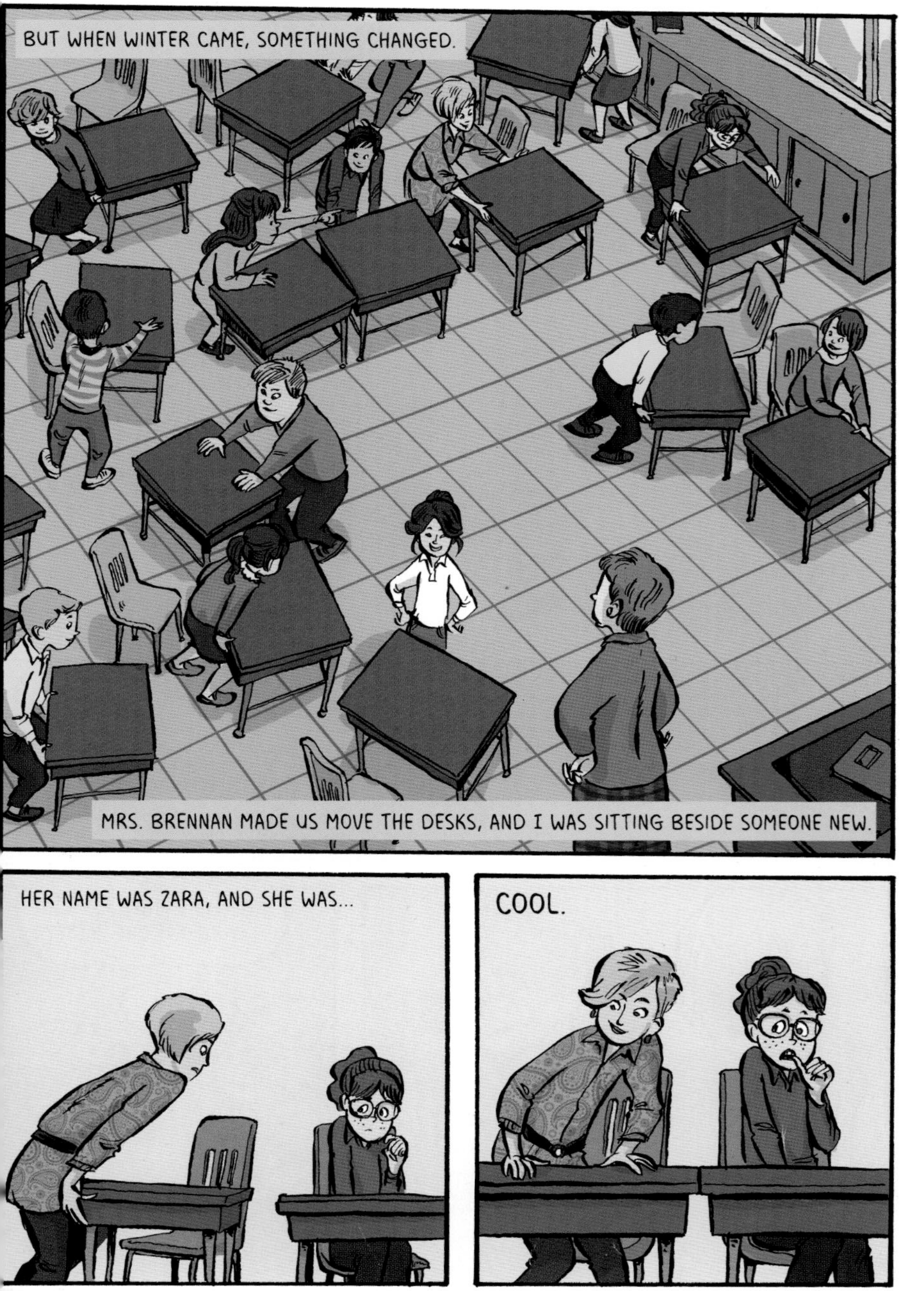
BUT WHEN WINTER CAME, SOMETHING CHANGED.
MRS. BRENNAN MADE US MOVE THE DESKS, AND I WAS SITTING BESIDE SOMEONE NEW.
HER NAME WAS ZARA, AND SHE WAS...
COOL.

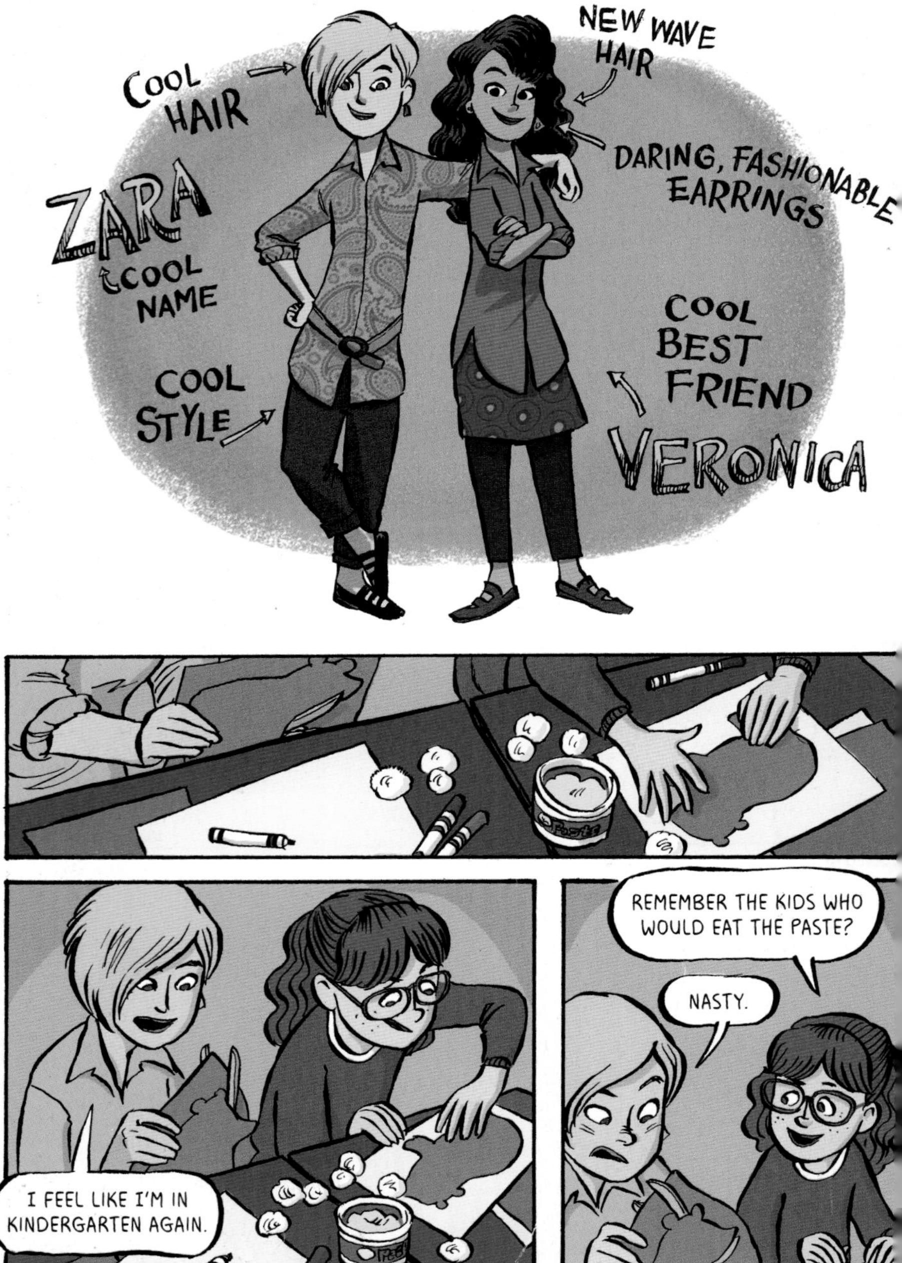
COOL HAIR
NEW WAVE HAIR
DARING, FASHIONABLE EARRINGS
ZARA
COOL NAME
COOL BEST FRIEND
COOL STYLE
VERONICA
I FEEL LIKE I'M IN KINDERGARTEN AGAIN.
REMEMBER THE KIDS WHO WOULD EAT THE PASTE?
NASTY.

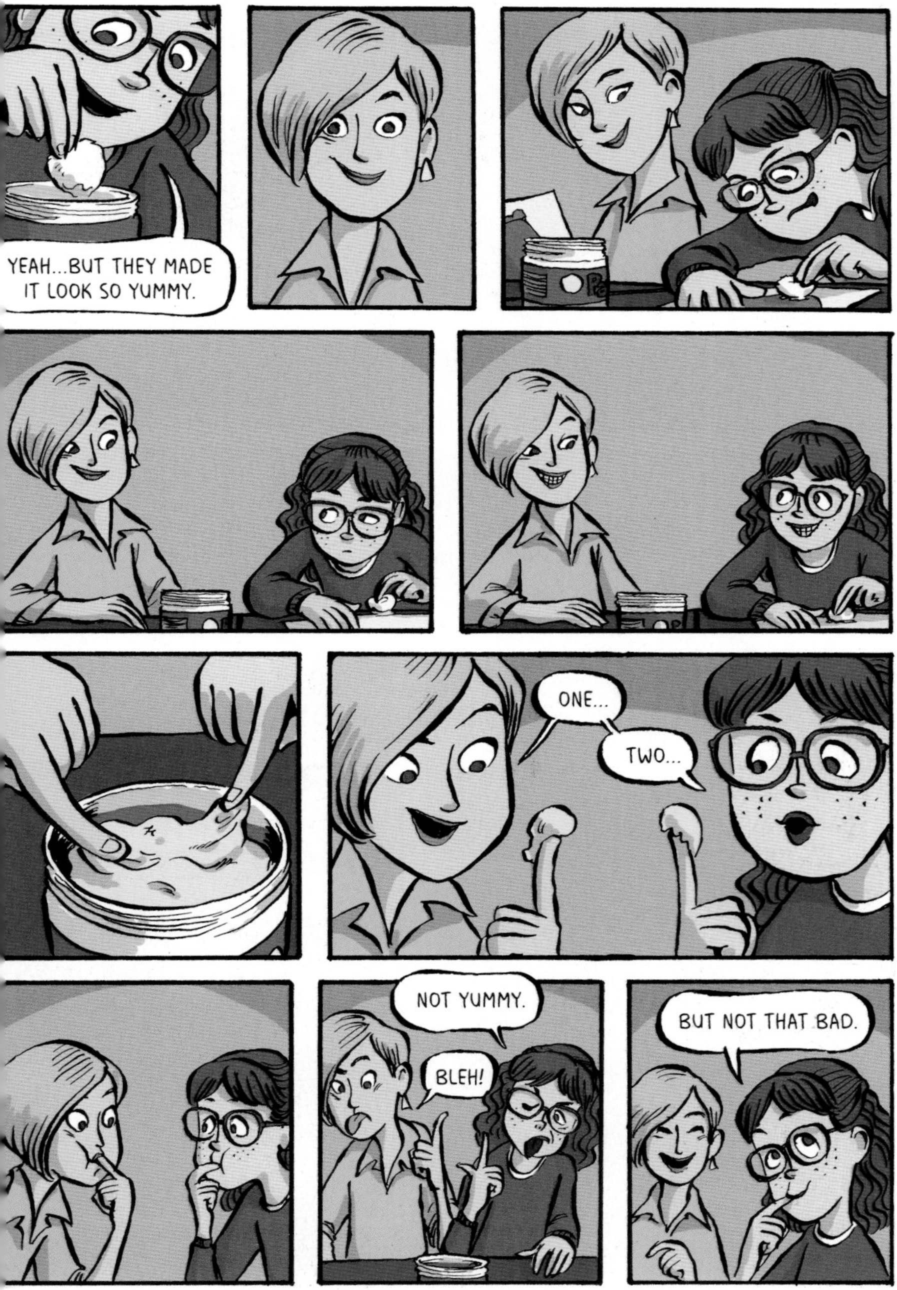
YEAH...BUT THEY MADE IT LOOK SO YUMMY.
ONE...
TWO...
NOT YUMMY.
BLEH!
BUT NOT THAT BAD.

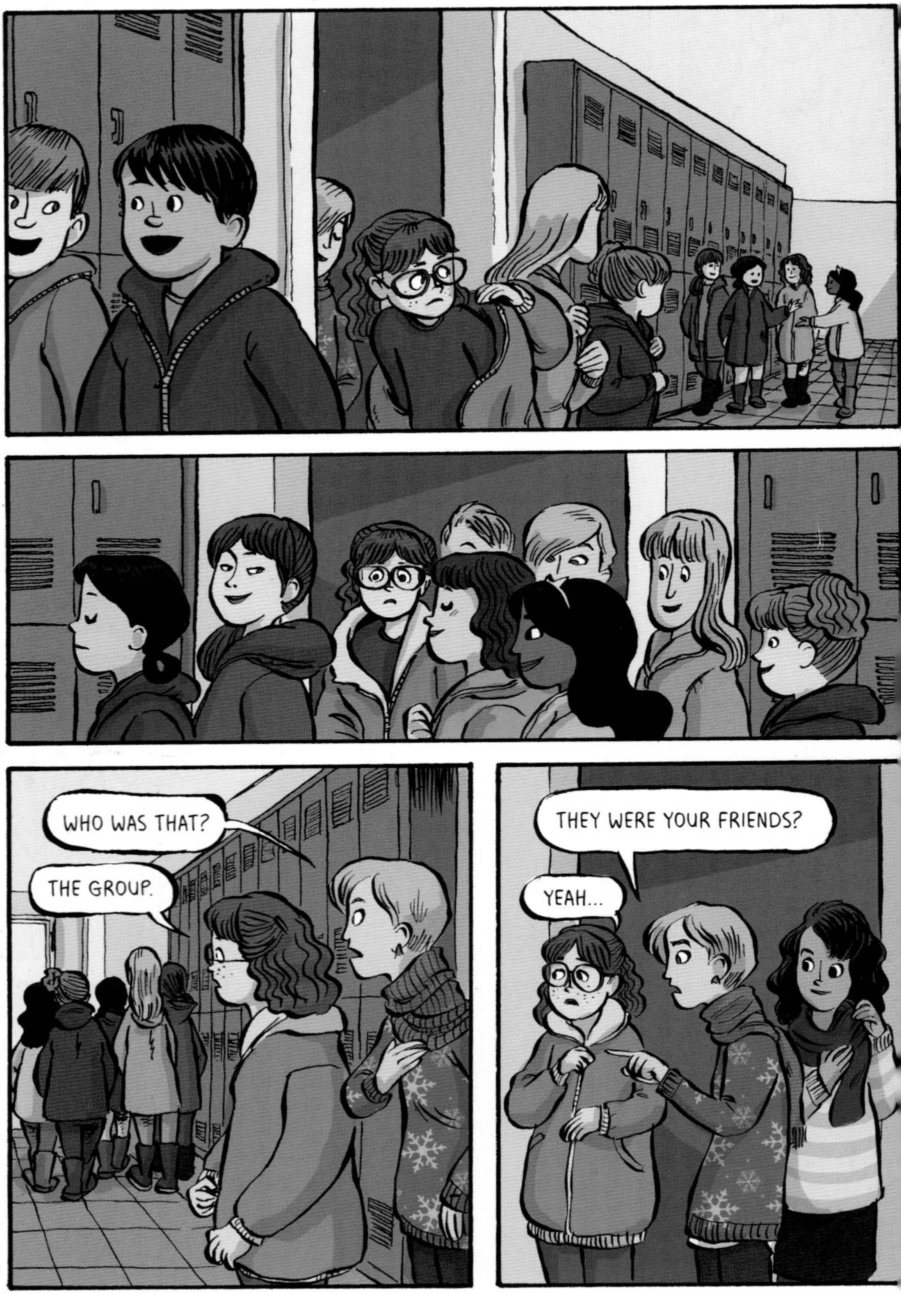
WHO WAS THAT?
THE GROUP.
THEY WERE YOUR FRIENDS?
YEAH...

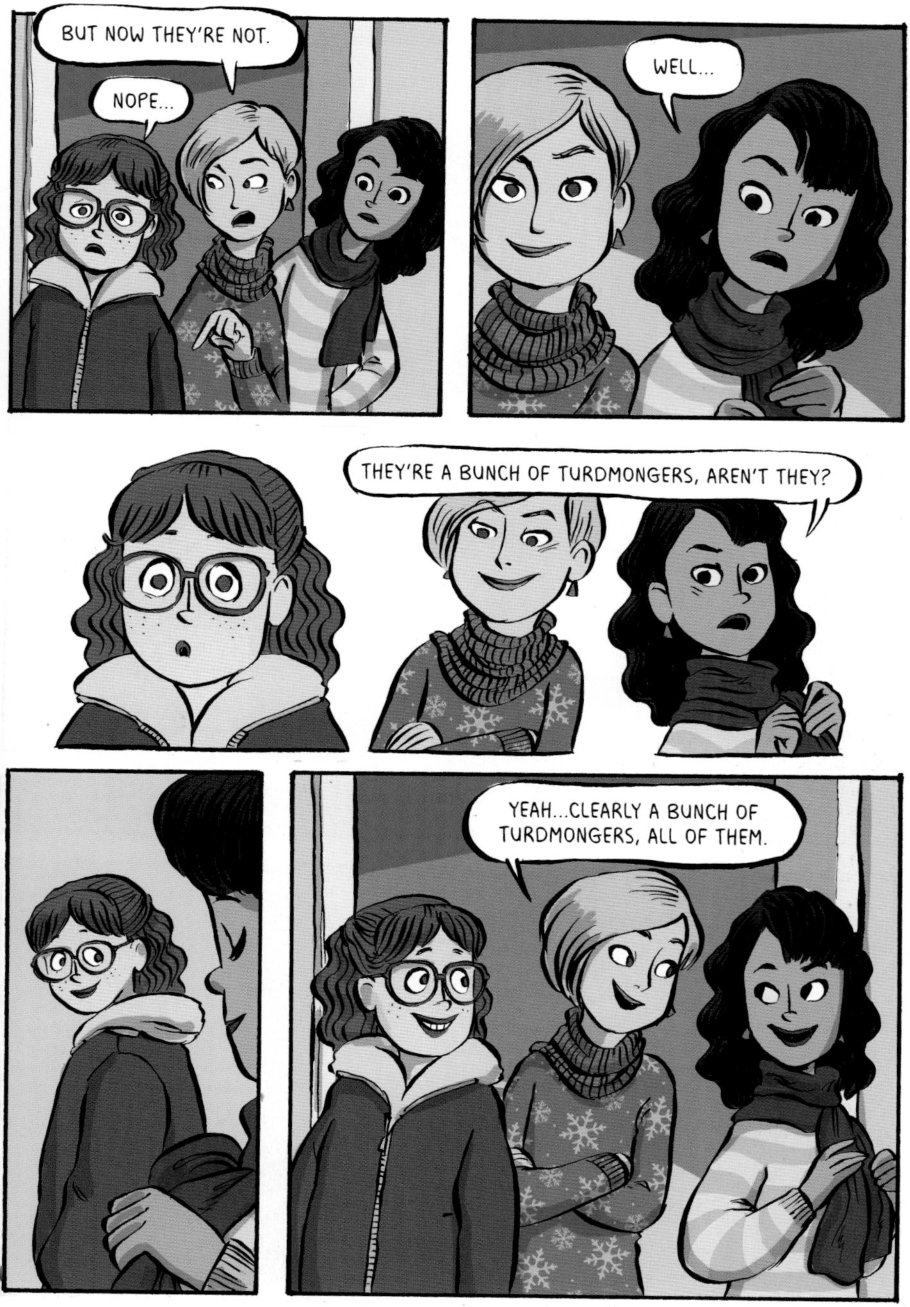
BUT NOW THEY'RE NOT.
NOPE...
WELL...
THEY'RE A BUNCH OF TURDMONGERS, AREN'T THEY?
YEAH...CLEARLY A BUNCH OF TURDMONGERS, ALL OF THEM.

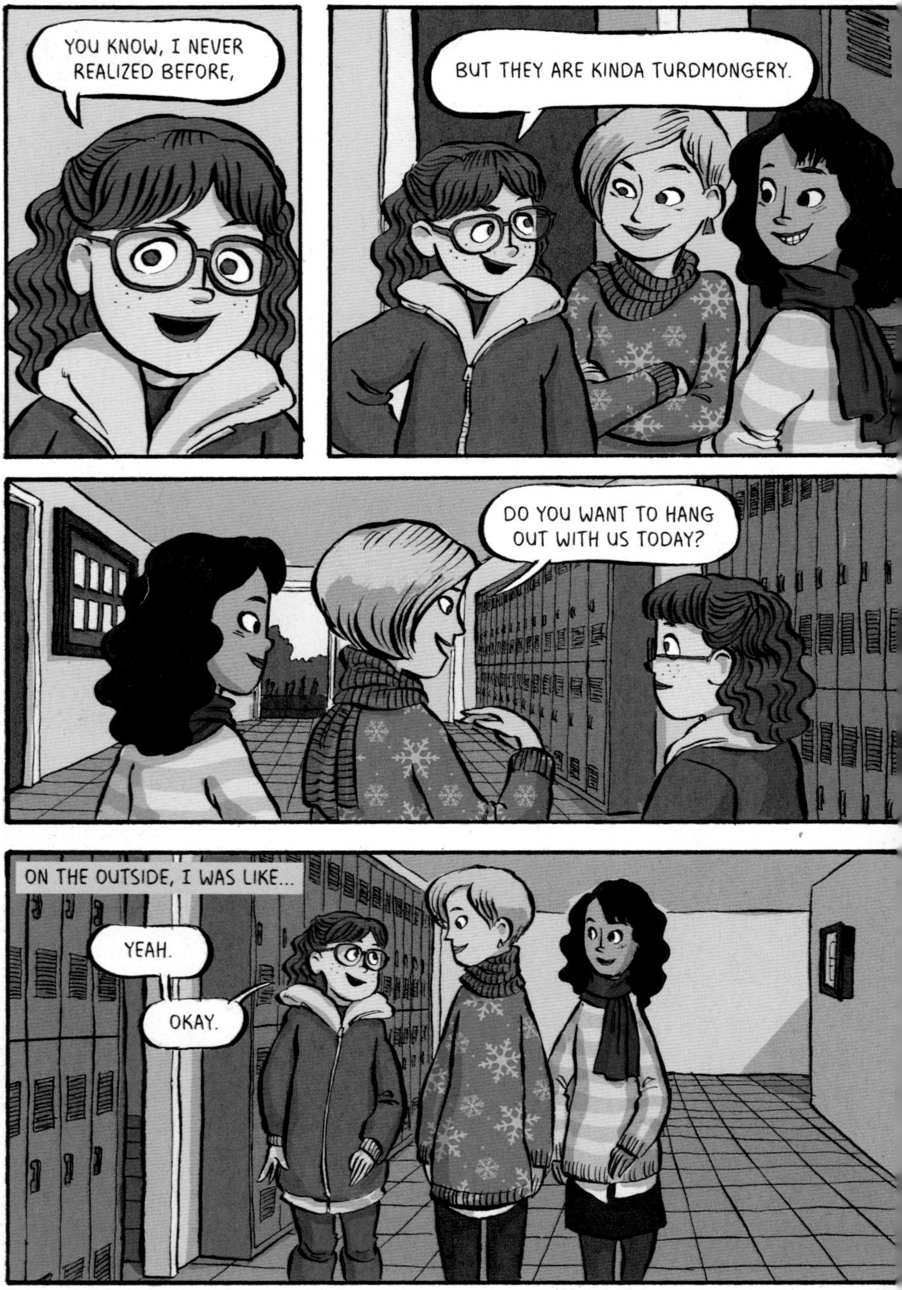
YOU KNOW, I NEVER REALIZED BEFORE,
BUT THEY ARE KINDA TURDMONGERY.
DO YOU WANT TO HANG OUT WITH US TODAY?
ON THE OUTSIDE, I WAS LIKE...
YEAH.
OKAY.

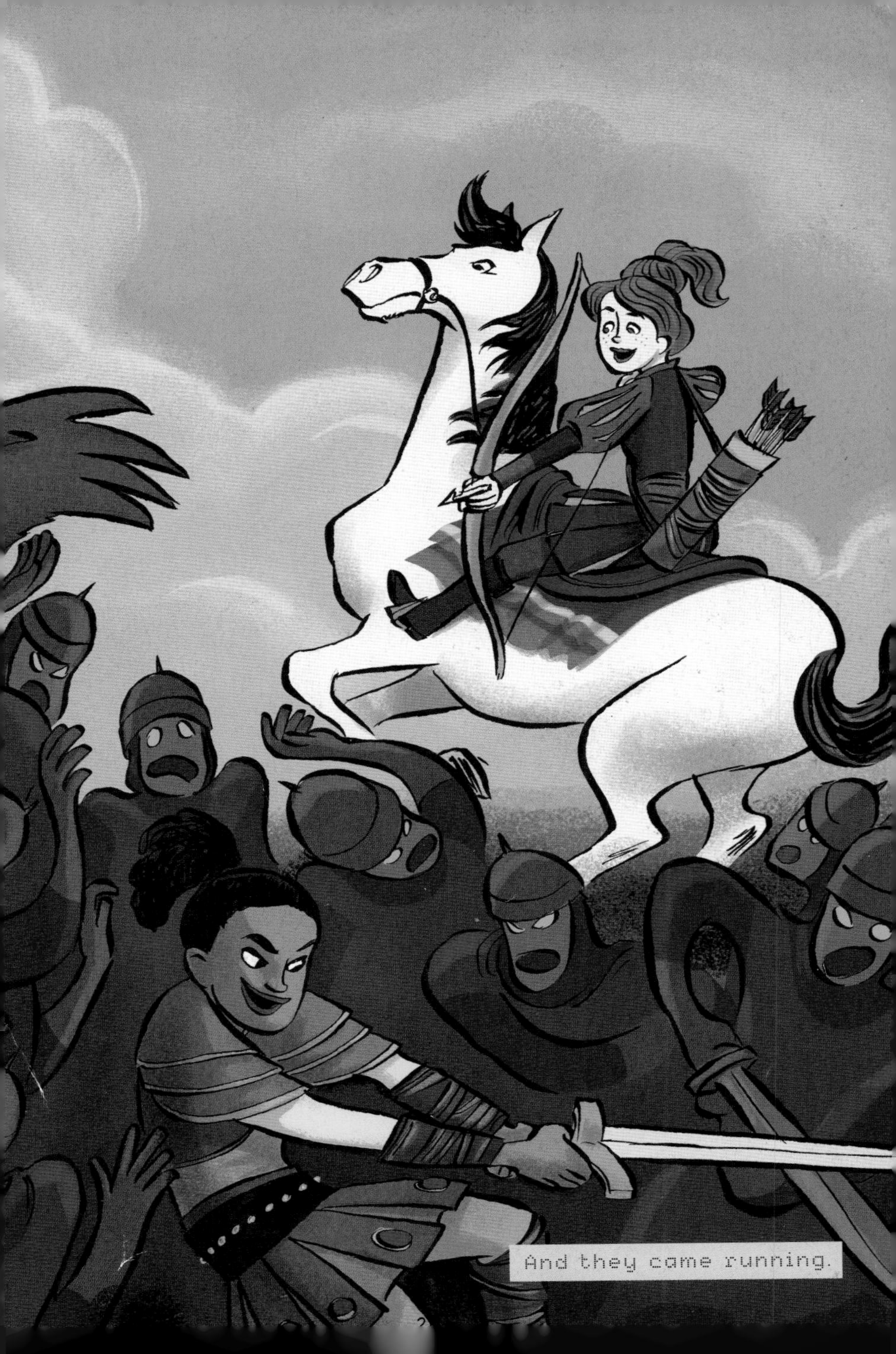
And they came running.

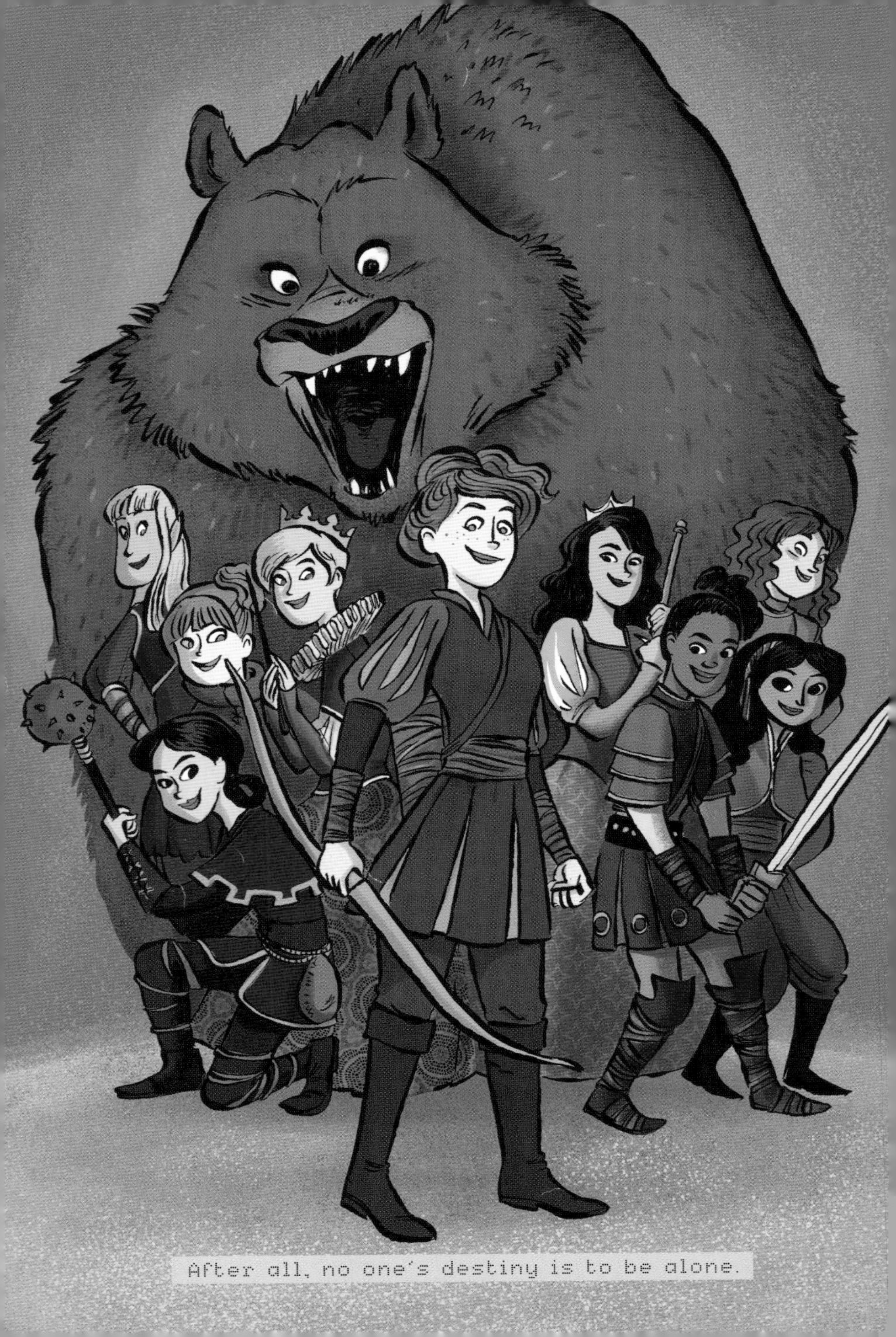
After all, no one's destiny is to be alone.

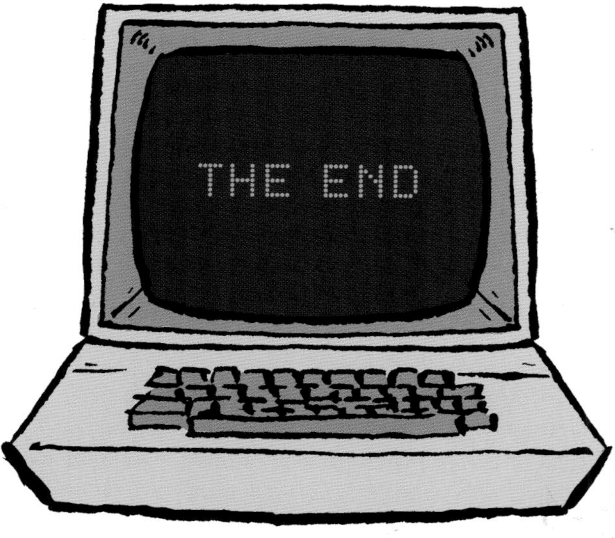
THE END

# Author's Note

Some have said that memories are the stories we tell ourselves about our past. *Real Friends* is the story I've been telling myself about my elementary school years. If you were to ask the other people portrayed in this book how it happened, surely the story they've been telling themselves would be different from mine.

I never thought I would write a memoir. For one thing, I didn't have a tragic or extraordinary childhood. I had kind parents who loved me. I had friends and many good times. But I decided to write this book in order to share how those years felt to me, in case you have felt or are feeling the same way. And then we can say to each other, "Hey, me too! Isn't that something? To realize I'm not the only one?"

Most of the events in this book really happened. Or I think they did. I've learned that memories aren't 100 percent accurate, and there's so much I didn't record in my journals. But I did my best. The parts I couldn't remember exactly, I wrote as they might have happened (like the conversation where Zara and I first became friends). A few parts I changed on purpose to help the story flow (like moving up the year Wendy left home). And I renamed everyone except myself because my flawed memory can't perfectly portray real people.

If this were a fiction, I probably would have resolved the relationship with Jenny, but in real life, it was never resolved. Even though little Shannon really did say "no" when Jenny asked to join the "new group," it was still hard for me to write it. After all, I believe in forgiveness and redemption. But I chose to include it because I think it's okay to make boundaries between ourselves and anyone who has bullied us. It's okay to say no.

Though my friend troubles didn't all go away in sixth grade, as I kept growing up, it did keep getting better. In high school I got to know the girl who had been my hiding-behind-the-shrub companion. Her situation in elementary school had been so much harder than what I'd been facing. I wonder if I could have seen her loneliness more clearly if I hadn't been so wrapped up in my own, and if we could have been friends for each other.

I was sick a lot, and though my loving mom took me to many doctors, we never figured out what was wrong. The mysterious stomachaches and some of those sad, anxious, yucky feelings were probably symptoms of an anxiety disorder and mild obsessive-compulsive disorder. Today there are lots of resources for kids with mental health disorders. Cognitive behavioral therapy is an effective tool for anxiety and OCD, and starting therapy when young can help tremendously. The website adaa.org is a helpful resource.

The sister who inspired the character of Wendy also struggled with undiagnosed behavioral health disorders. Back then, no one really knew what to do for kids whose brains worked a little differently. As she grew up, she found her own group—friends who realized how funny, clever, vibrant, and fun she was. Maybe our reconciliation in real life didn't happen as quickly as it does in this book, but it felt that way. We corresponded regularly whenever she lived out of state. She was the first person I talked to about my first kisses, my boy troubles, and my writerly dreams. As adults we became great friends, and she became a devoted, loving, brilliant mother.

She is so much more than I've been able to show in this book. As are the rest of my family; the people I call Jen, Jenny, and Adrienne; and even little Shannon. We are, all of us, so much more than we are at our worst and at our best.

Friendship in younger years can be especially hard because our worlds are small. In high school and beyond, I found many supportive, lifelong friends. If you haven't found your "group" yet, hang in there. Your world will keep growing larger and wider. You deserve to have real friends, the kind who treat you well and get how amazing you are.

## Kindergarten

*Awww . . .*

## 2<sup>nd</sup> Grade

*Here I am, looking super hand-me-down-ish and forgotten-in-the-middle child.*

### 3rd Grade

*When I first joined The Group.*

### 4th Grade

*The year I decided to be a writer.*

### 5th Grade

*My retake photo—this time
without glasses!*

# Acknowledgments

Special thanks from Shannon . . .

- to LeUyen Pham, who was exactly the right person to illustrate this book. This is as much your story as mine, Uyen. Thank you! Apologies to your family for all the long days and late nights you dedicated to this book. And cheers for Jane Poole and her magnificent help on the coloring.
- to Connie Hsu, my editor, who literally made this book possible. Thanks for taking my nonsense of a first draft and patiently talking me through twenty or so revisions until I got it right.
- to all the First Second and Macmillan folk who have taken such care of me and this book, including Gina Gagliano, Mark Siegel, Andrew Arnold, Danielle Ceccolini, Allison Verost, Erin Stein, Jon Yaged, Angus Killick, Jennifer Gonzalez, Simon Boughton, Lucy Del Priore, Katie Halata, Jill Freshney, Alexa Villanueva, and of course Connie Hsu, who I already mentioned but deserves being mentioned twice.
- to LeUyen Pham again, who is simply PHAM-TASTIC! (If that's not a thing yet, I'm going to make that a thing. You're welcome.)
- to Cece Bell, Jenni Holm, Emily Wing Smith, Aaron Hartzler, Raina Telgemeier, Coe Booth, and Sherri Smith, for the advice and inspiration.
- to the Bryner family, for the stories, the laughter, the forgiveness.
- to Ava Cabey and Avarose, Samantha Stewart, and Rebecca Jensen Maw, for friendship and insight.
- to Margaret Stohl and the YALLWEST crew, for huddling me in right when I needed it.
- and to Dean, Max, Maggie, Wren, and Dinah, who were the best beta readers in the history of the universe.

Special thanks from Uyen . . .

- to Shannon Hale. My head knows that you wrote this story. But my heart is still convinced that somehow you crawled inside my memories and handpicked all these events and feelings and insecurities from my childhood and called them your own. My husband likes to joke that if I had just swapped out the Salt Lake City neighborhoods for the Los Angeles suburbs, and your large Mormon family for my own large Vietnamese Catholic family, and lastly changed little Shannon's hair color from red to black, then this book is about me. Hopefully I've managed to crawl into your head and draw out your memories as well. You are forever a kindred spirit.
- to Connie Hsu, who went through every page, every panel, every face, and let me know when I got it just right. Like Ginger Rogers and Fred Astaire, we had to dance it just right, and you were the perfect dance partner. But which are you, Ginger or Fred?
- to Mark Siegel, for making me always believe I'm better than I am. It makes me never want to disappoint you.
- to the First Second and Macmillan crew, who I've worked with forever now it seems. How do you guys manage to do what you do with what little you have to do it with? I've never known a more devoted group than you. Special shout out to Andrew Arnold, who came out of nowhere and gave us that last push we needed over the finish line.
- to my colorists, Jane and Max, who pulled off the most amazing feat of labor since Hercules was challenged, and in far less time. I threw you into the deep end, and you're still talking to me. How is that possible? And I still owe you dinner . . .
- to Leo and Adrien, whose faces are still the faces of every character I draw. It is unbelievable how much I love you guys.
- to Alex. For absolutely everything.

**Shannon Hale** is the *New York Times*–bestselling author of many children's and young adult novels, including the popular Ever After High series and multiple award winners *The Goose Girl, Book of a Thousand Days,* and *Princess Academy,* a Newbery Honor book. She co-wrote the graphic novels *Rapunzel's Revenge* and *Calamity Jack* and the bestselling chapter book series The Princess in Black with her husband, Dean Hale. They live with their four children near Salt Lake City, Utah. **shannonhale.com**

**LeUyen Pham** is the *New York Times*–bestselling illustrator of The Princess in Black series with Shannon and Dean Hale and *Freckleface Strawberry* with Julianne Moore. She wrote and illustrated *Big Sister, Little Sister, The Bear Who Wasn't There,* and is the illustrator of numerous other picture books, including *The Boy Who Loved Math.* She lives and works in Los Angeles with her husband and her two adorable sons. **leuyenpham.com**